10/10

180.⁰⁰

Broadway

&

Broadway

An Encyclopedia of Theater
and American Culture

VOLUME 1: A–L

Thomas A. Greenfield, Editor

GREENWOOD
An Imprint of ABC-CLIO, LLC

A B C ● C L I O

Santa Barbara, California • Denver, Colorado • Oxford, England

Copyright 2010 by Thomas A. Greenfield

All rights reserved. No part of this publication may be reproduced, stored in a retrieval system, or transmitted, in any form or by any means, electronic, mechanical, photocopying, recording, or otherwise, except for the inclusion of brief quotations in a review, without prior permission in writing from the publisher.

Library of Congress Cataloging-in-Publication Data

Broadway : an encyclopedia of theater and American culture / Thomas A. Greenfield, editor.
   p. cm.
  Includes bibliographical references and index.
  ISBN 978–0–313–34264–6 (set: hardcover : alk. paper) — ISBN 978–0–313–34265–3 (set: ebook) — ISBN 978–0–313–34266–0 (vol. 1: hardcover : alk. paper) — ISBN 978–0–313–34267–7 (vol. 1: ebook) — ISBN 978–0–313–34268–4 (vol. 2: hardcover : alk. paper) — ISBN 978–0–313–34269–1 (vol. 2: ebook)
1. Theater—New York (State)—New York—Encyclopedias. 2. Broadway (New York, N.Y.)—History—Encyclopedias. 3. Broadway (New York, N.Y.)—Biography—Encyclopedias. I. Greenfield, Thomas Allen, 1948–
PN2277.N5B62   2010
792.09747′103—dc22   2009045720

14 13 12 11 10   1 2 3 4 5

Greenwood Press
An Imprint of ABC-CLIO, LLC

This book is also available on the World Wide Web as an eBook.
Visit www.abc-clio.com for details.

ABC-CLIO, LLC
130 Cremona Drive, P.O. Box 1911
Santa Barbara, California 93116-1911

This book is printed on acid-free paper ∞

Manufactured in the United States of America

For Alice Hermoine Rogstad
Suzanne Margaret Rogstad Greenfield
and
Alex Jee Rogstad Greenfield

Home with my own
when company's expected . . .
. . . well protected.

Contents

❧

Alphabetical List of Entries

Volume 1

Volume 2

Guide to Related Topics

☙

This list divides entry names (headwords) by broad topic. Note that some entries are listed under more than one topic.

Actors and Actresses

Andrews, Julie

Barrymore Ethel

Barrymore, John

Booth, Edwin

Brando, Marlon

Brice, Fanny

Cantor, Eddie

Channing, Carol

Cobb, Lee J.

Cohan, George M.

Cronyn, Hume

Davis, Ossie

Drake, Alfred

Ferrer, Jose

Fiske, Mrs. (Minnie Maddern)

Fontanne, Lynn. *See* Lunt, Alfred, and
    Fontanne, Lynn

Forrest, Edwin

Gilpin, Charles S.

Grey, Joel

Hagen, Uta

Harris, Julie

Harrison, Rex

Hayes, Helen

Jones, James Earl

Keene, Laura

Lane, Nathan

Lansbury, Angela

Le Gallienne, Eva

Lunt, Alfred, and Fontanne, Lynn

Lupone, Patti

Martin, Mary

McClendon, Rose

McDonald, Audra

Merman, Ethel

Raitt, John

Robards, Jason, Jr.

Robeson, Paul

Tandy, Jessica

Taylor, Laurette

Verdon, Gwen

Williams, Bert

Broadway and Main Street

High Schools, Theater Education in
High Schools, Theater Performances in
Regional Theaters

Touring Productions
Tourism

Broadway Entertainment Components

Broadway (Location)
Broadway's Theaters and Theater
    District
Critics

Off-Broadway
Playwrights
Producers

Choreographers and Dancers

Balanchine, George
Bennett, Michael
Champion, Gower
de Mille, Agnes
Fosse, Bob

Robbins, Jerome
Stroman, Susan
Tune, Tommy
Verdon, Gwen

Composers and Lyricists

Berlin, Irving
Bernstein, Leonard
Brown, Jason Robert
Comden, Betty, and Green, Adolph
Gershwin, George, and Gershwin, Ira
Gilbert and Sullivan
Hart, Lorenz
Herbert, Victor
Herman, Jerry
Kander, John, and Ebb, Fred

Kern, Jerome
Lerner, Alan Jay, and Loewe, Frederick
Lloyd Webber, Andrew
Loesser, Frank
Porter, Cole
Robbins, Jerome
Rodgers, Richard, and Hammerstein,
    Oscar, II
Sondheim, Stephen
Styne, Jule

Ethnicity, Gender, and Identity

African American Dramatic Theater
African American Musical Theater
Asians and Asian Americans
Gay Culture
Jewish American Musicals
Jewish American Playwrights

Latino and Latina Americans
Religion
Women and Broadway: The Early
    Years, 1845–1939
Women and Broadway: The Later
    Years, 1940–Present

Media and Journalists

Atkinson, Brooks
Critics

Nathan, George Jean. *See* Critics
Sullivan, Ed

Organizations

The Actors Studio
American Theatre Wing—Tony
    Awards
Disney Theatrical Productions
Federal Theatre Project
Group Theatre
Nederlander Organization

Neighborhood Playhouse
Provincetown Players
Shubert Organization. *See* Shubert
    Brothers
Theatre Guild
Theatrical Syndicate

Performing Arts, Entertainment, and Literature

Comic Strips
Dance and Choreography
European "Megamusicals"
Film
Musicals
New Media and Technology
Novels (American)
Operetta
Puppetry
Radio

Regional Theaters
Show Tunes: From Tin Pan Alley to
    Pop Radio
Show Tunes: The Rock Era, Disney,
    and Downloads
Solo Performance
Sports
Television
Vaudeville

Plays

Angels in America
Barefoot in the Park
The Black Crook
Cats
A Chorus Line
Company
The Cradle Will Rock
The Crucible
Death of a Salesman
*for colored girls who have considered
    suicide/when the rainbow is enuf*
Gypsy

Hair
In the Heights
Long Day's Journey into Night
My Fair Lady
Oh! Calcutta!
Oklahoma!
Othello
Our American Cousin
Our Town
Pal Joey
The Phantom of the Opera
Porgy and Bess

The Producers (The Musical)
A Raisin in the Sun
Rent
Show Boat

Shuffle Along
A Streetcar Named Desire
West Side Story
Who's Afraid of Virginia Woolf?

Playwrights and Authors

Albee, Edward
Anderson, Maxwell
Belasco, David
Booth, Edwin
Burrows, Abe
Champion, Gower
Clurman, Harold
Crothers, Rachel
Fierstein, Harvey
Fitch, Clyde
Glaspell, Susan
Hansberry, Lorraine. See *A Raisin in the Sun*
Hellman, Lillian
Hwang, David Henry
Inge, William
Kaufman, George S.
Kushner, Tony

Larson, Jonathan. See *Rent*
Laurents, Arthur
McNally, Terrence
Miller, Arthur
Norman, Marsha
Odets, Clifford
O'Neill, Eugene
Shakespeare
Shange, Ntozake. See *for colored girls who have considered suicide/when the rainbow is enuf*
Shaw, George Bernard
Simon, Neil
Wasserstein, Wendy
Wilder, Thornton
Williams, Tennessee
Wilson, August

Producers, Directors, Theater Owners, and Managers

Abbott, George
Disney Theatrical Productions
Fields, Lew
Fosse, Bob
Group Theatre
Kazan, Elia
Keene, Laura
Logan, Joshua
Mackintosh, Cameron
Merrick, David
Nederlander Organization
Neighborhood Playhouse
Nichols, Mike
Papp, Joseph

Pastor, Tony. *See* Vaudeville
Prince, Harold
Provincetown Players
Quintero, Jose
Richards, Lloyd
Shubert Brothers
Strasberg, Lee
Stroman, Susan
Taymor, Julie
Theatre Guild
Theatrical Syndicate
Wolfe, George C.
Ziegfeld, Florenz

Preface

∽

Broadway: An Encyclopedia of Theater and American Culture represents a review —in nearly 200 separate entries—of American theater's ongoing march toward self-definition within American culture. The perils inherent in undertaking such a review are painfully obvious and no less painfully numerous. They are as detail-bound as the fact that, during the week in which the encyclopedia was going into production, Yasmina Reza, a French novelist and playwright, became the first woman to win a second Tony Award for Best Play, thus adding new history to the two complicated issues of the influence (or lack thereof) of women and Europeans on Broadway. The perils are also as all-encompassing as the sobering knowledge that even an extensive list of cultural contexts and perspectives for exploring the topic will inevitably fall far short of being exhaustive.

What Is Included

Written by more than 60 scholars, researchers, and practitioners in the fields of theater and popular culture, the entries in *Broadway: An Encyclopedia of Theater and American Culture* provide basic and detailed information on key people, productions, and organizations that have shaped the character of Broadway and defined its place in American culture since the nineteenth century. Nearly all entries, each of which can be categorized as a *thematic essay*, a *profile essay* on a person or organization, or a *landmark production essay* focusing on a single production, end with further reading suggestions.

Unless otherwise noted, *landmark production essays* focus upon original Broadway productions. Certainly some revivals (such as the 1943 "Paul Robeson" *Othello*) and even a few out-of-town productions (such as the 1865 Washington, D.C., production of *Our American Cousin*, at which President Lincoln was assassinated) have earned their place as historical milestones. But, notwithstanding its oft-maligned artistic timidity, Broadway revels in the shock of the new and has primarily staked its claim in American culture and consciousness through momentous opening nights and historic first runs.

The encyclopedia concludes with an extensive bibliography of books and Web sites covering both broad and specific topics attendant to the study of the New York commercial theater scene. A glossary of selected historical theater terms and references elaborates upon the information contained in the entries, and a historical timeline at the front of the encyclopedia helps to put key people and events in context chronologically.

The principal purpose of this encyclopedia is to provide an extensive reference resource for assessing the ways in which Broadway commercial theater has both reflected and interacted with American culture at large from the nineteenth century to the present. College and high school students and faculty will in all likelihood make greatest use of the book, although it has been written and edited to be accessible and useful for the general reader interested in American theater. The encyclopedia builds upon the well-established scholarly principle that American culture, although certainly more than the sum of its parts, lends itself readily to fruitful examinations of key issues commonly associated with studies of modern civilization: the arts, religion, diversity and inclusion, communications and technology, political environment, etc. Each of these issues, of course, leads to considerations of key people and achievements that bring events to the fore and influence the direction of things to come. Those issues, people, and events (particularly historic Broadway productions) comprise the raw material for *Broadway: An Encyclopedia of Theater and American Culture.*

When discussions of cultural issues and Broadway appear in book form, they almost invariably do so in discrete, single topic publications: on women and theater, or on musicals; or they represent an individual biography, and so forth. This encyclopedia identifies and analyzes in a single source numerous key issues, persons, productions, and organizations that define Broadway as an American cultural phenomenon. Many entry topics will be familiar to most readers (the Broadway musical film, Rodgers and Hammerstein, *The Phantom of the Opera*) and others less so (the high school play, *The Black Crook*, puppetry, Joshua Logan). By design, well-known and relatively unfamiliar themes are given comparable weight and space within the book. For example, the article on Broadway puppetry is approximately as long as the article on Broadway films. The two subjects, while not equally familiar to most readers, are in fact equally revealing of Broadway's diversity as a wellspring for American creativity and, thus, equally important as considerations of Broadway's place in American culture.

Any discussion of Broadway, whether taking a narrow or a panoramic view, must come to grips with the question of who are the most significant people and what are the most significant productions. The 30 landmark productions and 115 profile subjects in this encyclopedia stand, respectively, in representation of the 100 or more Broadway productions that could reasonably be called "landmarks" or the hundreds of individuals who have made an important mark on Broadway in a creative or business capacity. In keeping with the eclectic nature of the encyclopedia and the eclectic nature of Broadway itself, the selection process took multiple approaches. In many cases Broadway's artists and audiences, past and present, helped us with our selection. Popular commercial success, while not always the central consideration, certainly commands respect in studies of popular culture. Indeed, this encyclopedia highlights several historic long-running, high-grossing productions and the people responsible for them, providing analysis and perspective on why and how they achieved the success that they did and/or the impact they had on other people and productions. To some extent, winners of major awards, especially awards that have some cachet with the general public such as Tony Awards and Pulitzer Prizes, were worthy of attention, particularly in those instances where the awards reflected important trends or characteristics about Broadway, its creators, or its audience. Breakthrough achievements, whether best documented through a biographical profile, a landmark production, or part of a thematic essay, provided excellent opportunities to note historic changes in Broadway and American culture, as when Bert Williams became the first black star of an otherwise all-white cast Broadway production (*Ziegfeld Follies*, 1910s) or when the musical *Hair* (1968) introduced rock music and postwar youth counterculture to the heretofore defiantly "middle-aged" Broadway audience of the 1950s and early 1960s. In each case, the entries point to issues, trends, ideas, and breakthroughs beyond themselves in open acknowledgement that the study of Broadway is a bit like Broadway itself. There are many players on the stage beyond those illuminated in the spotlight.

Acknowledgments

❧

I am deeply indebted to Kristi Ward, my first editor at ABC-CLIO–Greenwood Press, for developing the idea for this project with me and guiding me so capably through its nascent stages. Her successors at ABC-CLIO–Greenwood, Lindsay Claire, Anne Thompson, and Kathy Breit, were absolutely indispensable in helping me see it to completion. All four were a pleasure to work with.

In the three years of preparation for this book scarcely a week went by—and in the final weeks scarcely a day—when I did not seek the counsel of one or more members of my board of advisors. This highly generous and knowledgeable group included Professor Melanie Blood, Associate Dean of the School of the Arts at SUNY Geneseo; Professor Ray Miller of the Department of Theatre and Dance at Appalachian State University; William Charles Morrow of the Billy Rose Performing Arts Collection of the New York Public Library; Michael D. Kobluk, co-founder of American Theater Productions and former manager of the Spokane, Washington, Opera House, Convention Center, Coliseum and Stadium; Maryann Chach, Director of the Shubert Archive in New York; and Marty Jacobs, Curator of the Theater Collection at the Museum of the City of New York. Several of them, I am delighted to say, also contributed entries to this volume.

Sue Ann Brainard of SUNY Geneseo College Libraries and the aforementioned William Charles Morrow served as senior research associates on the project. Their professionalism, enthusiasm, and incomprehensible willingness to respond to my often unreasonable requests for assistance were sustained blessings I exploited repeatedly without shame or restraint.

I was the fortunate recipient of all manner of advice from many other friends, colleagues, and strangers brimming over with kindness. These included Professor Anne Fliotsos of Purdue University; Ben Hodges, editor-in-chief of *Theatre World*; Ben Pesner of the Broadway League; Professor Alyson McLamore of the music department at California Polytechnic State University, San Luis Obispo; Professor Anne-Marie Reynolds of the SUNY Geneseo School of the Arts; Stephen Marino, president of the Arthur Miller Society; Ken Cerniglia, dramaturg and literary manager of Disney Theatrical Productions; Albert Nocciolino, president of NAC Entertainment; Leslie Broecker, president of Broadway Across America–

Midwest; Professor Gerry Floriano of the School of the Arts at Geneseo; Dave Clemmons, owner and casting director of Dave Clemmons Casting; Robert Sagan, Director of Education and Outreach, and Linda Glosser D'Angelo, vice president of Operations, of the Rochester Broadway Theatre League in Rochester, New York; Gary McAvay, president of Columbia Artists Theatricals; Ellen Herzman of the English department at SUNY Geneseo; Tony Micocci, president of Micocci Productions, LLC; Molly Smith-Metzler of the Theatre Communications Group; Druscilla McConaughy; Marisa Fratto; and Alex Sovronsky.

These people gave me guidance, corrections, directions, and arguments—all of which accrued to the benefit of the book. In all instances, of course, I assume full responsibility for the content of the volume.

SUNY Geneseo provided me with travel funds from the English department, a Roemer Summer fellowship and a research travel grant from the Geneseo Foundation, and a one-semester research leave. I am deeply grateful to President Christopher Dahl; Professor Richard Finkelstein, my department chair in English; Anne Baldwin, director of Sponsored Research; and former Provost Kate Conway-Turner for supporting this project so enthusiastically over the past three years. I am also grateful to the staff and students of Geneseo's Writers House for feeding me so grandly, cheering me on, and occasionally suggesting that I take it down a notch.

The *sine qua non* of this encyclopedia was the "backstage crew": my students in several iterations of SUNY Geneseo Directed Study 399, which I conducted between 2006 and 2009. They served as my fact checkers, first drafters, co-authors, manuscript readers, data gatherers, therapists, insolent puncturers of trial balloons, and irritatingly formidable debaters on matters pertaining to this book. Nicole Katz, whose two and one-half year tenure with the project nearly equalled my own, is the first among equals. Her work is matched by the splendid contributions of Kevin Cunningham, Kaitlin Snyder, Nicholas Ponterio, Sarah Provencal, Laura Lonski, Christy Allen, Sean Roche, Rob Adamo, Mary Hanrahan, Caitlin Klein, Brian Balduzzi, Megan Lee, Michael Radi, Megan Zeh, Aaron Netsky, and Caitlin Nelson.

Every detail attended to in this book almost certainly came at the expense of a detail left unattended elsewhere. The burden of that equation fell with undue proportion on the shoulders of my wife and best friend of 34 years, Moine Rogstad, who supported my efforts with greater forbearance and dedication than I merited. I am deeply grateful for her love and encouragement.

Thomas A. Greenfield
New York City, June 2009

Introduction: Broadway and American Culture

On Saturday afternoon, May 30, 2009, President Barack and First Lady Michelle Obama left Washington, D.C., for an evening of dinner and theater in New York City. The president (and self-proclaimed dutiful husband) was making good on a long-standing "campaign promise" to take his wife to a Broadway show. The first couple dined in a small Greenwich Village restaurant and then went uptown by presidential motorcade to see August Wilson's *Joe Turner's Come and Gone*, the first Broadway revival of a Wilson play since the Pulitzer Prize winning author's death in 2005. The play had opened six weeks earlier to rave reviews and had just been nominated for six Tony Awards.

In a week whose political events would include the official announcement of General Motors' imminent bankruptcy and the first-ever major address by a U.S. president to the Muslim world, the First Couple's seemingly innocuous Broadway date ignited a storm of controversy. Pouncing on what they perceived as elitist Ivy League insensitivity to the plight of ordinary Americans—an oft-heard criticism of Obama during the 2008 presidential campaign—the Republican National Committee (RNC) linked the Obamas' Broadway date to the current economic crisis and condemned the outing as self-indulgent, imperious indifference to the suffering of American workers: "As President Obama prepares to wing into Manhattan's theater district on Air Force One to take in a Broadway show, GM is preparing to file bankruptcy and families across America continue to struggle to pay their bills."

An RNC spokesperson added, "if President Obama wants to go to the theater, isn't the Presidential box at the Kennedy Center (in Washington, D.C.) good enough?" (Politico).

Many observers felt that the RNC's criticism of the first couple's night out on Broadway contained a strongly implied rebuke of Broadway itself—as an upscale East Coast elitist indulgence alien to the world of Midwest factory workers and struggling families across America. Defenders of the president—and Broadway —responded in kind. Bloggers and media commentators noted that presidents are virtually never attacked politically for attending major sporting events, whose ticket prices can rival or even exceed those of Broadway shows (in other words, a pair of Broadway show tickets is just as "mainstream American" as two tickets to a Cubs game, and maybe even cheaper). Others cheered the Obamas for attending a challenging play by a major African American playwright and for setting a positive example in their pursuit of intellectual interests and support of American culture. And, no! The D.C. Kennedy Center, whose 2009 summer theater schedule consisted of touring company productions of shows no longer running on Broadway, is not "good enough." For live theater, an original *Broadway* production is the blue chip American brand—as it has been for at least a century. Notwithstanding the weighty issues confronting the nation as the Obamas took their seats at the Belasco, American professional theater found itself at the center of a debate over its place and identity in American culture.

It was hardly the first time.

America's professional theater, like its government, has deep roots in the nation's history as colonized territory. Unlike the government, however, the theater cannot point to a particular date on which it unequivocally declared or permanently won its independence from European culture. Indeed, as the diversity of scholarship and criticism on theater history makes clear, what might be viewed as the decolonization of American professional theater and postcolonial alignment with American culture at large is an ongoing production with countless dramatic rises and falls, perpetual cast and crew changes, improvisations, asides, technical errors, triumphant moments, and endless rewrites. (Apparently there is no finale and not much in the way of an intermission.)

American and Un-American Theater

The American theater's "Americanness" (and at times purported "Un-Americanness") has been a recurring flash point in the development of American theater dating back to the eighteenth century. In the late 1750s, the British "Hallam Company of Comedians from London," one of the first permanent professional theater companies in the colonies, changed its name to the "American Company" in response to the colonies' growing antipathy toward the British. In 1849 more than 20 people were killed outside of New York's Astor Place Opera House in protest of a touring British actor's appearance as Macbeth. (The protesters were, quite literally as it turned out, diehard fans of American Shakespearean actor Edwin Forrest.) Broadway in the first half of the twentieth century was a wellspring of flag-waving patriotism and nationalistic fervor, led by George M. Cohan's rousing patriotic shows and songs as well as the legendary war relief efforts of some of theater's leading women artists and producers. Yet the politically left-wing sensibilities of the Group Theatre and the Federal Theatre Project of the 1930s alarmed and alienated political and social conservatives in Congress and throughout the country. Those critics would wield enormous power over American popular culture in the 1940s and 1950s as the House Un-American Activities Committee (HUAC) sought to purge from the ranks of Broadway, Hollywood, and network broadcasting all vestiges of purported disloyalty, communist sympathy, and political dissent.

Debates over the meaning of American theater, of course, extend beyond politics to academic considerations of cultural identity. Many theater scholars argue that the Broadway musical in the twentieth century evolved from its European operetta roots into a distinctly American art form, earning comparable status as such with jazz or popular commercial filmmaking. Eubie Blake's *Shuffle Along* (1921), Jerome Kern and Oscar Hammerstein's *Show Boat* (1927), and Richard Rodgers and Oscar Hammerstein's *Oklahoma!* (1943) are frequently cited as milestone achievements in the Americanization of Broadway musical theater. These arguments, of course, brush up against the fact that the three longest-running Broadway shows in history are "megamusicals" created in Europe that transferred to Broadway from the London stage (*Cats*, Broadway opening, 1982; *Les Misérables*, 1987; *The Phantom of the Opera*, 1988). Moreover, venerated English and Irishmen William Shakespeare, George Bernard Shaw, and William S. Gilbert and Sir Arthur Sullivan were among the most frequently produced "Broadway writers" of the twentieth century. In some respects, Broadway is still drafting, or at least amending, its *Declaration of Independence.*

Diversity, Inclusion, and Exclusion on Broadway

The development of Broadway and American commercial theater is as much a function of the history of New York City as the history of the nation itself. New York City's special status as the birthplace of the American melting pot is among its most important historical distinctions. Yet, as a nurturer of ethnic and racial diversity, Broadway's record is decidedly mixed. From the late nineteenth century to the present, virtually all aspects of New York professional theater—musicals, vaudeville, and legitimate theater; performing, producing, and managing—provided rich opportunities for Jewish immigrant assimilation and advancement in American society. Yet few would dispute that African Americans, Asian Americans, and Latino/a Americans, large numbers of whom had emigrated and migrated to New York since the first decades of the twentieth century, have made significant contributions to Broadway theater while still being most often conspicuous on Broadway by their absence.

In the latter half of the twentieth century, as American intellectuals and politicians expanded the prevailing examinations of diversity and equality to include considerations of gender issues (especially women's rights) and sexual identity along with racial and ethnic equality, the role of women and issues of sexuality and sexual preference become important considerations in assessing the state of American culture, and certainly Broadway's place within it. Women stage performers, both as artistic talents and sexual attractions, have been central to the American commercial stage since the nineteenth century. In the late nineteenth and early twentieth centuries, women exerted a larger influence on Broadway as theater managers and producers than they do now (especially in the traditional sense of a "producer" as a single hands-on overseer of virtually all production considerations). In their unique position as collectively the most visible professional women in the country prior to World War I, Broadway theater women played a significant role in the suffragist movement, many of whose activities were centered in New York City and state. Yet today, the paucity of women directors, composers, and playwrights working on Broadway is widely viewed as bordering on scandalous, given the advancement of women in so many other creative fields in the past 40 years. In terms of industry employment, gays and lesbians have historically viewed Broadway and professional theater as among the more hospitable and supportive of American enterprises. The 1969 Stonewall Riots in New York City, which launched the modern gay/lesbian rights movement, provided a catalyst for increased visibility of gay theater artists and new openness about gay/lesbian themes in Broadway productions, including Martin Sherman's *Bent* (1979) and Harvey Fierstein's *Torch Song Trilogy* (1982).

Religious themes have provided popular, and occasionally controversial, Broadway fare for more than a century. Religion tends to make its presence felt on Broadway in historical or comedic shows, which perhaps explains in part why serious considerations of God and faith receive relatively little treatment in histories of commercial theater. The numerous, generally reverential dramatic representations of Saint Joan of Arc, probably Broadway's most frequently dramatized religious figure, stand with the seemingly ever-current retelling of the 1925 "Scopes Monkey Trial" in *Inherit the Wind* (1955); the celebratory backgrounding of Israel's struggle for independence in *Milk and Honey* (1961); the self-consciously hip retelling of Jesus' last days in *Jesus Christ Superstar* (1971); and the farcical analogy of a pre-Broadway out-of-town trial run as medieval religious quest in *Spamalot* (2005) constitute only a sample of the surprisingly large and diverse "catalog" of Broadway's religiously themed plays and musicals.

Broadway Theater and Her Sister Arts

All theater encompasses many art forms and American commercial theater is no exception. The tradition of Western theater we inherited from the ancient Greeks comprises plot, song, diction, and spectacle. To traditional disciplines of music, dance, and dramatic writing, American culture added most notably the Broadway film—especially the movie musical. The Broadway/Hollywood connection through adaptations of successful Broadway shows to commercial movies (and now frequently, especially through Disney Theatrical Productions, the adaptation of successful movies to Broadway shows) represents one of the most important and most exhaustively studied relationships between commercial theater and other popular art forms.

No less prominent is Broadway's relationship with the American popular music industry, especially the industry's traditional stock in trade—the popular hit show song or "single." The relationship between Broadway and popular songs reached its apex in the era of Tin Pan Alley (roughly 1880s to 1940), when Broadway served as the premiere vehicle by which songwriters would showcase new tunes and get them into the hearts, minds, player piano roles, night clubs, touring revues, and sheet music libraries of the American people. The relationship between Broadway and the music business became decidedly more complicated with the advent of radio as the principal way by which Americans first heard their soon-to-be favorite tunes. Nonetheless, the hit Broadway show tune and the "original cast album" remained staples of the music industry up through the 1970s. In the late twentieth century digital and Internet technology mounted a successful challenge to the radio and recording industries for primacy in distributing and marketing new popular music. This sea change in music distribution did not lessen Broadway musical producers' or composers' desire to get their songs and scores out of the theater and into the larger musical audience. But it certainly changed the marketing strategies. Today a "hit" Broadway tune might be as likely to find a national audience through YouTube, iTunes, and other file providers, or even a cell phone ring tone as through a recorded rendition heard on a radio or played on a CD purchased in one of America's rapidly disappearing record stores.

In addition to music and songwriting, dance reigns as among the most familiar of Broadway theater's constituent performing arts. Vaudeville tap dancing, "leg show" chorus kicks, and the refined disciplines of classical ballet and modern dance have all embraced and been embraced by musical theater throughout its history. Over the past 40 years, the increasingly common merging of the role of choreographer and director (i.e., Jerome Robbins, Bob Fosse, and more recently Susan Stroman) in a single Broadway show has greatly enhanced dance's position and prestige on Broadway—a fact graphically demonstrated at the 2009 Tony Awards by the dominance of *Billy Elliot: The Musical* (2008), the story of a working-class English boy's unbreakable determination to become a ballet dancer. Broadway theater's connections with other American arts and artists is hardly limited to its most conspicuous interrelationships with film, popular music, and dance. American novelists—from Harriet Beecher Stowe, to John Steinbeck, to James Michener, to Alice Walker—have found new audiences for their writings and new places in America's cultural consciousness by having their works adapted to the Broadway stage as musicals and plays. Although not as lofty as the novel, the American comic strip—a much underappreciated and underexamined popular art form—has found its way to the footlights. America's thriving community of puppet artists, given their long overdue spotlight by Jim Henson and the Muppets in the 1970s, have established a surprisingly strong presence on Broadway dating back to the 1920s. Recently *The Lion King* (1997) used masque and puppetry to bring non-Western theatrical motifs to a Broadway blockbuster and *Avenue Q* proved that puppet characters could interact as equals with "human" characters to the point of carrying a full-length show to a six-year plus run and a Tony Award for Best Musical. While arguably more vested in performance than art, the world of sports stands as theater's most formidable competitor for live entertainment dollars and press attention. Yet Broadway has on occasion happily mined the world of sports and America's fascination with athletic competition and heroes. The ethos and mystique of American sports have worked their way into Broadway legend through musical comedy (*Damn Yankees*, 1955), through searing social drama (*That Championship Season*, 1972), and in "real life" through the storybook evolution of champion gymnast Cathy Rigby from teenage world medalist to heralded musical theater star and producer.

Media and Technology

Almost all things cultural in America—from stage entertainment, to the music business, to film, to news and information packaging, and to political discourse —had to adjust to the sudden advent of radio broadcasting in the 1920s, followed in generational succession by the rise of television in the early 1950s and the Internet in the 1990s. Along the way Broadway has had to reconcile its traditions of intimate connection with a live audience and the practical need to stay relevant in a culture that subsumes every new phase of technology as soon as it comes along. The relationship between Broadway and modern media still appears tenuous at times, but thanks in large measure to a generation of directors, designers, and technicians who were educated, if not bottle-fed, with computer and digital technology, Broadway and new technology have made important strides together.

Roads, Regionals, and Class Acts

Broadway influences and is influenced by American culture in ways that are if not uniquely its own certainly peculiar to itself. Commercial theater earned its place in American culture the hard way, through word of mouth and through arduous touring long before radio and recordings, much less television and the Internet, could broadcast its riches across the country. American professional theater was a road business before New York or any other city had a professional theater district, and touring—from its wagon wheel beginnings to the multimillion dollar Broadway touring enterprise of today—is a critical and widely underdiscussed dimension of Broadway's impact on national culture. No less important a factor is the strength and resilience of American's regional (or resident) theaters. Regional theaters first made their names and drew their local audiences by providing outreach venues for preestablished hits and occasional experimental alternatives to the perceived homogenization of Broadway. Over the past 40 years, however, many regional theaters have flexed their muscles as discoverers and producers of new Broadway plays and musicals, touting (and often profiting handsomely from) their new role as Broadway producers in the hinterlands.

The recent craze of Disney Theatrical Productions' *High School Musical* play franchise, which, perhaps ironically, has never had a Broadway opening, has given national exposure to the long-overlooked relationship between Broadway and America's schools. Hiding in plain sight, the ubiquitous yet seemingly innocuous American "school play" has been a major factor in the way Americans learn to connect their own experiences to the world of Broadway theater. This has been especially true since the late 1960s when musicals like *Hair* (1968) and *Grease*

(1972) opened Broadway's doors to American teenage and even pre-teenage audiences. (Pre-teenagers now lay claim to proprietary ownership of musicals of their own, such as *Wicked* [2003] and *13* [2008].) No less important than the school play is the gradual ascendancy of the American playwright in the twentieth century from commercial hack, to respected writer, to author of canonical status. The ascendance in the twentieth century of major American playwrights into the realm of American literature and even world drama is due in large measure to the work of high school and college educators. In the mid-twentieth century, teachers began to insist that works by Thornton Wilder, Eugene O'Neill, Arthur Miller, and Tennessee Williams deserved to stand side by side in classroom "required reading" with the novels of Ernest Hemingway and F. Scott Fitzgerald as well as Western classics.

In some sense, *Broadway: An Encyclopedia of Theater and American Culture* aspires to do for the history of Broadway and American culture what a *Playbill Magazine* program, handed to each of us as we attend a Broadway show, does for a night in the theater. A reminder that there is more to what we see than what we are seeing, this reference book provides a number of contexts for viewing the "performance" that is theater's ever-evolving place in American culture. Profiles on selected artists and information on selected landmark productions flesh out and give context to discussion of larger cultural themes—more or less a behind-the-scenes look at how Broadway and American culture continuously define and redefine each other.

Enjoy the show.

Reference

"GOP takes aim at Barack and Michelle Obama's NYC trip." Retrieved May 30, 2009, from http://www.politico.com/news/stories/0509/23122.html.

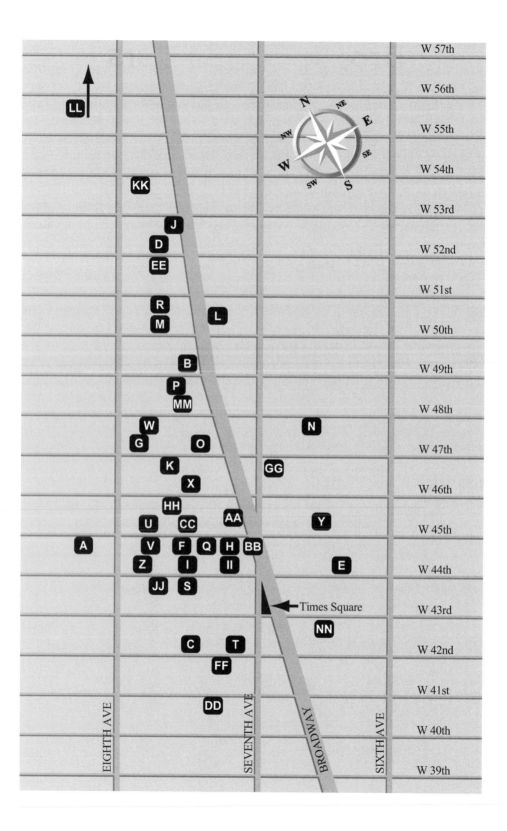

Broadway Theaters

A Al Hirschfeld
302 W. 45th St.

B Ambassador
219 W. 49th St.

I American Airlines
227 W. 42nd St.

D August Wilson
245 W. 52nd St.

E Belasco
111 W. 44th St.

I Bernard B. Jacobs
242 W. 45th St.

G Biltmore
261 W. 47th St.

H Booth
222 W. 45th St.

I Broadhurst
235 W. 44th St.

J Broadway
Broadway at 53rd St.

K Brooks Atkinson
256 W. 47th St.

I Winter Garden
1634 Broadway

M Circle in the Square
1633 Broadway/
235 W. Broadway

N Cort
138 W. 48th St.

O Ethel Barrymore
243 W. 47th St.

P Eugene O'Neill
230 W. 49th St.

Q Gerald Schoenfeld
236 W. 45th St.

R Gershwin
222 W. 51st St.

S Helen Hayes
240 W. 44th St.

T Hilton Theatre
213 W. 42nd St.

U Imperial
249 W. 45th St.

V John Golden
252 W. 45th St.

W Longacre
220 W. 48th St.

X Lunt-Fontanne
205 W. 46th St.

Y Lyceum
149 W. 45th St.

Z Majestic
247 W. 44th St.

AA Marquis
1535 Broadway

BB Minskoff
200 W. 45th St.

CC Music Box
239 W. 45th St.

DD Nederlander
208 W. 41st St.

EE Neil Simon
250 W. 52nd St.

FF New Amsterdam
214 W. 42nd St.

GG Palace
1564 Broadway/
47th St. and 7th Ave.

HH Richard Rodgers
226 W. 46th St.

II Shubert
225 W. 44th St.

JJ St. James
246 W. 44th St.

KK Studio 54
254 W. 54th St.

LL Vivian Beaumont
150 W. 65th St.

MM Walter Kerr
219 W. 48th St.

****NN** Henry Miller's Theatre
124 W. 43rd St.

*Henry Miller's Theatre was restored and opened as
an official Broadway Theater in the fall of 2009.

Timeline

❧

Year	Event
1664c.	The English peacefully take over lower Manhattan from the Dutch and rename the north-south trail known as "Heer Straat" Broadway.
1732c.	Early maps of New York City identify two theaters: the New Theatre on Nassau Street in lower Manhattan and the Theatre on Broadway.
1753	Lewis Hallam's London Company of Comedians, generally considered to be the first permanent professional theatrical company in the United States, arrives in New York from England.
1811	The Randel Plan for New York City requires Manhattan's avenues and streets in the relatively undeveloped area above (what is now known as) 14th Street to be constructed in uniform size and at right angles. Broadway remains a diagonal.
1826	The Bowery Theatre opens in 1826. Surviving numerous fires and even more numerous changes of ownership, it persists as the longest lasting American theater building to date. It closed permanently in 1929, under the name Fay's Bowery Theatre.
1847	Christy's Minstrels take up a ten-year residency in Mechanics Hall on Broadway, inaugurating a 25-year vogue of blackface minstrelsy in New York.
May 10, 1849	The Astor Place Riot. American theatergoers, in support of American actor Edwin Forrest, violently protest the appearance of English rival William Charles Macready as Macbeth at the Astor Place Opera House in New York.

Over 20 people are killed as military police break up the riot.

1864–1865 Edwin Booth performs his famous 100 Nights of *Hamlet* at the Winter Garden Theatre. The run gains sufficient cachet in theater history that it compels John Barrymore to play Hamlet 101 times in 1922, just to break Booth's record.

1866 *The Black Crook*, the first Broadway long-running hit musical, opens at Niblo's Garden. Produced by the theater's manager William Wheatley, the play runs for one year and grosses over $1 million.

July 1878 George M. Cohan, "Mr. Broadway," is born in Providence, Rhode Island. Cohan claimed the Fourth of July as his birthday although the issue has been disputed by some historians.

January 15, 1879 Gilbert and Sullivan's *H.M.S. Pinafore* opens on Broadway. Although it is their second Broadway show, it is their first hit and creates a sensation throughout the country. Gilbert and Sullivan productions will open on Broadway over 150 times in the next 100 years, the most of any modern era composer and/or lyricist of the twentieth century.

1880s–1940c. The Era of Tin Pan Alley, named for a section of midtown Manhattan where music publishing companies clustered to create and market (plug) songs. The principal source for generating popular music, including songs that would find their way into Broadway shows, "Tin Pan Alley" eventually became a descriptor for the music itself as well as the location of the music companies.

October 16, 1888 Playwright Eugene O'Neill is born in New York City.

June 9, 1891 Composer/lyricist Cole Porter is born in Peru, Indiana.

July 12, 1895 Lyricist Oscar Hammerstein II is born in New York City. With Richard Rodgers, Rodgers and Hammerstein become the premiere American composer/lyricist team in Broadway history.

1896 The Theatrical Syndicate is formed. Theater owners and entrepreneurs A. L. Erlanger, Charles Frohman, William Harris, Al Hayman, Marc Klaw, Samuel F. Nixon-Nirdlinger, and Fred Zimmerman consolidate their theater ownership, production, and booking interests. Within two years they had monopolistic control over the commercial theater industry in New York and nationwide.

1900   The Shubert Brothers, theater owners from Syracuse, New York, move to New York City to challenge the Theatrical Syndicate's control of commercial theater operations. By the start of World War I, they had replaced the Syndicate's monopolistic control of commercial theater with their own.

October 10, 1900   Actress Helen Hayes, "The First Lady of the American Theater," is born in Washington, D.C.

February 25, 1901   *The Governor's Son*, George M. Cohan's first Broadway show, opens. The 22-year-old wrote the book, music, and lyrics, and starred in the first of his 25 plus musicals and numerous plays. He soon becomes the first, and many assert the greatest, twentieth-century American star of Broadway musical theater.

June 28, 1902   Composer Richard Rodgers is born in New York City. He becomes the most prodigious and most decorated American composer of Broadway musicals in history.

1904   New York City formally renames Long Acre Square "Times Square."

November 7, 1904   Cohan's *Little Johnny Jones* opens on Broadway. The hit show contains the song "Give My Regards to Broadway," to this day the unofficial anthem of the theater district.

July 8, 1907   Florenz Ziegfeld stages the first *Ziegfeld Follies*, which polished vaudeville and burlesque traditions to create a historic family friendly variety stage show. He would mount these immensely popular revues almost annually until 1931.

1910   Bert Williams debuts in *Ziegfeld Follies* and performs with Ziegfeld until 1920. He eventually becomes a headline performer for Ziegfeld, the first black performer to headline a predominantly white cast musical or revue on Broadway.

May 26, 1913   Following a series of labor strikes, Actors' Equity Association (colloquially called "Equity") is founded in New York by 112 actors over the heated objections of many theater producers.

February 13, 1914
ASCAP (American Society of Composers, Authors and Publishers) is founded for the purpose of protecting copyrights and ensuring fair compensation for composers, lyricists, and their publishers for public performances of their works.

1915
The Provincetown Players, the Neighborhood Playhouse, and the Washington Square Players are established. Collectively they formed the nucleus of what came to be known as America's Little Theater Movement.

1915–1918
Jerome Kern and several collaborators write *The Princess Theatre Musicals*, a series of small shows for the intimate 299-seat Princess Theatre at 39th and Broadway. The shows represented an early example of American musical creators experimenting with sophisticated characterizations, plots, and songs—qualities that would later become standard features of American musicals.

1918
Playwright Jesse Lynch Williams's *Why Marry?* wins the first Pulitzer Prize for Drama.

1917c.–1930
The Harlem Renaissance. A period of flourishing African American arts and culture in the Harlem district of New York City and African American communities across the country. Mainstream Broadway plays and musicals soon show some increased involvement of African Americans and a growing influence of jazz as well as other aspects of African American culture on productions.

November 1, 1920
Charles S. Gilpin opens on Broadway in Eugene O'Neill's *The Emperor Jones*, becoming the first African American dramatic actor to perform the lead role in a Broadway play.

May 23, 1921
Eubie Blake and Noble Sissle's *Shuffle Along* opens. At 504 performances it becomes the longest-running production by an all African American creative team up to that time. It makes a partial break with the minstrelsy and "coon song" traditions of black musicals. The song "I'm Just Wild About Harry" is immortalized in American culture when it becomes Harry Truman's campaign song.

1927–1928
A generally accepted record of 264 or more shows open in one Broadway season, upwards of six times the number that open in a season today. The 1927–1928 season

is commonly cited as the historic high-water mark for new productions.

1927

Show Boat by Jerome Kern and Oscar Hammerstein II opens. *Show Boat* defies musical theater traditions of presenting spectacle as its main point of appeal, instead taking on social issues of race and class prejudice. The song "Ol' Man River" becomes an American classic concert song.

1929–1940

The Great Depression. Theaters in New York and across the country close or convert to movie houses. Theater production declines precipitously in New York.

1930

The League of American Theatres and Producers, Inc. (now known as the Broadway League) is founded by New York theater operators. The League negotiates collective bargaining agreements with various theatrical guilds and unions and otherwise promotes the interests of theater producers and presenters.

1935–1939

As part of the New Deal, the Roosevelt administration establishes the Federal Theatre Project (FTP), a government agency that keeps theaters open and theater artists employed around the country during the Depression. Supporters credit the FTP with saving professional theater from economic ruin. Critics rail against the left-wing themes of many of its productions and hail Congress's decision to suspend its funding in 1939.

November 8, 1939

Howard Lindsay and Russel Crouse's comedy *Life with Father* opens on Broadway. It runs for 3,224 performances over seven years, becoming the longest-running straight play in Broadway history to date.

March 31, 1943

Rodgers and Hammerstein's *Oklahoma!* opens. It ushers in a 25-year Golden Age of Musicals, in which strong integration of story, song, libretto, dance, and staging becomes the standard by which musicals are judged by critics and audiences.

October 19, 1943

The "Paul Robeson *Othello*" opens on Broadway. Running for 296 performances, it becomes the longest-running professional Shakespearean revival in American history.

April 6, 1947	The American Theatre Wing presents the first annual Antoinette Perry Awards (the Tony Awards) at the Waldorf-Astoria Hotel in Manhattan.
1947–1955c.	The House Un-American Activities Committee (HUAC) conducts investigations of alleged communist affiliations of prominent entertainment figures. Director Elia Kazan, choreographer Jerome Robbins, and actor Lee J. Cobb are among the notable Broadway figures who "named names" to the Committee. Playwrights Arthur Miller and Lillian Hellman refused to do so when called.
1949	Cole Porter's *Kiss Me, Kate* wins the first-ever Tony Award for Best Musical.
February 10, 1949	Arthur Miller's *Death of a Salesman* opens.
January 22, 1953	Arthur Miller's *The Crucible* opens. The two Miller plays are very successful despite their uncompromising criticism of, respectively, America's self-defeating idealization of appearances and the mindless "patriotism" of HUAC and its supporters. Over time the two plays became staples in high school and college English classes and theater programs, eventually "competing" against each other as the most performed and widely read American plays ever written.
March 5, 1955	NBC stages and broadcasts a live performance of the hit musical *Peter Pan*, directed by Jerome Robbins and starring Mary Martin. An estimated 60+ million viewers watch, a harbinger of future interactions between television and Broadway.
May 15, 1956	Alan J. Lerner and Frederick Loewe's *My Fair Lady* opens. It runs for six and a half years, eventually overtaking *Oklahoma!* as the longest-running musical up to that time.
November 7, 1956	Eugene O'Neill's *Long Day's Journey into Night* opens. It is considered by many critics to be the finest modern dramatic production ever to appear on Broadway.
March 11, 1959	Lorraine Hansberry's *A Raisin in the Sun* opens. It is the first major Broadway hit play written by an African American woman. The play is now viewed as a canonical work of American social drama and African American literature.

1961	*West Side Story* becomes the first film adaptation of a Broadway musical to win the Oscar for Best Picture.
October 10, 1962	Edward Albee's first full-length play, *Who's Afraid of Virginia Woolf?*, opens on Broadway. Controversies surrounding the production place the author in the center of debates about the present and future state of American playwriting, where he has remained ever since.
October 23, 1963	Neil Simon's *Barefoot in the Park* opens. Simon's third Broadway play, the smash hit makes him America's most popular comic playwright, a position he would not relinquish for over 25 years.
April 29, 1968	Gerome Ragni and James Rado's *Hair* opens on Broadway, ushering in the Rock (or Rock and Roll) Musical. Some historians cite *Hair* as signaling the decline of the "book" musical era or the Golden Age of Musicals that began with *Oklahoma!* in 1943.
June–July 1969	The Stonewall Riots in New York City effectively launch the modern gay/lesbian rights movement, resulting in new levels of visibility and openness regarding gay life and gay participation in commercial theater as well American society at large.
April 26, 1970	Stephen Sondheim's *Company* opens on Broadway, ushering in the "concept musical."
July 25, 1975	Michael Bennett's concept musical *A Chorus Line* opens. It revolutionizes the role of dance in late twentieth century Broadway musicals. It runs for almost five years, becoming the longest-running American-originated musical in Broadway history.
September 10, 1976	*for colored girls who have considered suicide/when the rainbow is enuf*, a self-labeled "choreopoem" by Ntozake Shange, opens on Broadway. With 742 performances it is the longest-running Broadway play ever written by an African American.
October 7, 1982	Andrew Lloyd Webber's *Cats*, produced by Cameron Mackintosh, transfers from London and opens on Broadway. The visual spectacle breaks all previous Broadway box-office records (18 years and over 7,400 performances) and ushers in the "European megamusical" as a Broadway phenomenon.

October 3, 1984   August Wilson's *Ma Rainey's Black Bottom* premieres on Broadway. *Ma Rainey* is the first of nine Broadway productions from Wilson's cycle of dramas about twentieth-century African American families—each set in a different decade of the twentieth century. The cycle is now acclaimed as a major achievement in modern American drama.

1986c.–1996c.   New York City and state governments with local businesses (especially the commercial theater industry) transform the theater district from a haven for drugs, prostitution, and pornography to a family-friendly tourist center. (Arguments persist to this day about precisely when the cleanup began and, predictably, to whom the lion's share of the credit for the cleanup should go.)

January 26, 1988   Andrew Lloyd Webber's *The Phantom of the Opera* opens on Broadway. In January 9, 2006, it became the longest-running and most lucrative show in Broadway history. In July 2009 *Phantom* was in the twenty-second year of its run, approaching 9,000 performances. Press estimates of the gross of all *Phantom* productions and merchandise exceed US$5 billion, making it the most lucrative single entertainment enterprise in history.

1988   David Henry Hwang wins the Tony Award for Best Play, *M. Butterfly*, becoming the first author of Asian or Asian American heritage to do so.

May 4, 1993   Tony Kushner's *Angels in America: Millennium Approaches* opens on Broadway. The highly innovative play powerfully dramatizes the political dynamics of the AIDS debate that figures prominently in American politics and culture during the 1980s and 1990s.

April 16, 1996   Jonathan Larson's *Rent* opens on Broadway. The posthumous 12-year run of the young author/composer/lyricist's musical brought the so-called "MTV generation" (or part of Generation X) to Broadway. *Rent* demanded of its audience nonjudgmental acceptance of homosexuality, bisexuality, and compassion for AIDS victims. The show and its creator have achieved iconic cultural standing among many young people during its high profile turn on Broadway.

1998   Julie Taymor becomes the first woman to win a Tony Award for Best Direction of a Musical (*The Lion King*).

	Garry Hynes becomes the first woman to win a Tony Award for Best Direction of a Play (*The Beauty Queen of Leenane*).
April 19, 2001	Mel Brooks's musical *The Producers* opens on Broadway. It wins 12 Tonys, the most for any production in the history of awards.
September 11, 2001	"9/11" has a devastating aftereffect on all air travel in the United States. Broadway, increasingly dependent on tourists since the arrival of mass appeal megamusicals and the cleanup of Times Square, suffers a one-season setback in ticket sales, new productions, and other economic indicators for the industry. A concerted promotional effort by the theater community and state and city governments results in evidence of a turnaround by 2003.
October 5, 2001	*Mamma Mia!* opens on Broadway. In spite of opening three weeks after "9/11," the show prospers. Still in its initial run in late 2009, it is the longest-running Broadway show that opened in the new millennium.
November 10– November 28, 2007	A prolonged strike by Broadway stagehands shuts down most Broadway shows for three weeks, including the lucrative Thanksgiving weekend. Losses to Broadway producers are estimated in the tens of millions of dollars.
March 9, 2008	*In the Heights* opens on Broadway and becomes the first mainstream hit musical by an all-Latino creative team. Composer/author Lin-Manuel Miranda brings long-neglected Latino culture to the Broadway stage. The show interweaves a multitude of urban music styles while artfully combining English and Spanish dialogue and lyrics in an homage to New York's Latino communities.
June 7, 2009	Playwright Yasmina Reza wins the Tony Award for Best Play, *God of Carnage*, becoming the first woman ever to win a second Best Play Tony Award. She won her first Tony Award in 1998 for *Art*.

Notes

Edwin Booth, 100 nights of *Hamlet*. Shattuck, Charles H. *Shakespeare on the American Stage: From Booth and Barrett to Sothern and Marlowe*. Washington, DC: Folger Shakespeare Library, 1987.

The Black Crook as first hit, a million-dollar musical. Kislan, Richard. *The Musical: A Look at the American Musical Theater.* Second ed., revised. Hal Leonard Corporation, 1995.

Thomas A. Greenfield/Caitlin Klein

ABBOTT, GEORGE (1887–1995)
DIRECTOR, PRODUCER, CO-WRITER, ACTOR

George Abbott's many accomplishments as a co-writer, director, **producer**, and actor make him one of the fathers of both American musical comedy and commercial theater. Using a combination of practical experience, common sense, and natural talent, Abbott reshaped the American **musical**. In a producing, writing, and directing career that lasted over 60 years, Abbott highlighted plot structure, demanded sound dialogue that enhanced characterization, and directed with a crispness and energy that produced consistently entertaining shows. This method would become famously known as "the Abbott touch" and garner Abbott many accolades and disciples.

Abbott was born in Salamanca, New York, in 1887. When he was a young boy, his family relocated to Cheyenne, Wyoming. Abbott would return to western New York as a young man to complete his education at the University of Rochester. He began his lengthy and rich association with the theater in 1913 as an actor, performing in New York City for over a decade in a variety of productions, including Gilbert and Sullivan **operettas** and early plays by John Howard Lawson and **Maxwell Anderson**. His interests extended to writing plays and, although he considered himself to be an undistinguished **playwright** of solo-written works, he displayed an early gift for co-writing that would bear fruit in later phases of his career. Abbott hit his stride in the 1920s co-writing such popular successes as *Broadway* (1926) and *Coquette* (1927). He was also earning a reputation as an astute director, bringing such plays as the aforementioned and Maurine Watkins's *Chicago* (1926) to the stage. He directed his first musical comedy, *Jumbo* (1935), with music and lyrics by **Richard Rodgers** and **Lorenz Hart**, by then among the elite Broadway composers of the day. Although *Jumbo* was successful, running 233 performances, his next effort with Rodgers and Hart was a smash. The ballet-themed musical *On Your Toes* (1936) ran for over 300 performances and established Abbott's model for what it took to produce a hit musical comedy. Every one of his best-known shows, from *On Your Toes* to *Once Upon a Mattress* (1959), boasted some of the greatest music that could be heard on a Broadway stage. The dialogue was fresh, snappy, and humorous in a timely way. And the list of choreographers who would move the choruses about in Abbott-directed plays, including **Jerome Robbins**, **George Balanchine**, and **Bob Fosse**, would further redefine musical theater.

After *Jumbo* and *On Your Toes*, Abbott became the most prolific and successful director of musical comedies for the next three decades. His ***Pal Joey*** (1940), *Where's Charley?* (1948), and *On the Town* (1944), which represented the auspicious Broadway debut for composer **Leonard Bernstein** and the librettist/lyricist team of **Betty Comden** and **Adolph Green**, were among the defining Broadway shows of the decade. He also directed and occasionally produced straight stage comedies, such as Clifford Goldsmith's school days hit *What a Life* (1938). In the 1950s, he would direct more historic hits, including **Irving Berlin**'s *Call Me*

George Abbott, right, with actress and singer Carol Burnett and her grandmother Mae White, posing at Broadway's Mark Hellinger Theater after the premiere of the new musical Fade Out—Fade In, *1964. Abbott directed the show and Burnett starred, with music by Jule Styne and book and lyrics by Betty Comden and Adolph Green. (AP Photo)*

Madame (1950), *The Pajama Game* (1954), *Damn Yankees* (1955), *Once Upon a Mattress* (1959), and *Fiorello!* (1959). Abbott's directing career would reach its peak with *A Funny Thing Happened on the Way to the Forum* (1962). It was his last original hit show but by no means the end of his career as a director or producer.

Abbott remained active throughout the 1960s and 1970s directing a range of shows from **John Kander and Fred Ebb's** Liza Minnelli star vehicle *Flora, The Red Menace* (1965) and the **gay**-themed comedy *Norman, Is That You?* (1970). He would also oversee short-lived revivals of his *Three Men on a Horse* (1935, revival 1969) and *The Pajama Game* (1954, revival 1973). In 1983 at age 95, he directed a hit revival of *On Your Toes*, capitalizing on a surge of audience interest in ballet that followed the improbable rise to pop stardom of former Russian dancer Rudolph Nureyev and other ballet artists. The production won the Tony Award for Best Reproduction (revival) of a Play or Musical.

Abbott would retire from the theater after this final success though his presence would continue to be felt through the many revivals of musicals, comedies, and dramas that benefited greatly from the "Abbott touch." He earned a slew of honors throughout his theater career, including two Tony Awards for Best Direction of a Musical (*Fiorello!* and *A Funny Thing Happened on the Way to the Forum*), three additional Tonys for Best Book of a Musical (*The Pajama Game, Damn Yankees,* and *Fiorello!*), plus two special Tony Awards. He also won the Pulitzer Prize for *Fiorello!* Abbott occasionally worked in Hollywood, often overseeing one or more aspects of film adaptations for his musicals. (Early in his career, he had even earned an Oscar nomination as screenwriter for the 1930 landmark war picture, *All Quiet on the Western Front.*)

Abbott's phenomenal productivity, innovativeness, longevity, and standard-setting success place him with the likes of **George M. Cohan** and **Flo Ziegfeld** as the producer/directors who shaped and defined the modern American musical.

George Abbott died from a stroke in 1995 in Miami Beach, Florida.

Darryl Kent Clark

Further Reading

Berger, Marilyn. "George Abbott, Broadway Giant with Hit after Hit, Is Dead at 107." *New York Times* (online). February 2, 1995. http://www.nytimes.com/1995/02/02/obituaries/george-abbott-broadway-giant-with-hit-after-hit-is-dead-at-107.html?scp=8&sq=%22george%20abbott%22&st=cse (accessed March 25, 2009).

Roberts, Jerry. *The Great American Playwrights on the Screen: A Critical Guide to Film, TV, Video and DVD*. New York: Applause, 2003.

THE ACTORS STUDIO
EDUCATIONAL INSTITUTION, PRODUCER, THEATER OWNER

Founded in the fall of 1947 by three alumnae of the **Group Theatre**, **Elia Kazan**, Cheryl Crawford, and Robert Lewis, the Actors Studio began simply as a workshop for gifted stage performers. However, it quickly became the U.S. center for teaching and promoting Method Acting, the most influential and controversial development in American acting since World War II.

At its inception, the Studio founders offered classes to New York actors but charged no tuition and handed out no diplomas; once an actor was accepted into the Actors Studio, membership was permanent. In essence, the studio was created to be a talent pool from which the three directors could cast their stage productions, independent of the demands and pressures of the commercial theater.

Only two months after its founding, however, the enormous Broadway success of **Tennessee Williams**'s *A Streetcar Named Desire* made leading man and Actors Studio student/member **Marlon Brando** famous, and unexpectedly put the Actors Studio at the center of what would become a seismic cultural shift in attitudes toward the theater. *Streetcar* director Kazan and most of the cast were affiliated with the Actors Studio, but it was Brando's well-publicized utilization of Method Acting that became a topic of sometimes heated public debate, pitting the psychological and internal exploration of Actors Studio modernists against the externalized, expressive stage grandeur of Broadway traditionalists. The Studio's carefully taught techniques of psychological exploration such as affective memory and "the private moment" were celebrated by some as a revolutionary step forward in acting, while others denounced those same tools as self-indulgent.

The arrival of Group Theatre co-founder and head acting instructor **Lee Strasberg** at the studio as a teacher in 1949 set the organization's course thereafter. Like Crawford, Kazan, and Lewis, Strasberg was a devotee of Method Acting, which derived from the theories of Russian director Konstantin Stanislavsky and which Strasberg had adapted for the Group Theatre in the 1930s. Within two years Strasberg became the Actors Studio's artistic director, a position he held until his death in 1982. While one-time colleagues such as Robert Lewis (who left the studio prior to Strasberg's arrival) and Stella Adler came to reconsider the importance of the Method and deemphasize its application in their own teaching, Strasberg remained a firm adherent of Method techniques. Under his tutelage, studio members focused primarily on contemporary American works by such playwrights as Williams, **Arthur Miller**, **William Inge**, etc., to the point where critics complained that training in the classics and period drama was neglected.

From the 1950s onward Actors Studio members worked extensively on **Broadway**, on **Off-Broadway**, and in live television. The studio trained a number of prominent actors who made a significant impact on Hollywood and Broadway, including Brando, James Dean, **Lee J. Cobb**, Rod Steiger, and later Paul Newman, Jack Nicholson, Al Pacino, and Willem Dafoe. The studio's best-known actresses include Anne Bancroft, Kim Stanley, Shelley Winters, and Geraldine Page.

For a number of years Strasberg resisted establishing an Actors Studio production company, but eventually in the early 1960s the studio ventured into the field with disappointing results on Broadway and disastrous results overseas. When the Actors Studio took Anton Chekhov's *The Three Sisters* to London as part of the World Theatre Festival in 1964, the production was greeted with catcalls, an experience that contributed to actress Kim Stanley's nervous breakdown and subsequent withdrawal from acting. After this, the Actors Studio returned to its primary function as a workshop.

In 1967 a California branch opened in West Hollywood. The studio struggled to adapt to changing times in the period after Strasberg's death, briefly closing in the late 1980s. However, affiliations developed since the 1990s with The New School and Pace University in New York City have provided the Studio with sufficient finances to sustain its educational mission.

Today the Actors Studio grants graduate degrees in acting, directing, and play-writing through its Actors Studio Drama School. Many people know the Studio best through its popular cable interview show *Inside the Actors Studio*, in which the school's colorful Dean Emeritus James Lipton interviews major figures from theater and film.

Although the Studio's influence has long since peaked, the fact that many principles of Method Acting are still widely taught and practiced serves as a measure of the Studio's lasting impact upon Broadway, Hollywood, and beyond.

William Charles Morrow

Further Reading

Hirsch, Foster. *A Method to Their Madness: The History of the Actors Studio*. New York: Da Capo, 2002.

Krasner, David. *Method Acting Reconsidered: Theory, Practice, Future*. New York: Palgrave Macmillan, 2000.

African American Dramatic Theater

Before Broadway: Nineteenth Century to the Harlem Renaissance

William Henry Brown's *The Drama of King Shotaway* (1823), the story of a slave uprising on the island of St. Vincent, is the first professional play known to have been written by an African American. The play was never performed in any mainstream theater but only at Brown's own short-lived African Grove Theater in New York. This theater was closed down by racist pressure from white theater owners, who feared that its growing popularity would affect ticket sales for the racially restricted seating sections of mainstream theaters. William Wells Brown's *The Escape; or, A Leap for Freedom* (1858) was the first black play published in America, but it, too, would not be seen on **Broadway**.

In the first part of the twentieth century black theater flourished mostly beyond the Broadway stage in community theaters, experimental groups, and black theater companies that were being established around the country. Overshadowed by the popular black **musicals** at the beginning of the century, serious drama by African Americans would get a slow start. One notable early twentieth-century pioneering theater group, the Lafayette Players, operating in a desegregated Harlem theater space in the 1910s, experimented with plays by African Americans beyond the limiting purview of the Broadway critics. W. E. B. Du Bois, one of the leading African American intellectuals and activists of the early twentieth century and a founder of the NAACP, recognized the power of the theater to both educate and proselytize. Although principally an essayist and editor, Du Bois's 1913 pageant *The Star of Ethiopia*, a sweeping history of African Americans, would be performed around the country, though not on Broadway. Another influential contribution to early African American theater would be Angelina Weld Grimké's *Rachel* (1916), a play about the effect of lynching on a middle-class African American family. *Rachel* kindled a debate among leading African American intellectuals over whether African American plays should be more concerned with racial issues or the playwright's personal interests and artistic aspirations. The debate inspired Du Bois to create the Drama Committee of the NAACP to encourage new black **playwrights**.

During the Harlem Renaissance of the 1920s, a historic surge of artistic creativity and political self-assertion within the black community of New York's upper Manhattan and beyond, African American writers and artists strengthened their position of influence among their fellow African Americans while attracting new levels of interest in their work among white audiences, producers, and mainstream press. African American literature and theater in particular benefited greatly from the Harlem Renaissance. Playwrights Langston Hughes and Zora Neale Hurston, stage performers **Paul Robeson**, **Charles S. Gilpin**, Pearl Bailey, and **Rose McClendon**, and McClendon's Negro People's Theater of Harlem all figured prominently in the Harlem Renaissance and eventually received recognition as important artists in the larger history of American theater. The period of the Harlem Renaissance also saw a few breakthrough appearances for African American artists on Broadway, especially playwrights.

The first Broadway drama by an African American playwright was Willis Richardson's one-act folk play, *The Chip Woman's Fortune* (1923), which tells the story of an impoverished but God-fearing family that survives the repossession of their Victrola. *Chip Woman* presented to Broadway a new image of the simple day-to-day life of most African Americans struggling to get by, leavened with a little light comedy that was not dependent on malapropisms or other vestiges of minstrel humor. Richardson never had another play produced on Broadway. The full-length *Appearances* (1925) by Garland Anderson was more sensational, depicting the trial of a morally upright bellhop unjustly accused of attacking a white woman (who turns out to be a mulatto). The play ran only a few weeks, possibly because, while it maintained a passive attitude toward the evident racism of its white characters, it did present the discomfiting issue of racism on stage. Anderson, a former bellboy himself, was concerned with conveying a more generalized message of self-worth and had struggled long and hard to get his play produced. Like Richardson, Anderson was unable to get any subsequent plays produced on Broadway.

Frank Wilson, a talented actor who had appeared in white-written dramas during the 1920s, such as Paul Green's *In Abraham's Bosom* (1926) and the title role in the Heywards' *Porgy* (1927), had his play *Meek Mose* (1928) produced at the famous Princess Theatre. Like Anderson, Wilson seemed wary of offending white patrons, and the play deflects what could have been a serious social commentary with deliberately comic black speech and passive heroes. Most critics dismissed it as too formulaic, and Wilson continued to have much greater success as an actor.

Novelist Wallace Thurman and William Jourdan Rapp's *Harlem* (1929) enjoyed a successful 100-show run with its salacious depiction of Harlem nightlife and introduction of the Slow Drag dance. Though some found its success encouraging, others found its depiction of African Americans to be degrading. Segregation was still a reality in New York, and Thurman, denied access to center seats, was forced to sit in the theater's black section for his own play. Although the play was predominantly Thurman's idea, having been developed from an earlier short story he had written titled "Cordelia the Crude," his white playwriting partner, Rapp, was always noticeably given primary billing. The pair were unable to find financing for their next play, *Jeremiah the Magnificent*, which was about a far less sexy topic, political activist and Pan-Africanist philosopher Marcus Garvey.

When the Depression overtook the American theater business, African American playwrights and performers were harder hit than their white counterparts. Although there were Negro Theater Units in the **Federal Theatre Project**, few works by African Americans saw Broadway production until after World War II. A notable exception to the Depression-era drought of African American authored plays on Broadway was Langston Hughes's surprise hit *Mulatto* (1935). An exploration of the issue of miscegenation, *Mulatto* was Hughes's first full-length play. It stunned many by running for 373 performances and touring successfully. Though melodramatic in form, its impact is intensified by its forthright approach to an inflammatory issue and Hughes's refusal to present miscegenation as it had been approached by white playwrights, namely, as a source of shame and self-disgust. Hughes would not have another Broadway success until 1947 with a musical version of Elmer Rice's *Street Scene* (1929), written with German composer Kurt Weill. Hughes's other efforts to bring his plays to Broadway were less successful, although they played well elsewhere. These included *Simply Heaven* (1957) and *Tambourines to Glory* (1963). *Mule Bone*, a play he wrote with Zora Neale Hurston, would not be seen on Broadway until 1991 when Lincoln Center mounted a production.

Aside from the work of Hughes, nine plays produced on Broadway through the Negro Theater Unit of the Federal Theatre Project included a controversial "voodoo" *Macbeth* (1936) set in Haiti and created by Orson Welles and John Houseman. The Federal Theatre also produced William Du Bois's *Haiti* (1938), a play about Haitian politics. Both plays depicted influential images of black nationhood. Frank Wilson wrote and directed *Walk Together Chillun* (1936), which, like Rudolph Fisher's *Conjur Man Dies* (1936), was more in the folk theater than Broadway theater tradition.

The Federal Theatre Project as a whole provided a good training ground for future African American artists. By 1940 black theater was firmly grounded in two widely respected theater companies: the American Negro Theater and the

Negro Playwrights' Company. Although the former's *Anna Lucasta* (1944), written by white playwright Philip Yordan, would be their only Broadway production, it was tremendously successful, running for 957 performances with an all-black cast.

The period between 1945 and the early 1960s saw a surge of African American playwrights entering the literary and theatrical mainstream with progressive and radical ideas about strengthening African American cultural identity. A committee was formed among Actors' Equity, the League of New York Theaters, the Dramatists Guild, the Negro Actor's Guild, and the NAACP to try to increase African American employment in Broadway shows, combat racial stereotyping in the theater, and encourage upcoming African American writers. Many African American plays of the period dealt with creating a positive identity for blacks in society. Louis Peterson is best known for his first play, *Take a Giant Step* (1953), a coming-of-age story, largely autobiographical, of a young black man, growing up in a predominantly white, middle-class area in Hartford, Connecticut. The young man faces the insidious racism meted out by his teachers and schoolmates. The play exposed Broadway's middle-class white audiences to the implications of their own innate racism. A young Lou Gossett Jr. garnered considerable attention playing the teenage lead and launched his vaunted stage, television, and film career. Similarly, Theodore Ward's *Our Lan'* (1947) saw moderate success in its attempt to reevaluate the African American's place in American culture. In 1941 Orson Welles, who had demonstrated a commitment to black themes in much of his theatrical work, produced and directed a respectable adaptation of Richard Wright's *Native Son*, co-written by Wright and Paul Green. *The Long Dream*, adapted by Ketti Frings from another of Wright's novels in 1960, was not as successful, closing after five performances. However, another black novelist, James Baldwin, would have more success with two plays: *Blues for Mister Charlie* (1964) and *The Amen Corner* (1965).

Lorraine Hansberry's **A Raisin in the Sun** (1959) gave African American drama its first bona fide Broadway hit. The play ran for over 500 performances, swept the Tony Awards, and won the New York Drama Critics Circle Award for Best Play of the Year over **Tennessee Williams**'s *Sweet Bird of Youth*, Archibald MacLeish's *J.B.*, and **Eugene O'Neill**'s *A Touch of the Poet*. Hansberry became an overnight celebrity, appearing on numerous talk shows and using these platforms as an opportunity to speak to a wider audience about the need for black social, political, and economic reform.

Hansberry's racial commentary is subtle throughout the play, which takes its title from a Langston Hughes poem about the way in which the dreams of African Americans are constantly deferred in America. *A Raisin in the Sun* depicts a middle-class African American family trying to advance itself against passive-aggressive resistance from a white neighborhood association. The plot draws heavily from Hansberry's own childhood when her family tried to settle in a white neighborhood near Chicago. While growing up, Hansberry experienced the tension between wanting to assimilate into mainstream society and maintaining pride in one's own culture. Her play articulated many of the mounting concerns held by African Americans and women of its day. The play has since become a standard work in high school and college literature courses and was the basis for the hit Broadway musical *Raisin* (1973).

Since then an increasingly vibrant Black Theater movement has pursued African American themes on and off Broadway. Many artists in this movement have attempted to create distinct dramatic forms that utilize aspects of African American performance from other arts to create unique theatrical presentations.

The sensitive portrayals of African American life offered by Baldwin, Wright, and Hansberry—despite their implicit warning not to trust whites—were conservative in comparison to many of the more vehemently militant pieces of the 1960s that demanded social revolution.

LeRoi Jones (who renamed himself Amiri Baraka in the late 1960s) had a large impact with highly creative but unmistakably angry plays including *Dutchman* (1964), which virulently attacked what he saw as racist issues and institutions. He was also a pivotal figure in advancing the arts in the Black Arts Movement of the 1960s, which advanced racial and political arts in the black communities of New York and beyond. Although Baraka's plays were never produced on Broadway, his work inspired others to create a strong "black aesthetic" in American theater and to reconsider the role of African Americans in American society and history. Baraka's influence on Broadway would be particularly evident a generation later in the successes of playwright **August Wilson**.

Charles Gordone's *No Place to Be Somebody* (1969) about a black bartender who tries to outsmart a white mobster syndicate was the first play by an African American to win the Pulitzer Prize. The play originated **Off-Broadway** but neither the original Broadway production nor a 1971 revival enjoyed long runs. Charles Fuller's *A Soldier's Play* (1982), which also won a Pulitzer, only played Off-Broadway, as had his earlier plays, *The Perfect Party* (1969) and *Zooman and the Sign* (1980). Richard Wesley would also be more successful beyond Broadway, although his *The Mighty Gents*, starring Morgan Freeman, briefly ran at the Ambassador Theater in 1978. Ron Milner saw three plays produced in Broadway theaters: *What the Wine-Sellers Buy* (1974), *Don't Get God Started* (1987), and *Checkmates* (1988), an all-star comedy with Ruby Dee, Denzel Washington, Marsha Jackson, and Paul Winfield in the cast.

Many women African American playwrights were also writing powerful dramas that addressed race relations and female roles. **Ntozake Shange** achieved extraordinary Broadway success, at least for her initial work, ***for colored girls who have considered suicide/when the rainbow is enuf*** (1976). She created a theatrical expression more closely related to African performance in her conception of the "choreopoem," with its ritualistic movement, dance, and mix of poetry and prose. Shange has since developed this format further in a series of Off-Broadway pieces. The Broadway run of *for colored girls*, at 742 performances, is the longest-running Broadway production of any play or musical ever written by an African American.

AFRICAN AMERICAN–THEMED PLAYS WRITTEN BY WHITES

Until the 1940s commercial plays with black themes were almost always written by whites. Edward Sheldon's *The Nigger* (1909), while attempting to address the issue of miscegenation, was viewed by critics as overly melodramatic. The first African American Broadway cast in a dramatic work appeared in a triptych of plays, *Three Plays for a Negro Theater* (1917) by Ridgely Torrence, a founder of the **Provincetown Players**. The Provincetown Players would offer the next significant presentation of an African American performer on Broadway: Charles S. Gilpin's 1920 performance in Eugene O'Neill's *The Emperor Jones*. Although critically popular, the play upset some African Americans in its presentation of blacks as exotic and primitive. Paul Green's *In Abraham's Bosom* (1926) depicted an African American idealist attempting to improve his rural community. W. E. B. Du Bois excoriated the play as white propaganda that depicted African Americans as unintelligent and defeatist. The rural, child-like innocents suggested by Marc Connelly's *The Green Pastures* (1930) were equally limiting, although some African Americans saw these folk representations as an improvement over past representations of blacks.

The presentation of Southern black life in Dorothy and DuBose Heyward's *Porgy* (1927), on which the 1935 musical *Porgy and Bess* was based, was deemed less condescending than some earlier plays. W. E. B. Du Bois, however, disliked *Porgy*, viewing it and plays such as Leon Gordon's *White Cargo* (1923) as presenting sexually explicit scenes of African Americans for sensationalism.

African American Drama Since the 1980s

The 1980s saw the emergence of August Wilson, arguably the most successful African American dramatist in history. Wilson left behind one of the tidiest canons of work—a play to explore the African American experience in each decade of the twentieth century. In interviews, speeches, and essays he called for African American theater to develop its own aesthetic, engaging in sometimes contentious debates with critics and fellow playwrights. While Wilson acknowledged an indebtedness to white dramatists, he singled out the influence of Baraka in viewing his art as standing firmly in a black dramatic and literary tradition that he saw as substantially different from that of white writers. Strongly opposed to color-blind casting (black actors playing traditionally white roles and vice versa), he was very vocal in pointing out the need for regional black theaters. Publicly voicing his personal politics, aesthetics, and future vision, Wilson insisted his stance was not separatist but rather insurance against the appropriation of black culture. Some would disagree, finding validity in all-black productions of *Waiting for Godot, Hello, Dolly!, Death of a Salesman*, or Lee Bauer's *Gospel at Colonus* (1988), which

Most of these early plays dwelled on issues of poverty, miscegenation, and what many whites perceived as exotic aspects of African American culture. However, African American critics and dramatists felt that much of this interest was spurious and counterproductive to increasing America's awareness of African American life. While many of these plays would seem irredeemably racist by today's standards, they offered African American actors more substantive roles than had been available in previous decades and helped demonstrate to mainstream audiences that African American actors could carry a show. These works also anticipated later plays that were decidedly less patronizing in their plea for racial tolerance, such as John Wexley's *They Shall Not Die* (1934), which foregrounded racial inequities in the legal system.

By the 1940s white playwrights were leaving behind the inanities of *Green Pastures* and tackling issues facing African Americans in a serious-minded way. Maxine Wood's *On Whitman Avenue* (1946), Dorothy Heyward's *Set My People Free* (1948), and Norman Rosten's *Mister Johnson* (1956) are examples of such endeavors. More recent plays, like Warren Miller and Tobert Rosse's *The Cool World* (1960), offered credible depictions of modern urban African American communities. Howard Sackler's *The Great White Hope* (1968), based upon the life of heavyweight champion boxer Jack Johnson, earned praise for its depiction of American hostility to black achievement. Herb Gardner's *I'm Not Rappaport* (1986) normalized an African American presence on stage in a friendship between an African American man and a Jewish man. The play focuses on age rather than race. While race remains a realistic element of the story, it does not drive the plot.

set Sophocles to a gospel swing, a validity that spoke of inclusion rather than assimilation. However, Wilson's outspokenness helped bring the role of African Americans in modern theater to the foreground in recent theatrical debates.

Wilson's first Broadway success, *Ma Rainey's Black Bottom* (1984), depicts the frustrations and struggles of black musicians in the 1920s. The play was developed under the tutelage of director **Lloyd Richards**, who had directed *A Raisin in the Sun* and 19 other plays on Broadway during his long career. Richards would guide Wilson through his next five plays until illness forced him to step aside after the production of *Seven Guitars* in 1996. Wilson's plays have all undergone extensive revision before arriving on Broadway. With two Pulitzer Prizes—for *Fences* in 1987 and *The Piano Lesson* in 1990—and a collection of other awards, Wilson is the most lauded African American playwright to date. His plays embody an exploration and reassessment of the cultural heritage of all African Americans. Wilson's success, and the greater influence of African American directors, such as Richards and **George C. Wolfe** with the Public Theater, allow for speculation that commercial theater producers might be increasingly willing to invest in the work of other up-and-coming African American playwrights, of which there are many.

One such up-and-coming playwright is Suzan-Lori Parks, who inventively explores issues of race, gender, and identity using historical characters, surrealism, and satire. She has written such controversial works as *Imperceptible Mutabilities in the Third Kingdom* (1989), *The America Play* (1994), and *Venus* (1996), as well as her Pulitzer Prize–winning, *Top Dog/Underdog* (2001). *Top Dog* was transferred from the Public Theater to Broadway by Wolfe in 2002 and starred rap singer Mos Def. (The casting of another rap singer, Sean Combs [aka P Diddy], would drive ticket sales in the 2004 revival of *A Raisin in the Sun*.)

Another recent trend has been the development of the one-person show by African American writers and performance artists. Anna Deavere Smith has been very successful in this genre. Smith's Broadway performance in 1994 of *Twilight: Los Angeles*, which recreated dozens of voices involved in the 1992 Los Angeles riots, caused an even bigger stir than her earlier Off-Broadway *Fires in the Mirror* (1992) and won her Tony Awards for Best Play and Best Actress.

In 2008, an all-black revival of Tennessee Williams's 1955 classic *Cat on a Hot Tin Roof*, directed by Debbie Allen, and a new play by white author George Stevens Jr., *Thurgood*, about the late Supreme Court Justice Thurgood Marshall, starring Laurence Fishburne, opened in Broadway's Broadhurst and Booth Theaters, respectively—a seeming testament to the integration, but not assimilation, of African American figures into mainstream culture and Broadway itself.

Susan C. W. Abbotson

Further Reading

Bean, Annemarie. *A Sourcebook of African-American Performance*. New York: Routledge, 1999.

Curtis, Susan. *The First Black Actors on the Great White Way*. Columbia: University of Missouri Press, 1998.

Elam, Harry J., Jr. and David Krasner, eds. *African American Performance and Theater History*. New York: Oxford University Press, 2001.

Gewirtz, Arthur, and James J. Kolb. *Experimenters, Rebels, and Disparate Voices*. Westport, CT: Praeger, 2003.

Hay, Samuel A. *African American Theater*. New York: Cambridge University Press, 1994.

Hill, Errol, ed. *The Theater of Black Americans*. New York: Applause, 1987.

King, Woodie, Jr. *The Impact of Race: Theater and Culture*. New York: Applause, 2003.

Krasner, David. *A Beautiful Pageant*. New York: Macmillan, 2002.

Molette, Carlton W., and Barbara J. Molette. *Black Theater: Premise and Presentation*. Bristol, IN: Wyndham Hall Press, 1986.

Woll, Allen L. *Black Musical Theater: From Coontown to Dreamgirls*. Baton Rouge: Louisiana State University Press, 1989.

———. *Dictionary of the Black Theater: Broadway, Off-Broadway, and Selected Harlem Theater*. Westport, CT: Greenwood Press, 1983.

AFRICAN AMERICAN MUSICAL THEATER

The story of African American or black theater is a complex one, largely due to the many ways in which one can interpret the terminology. There have been plays on Broadway both about and by African Americans, written by either African Americans or whites, and Broadway productions have variously included and excluded African Americans from sections of the audience, casts, and production teams. All of these variables can be seen as contributing to our national understanding of the African American experience and need some consideration in any assessment of Broadway's relationship to African American culture.

Blackface and the American Minstrelsy Tradition

During much of the nineteenth century, Broadway's onstage representations of African Americans were limited to roles played by white actors in blackface. Even plays featuring African American characters, such as George L. Aiken's tremendously successful adaptation of Harriet Beecher Stowe's *Uncle Tom's Cabin* (1852) or Dion Boucicault's *The Octoroon* (1859), did not cast black actors, as African Americans were banned from taking any major part in a white show. These depictions of African Americans were sentimental at best and later came to be the cause of much resentment among African American performers, writers, and the public at large. Aspiring African American actors, such as Ira Aldridge or James Hewlett, achieved some success in Shakespearean roles but mostly either abroad or in small theater companies beyond Broadway.

It would be through the popularity of the first indigenous American entertainment, the minstrel show, that African Americans would get their initial chance to be seen on the New York stage, but there were severe limitations to the image they were allowed to convey. As happily touted in a contemporary playbill, minstrel shows featured "shuffling, irresponsible, wide-grinning, loud-laughing Negroes" in a musical rendition of "darky life on the old Plantation" (Woll 1989, 1). Any attempt to show a more realistic portrait of African American life was berated as unseemly by white critics.

A white performer, Thomas Dartmouth Rice, reputedly created what would become the stereotypical minstrel-show representation of African Americans in 1832, when he appeared on stage as a "Kentucky cornfield Negro" during an interval of Solon Robinson's *The Rifle* at the Southern Theatre in Louisville, Kentucky. With a face colored by burnt cork and wearing raggedy clothing, he performed a routine based around a popular fiddle-and-dance tune "Jump, Jim Crow." His intention was to authentically emulate the song and dance of African Americans who worked on the Southern plantations. Rice would eventually make a career out of his Jim Crow character, developing him into longer routines he called "Ethiopian operas," such as *Long Island Juba, or Love by the Bushel* (1833). He even performed a burlesque version of *Othello* in 1845, playing the lead as Jim Crow, with Desdemona's handkerchief being replaced by a raccoon-hide towel.

Daniel Decatur Emmett developed the first full minstrel show in 1843, with the Virginia Minstrels. His intent was to create something entertaining and educational. The African American caricatures of Jim Crow and his urban brother "Zip Coon" or "Dandy Jim" were based on white perceptions of African American dress, manners, speech, song, and dance of African Americans in various regions of America and had the effect of making them appear to whites as docile cowards and fools. E. P. Christy and his Ethiopian Minstrels followed Emmett's lead and helped expand the form. During the 1840s minstrel troupes could be as small as four men, but as the decades advanced, the troupes grew larger and more numerous, with increasingly complex instrumentation and dance routines. By 1856, New York alone had five minstrel companies and the number kept growing. Minstrel shows formed the backbone of American popular entertainment for the next 50 years.

Initially, minstrel companies were composed entirely of white males. Female roles were played by men in drag, and many performers such as Edward Harrigan and Tony Hart—especially through their Mulligan Guard plays—grew famous by "blacking-up." In 1865 Charles Hicks organized the Georgia Minstrels, the first successful African American minstrel company, but the roles they played were the same as had been established by white performers. Such African American talents as W. C. Handy and Bessie Smith were expected to conform to these stereotypes, even down to using burnt cork on their faces just as white minstrel performers did.

Even with the decline of touring minstrel companies at the end of the century, blackface entertainment still made the leap to early Broadway musical comedy and revues. Lew Dockstader, a longtime blackface minstrel performer and producer, appeared in three of his own Broadway revues in blackface between 1906 and 1907. **Eddie Cantor**, a mainstay of the annual *Ziegfeld Follies* casts, performed in blackface during his earlier appearances in the 1910s. Most famously, Al Jolson appeared in blackface in various Broadway shows, stage concerts, and early "talkie" movies into the 1920s. However, Broadway interest in blackface waned shortly thereafter as artists and audiences grew tired of the dated entertainment form and its distortedly nostalgic nineteenth-century vision of America.

Beyond Minstrelsy

African American professional musical theater showed signs of growing beyond the minstrel show shortly after the Civil War. The 1870s saw the African American duo of Anna and Emma Hyer (professionally "The Hyer Sisters") from California fronting their family-owned production company and performing in Joseph Bradford's *Out of Bondage*, an episodic musical following the progress of a family from slavery to freedom. They also appeared in E. S. Getchell's *Urlina, the African Princess* with an exotic African setting. Even though the structure of the Hyers' shows borrowed from blackface minstrelsy, they proved that African Americans could independently mount a professional production as well as entertain audiences in roles other than those derived from minstrel stereotypes. Black theater's first influential departure from the minstrel show would be *The Creole Show* (1890), produced by Sam T. Jack, a white producer, and featuring a chorus line of African American women in what was likely an attempt to produce an African American show with the same sex appeal as the tremendously successful ***The Black Crook*** (1866)—generally viewed as the first American-written and American-composed musical that, notwithstanding its title, has nothing to do with African or Afro-American culture. A further development came with the musical farce *The Gold Bug* (1896) at the Casino Theatre in New York. Although this show had been penned by whites, it brought attention to the cakewalk performance of dancers **Bert Williams** and George Walker. Williams and Walker were attractive, dapper men who tried to avoid offensive racial stereotyping in their performances, albeit by becoming to some degree raceless. Williams and Walker's cakewalk was a syncopated song-and-dance routine based on slave parodies of the formal dances of white aristocrats. It evolved into a highly popular form of social dance by the early twentieth century, especially among African Americans.

The hour-long sketch *Clorindy, the Origin of the Cakewalk*, a collaboration between composer Will Marion Cook and poet Paul Laurence Dunbar, opened in New York's Casino Theatre in 1898. It was the first show written and performed by African Americans for white audiences. *Clorindy* was quickly followed by *A Trip to Coontown* (1898) by Bob Cole, a full-length comedy, for which Cole also formed the first professional African American theatrical stock (or repertory) company. Cole's title echoed that of *A Trip to Chinatown* (1891), a show that would be the long-run champion of Broadway for nearly 25 years. Cole's decision to appropriate for his shows the motifs and conventions of mainstream (essentially "white") Broadway musicals marked the key difference between Cole and Cook. Where Cook was interested in creating a new black aesthetic, Cole was more concerned with beating the whites at their own game, and the two men's respective works reflected their divergent ambitions. These early musical comedies still contained minstrel show elements, but through their continuous plotlines, these shows helped present a broader view of African Americans than the American stage had previously been exposed to. As a result of the efforts of both men, an increasing number of African American performers were employed in mainstream commercial theaters.

Williams and Walker, who were writers as well as performers, mounted several small shows in minor New York theaters at the turn of the century, including *The Policy Players* (1899) and *Sons of Ham* (1900), but they wanted to play major Broadway venues. This they would eventually do as performers with *In Dahomey* (1903), *Abyssinia* (1906), and *Bandana Land* (1908). Cook wrote the music for all three of these shows, inserting into the first two the newly popular romantic story line for African Americans of one day returning to Africa. Other African American writers were also making their mark, with such offerings as *Rufus Rastus* (1906), a musical extravaganza created by Ernest Hogan, Tom Lemonier, and Frank H. Williams, and *The Oyster Man* (1907) for which Flournoy Miller wrote the book and Hogan and Will Vodery the music. Two works by Cole and John Rosamond

Johnson, *The Shoo-Fly Regiment* (1907) and *The Red Moon* (1909), significantly extended the usual subject matter of African American productions. *The Shoo-Fly Regiment* follows an African American regiment from Alabama to the Philippines, and *The Red Moon* explores interrelations between African Americans and American Indians. By the close of 1911, there had been more than a dozen of these musicals produced on Broadway, but production of African American shows waned as many key figures died or moved on to new projects. Walker, Cole, and Hogan were all dead, and in 1910 Williams had moved on to **Flo Ziegfeld**'s *Follies*. Although Williams's resulting stardom over the next nine years made major inroads for the future of racial integration of the Broadway stage, it left the growing genre of the black musical short on known talent.

Black musicals triumphantly returned in 1921 with the amazing success of **Shuffle Along**, which ran for 504 performances. *Shuffle Along* brought Eubie Blake and Noble Sissle to the fore as writers and Adelaide Hall, Flournoy Miller, and Aubrey Lyles to the fore as performers. (Miller and Lyles's stage performance would later provide the inspiration for *Amos and Andy*, the hit 1930s radio comedy that featured white actors caricaturing African Americans using broad exaggerations of ostensibly black speech patterns and malapropisms.) Even though *Shuffle Along* borrowed generously from minstrel plot and structure, its fast pace, imaginative score of hit songs that combined ragtime with **operetta**, and stunning choreography legitimized the black musical on mainstream Broadway and created opportunities for more African American entertainers to show their talents. Blake and Sissle would try to repeat their success, but only came close with *The Chocolate Dandies* (1924). *The Chocolate Dandies* was an early star vehicle for the then teenaged singer/actress/comedienne Josephine Baker, who in the next ten years would become the toast of Europe and America for her sensual, exotic stage and concert performances. Blake and Sissle's work spawned imitators, several of whom showed considerable talent. Among the more successful followers of Blake and Sissle were James Johnson and Cecil Mack, whose *Runnin' Wild* (1923) introduced the 1920s signature dance craze the Charleston, and Lew Leslie's *Blackbirds of 1928*, which notably brought song-and-dance man Bill "Bojangles" Robinson to the public eye. *Blackbirds* even beat *Shuffle Along*'s pacesetting Broadway run by about two weeks with 518 performances. Leslie had also featured Florence Mills in some of his earlier revues.

However, white investors soon grew aware of the evident profitability of these black musicals. While their versions kept the African American performers on stage, African Americans found themselves being increasingly replaced by white talent behind the scenes as writers, directors, and producers.

In 1922 **George Gershwin** had written a 20-minute Harlem opera *Blue Monday Blues* for inclusion in that year's *Scandals* (a series of nine Tin Pan Alley tune-laced Broadway revues to which Gershwin contributed between 1919 and 1929). The short piece was performed by white actors in blackface. The audience was uncertain about how to respond, given that blackface was so strongly associated with broader, "traditional" comedy. The piece was quickly pulled, but Gershwin was drawn to what he recognized as the African American underclass and its culture within a wider American culture. He would finally capture this vision in *Porgy and Bess* (1935), based on the successful 1927 play *Porgy* by the white husband and wife writing team of DuBose and Dorothy Heyward. With *Porgy and Bess* Gershwin introduced a reasonably representative, nonoffensive (for the time) black vocal idiom into serious musical theater and raised the bar on the type of music typically sung by African Americans on stage. **Jerome Kern** and **Oscar Hammerstein**'s 1927 *Show Boat*, with its concern over miscegenation and its depiction of African American life on the Mississippi, also made significant inroads into representing blacks seriously and sympathetically on the musical stage. Following in the shoes of Gershwin, Harold Arlen, another white musician, wrote several serious musicals for African American principal actors. He began with music for the 1943 movie version of *Cabin in the Sky*, which would be the first black-performed Broadway musical to be adapted to a commercial Hollywood film. Arlen also presented an early integrated cast in *Bloomer Girl* (1944), the all-black *St. Louis Woman* (1946), which starred Pearl Bailey, and *Jamaica* (1957), which was originally written as a vehicle for Harry Belafonte but revamped for Lena Horne when Belafonte grew ill. *Jamaica* would run for 555 performances. It featured **Ossie Davis** who, after having played small roles on Broadway since 1946 and having developed expertise in all phases of African American community theater since the 1930s, went on to become one of the most active and venerated African American theater and film stars of the century. Horne, meanwhile, would not return to a Broadway stage until 1981 in her award-winning special event show *Lena Horne: The Lady and Her Music*.

This period also saw the vogue of some imaginative and successful musical adaptations of established works featuring largely or all-black casts. Two adaptations of **Gilbert and Sullivan**'s 1880s opera *The Mikado* proved successful in New York in 1939: *The Hot Mikado* with Bill Robinson given a new lease on his performing life as the Mikado and *Swing Mikado* produced by the New York Negro Unit of the **Federal Theatre Project**. *Swingin' the Dream* (1939), a blues- and jazz-infused adaptation of Shakespeare's *Midsummer Night's Dream*, saw moderate success, but *Carmen Jones* (1944), an African Americanized version of Bizet's opera created by Oscar Hammerstein II, was enormously successful. Kurt Weill and **Maxwell Anderson** wrote a musical version of Alan Paton's 1948 novel *Cry, the Beloved Country* about racial strife in South Africa. The show was titled *Lost in the Stars* and ran for a respectable 273 performances in 1949. Even while white composers continued to dominate Broadway musicals—famous African American jazz composers Fats Waller and Duke Ellington had only mild success with music they wrote for Broadway—the era was seeing a growing integration of blacks into white shows. Several popular musicals of the late 1940s and early 1950s advanced the theme of racial tolerance—reflecting the advent of racial integration and civil rights in national politics during those decades. Among the most famous of these shows were *Finian's Rainbow* (1947), *South Pacific* (1949), and *The King and I* (1951), although these productions did not deal with African American themes *per se*. In 1964, **Clifford Odets**'s 1937 drama *Golden Boy* was adapted into a musical, in which the lead, originally written as an Italian

American, was now played by Las Vegas "rat pack" singer/actor Sammy Davis Jr., who was the most famous African American entertainer at the time. The show was a critical and commercial success, running for nearly two full Broadway seasons.

Ossie Davis and his wife, Ruby Dee, had starred in Davis's successful drama about a traveling preacher, *Purlie Victorious*, in 1961. The 1970 musical *Purlie*, which was developed from this show, went on to run for 689 performances, winning a Best Musical Tony. Other Tony Award musical hits of the 1970s with African American casts were also based on earlier material. *Raisin* (1973), adapted by Robert Nemiroff from his late wife's landmark play **A Raisin in the Sun** (1959), and *The Wiz*, based on L. Frank Baum's *The Wizard of Oz* (1900), each ran for over 800 performances.

The 1970s saw an increased presence of African American composers on Broadway. Micki Grant, who had performed in Langston Hughes's 1963 play with music *Tambourines to Glory*, contributed two successful black revues, *Don't Bother Me, I Can't Cope* (1972) and *Your Arms Too Short to Box with God* (1976). Melvin Van Peebles who, while earning fame as a groundbreaking Hollywood filmmaker, also had some Broadway hits in the early 1970s: *Ain't Supposed to Die a Natural Death* (1971) and *Don't Play Us Cheap* (1972). Van Peebles's works introduced Broadway audiences to far more edgy portrayals of African American life than they had seen before on commercial stages. Linda Hopkins won accolades for her turn as Bessie Smith in *Me and Bessie* (1975), which also heralded a growing interest in biographies of famous African Americans (the non-musical *I Have a Dream*, exploring the life of Martin Luther King Jr., would run for three months in 1976).

In 1978 the outspoken actress Eartha Kitt, who had had some Broadway success in the 1950s with *Mrs. Patterson* (1954) and *Shinbone Alley* (1957), returned to the Broadway stage in the hit musical *Timbuktu!* That year also saw *Robeson*, a controversial piece by Philip Hayes Dean, based on the life of singer/actor **Paul Robeson** and starring **James Earl Jones**. Reactions pointed to the power of the stage to shape an image, as Robeson's son complained about what he felt was a skewed depiction of his father. The show lasted for only 77 performances amid a heated debate, then transferred to **Joseph Papp**'s Public Theater for a much longer run. It has been revived twice on Broadway since, with Avery Brooks in the lead role.

The 1970s also witnessed the growth of new kinds of black musicals, including a string of what composer Lehman Engel called "folio" shows, which may have been Broadway's reaction to some of the startling rock musicals that had begun to invade commercial theater as well as a nostalgic counterpoint to the popular black-influenced disco and funk club music of the day. These pieces presented an assortment of songs by past African American composers: *Ain't Misbehavin'* (1978), *Eubie!* (1978), and *Sophisticated Ladies* (1981), respectively, featured songs by Fats Waller, Eubie Blake, and Duke Ellington. The latter two starred singer/dancer Gregory Hines, who would also appear in George C. Wolfe's *Jelly's Last Jam* (1992) about Jelly Roll Morton. There were also successful song and story revues such as *Bubbling Brown Sugar* (1976) and *Tintypes* (1980), which featured music by an assortment of earlier African American songwriters, including

Bert Williams. The 1970s also saw revivals of two "Golden Age" musicals with all-black casts. In 1975 Pearl Bailey, a popular night club and recording artist, starred in a revival of *Hello, Dolly!* (1964). The following year Robert Guillaume starred in a revival of *Guys and Dolls* (1950). Collectively these shows reflected a growing national recognition of the importance of African American culture in American culture.

Following the successful inroads made by **Stephen Sondheim** in his more loosely structured musicals based upon concepts and close delineation of character rather than linear story line, Tom Eyen's *Dreamgirls* (1981), a rags-to-riches melodrama of how black music had been historically dominated by white taste and corporate ownership, ran for 1,522 performances. Since the racially integrated cast of musicals like *Hair* in 1968, African Americans were increasingly used on stage indiscriminately to create casts that reflected a growing multicultural society. Although there continue to be musicals with predominantly African American casts or concerns, they have lessened in number. Some notable recent successes include Queen Esther Marrow's *Truly Blessed* (1989), based on the life of Mahalia Jackson, Lynn Ahrens's *Once on This Island* (1990), and *Bring in 'Da Noise, Bring in 'Da Funk* (1996), based on a book by Reg E. Gaines, which ran for 1,135 performances. The show made a star of dancer Savion Glover, who had first appeared in the 1989 revue *Black and Blue* and *Jelly's Last Jam*.

Currently on Broadway there are two long-running musicals that prominently feature African Americans, albeit the creative talents behind them are largely white. Pop composer Elton John and Tim Rice's *The Lion King* opened in 1997, one of only a small handful of Broadway shows to have run for over ten years and 4,000 performances. *The Lion King*, which earned six Tonys in its opening year, owes much of its success to magnificent choreography by Garth Fagan, an African American modern dancer and choreographer based in Rochester, New York. **Marsha Norman**, a white playwright who won the Pulitzer Prize for her 1983 play *'night Mother*, rendered a stage adaptation of Alice Walker's novel *The Color Purple*, which had won the Pulitzer Prize for fiction in that same year. The opening of the Broadway musical of *The Color Purple* (2005) was widely heralded for being television star and mogul Oprah Winfrey's debut as a Broadway producer. While recent decades have seen fewer African Americans writing successful musicals, African American onstage performers have maintained a strong presence on contemporary Broadway. *See* **African American Dramatic Theater**.

Susan C. W. Abbotson

Further Reading

Bean, Annemarie. *A Sourcebook of African-American Performance*. New York: Routledge, 1999.

Curtis, Susan. *The First Black Actors on the Great White Way*. Columbia: University of Missouri Press, 1998.

Elam, Harry J., Jr. and David Krasner, eds. *African American Performance and Theatre History.* New York: Oxford University Press, 2001.

Gewirtz, Arthur, and James J. Kolb. *Experimenters, Rebels, and Disparate Voices.* Westport, CT: Praeger, 2003.

Hay, Samuel A. *African American Theatre.* New York: Cambridge University Press, 1994.

Hill, Errol, ed. *The Theatre of Black Americans.* New York: Applause, 1987.

King, Woodie, Jr. *The Impact of Race: Theatre and Culture.* New York: Applause, 2003.

Krasner, David. *A Beautiful Pageant.* New York: Macmillan, 2002.

Molette, Carlton W., and Barbara J. Molette. *Black Theatre: Premise and Presentation.* Bristol, IN: Wyndham Hall Press, 1986.

Woll, Allen L. *Black Musical Theatre: From Coontown to Dreamgirls.* Baton Rouge: Louisiana State University Press, 1989.

———. *Dictionary of the Black Theatre: Broadway, Off-Broadway, and Selected Harlem Theatre.* Westport, CT: Greenwood Press, 1983.

ALBEE, EDWARD (1928–)
PLAYWRIGHT

The life and work of Edward Albee have come to represent the rebellious spirit of late-twentieth-century American theater and culture. His 30-plus plays, in their scrutiny of American values and their representation of the disenfranchised and disaffected, have influenced a generation of American **playwrights**, including Sam Shepard, David Mamet, **Terrence McNally**, and John Guare—all of whom found in Albee the bohemian spirit that epitomized New York City culture during and after the 1960s. Albee is generally regarded as the most important American playwright of his generation and, as such, the literary heir to the likes of **Eugene O'Neill**, **Arthur Miller**, and **Tennessee Williams**. Variously embraced and rejected by Broadway throughout his career, Albee helped acclimate **Broadway** theater to innovative **Off-Broadway** and European sensibilities, including the Theater of the Absurd, daring explorations of sexuality, and unconventional uses of language to reveal deeply personal and complex human emotions.

Critics often invoke Albee's personal life in describing his plays, drawing on his adoption as an infant by Frances and Reed Albee, heir to the famous Keith-Albee theater **vaudeville** circuit. Growing up in Larchmont, New York, in an affluent, but indifferent, environment, Albee left home at a young age at odds with his parents' politics and morality. Indeed, in his Pulitzer Prize–winning drama *Three Tall Women* (1994), Albee writes about the relationship between a mother and her gay son from her perspective.

Prior to his 1962 Broadway debut, Albee created a stir in professional theater circles with several revolutionary Off-Broadway productions in 1960 and 1961. *The Zoo Story* (which had its world premiere in Germany in 1959), *The American Dream*, *The Sandbox*, and the *Death of Bessie Smith* signaled a new direction in

American playwriting, away from narrowly realistic or impressionistic "conversational" plays toward dramas that explored, often literally, the animalistic nature of human communication and relationships.

The most important of these early works, which are still widely read and frequently performed in professional and university theaters, is *The American Dream*. First produced in 1960, *The American Dream* marked the Americanization of the European-based Theater of the Absurd movement. Opening with a middle-class wife babbling inanely about mundane events while her husband pretends to listen, *The American Dream* is a direct homage to Romanian Eugene Ionesco's 1950s Absurdist classic *The Bald Soprano*. Albee's play also stresses many of the same issues: the breakdown of language, the corruption of values in the middle-class family, and the substitution of the artificial for the real in language, human relationships, and social values.

Albee enjoyed an auspicious Broadway debut with **Who's Afraid of Virginia Woolf?** in 1962. The production earned rave reviews and Tony Awards for the 34-year-old playwright, both leading actors (Arthur Hill and **Uta Hagen**), and Alan Schneider as Best Director. Many critics believe that *Virginia Woolf* remains the best and most important play of his entire career. Albee followed *Virginia Woolf* with an ambivalently received dramatic adaptation of Carson McCullers's novella, *The Ballad of the Sad Cafe* (1963). His next play, the highly regarded *Tiny Alice* (1964), enjoyed a respectable Broadway run for a serious drama as did the Pulitzer Prize–winning *A Delicate Balance* (1966). These two plays, following closely on the success of *Virginia Woolf*, established Albee as an important new voice in American drama and Broadway theater.

However, shortly thereafter, Albee suffered a now notorious string of Broadway disappointments. His adaptations of James Purdy's *Malcolm* (1966) and Vladimir Nabokov's *Lolita* (1981) were critical and commercial failures. His original dramas *All Over* (1971), *The Lady from Dubuque* (1980), and *The Man Who Had Three Arms* (1983), a supposedly autobiographical play about a man who achieves success and fame when he grows the titular appendage, fared no better. *Seascape* in 1975 won the Pulitzer Prize and a Best Play Tony nomination, but Broadway

Edward Albee, 1962. (AP Photo)

audiences recoiled at the surrealistic complexity of the work. For much of the 1970s and 1980s, Albee worked in Europe, often directing his own plays to generally more receptive audiences and critics. He also developed strong producing relationships with regional theaters in the eastern United States, especially the Hartford Stage Company in Connecticut and the McCarter Theatre in Princeton, New Jersey. While only sparingly bringing new plays to Broadway after 1980, periodic revivals of earlier plays—including *Who's Afraid of Virginia Woolf?* in 1976 and 2005 and *A Delicate Balance* in 1996—sustained him as an esteemed if not dominating presence in American commercial theater.

Three Tall Women in 1994 marked Albee's successful return to New York theater and precipitated a late-career resurgence of interest in his work. Although the play did not have a Broadway opening, it played and toured successfully throughout the United States and enjoyed a critically acclaimed run in London's West End. The play won the Pulitzer Prize and heralded a comeback for Albee as a major literary figure. In 2002, at age 74, Albee stunned Broadway with *The Goat, or Who Is Sylvia?*, a deadly serious exploration of a 20-year marriage thrown into crisis when the husband falls hopelessly in love with a goat. The play was by far Albee's biggest Broadway success since *Virginia Woolf* 40 years earlier. It ran for over 300 performances and earned Albee the Tony Award for Best Play—his first since *Virginia Woolf.*

In 2007–2008, in honor of Albee's eightieth birthday, the Off-Broadway season was unofficially named in his honor. The season heralded the production of his new plays *Me, Myself and I* at the McCarter Theatre and the two-act *Peter and Jerry* based on the original *Zoo Story.* In addition, the season saw the revival of the double bill *The American Dream* and *The Sandbox* directed by the playwright, and the official New York premiere of *Occupant*, a biographical play about his friend, the sculptress Louise Nevelson. In an indirect tribute to Albee's contribution to the American theater, the 2007–2008 season on Broadway was also distinguished by plays that scrutinize the dysfunctional family, including the 2008 Pulitzer Prize–winning *August: Osage County* by Tracy Letts as well as major revivals of Harold Pinter's *The Homecoming* and Tennessee Williams's *Cat on a Hot Tin Roof.*

The winner of two Best Play Tony Awards, a Lifetime Achievement Tony Award, and three Pulitzer Prizes, Albee is widely credited with shaking Broadway drama out of its artistic complacency and inspiring other American playwrights to do the same. In his unpredictability and his refusal to imitate earlier successes, Albee is difficult to categorize. For five decades he has written forcefully in all manner of dramatic styles: naturalism, expressionism, symbolism, satiric farce, tragicomedy, and metaphysical allegory. In so doing he expanded the artistic range of late twentieth-century American drama while infusing American playwriting with an astonishing level of creative energy and insight into the human condition.

Isa Goldberg

Further Reading

Albee, Edward. *Stretching My Mind: The Collected Essays 1960 to 2005.* New York: Da Capo Press, 2005.

Gussow, Mel. *Edward Albee: A Singular Journey: A Biography.* New York: Simon and Schuster, 1999.

Horn, Barbara Lee. *Edward Albee: A Research and Production Sourcebook.* Westport, CT: Praeger, 2003.

AMERICAN THEATRE WING—TONY AWARDS

Although best known today as the administrator of Broadway's Tony Awards, the American Theatre Wing grew out of two proud historical traditions—neither of which initially involved bestowing awards. "The Wing's" original mission involved mounting relief and charity projects on behalf of American war efforts and, later, educating aspiring theater professionals.

The Wing evolved out of the Stage Women's War Relief Fund, which was founded at the beginning of America's involvement in World War I. The Fund was established by a group of women theater professionals, most notably playwright **Rachel Crothers**. The goal of the organization was to provide aid in the war effort. The women collected clothes and food for the armed forces and opened the first Stage Door canteens in New York for the entertainment and nourishment of servicemen. At the close of the war, the women continued their charitable and service activities, inspiring formation of a short-lived brother organization by a group of theater men.

In 1939, with the increasing likelihood that America would enter World War II, government officials asked Crothers to reactivate the Stage Women's War Relief Fund, soon thereafter renamed the Theatre Wing of Allied Relief. Director Antoinette Perry, actress Vera Allen, and other notable theater women joined Crothers in this renewed effort. More Stage Door canteens opened in New York and across the country. Theater luminaries such as actress Gertrude Lawrence and lyricist/composer Dorothy Fields temporarily put aside their professional careers to work on committees for the Wing and help sustain the canteens. The Wing also sent entertainers to visit hospitals and entertain troops overseas. Through much of this period, Antoinette Perry served as the Wing's chairman of the board and secretary.

Adding to the local effort were the Wing-sponsored Lunchtime Follies, modeled after the Entertainments National Service Association in England. The Follies consisted of skits, short plays, songs, and dances performed at factories around the country. The entertainments included both moral lessons and propaganda designed to amuse workers, enhance their productivity, and rouse their patriotic support of the war effort. Adolf Hitler was frequently parodied, shown lamenting the fact that his mother was not around for her daily beating and ranting against dogs that resembled Jews. Songs encouraged male workers in particular to increase their productivity. (One such song, "On Time," involved a woman singing about how much she loved men who got to work on time and worked hard, all the while hinting of the rewards she might have in store for them.)

Following the close of World War II the Wing turned its attention to the veterans, serving in hospitals and establishing recreation programs for returning servicemen and women. In addition, the Wing became involved in recruiting and training new theater professionals, sending them around the country to help veterans readapt to home life with their families. It also opened up theater educational programs for returning veterans. Vera Allen, director Mary Hunter, and actor Winston O'Keefe founded the American Theatre Wing Professional School in 1946. **Alfred Lunt** and Ray Bolger were among the Broadway stars who taught at the school.

The Wing continues its tradition of education to this day, most notably with the "Working in the Theatre" seminars it has conducted every spring and fall since 1973. Theater professionals from actor Brian Dennehy to composer **Stephen Sondheim** have shared their experiences with aspiring theater professionals. Isabelle Stevenson, president of the American Theater Wing from 1966 to 1998, created and hosted the seminars. Until her death in 2003, she promoted them every year during the televised annual Tony Awards ceremony.

The Antoinette Perry (Tony) Awards

The Antoinette Perry Awards or "Tony Awards," named for the former chair of the board and secretary of the American Theatre Wing, represent the highest honor a Broadway play, **musical**, performer, designer, director, or writer can receive. Founded in 1947, they are administered by the American Theatre Wing and voted on by over 700 theater professionals. The fame and prestige of the Tony Awards at once sustain and overshadow their namesake's place in theater history.

Beloved and respected as a pioneering woman director, a notorious perfectionist, and a leader in creating opportunities for African American actors, Antoinette Perry (1888–1946) directed 19 Broadway dramas and comedies between 1928 and 1944. She was also famously generous to theater colleagues, frequently loaning or giving money to actors and directors who were struggling financially. Her generosity would come back to haunt her when the stock market crashed in 1929. She found herself saddled with $2 million of debt. Perry gradually rebounded professionally, capping her illustrious career by directing the original Broadway production of the hit Pulitzer Prize–winning play *Harvey* (1941). Perry died in 1946 of a heart attack at the age of 58.

In 1947 friends and colleagues of Perry proposed that the Wing honor her memory by establishing a series of awards in her name for excellence in theater. At the inaugural ceremony on April 6, 1947, Perry's friend and frequent producer Brook Pemberton, while presiding over the event, called one of the awards a "Tony." The nickname stuck. **José Ferrer** and Fredric March were co-winners of the inaugural best actor honors while **Helen Hayes** and Ingrid Bergman shared the award for best actress. **Arthur Miller** won as best author for his play *All My Sons*.

In 1949, the original awards—lighters and money clips for men, compacts for women, and scrolls for all winners—were replaced by the now familiar Tony medallion. In 1967 the Wing, while maintaining administrative oversight of the Awards, sought the involvement of the League of New York Theatres (now called the Broadway League) as the annual awards ceremony expanded its venue selection from hotel ballrooms, to Broadway theaters, to its current home in Radio City Music Hall. That year also marked the first year the Tony Awards ceremony was televised, as it has been annually ever since.

Currently, the scheduled three-hour (but often longer) Tony Awards program, broadcast on CBS since 1978, serves as a grand commercial for the New York theater scene. A major highlight for viewers is the live Broadway-cast scenes and numbers from current shows interspersed between award presentations. Although in any given year ratings and critical response can please or disappoint its producers, the Tony Awards ceremony is a firmly established part of network **television**'s annual awards show lineup along with the Academy Awards, the Emmy Awards, and the Grammy Awards. With the advent of YouTube, audiences around the world enjoy recent and past Tony Award show performances 24 hours a day, with "Tony clips" from hit shows like *The Lion King* (1997; Tony Award show, 1998) and *Dreamgirls* (1981; Tony Award show, 1982) exceeding, respectively, half a million and one million views.

Thomas A. Greenfield and Aaron Netsky

Table 1
Tony Award Winners for Best Plays

Year	Play	Playwright
1948	*Mister Roberts*	Thomas Heggen and Joshua Logan
1949	**Death of a Salesman**	Arthur Miller
1950	*The Cocktail Party*	T. S. Eliot
1951	*The Rose Tatoo*	**Tennessee Williams**
1952	*Four Poster*	Jan De Hartog
1953	**The Crucible**	Arthur Miller
1954	*Teahouse of the August Moon*	John Patrick
1955	*The Desperate Hours*	Joseph Hayes
1956	*The Diary of Anne Frank*	Frances Goodrich and Albert Hackett (adapted by); Anne Frank
1957	**Long Day's Journey into Night**	**Eugene O'Neill**
1958	*Sunset at Campobello*	Dore Schary
1959	*J.B.*	Archibald MacLeish
1960	*The Miracle Worker*	William Gibson
1961	*Becket*	Jean Anouilh
1962	*A Man for All Seasons*	Robert Bolt
1963	**Who's Afraid of Virginia Woolf?**	**Edward Albee**
1964	*Luther*	John Osborne
1965	*The Subject Was Roses*	Frank D. Gilroy
1966	*The Persecution and Execution of Marat as Performed by the Inmates of the Asylum of Charenton Under the Direction of the Marquis de Sade*	Peter Weiss; English version by Geoffrey Skelton
1967	*The Homecoming*	Harold Pinter
1968	*Rosencrantz and Guildenstern Are Dead*	Tom Stoppard

Table 1 (continued)

Year	Play	Playwright
1969	*The Great White Hope*	Howard Sackler
1970	*Borstal Boy*	Frank McMahon
1971	*Sleuth*	Anthony Shaffer
1972	*Sticks and Bones*	David Rabe
1973	*That Championship Season*	Jason Miller
1974	*The River Niger*	Joseph Walker
1975	*Equus*	Anthony Shaffer
1976	*Travesties*	Tom Stoppard
1977	*The Shadow Box*	Michael Cristofer
1978	*Da*	Hugh Leonard
1979	*The Elephant Man*	Bernard Pomerance
1980	*Children of a Lesser God*	Mark Medoff
1981	*Amadeus*	Peter Shaffer
1982	*The Life and Adventures of Nicholas Nickelby*	David Edgar (adapted by); Charles Dickens
1983	*Torch Song Trilogy*	Harvey Fierstein
1984	*The Real Thing*	Tom Stoppard
1985	*Biloxi Blues*	**Neil Simon**
1986	*I'm Not Rappaport*	Herb Gardner
1987	*Fences*	August Wilson
1988	*M. Butterfly*	David Henry Hwang
1989	*The Heidi Chronicles*	**Wendy Wasserstein**
1990	*The Grapes of Wrath*	Frank Galati (adapted by); John Steinbeck
1991	*Lost in Yonkers*	Neil Simon
1992	*Dancing at Lughnasa*	Brian Friel
1993	***Angels in America***: *Millenium Approaches*	**Tony Kushner**
1994	*Angels in America: Perestroika.*	Tony Kushner
1995	*Love! Valour! Compassion!*	**Terrence McNally**
1996	*Master Class*	Terrence McNally
1997	*The Last Night of Ballyhoo*	Alfred Uhry
1998	*Art*	Yasmina Reza; Translated by Christopher Hampton
1999	*Side Man*	Warren Leight
2000	*Copenhagen*	Michael Frayn
2001	*Proof*	David Auburn
2002	*The Goat, Or Who Is Sylvia?*	Edward Albee
2003	*Take Me Out*	Richard Greenburg
2004	*I Am My Own Wife*	Doug Wright
2005	*Doubt*	John Patrick Shanley
2006	*The History Boys*	Alan Bennett
2007	*The Coast of Utopia, Parts 1, 2, and 3*	Tom Stoppard
2008	*August: Osage County*	Tracy Letts
2009	*God of Carnage*	Yasmina Reza; Translated by Christopher Hampton

Sources: Internet Broadway Database. http://www.ibdb.com/advancesearchaward.asp; American Theatre Wing. "Tony Awards" [Search Past Winners]. http://www.tonyawards.com.

Further Reading

American Theatre Wing. http://americantheatrewing.org/.

The Official Website of the American Theatre Wing's Tony Awards. Retrieved April 20, 2009, from http://www.tonyawards.com/en_US/index.html.

Stevenson, Isabelle, ed. *The Tony Award.* New York: Crown, 1980.

Anderson, Maxwell (1888–1959)
Playwright, Producer, Lyricist

A Pulitzer Prize–winning playwright with over 25 Broadway plays to his credit, (James) Maxwell Anderson was among the most distinguished and successful **playwrights** in the period from the 1920s to the 1940s, when serious dramatists were staking their claim for attention and audiences on **musical**-dominated **Broadway**. A **critic** as well as a playwright, Anderson published one of the first major essays to analyze American drama in terms of formal aesthetics. A founding member of the Playwrights' Company in 1938, a production company dedicated to ensuring the viability of high-quality drama on Broadway, Anderson was a pioneer in establishing serious dramatic literature as a staple of modern Broadway theater.

Anderson was born in Pennsylvania. During his childhood his family moved often around the Midwest. He graduated from the University of North Dakota and later studied at Stanford University, eventually becoming a high school English teacher and college professor. In 1917 he was fired as head of the English department at Whittier College in California for supporting a student pacifist movement. Shortly thereafter, Anderson moved to New York City and became a writer, publishing editorials, book reviews, and poetry in various newspapers and magazines.

Influenced by **Shakespeare** and verse drama and classical Greek tragedies, Anderson launched his professional playwriting career with a verse play *White Desert* (1923), which had a brief, unsuccessful run on Broadway. His next play marked his first Broadway success. *What Price Glory* (1924), a disillusioned reflection on World War I and its devastating effects on soldiers who fought in it, ran for a full year and over 433 performances. Co-written with friend and war veteran Laurence Stallings, the play drew its dramatic impact largely from the loud bravado-laced talk of young, bellicose servicemen. *What Price Glory* brought Anderson fame in the Broadway community and corresponding infamy in the press for its decidedly unglamorous depiction of soldiers at war. Members of the U.S. military and government threatened to prosecute Anderson for defamation of the army.

Anderson achieved even greater fame and recognition for his work in the 1930s, in the minds of many rivaling **Eugene O'Neill** as the foremost American playwright of the decade. *Elizabeth the Queen* (1930), the first of three Tudor dramas he would take to Broadway, was a critical success and a rare modern application of Shakespearean blank verse in commercial theater. Representing a passionate romance between the aged Queen Elizabeth I and her lover, Lord Essex (played by Broadway's most popular husband-and-wife team, **Alfred Lunt and Lynn Fontanne**), the play examined the temptations of political power and the tragedy of amorous betrayal. Anderson eclipsed this work in 1933 with *Mary of Scotland*, a critical and commercial hit that starred **Helen Hayes** as the morally courageous Mary pitted against manipulative young sister Elizabeth. The third play, *Anne of a Thousand Days* (1948), completed the trilogy, again exploring themes of sex and political power. Anderson's grounding in Shakespearean drama was also the influence for 1933's *On Both Your Houses*, a tale of political corruption and individual heroics that earned Anderson the 1933 Pulitzer Prize for Drama.

Anderson's later successes included several historical American war epics, including *Valley Forge* (1934), in which Anderson dramatizes George Washington holding together the American resistance during the famed brutal winter of 1777–1778. The play was widely viewed as an allegory for President Franklin Roosevelt's political courage during the Great Depression. In *Key Largo* (1938), a weak-willed American soldier working for the fascist forces of Spain's tyrannical dictator Francisco Franco comes to understand the immorality of his position and repents. The hero's change of heart reflected Anderson's own shift away from pacifism in the face of burgeoning fascist movements in Europe during the 1930s. In *Candle in the Wind* (1941) and *The Eve of Saint Mark* (1942), Anderson became something of an American patriotism propagandist glorifying the sacrifices, including the deaths, of young serviceman.

In addition to writing literate successful dramas, Anderson played an important role in the intellectual and academic legitimization of the American play as meaningful dramatic literature. In 1939 he published the highly influential *The Essence of Tragedy and Other Footnotes and Papers*, one of the first attempts to systematically analyze American plays as true tragedies and significant works of literature. Anderson's criticism would influence Arthur Miller's more famous essay on modern American tragedy, "Tragedy and the Common Man" (1949).

Anderson continued to write plays for the remainder of his life. His final Broadway play, *The Day the Money Stopped* (1958), opened one year before his death. That show flopped but it had been preceded by the highly successful and harrowing *The Bad Seed* (1954), about an 11-year-old girl who is a skilled and remorseless serial murderess. In 1949 he collaborated with Kurt Weill on a popular musical, *Lost in the Stars*, for which he wrote the book and the lyrics to the show's 15 songs.

Anderson also wrote dozens of **film** and **television** scripts, including numerous adaptations of his own more famous works, including *What Price Glory* and *The Bad Seed*. Early in his career he received an Oscar nomination as one of the screenwriters for the 1930 classic war film *All Quiet on the Western Front*, adapted from Erich Maria Remarque's novel. Anderson also wrote a book of poetry and numerous essays on matters related to theater and culture.

With the exception of Eugene O'Neill and, debatably, **Thornton Wilder**, no other writer before World War II did as much to prove that Broadway could make room for highly literate, intellectually demanding American plays, and still succeed commercially.

Anderson died on February 28, 1959, in his home in Stamford, Connecticut, after suffering a stroke.

Thomas A. Greenfield and Robert A. Adamo

Further Reading

Clark, Barrett H. *Maxwell Anderson: The Man And His Plays*. Whitefish, MT: Kessinger Publishing, 2007.

Horn, Barbara Lee. *Maxwell Anderson: A Research and Production Sourcebook*. Westport, CT: Greenwood Press, 1996.

ANDREWS, JULIE (1935–)
ACTRESS

Dame Julie Andrews made an enormous impact on Broadway **musicals** during their Golden Era despite having appeared in only three shows during this time and four in her entire career. She had the lead role in every Broadway show in which she was cast, starting with her debut at age 19 in *The Boy Friend* (1954). Two of her later roles, Eliza Doolitte in *My Fair Lady* (1956) and Guinevere in *Camelot* (1960), are among the most memorable Broadway characters to emerge from this period. Over time these roles, and Andrews's association with them, have taken on nostalgic qualities, invoking the postwar innocence of America before civil unrest, the sexual revolution, and political assassinations of the late 1960s and 1970s. Andrews's starring role as Maria in the 1965 film version of *The Sound of Music* (1965), the most commercially successful Broadway-to-film adaptation made in the twentieth century, significantly enhanced her popular reputation as a "Broadway" musical star, even though she actually spent relatively little time on Broadway.

Born Julia Elizabeth Wells in Walton-on-Thames, Surrey, England, Andrews performed on **radio**, on **television**, and in small theater productions while growing up. She immigrated to America while still in her teens, hoping to break into Broadway. Producer Cy Feuer, coming off the successes of *Guys and Dolls* (1950) and *Can-Can* (1953), cast two unknown young English actors for the leads in *The Boy Friend* (1954): John Hewer and Andrews, both of whom received excellent reviews. For a show with unknown lead actors, the 14-month run was a clear success. Hewer later returned to England and never worked on Broadway again. Not so, Julie Andrews.

Her reputation from *The Boy Friend* was sufficient to earn her the lead role of Eliza Doolittle (after American star **Mary Martin** famously turned it down) in **Alan J. Lerner and Frederick Loewe**'s *My Fair Lady* (1956). She would play opposite **Rex Harrison**, an icon of British film and theater comedy and a tone-deaf singer. The theatrical chemistry between the 48-year-old Harrison and 22-year-old Andrews was astonishing. While Harrison elegantly talked his way through his songs, Andrews soared in showstopping numbers "I Could Have Danced All Night" and "Wouldn't It Be Loverly." She also stood toe to toe with Harrison in their comic scenes and duets, especially "The Rain in Spain." Although Harrison stayed with the show for only 20 months of its six-year run, Andrews and Harrison —who never worked together again on stage—endure as one of the most brilliantly conceived and executed "boy–girl" pairings in Broadway history. Although she lost the Tony for Best Actress to Judy Holliday in *Bells Are Ringing* (1956), Andrews's Eliza Doolittle has since emerged as one of Broadway's legendary performances.

Lerner and Loewe played to their strength when they cast Andrews as Queen Guinevere in their next show, *Camelot*, which they co-produced as well as wrote. Although the show suffered some criticism, perhaps unavoidably, in comparison to *My Fair Lady*, Andrews triumphed again. The play ran for a healthy three years and, although the show's big song, "If Ever I Would Leave You," went to Broadway newcomer Robert Goulet as Lancelot, Andrews's solid delivery of "The Lusty Month of May" and "I Loved You Once in Silence" made those songs popular.

As it did for many successful Broadway performers, Hollywood was beckoning to Andrews, and she did not require much persuading. She received solid notices for her performance in a made-for-television musical, **Rodgers and Hammerstein**'s *Cinderella* (1957). When she began doing feature **films**, Andrews took Hollywood by storm—much as she had done when she first performed on Broadway. In 1964, she starred in two hit movies: *The Americanization of Emily* and Disney's hit musical fantasy *Mary Poppins* (1964), for which Andrews won the Oscar for Best Actress. She next starred in *The Sound of Music* (1965) which, 45 years later, still enjoys remarkable popularity through video sales, rentals, and television broadcasts. While in Hollywood she met film director and producer Blake Edwards, whom she married in 1969. She has enjoyed a successful film career ever since.

Andrews returned briefly to Broadway in a replacement/cameo appearance for **Stephen Sondheim**'s revue, *Putting It Together* (1993). In 1995, she starred in her most recent, and in all likelihood final, Broadway production, *Victor/Victoria* —a stage adaption of her 1982 movie. Husband Blake Edwards produced both the film and the show. This time, the ingénue of the 1950s was back as a 60-year-old drag performer. **Critics** swooned, audiences were thrilled to see her live, and the show ran for a solid two years. In 1998, the year following the Broadway run of *Victor/Victoria*, Andrews lost her singing voice in a throat operation. Her highly publicized malpractice suit against her surgeon resulted in her receiving an undisclosed, but presumptively large, settlement. In recent interviews she has allowed that, while she has recovered some singing capacity, she has "put to bed" any thoughts of carrying a substantial singing role on stage or film.

With no Tony Awards to her credit and only two stage roles of historic significance, Andrews is an atypical Broadway "legend." Yet her few roles have made a remarkable contribution to Broadway history. Moreover, her Broadway career has enhanced even as it has benefited from the interconnected relationship that Broadway and Hollywood have enjoyed over the past 75 years.

Thomas A. Greenfield and Caitlin Klein

Further Reading

Andrews, Julie. *Home: A Memoir of My Early Years*. New York: Hyperion, 2008.

Windeler, Robert. *Julie Andrews: A Life on Stage and Screen*. Thorndike, ME: Thorndike Press, 1998.

ANGELS IN AMERICA

Angels in America, **Part One:** *Millennium Approaches*
Broadway Run: Walter Kerr Theatre
Opening: May 4, 1993
Closing: December 4, 1994
Total Performances: 367
Writer: Tony Kushner
Original Music: Anthony Davis
Additional Music: Michael Ward
Director: George C. Wolfe
Produced by Jujamcyn Theaters; Center Theatre Group/Mark Taper Forum, Margo Lion, Susan Quint Gallin, Jon B. Platt, The Baruch-Frankel-Viertel Group, Frederick M. Zollo, and others.
Cast: Kathleen Chalfant, David Marshall Grant, Marcia Gay Harden, Ron Leibman, Joe Mantello, Ellen McLaughlin, Stephen Spinella, Jeffrey Wright (all in multiple roles)

Angels in America, **Part Two:** *Perestroika*
Broadway Run: Walter Kerr Theatre
Opening: November 23, 1993
Closing: December 4, 1994
Total Performances: 217
Written by: Tony Kushner
Original Music by: Anthony Davis
Director: George C. Wolfe
Produced by Jujamcyn Theaters; Center Theatre Group/Mark Taper Forum, Margo Lion, Susan Quint Gallin, Jon B. Platt, The Baruch-Frankel-Viertel Group, Frederick M. Zollo, and others.

Cast: Kathleen Chalfant, David Marshall Grant, Marcia Gay Harden, Ron Leibman, Joe Mantello, Ellen McLaughlin, Stephen Spinella, Jeffrey Wright (all in
multiple roles)

In 1993, **Tony Kushner** shook the foundations of the relationship between sexual
identity and power with his *Angels in America*: Parts One and Two. *Angels* opened
on Broadway in May and November 1993, respectively, and radically expanded
the manner in which pointed political and social drama could be written and
staged. Presented in two separate parts, each running approximately three hours
long, the play is highly unrealistic, with fantasy sequences, actors playing multiple
characters who share a connection, juxtaposed "split scenes" that exhibit relationships in the action, ghosts who represent the main character's ancestors visiting
him at his bedside, and an angel with "great opalescent gray-silver wings" floating
above a bed on stage. Even the name of the main character, "Prior," is allegorical
rather than realistic, signifying a connection to the historical past—what has come
"prior." *Angels* blurs the boundaries between imagination and the real in order to
comment on the surrealistic political realities of living with AIDS in America.

Kushner's acknowledgment of a historical past is evident from the play's title.
Kushner's Angel was inspired by the German-Jewish cultural critic Walter Benjamin's "Theses on the Philosophy of History" (1940). In his essay, Benjamin
describes the angel in Paul Klee's 1920 painting, *Angelus Novus*. For Benjamin,
the movement of history is not one of steadfast forward motion intent on progress,
but a messier intersection of past and present. Benjamin pictures the angel of history with his face turned toward the past, viewing piles of wreckage and yet unable
to stay and remedy the destruction because a storm from Paradise is propelling him
into the future, to which his back is turned. The storm is what Benjamin sees as
"progress," while the pile of debris that is history grows skyward. The Angel of
history who greets the main character, Prior, at the end of *Angels in America: Millennium Approaches*, Part One, is not only an overtly antirealistic device in this
play's "fantasia," but a reminder that the future bears the past along with it.

Another strong antirealistic aspect of the play is its interaction between fictional
characters and characters that represent key historical figures from various decades, such as McCarthy-era lawyer Roy Cohn and convicted (controversially)
Cold War–era spy Ethel Rosenberg, who appears as a ghost. Kushner sets the play
in 1985–1986 during Ronald Reagan's presidency (with an epilogue set in 1990).
By the time President Reagan's administration had formally acknowledged AIDS
in 1987, believing it to be a disease that only affects the marginalized—gay men
—over 20,000 Americans had died of the disease. The Reagan view of AIDS as
a "homosexual disease" and the moral condemnation associated with that view
are powerfully addressed in *Angels*. When Prior's ancestors—a thirteenth-
century British squire and an elegant seventeenth-century Londoner—appear, they
announce how they had each died of different "plagues," one that originated from
fleas on rats, the other from the water supply. They understand AIDS as another
plague, a view intended to depoliticize AIDS, connecting it to the history of disease. Through the ancestors, Kushner refutes the "Religious Right" argument that

AIDS is moral punishment against gay men—a view that gained considerable public attention during the Reagan era. *Angels* movingly personalized difficult political issues—a trademark of American social drama since **Clifford Odets**'s plays of the 1930s—but did so in a context of spectacular staging, nonlinear storytelling, and fantasy images.

Angels in America also illustrates links to McCarthyism during the 1950s in order to examine issues of power and persecution in American history. Kushner directly employs characters from the McCarthy era—Roy Cohn and the ghost of Ethel Rosenberg—to explore the complexities of how the political is related to the personal during the AIDS crisis of the 1980s and 1990s.

The connection Kushner draws between sexual identity and power is most clearly revealed in the character of Cohn. When Cohn is informed that he has AIDS, he refuses to admit he has the disease. Protesting that AIDS affects mostly "homosexuals and drug addicts," he insists he has liver cancer. Even though Cohn admits to having sex with men, he rejects the label "homosexual" as part of his identity. In a key speech to his doctor he denies the common notion that sexual labels signify "who someone sleeps with," pointing out instead that labels reveal one thing only: social and political "clout." In developing the character Roy Cohn as self-defined by his power, Kushner invokes the legacy of the real Roy Cohn—a ruthless young staff attorney for Joe McCarthy and a closeted gay man who persecuted gays. Cohn survived McCarthy's downfall to become an influential power broker and a member of President Reagan's social circle. To assert his power in the face of his doctor's AIDS diagnosis, the character Roy Cohn disdainfully rejects all association with homosexuals. Ultimately, however, social clout turns out to be useless in a battle with disease of the body, and Roy Cohn dies of AIDS while Prior survives both physically and emotionally. *Angels in America, Perestroika*, Part Two, ends with Prior breaking the fourth wall, demanding visibility and a rightful place in society for victims of AIDS: "We won't die secret deaths anymore ... We will be citizens."

Angels in America was the most heralded American Play of the 1990s, winning four Tony Awards, including Best Play, as well as the Pulitzer Prize for Drama and numerous other awards. (In 2003, Kushner developed a screenplay for an enormously successful and highly regarded **television** miniseries adaptation of *Angels*.) The play also upends the long-standing notion that, but for the occasional experimental "think piece," mainstream American social drama follows the tradition of realism: a dramatic style that seeks to reproduce the surfaces of reality, with stage settings that reflects a specific place and time, and characters written to mirror the speech, dress, and behavior of their middle-class audiences. By contrast, *Angels*, with its sprawling, sometimes oddly interconnected story lines and collage of fictitious, "real," and historic characters, makes its political points with imagery, symbol, and vignette as much as with linear narrative. Furthermore, the play's wide public acceptance contributed directly to contemporary public discussion of AIDS policies and gay/lesbian rights. In so doing, *Angels in America* joined such elite company of successful Broadway social plays as **Arthur Miller**'s *The*

Crucible (1953) and Lorraine Hansberry's *A Raisin in the Sun* (1959), which became in and of themselves effective catalysts for contemporary political debate.

Annette Saddik

Further Reading

Fisher, James. *Understanding Tony Kushner.* Columbia: University of South Carolina Press, 2008.

Geis, Deborah R., and Steven F. Kruger, eds. *Approaching the Millennium: Essays on Angels in America (Theater: Theory/Text/Performance).* Ann Arbor: University of Michigan Press, 1998.

ASIANS AND ASIAN AMERICANS

For well over a century theater artists of Asian descent have been subjected to persistent discrimination in the workplace and demeaning caricature on the stage. In the face of traditions rooted in years of established and unquestioned theatrical practice, they have had to struggle constantly to secure dignified work. Like many ethnic groups, their story is one of perseverance and courage in seeking equal treatment in American commercial theater.

American Yellowface: The Beginnings to 1945

While historians have written extensively about discriminatory portrayals of Asians in American cinema, they have focused comparatively little attention on those Broadway practices that laid the groundwork for the likes of filmdom's Charlie Chan, Mr. Moto, and Fu Manchu. As white performers and writers caricatured African Americans in blackface minstrel shows well into the twentieth century, they also caricatured Asian characters through "yellowface," a practice that involved makeup, costumes, properties, and so-called "acting techniques." To a yellow greasepaint base, Caucasian (and on occasion African American) performers added exaggerated, upswept, "slanted" eyes and eyebrows, bee-stung lips, and long fingernails as well as various "Asian" props and costumes. (Any sense of cultural accuracy was immaterial so long as props and costumes manifested a vague sense of "Orientalia.") To augment the makeup design, Caucasian actors generated a vocabulary of affected "Asian gestures" and "Asian accents," reversing "r's" and "l's," taking tiny steps, making delicate gestures, ubiquitous bowing, and oftentimes speaking outright gobbledygook as ostensibly "realistic" renderings of Asian languages.

Charles T. Parsloe (1836–1898) was the first American actor to parlay the "stage Chinaman" into a lucrative career. His Hop Sing in Bret Harte's melodrama *Two Men of Sandy Bar* (1876) ran successfully at Union Square Theater and set the standard by which subsequent stage Chinamen would be judged. Favorable reviews bred more success and the following year found Parsloe on Broadway as the title character in Harte and Mark Twain's *Ah Sin* (1877). Parsloe again impressed audiences and **critics** for projecting such "realistic" ethnic characteristics as Chinese cleverness and rascality. Parsloe went on to play stage Chinamen for the next 14 years, including a number of Broadway productions: *The Danites* (1879), murder mystery *My Partner* (1879), Bill Nye's *The Cadi* (1891), and the Goodwin-Cheever burlesque *Evangeline* (1896). He died an exceedingly wealthy man that same year, having set what became the theatrical standard by which white audiences would continue to judge verisimilitude of stage Chinamen.

In the wake of Parsloe's success, a raft of Caucasian actors put their hands to dramatizing Asian characters, becoming acknowledged connoisseurs of "all things Asian." Producers regularly sought out their talents. Among the most noteworthy of these performers were Blanche Bates, who appeared as Cio-Cio-San in **David Belasco**'s *Mme. Butterfly* (1900) and Yo-San in Belasco's *The Darling of the Gods* (1902); and Allen Atwell, who played Oku in George Broadhurst's *Bought and Paid For* (1911, revival 1921). Yellowface thus became viewed as "truthful" representation of Asian characterization to the point that white actors playing Asian characters on stage faced press excoriation if they failed to measure up to the standards of Bates, Atwell, and the other leading yellowface actors of the day. In reviews that praised yellowface performances as "truthful," "accurate," and "excellent," critics reinforced the validity of what Broadway, for the most part, now understands as demeaning Asian stereotypes. These stereotypes would soon be appropriated by the emerging American film industry and prove stubbornly difficult to uproot.

The promulgation of yellowface acting could not have occurred without **playwrights** and **producers** providing "yellowface plays," each genre of which had its own peculiar formula that required stock type Asian characters to appear in proscribed, predictable, and demeaning situations. Exotic extravaganzas, for example, were short on plot and long on pageantry in settings and costumes. W. T. Moncrieff's *The Cataract of the Ganges* (1873) was a popular example of these "Oriental" spectacles. Despite the luxurious production elements, producers evinced a marked propensity for conflating Asian cultures as interchangeable. *The Cataract of the Ganges*, despite its Indian setting, boasted a third act troupe of Bedouin Arabs. *Aladdin* (1895) at the Broadway Theatre was somehow and without explanation transposed to China from its western Asian roots.

The "Asian melodrama" of the 1920s provided the inspiration for dastardly Fu Manchu and Dragon Lady stereotypes. These melodramas cast Asian characters as opium traffickers (*The Poppy God*, 1921), treacherous Chinese madams (*The Shanghai Gesture*, 1926), stealthy, hissing Indians (*The Ghost Parade*, 1929), and in one case, a character who is *both* a Chinese laundryman *and* an evil opium den owner (Ling Foo in *The Scarlet Fox*, 1928). The "positive" Asian melodramatic character was typified by the asexual, soft-spoken Chinese detective Charlie Chan, first played on Broadway by William Harrigan in *The Keeper of the Keys* (1933).

Titillating interracial love stories also bred success in the first half of the twentieth century. The happy union of an Asian woman with a Caucasian man was an acceptable theme. However, such dalliances generally ended in tragedy as in Belasco's rendition of *Mme. Butterfly*. Samuel Shipman and John B. Hymer's *East Is West* (1918) about adorable Ming Toy and her dashing American lover Forrest Winant was so popular it was revived and made into two films (1922 and 1930). On the other hand, sex between an Asian man and a Caucasian woman was invariably portrayed as destructive, and such dramas often had spectacularly dire endings. In Lincoln Osborne's *Uptown West* (1923), Sakamoto, the Japanese husband, commits ritual suicide onstage after his biracial child is killed in a car accident and his Caucasian wife rejects him for a white man.

By the time the United States entered World War II, Broadway audiences knew well their favorite Asian stock types. Male characters were asexual, bumbling valets, servants, cooks, gardeners, and laundrymen, or evil, degenerate crooks and opium dealers who preyed on white girls. Asian women were adorable, sexually available sweethearts who provided comic double entendre, or conniving villainesses providing titillating glimpses of breast and leg. With extremely rare exceptions, all were played by Caucasian actors in yellowface. Authentic Asian and Asian American performers were considered to look and sound "too Asian" to be accepted as "real."

Even well-known performers like Anna May Wong and Sessue Hayakawa fared better in **film** than they did in theater. Wong, generally acknowledged as the first Chinese American movie star, played Broadway only once, as a gangster's moll in *On the Spot* (1931), but appeared in over 60 films and television episodes during her career. Hayakawa performed in *The Love City* (1926), oversaw "Japanese authenticity" for a cast of yellowface Caucasians in *Namiko-San* (1927), and performed in the short-lived *Kataki* (1959). After *Kataki*, however, he never returned to Broadway but appeared in over 100 films and television programs.

Lesser known Asian and Asian American actors continued to knock on producers' doors prior to World War II despite discriminatory casting practices that restricted them to playing stereotyped supernumeraries while their Caucasian colleagues garnered the high profile "Asian" leads and rave reviews. Few were able to earn a living in the acting business, and certainly none became Broadway regulars.

The experience of Sachiro Oida, who made his Broadway debut as the comic servant Satsuma in the farce *On the Quiet* (1901), was typical. Oida was the sole Asian performer to appear on Broadway during the 1901–1902 season. Yet in the same year, Broadway provided numerous Asian roles that went to Caucasian yellowface performers: The lion's share of the cast of Belasco's *Mme. Butterfly* and two revival casts for the musical *San Toy*; Stanley Murphy as the Chinese cook Sam Wong in *Arizona*; Faye Templeton as a plump Japanese geisha in *Hoity-Toity*; Marie Murphy as Omyama San in the musical *The Liberty Belles*; Ferdinand Bonn in the title role of *Kiwito*; and the season closer, the British import musical *A Chinese Honeymoon*, which fell in line with established casting practices. Like Ah Wung Sing, Oida vanished from Broadway when *On the Quiet* closed.

If there was an Asian actor who stood out in the first half of the twentieth century, it was Tsunetaro Tamamoto, a classically trained Japanese actor who emigrated to the United States around the turn of the century. He worked consistently between 1909 and 1923, appearing in 13 Broadway productions in addition to 23 films. Not willing to sit on the sidelines, Tamamoto made headlines wherever he went, even unveiling a plan for what would have been the first Asian American theater company before retiring from the stage altogether. He found more work than his predecessors, but the quality of the roles to which he was relegated, despite his acknowledged talent, did not satisfy him.

World War II to 1988

The World War II years continued to see a paucity of dignified roles for Asian performers. With the United States at war with Japan and Japanese American citizens incarcerated in internment camps, images of Japanese characters invariably reflected America's intense phobia about Japan and Japanese Americans. **Irving Berlin**'s musical revue *This Is the Army* (1942) featured a number titled "Aryans Under the Skin," which presented a singing and dancing chorus of "Japs" and Germans. The same year, Walter Kerr's **musical** *Count Me In* showcased a special dance number for a "grinning Jap quartet." Actors of Chinese ancestry could find the same tired houseboy roles that were offered to them before the war. Peter Goo Chong (1898–1985) portrayed a Chinese houseboy in *Little Darling* (1942) and received appreciative reviews for his character's humorous butchering of the English language. Frederick Munn Szeto and Chueck Ming Chin, in the only Broadway appearance of their careers, actually alternated in a miniscule role, that of "Chinatown" in Jack Kirkland's *Suds in Your Eye* (1944).

The musical *Lute Song* (1946), which played 142 performances on Broadway, was a forerunner of things to come. Based on Gao Ming's fourteenth-century Chinese classic *Pipa ji*, this American adaptation featured an entire yellowface cast, including **Mary Martin**, Mildred Dunnock, Yul Brynner, and longtime "stage Asian" Clarence Derwent. Not a single Asian actor appeared in either this version or the 1959 City Center revival, both of which received generally favorable reviews.

Between 1949 and 1958 **Richard Rodgers and Oscar Hammerstein II** collaborated on three musicals with Asian characters and themes: *South Pacific* (1949), *The King and I* (1951), and *Flower Drum Song* (1958). One more, *Oklahoma!* (1943), featured an Asian character, Ali Hakim, ostensibly of Southwest Asian descent. The four musicals represent a much-loved, oft-produced body of work and have been given countless revivals, from secondary schools and community theaters to professional regional theaters and Broadway. The pattern of their casting reveals much about the opportunities available, but only recently granted, to Asian American performers.

Oklahoma!'s Ali Hakim is a case in point. In the 1943 premiere the Russian-born Joseph Buloff took the part of the Persian peddler. Through three revivals

(1951, 1953, 1979), non-Asians played the role. It was not until Indo-American Aasif Mandvi was cast in the 2002 revival that an actor of Asian descent was tapped to play this Asian role. *South Pacific* takes place during World War II in the Pacific theater of war with a plot that revolves around a love affair between the Arkansan Nellie Forbush and Emile de Becque, a Frenchman who is the father of two biracial children. The book also follows a subplot about an interracial relationship between a white man and a Polynesian woman. In both the 1949 premiere and its 1955 revival at City Center, non–Asian American performers took the Polynesian roles of Liat and her mother Bloody Mary.

The King and I (1951), set in nineteenth-century Siam, follows the story of Anna, a widow who has come to teach English to the children of the king, played by Yul Brynner. (Brynner had cut his teeth on yellowface in *Lute Song*.) The cast of 60 performers in the original production featured a majority of Caucasians with a few actors of Latino descent and only three Asian American performers in dancing—not speaking—roles: Baayork Lee, Yuriko, and Michiko. A 1977 revival featured more Asian American performers with June Angela playing the featured role of Tuptim and Hye-Young Choi as Lady Thiang. Brynner returned as the king in the 1985 revival. It was not until the 1996 revival that Philippines-born Lou Diamond Phillips portrayed the king accompanied by a largely Asian American cast.

Flower Drum Song has been criticized for its reinscription of Asian stereotypes —Lotus Blossom "good girl" Mei-Li (Miyoshi Umeki), Dragon Lady "of loose morals" Linda Low (Pat Suzuki), the dutiful son under his father's control, Wang Ta (Ed Kenney). Nevertheless, it remains in a category of its own. *Flower Drum Song* is a classic American book musical with big dance numbers, a score that includes hit songs such as "Love Look Away," and, most important, one that portrays Asians not as unassimilable "foreigners" but as Americans with a foot in both Asian and American cultures. For all its advances, however, racist casting practices were evident in the original production of *Flower Drum Song*. Although the cast was nearly entirely Asian American, two plum roles went to Caucasian and African American actors sporting taped eyelids: nightclub owner Sammy Fong played by Caucasian actor Larry Blyden and Auntie Liang played by African American Juanita Hall, who was eventually chosen for the 1961 film version over Anna May Wong.

In 2002 *Flower Drum Song* became the only Rodgers and Hammerstein musical to appear on Broadway with an adapted script. The preeminent Chinese American dramatist **David Henry Hwang** requested permission of the Rodgers and Hammerstein estate to rework the libretto, maintaining its theme of acculturation in the face of tradition and generational conflict but eliminating its originally well-intended but ultimately racist imagery and references. This time all the roles were cast appropriately, and the production headlined talented Asian American performers, including Randall Duk Kim and Jodi Long as Wang and Liang, respectively, and Lea Salonga, who had received a Tony Award for her portrayal of Kim in the hit musical *Miss Saigon* (1991), as leading lady Mei-Li.

For all Rodgers and Hammerstein's efforts, considered inclusive and even socially daring writers in their time, their musicals nevertheless continued to reinforce those practices established in the prewar years of casting Caucasian performers in starring yellowface roles and relegating actors of Asian descent, when they appeared at all, to small supernumerary parts. After World War II, Asian actors were still largely excluded from playing Asian characters as evidenced by the casting of such shows as *Yours Is My Heart* (1946), *The Carefree Tree* (1955), *A Majority of One* (1959), and *Christine* (1960). Casting directors relied upon yellowface even for Asian play scripts or English-language adaptations of Asian materials. In *Rashomon* (1959) Caucasian Americans and two Europeans, Oscar Homolka and Akim Tamiroff, were chosen for the all-Japanese cast of characters over the Japanese American actor Mako, who was told he looked "too Japanese" to play a role next to his Caucasian colleagues.

It was a rare occasion in the 1950s and 1960s when an Asian actor played a dignified Broadway role as when Sessue Hayakawa played Kimura in Shimon Wincelberg's World War II drama *Kataki* (1959). *The World of Suzie Wong* (1958) is more typical of the time. Eurasian actress France Nuyen played the "whore with a heart of gold," irresistible and sexually available to her Caucasian leading man, William Shatner. Thus, in both casting and writing, little actually changed during the years immediately after World War II. Cutting-edge Asian American designers, however, were able to establish long-standing, productive careers. Costume designer Willa Kim and set designer Ming Cho Lee launched their 50-year careers, paving the way for younger artists, such as lighting designer Victor En Yu Tan.

Between 1968 and 1972, buoyed by America's cultural upheaval over the Vietnam War, feminism, and minority rights, Asian American actors began organizing to openly oppose inequitable practices in American theater. Alvin Lum led the New York–based Oriental Actors of America (OAA), picketing productions that practiced yellowface casting and pursuing discrimination suits against theatrical producers. With *Here's Where I Belong* (1968, a musical version of John Steinbeck's novel *East of Eden*), *Lovely Ladies, Kind Gentlemen* (1970, a musical version of the 1953 hit play *Teahouse of the August Moon*), and two Lincoln Center productions—*The Good Woman of Setzuan* (1970) and *Narrow Road to the Deep North* (1972)—OAA focused public attention on discriminatory practices that resulted in Asian American actors suffering from the highest unemployment rate of any group in the theater business. OAA ultimately took its cases to the New York State Division of Human Rights but lost when the commissioner ruled that Lincoln Center was simply exercising its artistic freedom in casting Caucasian, African American, and Latino performers in Asian roles. As a result of the court battle, a small role in *Narrow Road*, that of "A Child," eventually was given to one Toby Obayashi, who never appeared in another Broadway show.

Another milestone for Asian American actors came with **Stephen Sondheim**'s *Pacific Overtures* (1976) about Commodore Matthew Perry's 1853 arrival in Japan. Unique in the annals of Broadway for its reliance upon Japanese Kabuki techniques, the production featured an entirely Asian American cast, including Mako, Yuki Shimoda, Sab Shimono, Alvin Ing, Soon-Teck Oh, Conrad Yama, Ernest Abuba, Gedde Watanabe, and Tom Matsusaka.

David Henry Hwang, The *Miss Saigon* Controversy, and Beyond

David Henry Hwang became the first Asian American playwright to receive a Tony Award for Best Playwright with his drama of espionage and gender politics, *M. Butterfly* (1988). Drawing upon a true story about a French diplomat who fools himself into believing that his lover, a Beijing opera female impersonator, is indeed a woman, Hwang examines the extent to which stereotypes distort both individuals' and nations' ability to perceive truth. B. D. Wong created the role of the lover, Song Liling, becoming the first Asian American actor to win the Tony Award for Best Actor in a Play. In 1990 Hwang, B. D. Wong, and Tisa Chang— in an incident reminiscent of OAA protests—found themselves confronting British producer **Cameron Mackintosh** in one of Broadway's most public controversies of the past several decades. Mackintosh, the producer behind some of Broadway's longest-running blockbusters, including ***Cats*** (1982) and ***The Phantom of the Opera*** (1988), was set to unveil on Broadway his *Miss Saigon*, a *Madame Butterfly* story set during the Vietnam War. The show had successfully run in London, and the American production boasted advance ticket sales of $25 million, a record for its time. Mackintosh's production team had undertaken a worldwide audition tour to find the performer to play Kim, the "Miss Saigon" of the title, choosing the Filipina Lea Salonga. However, Mackintosh insisted that no Asian American man was strong enough for the potentially career-making role of the Eurasian Engineer. This was a questionable claim, considering *Shogun the Musical* (1990), which had closed on Broadway some four months prior to *Miss Saigon*'s opening, starred powerful Asian American actors, including Alan Muraoka and Francis Ruivivar. Moreover, in the London production Jonathan Pryce had worn yellow greasepaint and prosthetic eyepieces intended to give the appearance of an eye skin fold—essentially recycling nineteenth-century yellowface practices.

Hwang, Wong, and Chang mobilized artists in the Asian American theater community to take their case to their union, Actors' Equity Association (AEA), which initially supported them. However, Mackintosh made it clear he stood ready to cancel the production, thereby depriving a large number of Asian American actors any work at all, and Equity reversed its decision. AEA eventually ruled that Mackintosh could bring his star to Broadway, but Pryce was prohibited from wearing the offensive makeup in the production. The union also stipulated that replacements were to be Asian Americans after Pryce left the cast. All the actors who followed Pryce as The Engineer were indeed Asian American: Raul Aranas, Tony C. Avanti, Joseph A. Foronda, Norman Wendell Kauahi, Ming Lee, Paul Matsumoto, Ray Santos, Herman Sebek, Luoyong Wang, and, notably, Alan Muraoka and Francis Ruivivar who had starred in *Shogun the Musical*. *Miss Saigon* ran for ten years, becoming one of Broadway's most commercially successful musicals. The protest surrounding the original Broadway casting brought widespread attention to long-standing discriminatory practices against actors of Asian descent in American theater.

Although Asian American actors cannot be said to be on equal footing with Caucasian or arguably with African American and Latino performers, bias against them is no longer an unspoken, *de facto* condition of theatrical employment. In the "Post-*Miss Saigon* Era," the majority of successful Asian American playwrights and directors work in regional theater, not Broadway, and Asian American actors augment their Broadway work in regional and ethnically specific theaters or **Off-Broadway**. The most consistently visible Asian American theater performers have found acceptance as dancers in musicals rather than in leading dramatic roles. B. D. Wong has been able to break the "bamboo ceiling" by playing in color-blind productions such as the revival of *You're a Good Man, Charlie Brown* (1999) in which he played Linus, and David Henry Hwang has collaborated on non-Asian-related productions, writing libretti for *Aida* (2000) and *Tarzan* (2006).

Nonetheless, the majority of opportunities for Asian American theater artists still comes from projects that rely upon their ethnicity: B. D. Wong portrayed The Reciter in the Amon Miyamoto-directed revival of *Pacific Overtures* (2004), and has had to look toward television (*Oz, Law & Order SVU)* for more lucrative employment. David Henry Hwang's short-lived *About Face* (1996) and *Golden Child* (1998) have not matched the critical accolades received by *M. Butterfly*, and his adaptation of *Flower Drum Song* (2002) ran a disappointing five months.

Thus, although opportunities for Asian and Asian American actors on Broadway have increased in terms of quantity, they have not consistently improved in terms of quality; they tend to be neither high paying nor star making. The elimination of yellowface, whether in casting or writing, is a battle still being fought. The rosters of hundreds of Broadway shows reveal numerous Asian Americans who were able to secure one or two small roles in shows that called specifically for someone of Asian origin before so many, like Ah Wung Sing over a century ago, disappeared from the Broadway stage.

Randy Barbara Kaplan

Further Reading

Lee, Esther Kim. *A History of Asian American Theater.* Cambridge, U.K.: Cambridge University Press, 2006.

Lee, Josephine. *Performing Asian America.* Philadelphia: Temple University Press, 1998.

Moon, Krysten. *Yellowface: Creating the Chinese in American Popular Music and Performance, 1850s–1920s.* Piscataway, NJ: Rutgers University Press, 2005.

ATKINSON, BROOKS (1894–1984)
THEATER CRITIC, THEATER HISTORIAN

Renowned for his stylish, sophisticated theater reviews, (Justin) Brooks Atkinson was instrumental in both chronicling and championing American theater's evolution from a mere popular entertainment vehicle to a formidable modern art form. Born in Melrose, Massachusetts, Atkinson attended Harvard University, graduating in 1917. Starting out as a beat reporter for the *The Daily News* in Springfield, Atkinson joined *The Boston Evening Transcript* as a crime reporter and later assistant drama critic in 1919. Atkinson moved to New York City, accepting the position of drama **critic** for the *New York Times* in 1925. He held that post continuously for 35 years except for a Pulitzer Prize–winning tenure as a *Times* war correspondent during World War II.

Atkinson's theater reviews were highly respected for their pointed insights, engaging wit, high standards, and gracious manner—all of which earned him considerable favor with the theater-going public and the professional theater community. Through his popularity with readers, open support of artistic experimentation, and longevity with the *Times*, Atkinson became one of the first American theater critics whose influence grew well beyond the sphere of opening night praises and pans. Atkinson's admiration for early productions of **Eugene O'Neill**, **Tennessee Williams**, **Arthur Miller**, and **Edward Albee** helped ensure a permanent place for literary playwriting in American commercial theater. In the 1940s and 1950s Atkinson was among the first observers to point out that composers and lyricists like **Rodgers and Hammerstein**, **Lerner and Lowe**, and Meredith Willson were introducing thematic unity, literary sophistication, character-specific songs, and other important groundbreaking approaches in the way **musicals** were being written and staged. At about that same time Atkinson began to champion **Off-Broadway** theater, whose productions had heretofore been largely relegated to nontheatrical venues such as basements and storefronts. By 1960, Atkinson's support of New York's stronger fringe theaters had helped transform Off-Broadway into "legitimate theater." His reviews helped expand the audience for Off-Broadway and led to the early transfer of several Off-Broadway plays to legitimate theaters decades before such transfers were commonplace (*see* **Off-Broadway**). Atkinson earned still more adulation from the theater community in the late 1940s and early 1950s for his public condemnations of the House Un-American Activities Committee (HUAC) and Senator Joe McCarthy's inquiries into alleged communist activities of many prominent Americans, including film and theater artists.

In addition to his work as a critic, Atkinson wrote several books on Broadway, including *Broadway Scrapbook* (1947), *Broadway* (1970), and *The Lively Years: 1920–1973* (1974). Atkinson's Broadway books chronicle the major transformations of American theater in the twentieth century, most of which he saw firsthand. A prodigious literary scholar as well, Atkinson wrote and edited books on Henry David Thoreau and Ralph Waldo Emerson.

Atkinson retired as the *Times* drama critic in 1960 but continued to write a column titled "Critic-at-Large" for five more years. In that same year the Mansfield Theatre in the **Broadway theater district** was renamed the Brooks Atkinson Theater in his honor. He was awarded a special Tony Award in 1962 for his work with the *New York Times*.

Atkinson died of pneumonia in Huntsville, Alabama, where he had lived during the final years of his life.

Thomas A. Greenfield and Kevin Cunningham

Further Reading

Atkinson, Brooks. *Broadway.* New York: Macmillan, 1970.

Barranger, Millie S. *Theatre: A Way of Seeing.* 6th ed. Florence, KY: Cengage Learning, 2005.

Connolly, Thomas F. *George Jean Nathan and the Making of Modern American Drama Criticism.* Madison, NJ: Fairleigh Dickinson University Press, 2000.

BALANCHINE, GEORGE (1904–1983)
CHOREOGRAPHER

What Picasso was to modern art and Proust to the modern novel, George Balanchine was to modern ballet. More than anyone else, he was the first person to understand and cultivate the riches that Broadway **musical** dancing and concert ballet could bring to one another. His humble beginnings in Russia and his early triumphs in Russian and European ballet made him an unlikely prospect to become a historic innovator on Broadway during the era of **George Abbott**, **Richard Rodgers** and **Lorenz Hart**, and **Cole Porter**. But, indeed he did.

Balanchine was born in St. Petersburg, Russia, on January 22, 1904. His father was a composer and collector of folk songs and his mother was an amateur pianist. His keen and sophisticated knowledge of music informed his work as a choreographer. By the age of nine, he was admitted to the Imperial School of Theatre and Ballet. He would later describe himself as a "cloud in trousers." Though he came from a family of modest means, his life was filled with music, dance, and art. While the Russian Revolution closed the school for a time and resulted in extreme hardships for the dancers, students, and teachers, Balanchine eventually graduated in 1920 and was soon admitted into the corps de ballet of the Imperial Ballet Company at the Maryinsky Theatre. From the very beginning, his precocious choreographic interests were recognized and encouraged by his teachers and fellow dancers.

In 1924, when ballet impresario Sergei Diaghilev offered Balanchine the position of choreographer for his Diaghilev Ballet Russe in Paris, the world's pre-eminent ballet company, Balanchine and his bride, Tamara Gevergeva, defected to France. He was 20 years old. During his four and a half year tenure with the

Diaghilev Ballet Russe, Balanchine honed his skills as a choreographer. Two of his dances from this period continue to be revived and admired to this day. One of them is *Apollo*. Choreographed in 1928 to a score by Igor Stravinsky, this paean to the creative process took the legend of Apollo and his muses for its subject. For many dance historians, this ballet initiated the neoclassic approach to ballet—diminished story line and setting with emphasis on classical dance technique—that characterized so many of Balanchine's subsequent ballets. The second was *The Prodigal Son*, choreographed in 1929. If the first ballet was abstract and pure in its execution, this was dramatic and evoked powerful emotions with a keen intensity on the part of its performers.

Between 1929 and 1936, the period between Diaghilev's death and his first triumph with a Broadway musical, Balanchine's choreographic life was diverse and varied. He continued choreographing ballets for the resurrected Ballet Russe de Monte Carlo and at the same time, he choreographed a series of revues for the Englishman Charles B. Cochran that included *Cochran's 1930 Revue* and *Cochran's 1931 Revue*. In 1933 Balanchine formed a small ballet company, *Les Ballets 1933*, in England. It was his work with this dance ensemble that caught the attention of ballet impresario Lincoln Kirstein. Kirstein convinced Balanchine to emigrate to the United States to establish an American ballet company and school.

What Balanchine discovered in America was a country that viewed ballet more as a part of musical theater and operatic production rather than the concert stage. In many cases, serious dance was left to the early modern dance pioneers rather than their ballet counterparts. While training dancers for his ballet aesthetic and building an audience for serious ballet as a concert form, Balanchine accepted an offer from Richard Rodgers and Lorenz Hart to choreograph their musical, *On Your Toes* (1936), an unusual piece for mainstream Broadway at the time.

The composer/lyricist duo of Richard Rodgers and Lorenz Hart was at the peak of its powers in 1936 and could afford to take chances with the material written for this Broadway musical. In this musical, the lead character, a **vaudeville** tap dancer played by Ray Bolger, falls in love with a Russian ballerina, played by Balanchine's now former wife, Tamara Geva. The musical includes vaudeville soft shoe, production numbers, a "conventional" ballet, and the show's signature piece, "Slaughter on Tenth Avenue." In this final ballet, the ballerina is killed by mobsters while the former vaudevillian dances his anger out in tap shoes. In choreographing this piece, Balanchine combined jazz dance with tap and ballet in what has now come to be recognized as a landmark production in the history of musical theater dance. Apart from the inventiveness of his choreography, Balanchine became the first Broadway "dance director" to insist that he be credited as *choreographer* rather than the common, more prosaic dance director appellation.

In total, Balanchine spent 16 years choreographing, and in some cases directing, musical comedies, **operettas**, revues, and serious musical theater. Some of his work was traditional but his choreography was not formulaic. He tried to discern the purpose and function of the dance in each of these musical theater forms and then construct them in a way that would be both entertaining and of high quality.

He continued to collaborate with Rodgers and Hart on several more musical comedies including *Babes in Arms* (1937), *I Married an Angel* (1938), and *The Boys from Syracuse* (1938). His most conventional work was reserved for operettas like *Rosalinda* and *Song of Norway.*

Balanchine created one of his most innovative productions in 1940 when he directed and choreographed *Cabin in the Sky* by Vernon Duke (composer) and John La Touche (lyricist). Inspired by African American folklore, it told the story of Little Joe trying to make his way to heaven while being tempted by a sensuous Georgia Brown, played by renowned dancer Katherine Dunham, and by Lucifer Jr. Balanchine collaborated with Ms. Dunham on the choreography, which combined his classical ballet with her unique and vibrant African- and Caribbean-based movement vocabulary. While critics were unclear about how to describe what they saw and what it meant in terms of musical theater dance, *Cabin in the Sky* was generally recognized as an artistic if not a commercial success. This collaboration would continue to inform Balanchine's approach to ballet on the concert stage and to demonstrate to future Broadway musical theater choreographers the importance of incorporating an Africanist aesthetic into the Broadway dance vocabulary.

Balanchine ended his career on the Broadway musical theater stage with a conventional approach to the musical *Where's Charley?* (1951) and a flop with *Courtin' Time* (1951). Nonetheless, throughout his Broadway career he set a high standard for musical theater dancers and choreographers by raising the bar regarding the technique expected of the dancers and pointing the direction for future choreographers to more conscientiously integrate dance into the fabric of the musical. Balanchine challenged himself to learn what he could from the best in American music, be it jazz, popular, or classical, and from new forms of American dance as exemplified by tap dancer Ray Bolger and the Caribbean-based dance of Katherine Dunham. He showed the world of Broadway stage that ballet could combine with native American dance forms in exciting and new ways. He would also take what he learned from the Broadway musical back to the concert stage and create some of the most interesting and innovative American ballets.

By 1948, Balanchine and Lincoln Kirstein had the financial means, the dancers, and the audience to establish one of the world's most distinguished ballet companies—the New York City Ballet. Until his death in 1983, Balanchine worked principally in the United States, creating ballet with the best composers, including friend and fellow expatriate Igor Stravinsky. Balanchine also attracted the best Russian ballet defectors to the West, including Rudolf Nureyev and Mikhail Baryshnikov. His impact on the concert stage is immeasurable. His contribution to the musical theater stage is yet to be fully appreciated.

Ray Miller

Further Reading

McDonagh, Don. *George Balanchine*. Boston: Twayne Publishers, 1983.

Taper, Bernard. *Balanchine: A Biography*. New York: Times Books, 1984.

BAREFOOT IN THE PARK

Broadway Run: Biltmore Theatre
Opening: October 23, 1963
Closing: June 25, 1967
Total Performances: 1,530
Preview: October 21, 1963
Total Previews: 2
Writer: Neil Simon
Director: Mike Nichols
Producer: Saint Subber
Cast: Elizabeth Ashley, Robert Redford, Mildred Natwick, Herbert Edelman, Kurt Kasznar, and Joseph Keating

Although it was his third script to be produced on Broadway, **Neil Simon**'s ascent to his present status as America's most successful playwright in history effectively begins with *Barefoot in the Park*. At 1,530 performances covering nearly four years, *Barefoot* achieved to that point the second longest Broadway run of any nonmusical production since the 1940s. (Jean Kerr's *Mary Mary* had run longer: 1,572 performances between 1961 and 1964.) The play served notice that playwright Simon and first-time Broadway director **Mike Nichols**, having cut their teeth in television writing and club comedy, respectively, had graduated to Broadway with their astonishing gifts for naturalistic comedy writing and staging. With **musicals** commanding ever more attention of **producers** and theatergoers and the commercial fortunes of serious **playwrights** such as **Tennessee Williams**, **Arthur Miller**, and **Lillian Hellman** in decline, *Barefoot in the Park* inaugurated Neil Simon as the unlikely but undisputed master of "the Broadway play" from the 1960s through the 1980s.

Much like Simon's first play, the impressive debut comedy *Come Blow Your Horn* (1961), and numerous plays thereafter, *Barefoot in the Park* exacts its comedy by thrusting an "odd couple" together in close quarters. As *Barefoot in the Park* opens, earnest and handsome young attorney Paul Bratter and lovely free spirit Corie have recently met, had a whirlwind courtship, married at the peak of their considerable mutual attraction, and set up "house" in a small apartment on the top floor of one of New York's infamous, multidwelling brownstones.

As the realities of youthful poverty, the demands of Paul's career, and all manner of housing malfunctions encroach upon the newlyweds' bliss, Simon establishes the predominating comic tension for the play. Paul presses Corie to tack their marriage toward meeting responsibilities and embracing the pragmatism of upward mobility. However, Corie, at first flirtatiously and then militantly, challenges Paul to maintain the devil-may-care spontaneity that engendered their love in the first place and, on some level, seems to be all that is keeping her alive. In Simon's comic world of tortured but inevitable compromise, lions will lie down with lambs. Paul and Corie ultimately work things out, but not until Paul gets in touch with his inner free spirit by agreeing to, of course, walk barefoot in the park.

Robert Redford in a scene from Barefoot in the Park, *one of the biggest hits of the 1964 season on Broadway. (AP Photo)*

Along the way a sardonic neighbor, Corie's mother, and repairmen of various stripes come and go, offering wry commentary on modern life and imbuing the show with the special comic energy that only exquisitely timed, inconvenient entrances and exits can provide.

For his part, Nichols was widely praised for his skillful management of Simon's wisecrack-laden dialog and for his handling of what was to become a Simon stage comedy trademark: agitated verbal and physical congestion of anxious characters large and small. Critics raved about Nichols's ability to punctuate the action with a deceptively subtle running gag: everyone who enters the apartment (and, thus, the stage) after ascending the unseen five flights of steps does so in a state of increasingly elaborate, scene-stealing exhaustion. By Act II, Nichols had built an altogether independent comic arc into the play as audiences, attentive to the rapid-fire action and repartee on stage, nevertheless were compelled to keep a watchful eye on the apartment front door to see who would burst through next and stop the show. Nichols won the Tony for Best Director and would go on to become among the most successful Broadway and Hollywood directors of the past 40 years. He would continue to work with Simon periodically, directing four additional Neil Simon plays on Broadway as well as the highly successful **film** adaptation of Simon's *Biloxi Blues* (play, 1985; film, 1988).

Barefoot in the Park also ended the Broadway career of its lead actor, but it did so to great effect. Before originating the role of Paul Bratter, 26-year-old Robert Redford had been struggling in **television** in both New York and Hollywood, doing one-episode appearances on various television series and taking the occasional Broadway role. Yet it was Broadway that actually launched Redford to Hollywood stardom. After his success in *Barefoot in the Park* Redford began landing solid roles in prestigious Hollywood films, such as *Inside Daisy Clover* (1965) with Natalie Wood and *The Chase* (1966) with Marlon Brando. His first starring role in a major film was, in fact, as Paul Bratter for the 1967 film adaptation of *Barefoot in the Park*. (Corie would not be played by the very capable but still relatively unknown Elizabeth Ashley, who had co-starred with Redford on Broadway, but by the decidedly more famous Jane Fonda.) The film adaptation of *Barefoot in the Park* proved to be a triumph for all involved, especially Redford. He has been one of Hollywood's most influential actors, directors, and producers ever since and has never done another Broadway play.

Barefoot in the Park consecrated Simon's approach to middle-class family comedy that, although not original with him in concept, became his element over the next 40 years. *Barefoot in the Park* displays Simon's masterful development of natural, believable characters and relationships within a torrent of punch lines and stage schtick. He was often criticized in the 1960s by academics in particular for writing to formula and for seeming to repeat himself in later plays featuring clashes of pairs, such as *The Odd Couple* (1967) and *The Sunshine Boys* (1972). But audiences knew better and, eventually, the "intellectual community" was able to see past the commercial success of *Barefoot in the Park* and accept it as the harbinger of a theatrical phenomenon that it was.

Thomas A. Greenfield

Further Reading

Greenfield, Thomas Allen. *Work and the Work Ethic in American Drama, 1920–1970.* Columbia: University of Missouri Press, 1982.

Koprince, Susan. *Understanding Neil Simon.* Columbia: University of South Carolina Press, 2002.

Simon, Neil. *Rewrites: A Memoir.* New York: Simon and Schuster, 1998.

BARRYMORE, ETHEL (1879–1959)
ACTRESS, DIRECTOR

Despite her fame on two continents and the theatrical immortality of her family name, Ethel Barrymore remains something of an enigmatic figure in the history of American theater. During her lifetime, she was viewed by some as a privileged ingénue whose first theatrical successes came unearned and too early. On the other hand, she was also seen as something of a young victim of a star-making system that marketed her name, looks, and charm at the expense of her talent. She eventually overcame whatever burdens encumbered the early phases of her artistic development to become the most distinguished Broadway actress of the 1920s—a period when both women and serious drama began to establish themselves on modern Broadway. An unanticipated comeback success in 1940 extended her legend and legacy throughout the first half of the century.

Barrymore was born in 1879 to Herman Blyth (a famous actor later known by the stage name Maurice Barrymore) and Georgiana Drew Barrymore, who themselves had several prominent relatives in the theater business. The Barrymores' social connections saw Ethel and her brothers, the famous actors **John** and Lionel Barrymore, accompanying their parents to Europe for extended stays. During these sojourns the Barrymore children met their parents' celebrated friends and colleagues, including producer Sir Henry Irving and playwright Oscar Wilde. After the death of Georgiana when Ethel was 13, she entered a convent where she completed her formal education. At this time she showed a greater interest in concert piano than theater.

Nevertheless, by age 15 she was acting professionally thanks to the patronage of her relatives. In New York she appeared in Richard Brinsley Sheridan's eighteenth-century classic *The Rivals* (1894) and the contemporary British comedy *The Bauble Shop* (1894), earning immediate popularity as a promising youthful actress and celebrity child of America's premiere acting family. Among the people she met during this period was Broadway producer and **Theatrical Syndicate** co-founder Charles Frohman, who would later take her under his wing as a protégé. Barrymore's visibility among the social and intellectual elite grew when she appeared on Broadway and later on tour with her uncle John Drew in the contemporary British drama *Rosemary* (1896). During the *Rosemary* tour, she accepted an invitation to perform in the London production of *Secret Service*, written by Barrymore family friend William Gillette. Barrymore would stay in London long enough to finish the run of *Rosemary* and perform in *Peter the Great* for Henry Irving.

Upon returning to the United States, Ethel was cast by Frohman to star in **Clyde Fitch**'s *Captain Jinks of the Horse Marines* (1901). The comedy was a big hit, turning the 21-year-old ingénue into a bona fide Broadway star. She would remain under Frohman's exclusive management (and that of his company) for 20 years. Frohman cast her in light comedies (like Hubert Henry Davies's *Cousin Kate* [1903]) that featured her youthful girlish appeal as well as in challenging dramatic roles (such as Henrik Ibsen's *A Doll's House* [1905]) in the hopes of molding her into the leading actress of the day. Some critics and historians speculate that Frohman rushed her too quickly into the more ambitious roles, a move that likely had an inhibiting effect on the development of her talent (Izard 352–353). During this ten-year period she performed in 17 Broadway plays, becoming Broadway's most famous actress, if not its most accomplished.

Barrymore did not seem to chafe under Frohman's tutelage. However, for several years after his death in 1915 she still had contractual obligations to his company, which eventually displeased her. By 1921, she was free of those obligations and, in her forties, entered her professional and artistic adulthood. Her first projects after leaving Frohman's company marked a significant artistic departure from her earlier work, with a strong emphasis on challenging formidable roles. She played Juliet in a 1922 production of *Romeo and Juliet*, and later Ophelia in *Hamlet*, followed by Portia in *The Merchant of Venice* (1925). Perhaps the role for which she is most famous is the original Constance Middleton in 295 performances of W. Somerset Maugham's *The Constant Wife* (1926). She then starred and directed a religious play, Spanish writer Gregorio Martinez Sierra's *The Kingdom of God* (1928). *The Kingdom of God* was the first play produced in the Ethel Barrymore Theatre, built and named in her honor by the **Shubert Brothers**. Although not every project succeeded (critical reaction to *Romeo and Juliet* was particularly harsh), her acting matured gradually. By the end of the decade she had established herself as Broadway's most venerated dramatic actress.

In the 1930s she began directing as well as acting on Broadway, commanding respect from audiences and **critics** if no longer indisputably Broadway's leading female performer. In 1940, as her storied career seemed to be winding down, she scored the greatest single triumph of her career as the amiable schoolteacher Miss Moffat in Emlyn Williams's *The Corn Is Green*. She would play this role over a thousand times—over 500 times on Broadway. The role, considered by many to represent the pinnacle of her talent and achievement as an actress, solidified her place of singular distinction for stage actresses of her time.

Like most stage performers who came of age with the **film** industry, Barrymore acted in films at various times throughout her career. She was generally disdainful of the film industry, and her efforts in the silent era of the 1910s and the early talkies of the 1930s were undistinguished. She fared better later in life, winning an Oscar for best supporting actress in *None But the Lonely Heart* in 1944.

Barrymore died in 1959 in her home in Beverly Hills, California, from heart disease.

Thomas A. Greenfield and Megan Lee

Further Reading

Izard, Forrest. *Heroines of the Modern Stage*. New York: Sturgis and Walton, 1915.
Peters, Margot. *The House of Barrymore*. New York: Alfred A. Knopf, Inc., 1990.

BARRYMORE, JOHN (1882–1942)
ACTOR

Known as "The Great Profile" for his distinguished looks, charismatic stage presence, and classical acting style, John Sidney Blyth Barrymore was the most famous member of America's premiere theatrical family. Generally considered the best American Shakespearean actor of the twentieth century, his Broadway performances in *Richard III* and *Hamlet* during the 1920s helped establish modern American commercial theater's reputation and confidence for staging world-class Shakespearean productions. Moving into **film** acting shortly after establishing himself as a Broadway star, Barrymore became an early prototype of the actor who parlays New York stage success into Hollywood film stardom and fashioned one of the first truly successful bicoastal acting careers.

Barrymore grew up in Philadelphia. He was raised principally by his maternal grandmother, Louisa Lane Drew, who operated a popular Philadelphia theater. His father, under the stage name Maurice Barrymore, and mother, Georgie, were also American stage actors. After an early attempt to become a painter and illustrator, Barrymore entered the family business of acting when he was in his early twenties. He debuted on Broadway in **Clyde Fitch**'s comedy *Glad of It* (1903). Reviewers praised Barrymore's stage presence and strong physicality, noting similarities with his father's acting style. For the next ten years he continued working on Broadway in a variety of comedies and popular dramas, earning fame and

The acting Barrymore clan gathers in Hollywood, 1932. Seated, from left to right: Irene Fenwick (wife of Lionel Barrymore); Lionel Barrymore; Ethel Barrymore; Dolores Costello (wife of John Barrymore) holding daughter Dolores Ethel Barrymore; John Barrymore, holding John Barrymore Jr. Standing, from left to right: Ethel's three children, John, Ethel, and Samuel Colt. (AP Photo)

audience adoration for his comedic talents and his dashing good looks. He was a particular favorite of director Arthur Hobson, who would figure prominently in his later ascent to legendary status.

Barrymore's early stage successes gave him an entree to film stardom. In the 1910s, Hollywood producer Adolph Zukor formed the Famous Players Film Company, specializing in adapting stage hits into films. The handsome, famous, and talented Barrymore was a logical choice to make the transition from stage to screen. Barrymore's first film was a sentimental drama, *An American Citizen* (1914). He was drawn immediately to Hollywood living, the higher pay, and the less demanding work requirements of starring in a film than starring in an eight show per week play. In each of the next five years, Barrymore would appear in numerous films, coming back east to appear annually in one or two Broadway shows as well. His more notable plays during this period included hits *The Yellow Ticket* (1914), *Kick In* (1914), and two productions of a comedy, *The Jest* (1917, 1919). In the meantime he starred for Zukor's Famous Players in *The Dictator* (1915) and *Dr. Jekyll and Mr. Hyde* (1920) as well as several other films.

By 1920, Barrymore was a star in both New York and Hollywood—a rarity for that time—and had developed an extensive network of friends and collaborators in both the film and theater industries. Sensing that Barrymore had not yet reached his artistic or commercial potential in theater, a coalition of some of Broadway's leading talents—producer/director Arthur Hopkins and voice teacher Margaret Carrington among them—assembled a repertory theater company around Barrymore. Under Hopkins's familiar direction and with speech instruction from Carrington (vocal dynamics being among Barrymore's few acting weaknesses), Barrymore took on two **Shakespeare** roles that secured his legacy on Broadway—and to some extent that of Shakespeare's as well.

A limited run in *Richard III* (1920) was an unbridled triumph, hailed by **critics** as a defining moment in the history of American acting. What shortcomings Barrymore might have had in vocal technique were more than tended to by Carrington's instruction and Barrymore's own ambition and talent. Barrymore and company outdid themselves two years later with a production of *Hamlet*, which ran for a record 101 performances, beating previous record holder **Edwin Booth**'s historic 100-nights-of-*Hamlet* run from 1865. *Hamlet* earned Barrymore $1,000 a week. For the next several years he turned *Hamlet* into a franchise for himself. He took the show on tour in 1923, shattering American box-office records for a road Shakespeare production. Daring to go where few American Shakespearean actors would go before, he put together the finances to bring *Hamlet* to London in 1925. Despite terrible reviews, including an acerbic drubbing from **George Bernard Shaw**, he sold out the entire England run and pocketed a handsome profit for his troubles.

Hamlet had elevated Barrymore to the heights of theatrical acclaim and, in so doing, significantly elevated his marketability in Hollywood. In 1926—approaching age 40, discontented with the rigors of Broadway and touring, and drawn to Hollywood's riches—Barrymore signed a lucrative multiple picture contract with Warner Brothers studio. He would not return to Broadway until 1940. He made numerous movies during this time, including some classic American films: *Moby*

Dick (1930), *Grand Hotel* (1932), and *Dinner at Eight* (1933). His legend was no less enhanced by his personal excesses, including binge drinking, binge spending, multiple marriages, multiple affairs, and multiple divorces. He filed for bankruptcy in 1937 even though he had made five films that year.

Numerous entreaties from New York friends and well wishers to get him to return to Broadway had gone unheeded throughout the 1930s, until he agreed to play a small part—a caricature of himself—in the first and only Broadway play by two Hollywood writers: *My Dear Children* (1940) by Catherine Turney and Jerry Horwin. Publicity announcing Barrymore's long-awaited return to New York theater spiked advance ticket sales to a then near record $50,000. However, from the play's opening night Barrymore was engagingly horrendous—missing lines and entrances, recklessly ad-libbing, shamelessly scene stealing—all to the delight of audiences. The play ran for 117 performances, until Barrymore bid the show and Broadway an abrupt farewell to take up his final Hollywood film offers. He died in 1942 in Los Angeles of cirrhosis of the liver, a condition doubtless aggravated by his excessive alcohol consumption. His acting brother Lionel and acting sister Ethel survived him. His granddaughter, Drew Barrymore, has been a major film star and Hollywood personality for 20 years

Barrymore's life of spectacularly high achievement, volatile changes of mood and mind, and dissolute personal behavior made him a theatrical legend even before his death. His once awe-inspiring, room-filling stage presence made for easy mockery, even self-mockery, toward the end of his career. With the rise of American Method Acting in the 1940s—with its emphasis on internalized feelings and controlled character development—Barrymore's riveting stage postures and grand gestures became fodder for theatrical nostalgia and even derision. Yet in the 1920s, Barrymore gave a young American theater outrageous ambition, transcendent self-confidence, and ferocious star power that many jaded theater artists of today would envy—even if they chided themselves for doing so.

Thomas A. Greenfield and Brian Balduzzi

Further Reading

Fowler, Gene. *Good Night, Sweet Prince*. New York: Viking, 1944.

Kobler, John. *Damned in Paradise: The Life of John Barrymore*. New York: Atheneum, 1977.

Taylor, Phil and Paul Nicholas. *Barrymore: A Man Possessed.* London: Metro Publications, 2002.

BELASCO, DAVID (1853–1931)
PRODUCER, DIRECTOR, WRITER, PERFORMER, THEATER MANAGER

A legendary **producer**, director, **playwright**, and dynamic life force in New York theater for five decades, David Belasco left two distinctly different legacies to the

A 1929 photo of producer David Belasco, relaxing in Atlantic City, New Jersey. (AP Photo)

history and culture of Broadway. At the peak of his powers Belasco became the public embodiment, and eventually a clichéd stereotype, of the megalomaniacal, self-obsessive producer/tyrant. Credited with mounting some 100 Broadway shows, his single vision for his productions reportedly extended into every aspect of his life and often imposed itself into the lives of the people around him. On the other hand, theater historians note Belasco as a groundbreaking, meticulous craftsman in theatrical lighting and set design who first brought truly complex, sophisticated, modern realistic staging to Broadway.

Of Portuguese-Jewish ancestry Belasco was born in San Francisco, the son of immigrants from England. His father had been a stage performer in London and supported his son's youthful passion for theater. During childhood, Belasco's family moved to Vancouver and back to San Francisco. The senior Belasco aided his son in meeting theater professionals living in or passing through both cities. In his teens Belasco appeared in some professional productions in California and Nevada, playing small parts and landing odd jobs for various theater companies. By his early twenties, Belasco had befriended and worked with **Edwin Booth**, renowned playwright and actor James Herne, and the legendary melodramatist Dion Boucicault—the latter having influenced Belasco's initial forays into playwriting and directing.

In the 1870s Belasco became involved in theater management. His principal engagement during this period was as assistant and then stage manager for San Francisco theater owner Thomas Maquire for whom he worked variously as a producer's secretary, minor actor on call, resident playwright, and stage manager. Maguire's two principal theaters, Maguire's New Theatre and Baldwin Academy of Music, specialized in attracting major touring performers and shows, and the ambitious, young Belasco used his association with Maguire to advance his reputation among American theater's artists and producers.

Although still in California, Belasco earned his first New York playwriting credit in 1880, when a **touring production** of his play *Hearts of Oak*, which had premiered at the Baldwin, played briefly at the prestigious Fifth Avenue Theatre. By Belasco's own admission the play was lacking in quality, but the laborious stage detail Belasco had insisted upon—actual water in pitchers, real beans in bean bowls, and so on—foreshadowed the new territory in realistic staging he would later bequeath to modern Broadway. In 1882 a second piece, *La Belle Russe*, played in New York after opening at the Baldwin. However, negotiations for the tour caused a rift between Maguire and Belasco, and Belasco made the first of what would be his two moves to New York.

Through Broadway connections established in California, Belasco quickly secured the job of stage manager of the Madison Square Theatre, another high-profile Broadway theater of the day. While managing the Madison, he oversaw a hit production of *Young Mrs. Winthrop* (1882) by veteran playwright Bronson Howard and a successful run of his own play *May Blossom* (1884). He returned to San Francisco to direct a season at the Baldwin, now under new ownership, only to move to New York permanently in 1886 at the behest of producer and owner of Broadway's Lyceum Theatre, Daniel Frohman (another of the Broadway luminaries Belasco had befriended in California).

From 1886 to 1890, Belasco virtually homesteaded in Frohman's Lyceum, directing and writing several productions. He struck up a writing partnership with Henry C. DeMille (father of film director Cecil B. DeMille and grandfather of choreographer **Agnes de Mille**). The pair wrote four consecutive popular hits: *The Wife* (1887), *Lord Chumley* (1888), *The Charity Ball* (1889), and *Men and Women* (1890), all but the last staged at the Lyceum. While not masterpieces, the four plays, all chronicling the vicissitudes of life in New York high society, were well crafted to popular tastes and the productions were widely praised for their staging.

By 1890 Belasco had established himself as a major Broadway author and director. He soon began what became a notorious string of involvements with aspiring actresses. The first of these relationships, with Mrs. Leslie Carter, caused a break between Belasco and the appearance-conscious Daniel Frohman. Nevertheless, Belasco continued to write and stage new plays. He wrote the Western panorama drama *The Girl I Left Behind Me* (1893) for Daniel Frohman's brother Charles, a more successful producer than Daniel, to open and dedicate Charles's new Empire Theatre. Although containing stereotypical representations of Native Americans that would be unacceptable today, the play was, for its time, regarded as a distinguished contribution to American playwriting. Belasco introduced innovative applications of offstage sound to build and clarify tensions between Native Americans and white soldiers.

Although he had been a successful Broadway playwright and director for a decade, *The Heart of Maryland* (1895) established Belasco as an independent producer—the role that would bring him lasting fame and infamy. In one of the most memorable staging feats of the decade, star Mrs. Carter swung to and fro onstage from a bell clapper to keep it from ringing and, thus, signaling death for her captured lover. The extravagance of the play marked something of a watershed for Belasco, who would thereafter gradually turn to more subtle, naturalistic staging.

From 1895 until his death in 1931 every Broadway season brought at least one original or new revival of a Belasco production. During this period, Belasco brought major innovations to theatrical lighting and stagecraft. His relentlessly doctrinaire naturalism set new standards for Broadway production values. He famously imported eighteenth-century French furnishings for *Du Barry* (1901) about King Louis XV's mistress. For a forest scene in *Tiger Rose* (1917) he covered the stage floor with real, fresh pine needles, which released their scent as the actors walked upon them every night. Although sometimes criticized for gimmickry, Belasco believed, as did the leading European naturalist dramatists of his day, that meticulous, intelligent stage setting focused and intensified the experience of the play for both actors and audience. **Critics**, audiences, and other producers took notice.

Even more lasting than his staging innovations was his complete reconception of lighting as an integral part of the artistic and emotional design of a play. He is credited with being the first American producer to eliminate clumsy, conspicuous footlights by moving toward ceiling-anchored full-stage front lighting—now standard operating procedure in theatrical lighting. Belasco also developed unified lighting "scores" that supported the arc of a play's story and character development. His use of lighting to stage the presence of onstage spirits, whether in a **Shakespeare** production or his own *The Return of Peter Grimm* (1911), was also revolutionary. In numerous productions, his control of the emotional impact of lighting transitions between day and twilight or night and day explored detail heretofore unknown in the theater. He famously boasted that he could "double" the power and persuasiveness of a character's speech by lighting alone.

No shrinking violet, Belasco claimed to have been as innovative in his directing techniques for actors as he had been in staging and lighting. Some historians are reluctant to go that far, since he never wrote down his theories for directing (as he did in his numerous prompt books for staging and lighting). However, he was unquestionably astute—perhaps as no other director and producer of his time— about anticipating what an audience wanted from theater and then teaching the audience to want something better.

Belasco was by far the most formidable and successful independent producer of the first half of the twentieth century, competing as no one else could against (and at times working independently with) the successive Broadway monopolies held by the **Theatrical Syndicate** and the **Shubert Brothers** from the late 1890s through the Depression. In 1907 he commissioned the building of his own theater on 44th Street, which he named after himself in 1910. The Belasco is still one of Broadway's active historic theaters.

In his lifetime and his legacy, Belasco personified the successes and excesses of young modern Broadway: shameless self-promotion and awe-inspiring triumphs, formulaic pap and cutting-edge creativity, self-indulgent hedonism and consummate professionalism.

Belasco died in New York City of aftereffects of a heart attack on May 14, 1931. His final production, *Tonight or Never*, which he had produced and directed, had opened six months earlier and was still running in the Belasco Theatre on the night he died. One last hit.

Thomas A. Greenfield

Further Reading

Dorbian, Iris. *Great Producers: Visionaries of the American Theater.* New York: Allworth Press, 2008.

Winter, William. *The Life of David Belasco V1.* Whitefish, MT: Kessinger Publishing, 2008.

BENNETT, MICHAEL (1943–1987)
CHOREOGRAPHER, DANCER, DIRECTOR, PRODUCER

Michael Bennett (born Michael DeFiglia) was one of the most innovative and successful Broadway choreographers and directors in American theater history. He was among the most influential theater director/choreographers of the past 30 years, having infused the contemporary Broadway **musical** with an enlarged, invigorated focus on dance. Three of his shows, *Company* (1970), *A Chorus Line* (1975), and *Dreamgirls* (1981), stand among the most significant Broadway musicals of the late twentieth century.

Born in 1943 in Buffalo, New York, Bennett began dance lessons in childhood. Prior to completing high school he appeared in a national and European **touring production** of *West Side Story* (1957), a breakthrough musical in the use of dance to establish dramatic tension within the plot. After completing the tour, Bennett began a career as a New York–based theatrical dancer and choreographer. While still in his teens he danced in the **Betty Comden and Adolph Green** success *Subways Are for Sleeping* (1961) and became an assistant choreographer for author/lyricist James Lipton's *Nowhere to Go But Up* (1962). He remained active on Broadway through his early twenties dancing in *Here's Love* (1963) and *Bajour* (1964).

In 1965 Bennett took a one-year hiatus from Broadway, finding anonymous national popularity in Hollywood as a regular dancer on NBC's hit pop music **television** revue *Hullabaloo!* "The *Hullabaloo!* Dancers" became famous in their own right for their exaggerated, trendsetting youth dances performed as guest stars such as Diana Ross and the Supremes, the Kinks, and Sammy Davis Jr. sang amid

Michael Bennett, shown in a photo circa 1980s. (AP Photo)

their flailing limbs and scene-stealing hip moves. The dancing on *Hullabaloo!* hinted at the commanding energy Bennett would bring to his later Broadway productions.

While doing *Hullabaloo!* Bennett met and formed a lasting relationship with fellow *Hullabaloo!* dancer, Donna McKechnie. Bennett and McKechnie worked together repeatedly throughout his career. (McKechnie won a Tony Award for her role in Bennett's *A Chorus Line*. The two were married briefly in 1976.)

Soon after returning to Broadway, Bennett launched a career as a solo Broadway choreographer, first in the short-lived *A Joyful Noise* (1966) and then in *Henry, Sweet Henry* (1967). Neither show was commercially successful, but Bennett's imaginative choreography won Tony nominations for each show and earned the admiration of the Broadway community.

Bennett's reputation took a quintessential leap forward with his next series of projects. His first genuine Broadway hit as a choreographer, *Promises, Promises* (1968), ran for three years and placed the 25-year-old Bennett squarely in the company of some Broadway titans who were also involved with the production. These included author **Neil Simon** and producer **David Merrick**, respectively the most successful **playwright** and producer of the decade. The following year Bennett choreographed *Coco*, the musical biography of Parisian fashion designer Coco Chanel. The show marked Katharine Hepburn's return to Broadway after a 17-year absence. Despite enormous preproduction publicity and excellent advanced sales, the show could not sustain an audience after Hepburn's departure several months into the run. The show was a financial failure, but Bennett continued to impress the industry as well as the public, and *Coco* earned Bennett a third Tony nomination.

During this period Bennett collaborated with composer and lyricist **Stephen Sondheim** in *Company* (1970), *Follies* (1971), and *Twigs* (1971), serving as both director and choreographer for the latter two. The collaborations with Sondheim, while not yielding huge box-office success, were significant in a number of ways. *Company* is generally viewed as marking a defining stage in the evolution of the American musical, marking a break from the linear-plot book musicals of the **Rodgers and Hammerstein** era into darker, more impressionistic treatments of stories and character relationships. *Follies*, also structured as a "concept" musical, earned Bennett his first Tony Awards for direction and choreography.

Bennett won a second Tony Award for choreography for the critically acclaimed but short-lived *Seesaw* (1973), a highly troubled production even by Broadway standards that Bennett essentially restaged when producers called him in to "save" the struggling show. The all-but-forgotten production is now best known as the musical Bennett did before *A Chorus Line.*

Bennett's reputation exploded into legend with *A Chorus Line*, which became the longest-running show in Broadway history up to that time: 6,137 performances when it closed in 1990 after a run that lasted almost 15 years. (As of October 2009 it was still the longest-ever running Broadway show that originated in the United States.) As director, producer, and "conceiver" of the show, Bennett fashioned the production from taped conversations and interviews with numerous musical chorus dancers, whose onstage anonymity and practiced enthusiasm masked the punishing, sometimes desperate lives they led. For Bennett a dancer's audition became a convincing metaphor for success, failure, love, heartbreak, and the Darwinian-like selection process governing artistic competition and the pursuit of dreams. The play's seven Tony Awards, Pulitzer Prize, successful Broadway revival (2006), national tours, **film**, and untold numbers of school and community productions stand as the signature triumph of the choreographer as *auteur* and overlord of the American musical. Thanks to Bennett's *A Chorus Line* and the countless dance academy tour groups from across the country that flocked to see it in the Shubert Theatre, dance-driven musicals have established an enduring presence on Broadway.

Bennett's next big hit was *Dreamgirls* (1981), which, with 1,521 performances, was one of the longest-running Broadway shows ever to feature both African American performers and African American–based content. (Only 1978's *Ain't Misbehavin'*, a tribute show based on the music of Fats Waller, ran longer.) Loosely based on the 1960s rise of the Supremes, Diana Ross, and Motown Records' founder Berry Gordy, the show remained true to Bennett's vision of featuring extended musical numbers while all but eliminating dialogue-driven peak moments and scenes. While generally devoid of traditional discrete dance numbers, the entire musical is set to music and motion. *Dreamgirls* earned Bennett another Best Musical Tony Award and secured his election to the Theatre Hall of Fame in 1986. *Dreamgirls* experienced a rebirth of public affection in 2006, a quarter of a century after its Broadway opening, in one of the most commercially successful Brodway musical-to-film adaptations in history. (In 2009, the film *Dreamgirls* ranked third in North American box-office receipts for all such Broadway musical film adaptations behind the film versions of *Chicago* and *The Sound of Music.*)

Bennett continued working until shortly before his death in 1987 but never mounted another new Broadway show after *Dreamgirls*. He died in Tuscon, Arizona, of lymphoma resulting from AIDS. His accomplishments in the 1970s and 1980s secured what remains today a prominent role for dance innovation in Broadway musicals.

Thomas A. Greenfield and Nicole Katz

Further Reading

Kelly, Kevin. *One Singular Sensation: The Michael Bennett Story.* New York: Zebra, 1991.

McKechnie, Donna, and Greg Lawrence. *Time Steps: My Musical Comedy Life.* New York: Simon & Schuster, 2006.

BERLIN, IRVING (1888–1989)
COMPOSER

Through his songwriting Irving Berlin ([Israel] Isadore Beilin, alt. Baline) translated American sensibilities and major moments in American history into memorable lyrics. A tunesmith who began work on the streets of New York, Berlin ended his career having impacted all major commercial musical outlets from sheet music to ASCAP (the composers union), from player pianos to records, from **radio** to **television**, **film**, and, of course, Broadway. In addition, he was one of only a handful of Broadway power brokers of his time willing to advocate for equal treatment of talented African American performers.

Emigrating from Russia in 1893, the Beilins, a large Jewish family, struggled to survive on New York's rough Lower East Side. Despite lacking formal music training, their youngest son Israel (or "Izzy") began a stint as a singing waiter in the notorious Pelham Café, a bar known for its criminal element. It was here in 1907 that he wrote his first song lyric titled "Marie from Sunny Italy." After shopping the song around Tin Pan Alley, he succeeded in getting it published. Perhaps the most lasting impact from this song came in the form of his accidental *nom de plume*, a misprinting by the sheet music publisher of Berlin for Beilin. Although early success was gradual, eventually Henry Waterson, an influential Tin Pan Alley music publisher, hired Berlin as a staff lyricist. Berlin was nothing if not prolific, reputedly publishing over five songs a week while accumulating a trunkful of thwarted efforts he intended to rework later. Inspired by the song-and-dance numbers of Broadway **vaudeville** star **George M. Cohan** and the minstrel-influenced folk songs of Stephen Foster, Berlin blended syncopated rhythms with easily discerned lyrics, filling his songs with local color and recognizable sentiments.

As his songs gained fame, famous performers from Broadway's vaudeville shows sought out his songs. Berlin composed for such popular vaudevillians as Al Jolson, **Fanny Brice**, and **Bert Williams**. His first megahit song, "Alexander's

Ragtime Band," was first performed professionally in 1911 by a vaudeville-headlining comedienne named Emma Carus. The song remains a popular sing-along and piano-bar number to this day. Soon Berlin was composing entire musical comedy revues for Broadway. The first was *Watch Your Step* (1914), starring nationally renowned ballroom dancers Vernon and Irene Castle, followed by *Stop! Look! Listen!* (1915). Berlin's career as a **show tune** composer appeared to be short-lived as he was drafted into the Army in 1918, a few months after being naturalized as a U.S. citizen. Berlin seems to have had few military talents, and his commanding officer soon recruited him to assist with a musical fund-raiser, ultimately producing what Berlin would turn into a military-themed Broadway show, *Yip, Yip Yaphank* (1918) and later adapted as *This Is the Army* (1943).

Shortly after completing his tour of duty, Berlin built his own theater, the Music Box on West 45th Street, in order to mount musical revues. The first of these was *The Music Box Revue of 1921*. Never afraid of experimenting with a new medium for showcasing his songs, Berlin soon began contributing material to Hollywood films, including "Blue Skies" featured in the first full-length talkie *The Jazz Singer* (1927), starring Al Jolson. He went on to write dozens of songs for various studios, including two songs for the first major all-black musical film *Hallelujah* (1929) and three for the Marx Brothers, including the 1929 film adaptation of the Berlin–**George S. Kaufman**–Marx Brothers' Broadway musical farce *The Cocoanuts* (1926).

Back on Broadway Berlin joined forces with Kaufman's collaborator Moss Hart on *Face the Music* (1932), *As Thousands Cheer* (1933), and *Louisiana Purchase* (1940). Of these the most lasting was *As Thousands Cheer*, which based music and scenes on current newspaper headlines. The show featured several hits, including "Easter Parade," "Heat Wave," "Harlem on My Mind," and, most powerfully, "Supper Time" sung by Ethel Waters about a housewife who has just heard of her husband's lynching. Waters's appearance in *As Thousands Cheer* marked one of the first times an African American woman had a featured role in a predominantly white Broadway musical cast.

Viewed by current social standards, Berlin's relation to issues of race was complicated; however, past theatrical practices of minstrelsy and blackface were accepted stage conventions throughout the early twentieth century. Blackface had, for instance, been featured in sketches in Berlin's army show. Nevertheless, returning to the armed forces during World War II to remount his patriotic musical revue, Berlin insisted on including black recruits on stage, which meant his was the only integrated unit in the army. Further, Berlin insisted that his company perform exclusively in cities where blacks could stay in hotels with whites. Similarly, when, during *As Thousands Cheer*, white cast members objected to Ethel Waters joining them during the curtain call, Berlin retorted with an ultimatum: either the entire company would be on stage or none would—from then on, all the performers stood together.

Berlin's versatility and adaptability allowed him to expand his musical range with the changing times and tastes of popular music and theater. As book musicals rather than revues became the standard after the 1930s, Berlin began writing more cohesive stories set to music. He also continued to write songs in Hollywood, contributing some of his most lasting material for movies featuring Fred Astaire dance numbers, the films *Top Hat* and *Holiday Inn* among them. In the latter, Bing Crosby sang Berlin's immortal "White Christmas." Among the film musicals Berlin worked on during this time was *Alexander's Ragtime Band* (1938), for which he combined old songs with new compositions and provided the first occasion to work with **Ethel Merman**. Soon, he would write several Broadway musicals starring Merman, including his last original hit musical, *Call Me Madam* (1950), which won Tony Awards for both Berlin and Merman, and, his longest-running success, *Annie Get Your Gun* (1946), which offered numerous showstoppers from "You Can't Get a Man with a Gun" to "There's No Business Like Show Business." Berlin concluded his output of original musicals rather anticlimactically with the short-lived *Mr. President* (1962). Nevertheless, even today hardly a Broadway season passes without the inclusion of one or more of Berlin's songs in a production or a full revival of one of his hit shows.

Berlin lived the latter part of his life out of the limelight. He died on September 22, 1989, at the age of 101, in New York City, essentially having been retired from songwriting for over 20 years. Berlin's songs captured the American spirit and imagination. Perhaps his most lasting contribution to American culture involves Kate Smith's rendition of "God Bless America." Originally written for the 1918 military musical comedy *Yip, Yap Yaphank* but removed by Berlin as being too somber for the show, "God Bless America" never fell out of popularity once Smith started singing it regularly on her radio program in the late 1930s. The song became an anthem for national unity after the attack on the World Trade Center on September 11, 2001, when Berlin's music did what it had always done: soothed the spirit, touched the heart, and told a story with moving lyrics melded perfectly with a memorable score.

Felicia J. Ruff

Further Reading

Bergreen, Laurence. *As Thousands Cheer: The Life of Irving Berlin*. New York: Da Capo Press, 1996.

Leopold, David. *Irving Berlin's Show Business: Broadway—Hollywood—America*. New York: Harry N. Abrams, 2005.

BERNSTEIN, LEONARD (1918–1990)
COMPOSER, CONDUCTOR, PIANIST

Best remembered by Broadway enthusiasts as the composer of *West Side Story* (1957), Leonard (Louis) Bernstein was one of the most influential figures in all of twentieth-century American music. More than any other modern American

Leonard Bernstein working on a musical score in his apartment in New York City, 1945. (AP Photo)

composer, Leonard Bernstein narrowed the artistic and cultural gap between classical and popular music for the ultimate benefit of both. Combining classical forms and idioms with popular music traditions, Bernstein expanded the boundaries of both Broadway musical and symphony orchestra composition. Rupturing the stereotypical demur, behind-the-scenes persona of the classical composer/conductor, Bernstein moved easily among New York City's intellectual circles of famous artists, journalists, and politicians—relishing the limelight and using his fame to promote his numerous creative projects, charitable works, and social causes.

Born in Lawrence, Massachusetts, to a Jewish family who were steadily pulling themselves into the upper-middle class, Bernstein graduated from Boston Latin School—a prestigious prep school for Ivy League aspirants. From 1934 to 1939, he attended Harvard University where he majored in music and intensively pursued professional interests in composition, conducting, and musical theater. He conducted his own incidental music for a Harvard production of Aristophanes's *The Birds* and directed a production of Marc Blitzstein's ***The Cradle Will Rock***. During his college years he met and was mentored by conductor Dimitri Mitropoulos as well as Aaron Copland. During this time he also met **Adolph Green**, who would become a major Broadway lyricist as well as Bernstein's lifelong friend and frequent collaborator. Bernstein spent the summer after graduation in New

York City, where he accompanied The Revuers, a musical variety act that performed at the famed Village Vanguard in Greenwich Village. The group included Green as well as Green's future writing partner, **Betty Comden**.

Following graduation from Harvard, Bernstein spent two years at Philadelphia's Curtis Institute of Music, earning a diploma in conducting and honing his conducting skills. During the early 1940s he had the opportunity to work at the famed Tanglewood summer festival of theater and dance in the Berkshire Mountains, where he was mentored by the Boston Symphony Orchestra's conductor Serge Koussevitzky. In something of a surprise move Bernstein was named as assistant conductor of the New York Philharmonic by principal conductor Arthur Rodzinski. He was all of 25 years old. He made his celebrated professional conducting debut later that year, filling in for the ailing Bruno Walter. Critics raved and Bernstein was on a meteoric path to becoming an internationally renowned conductor. Nevertheless, he continued composing music.

Despite his youth, the quality of his compositions and his growing network of friends among the rising and established stars of the performing arts in New York led to early successes. Bernstein scored the accompaniment for a new work by the New York Ballet Theatre's promising young choreographer, **Jerome Robbins**. The new piece, featuring three sailors on shore leave, became "Fancy Free," one of Robbins's early signature dance compositions. Conceptually this ballet evolved into Bernstein's first Broadway success, *On the Town* (1944), with lyrics by good friends Comden and Green. The show ran for a healthy 462 performances, generated a now classic Broadway song ("New York, New York"), and unleashed the nascent talents of Bernstein, Comden, Green, Robbins, and star Nancy Walker on Broadway for decades to come. Bernstein would compose small pieces for other Broadway shows throughout the decade, but would take up writing full shows again in the 1950s.

Even with the allure of Broadway success, European conducting invitations followed. From the artistic pinnacles, such as directing Maria Callas in *Medea* at Milan's famous opera house La Scala, to the heart-wrenchingly painful, such as conducting Holocaust survivors who had performed in a concentration camp orchestra, Bernstein's career was becoming the stuff of legend. Not content to limit himself to stardom in only conducting, classical composition, and Broadway composition, he also lent his talents to Hollywood, composing the score for **Elia Kazan's** *On the Waterfront* (1954).

Throughout the 1950s and while continuing his professional affiliations in the classical musical world, Bernstein accelerated his musical theater efforts. He composed another hit with Comden and Green, *Wonderful Town* (1953), which won the Tony Award for Best Musical. *Candide* (1956) won some critical acclaim but was commercially unsuccessful. He followed *Candide* with *West Side Story* (1957), collaborating with young lyricist **Stephen Sondheim** and director/choreographer Jerome Robbins. *West Side Story* elevated Bernstein's stature on Broadway from success to superstar.

West Side Story represented a new direction in Broadway musicals on a number of levels. The subject matter was uncommonly serious for a mainstream musical: a

New York racial gang conflict rendition of Shakespeare's *Romeo and Juliet*. Furthermore, the show placed new demands on the performers, who were expected to dance, sing, and act; previously these skills were not integrated in the way that Robbins's direction and the new material now required. *West Side Story* ran for over 700 performances and produced several enduring hit songs, including "Tonight," "Maria," and "Something's Coming." With its staging of multiple simultaneous scenes and dynamic choreography in a congested urban setting (fire escapes, roof tops, tiny balconies), it is still regarded as one of the most influential and artistically brilliant **musicals** in history.

By the late 1950s, Bernstein no longer needed to prove himself professionally and could concentrate on developing new music audiences through connecting classical music with new media. He brought classical music to live **radio** broadcasts and several televised concerts for the famed half-hour CBS *Omnibus* **television** series. Bernstein's appearances on *Omnibus*, wherein he combined his extensive knowledge of music with a masterful ability to communicate on television, are widely viewed as the highlights of that outstanding series. Bernstein eventually won Emmy Awards for his television work and Grammy Awards for his recordings, making him one of only a handful of artists to have won the highest peer-granted awards in theater, recording, and television.

Along with singer Harry Belafonte, Bernstein was an early champion of what was to be known decades later as "World Music"—an approach to American music performance, broadcast, and appreciation in the context of multiple traditions, both indigenous and international. He composed, conducted, and performed in a variety of American musical styles as far ranging as jazz and **show tunes** and integrated composers such as **George Gershwin**, Charles Ives, and Aaron Copland into symphony programs alongside the European masters, particularly Mahler and Beethoven.

Bernstein also crossed the classical music world with international politics. These efforts included concerts in Israel to mark the reunification of Jerusalem, tours to the Soviet Union that included "The Age of Anxiety," based on the poetry of W. H. Auden, and the "Berlin Celebration Concerts" where he conducted Beethoven's *Ninth* on both sides of the Berlin Wall during its dismantling. By 1970 Bernstein had become so well-known for fundraising and social activism—in addition to his still prodigious musical career—that he was famously caricatured by cultural critic Tom Wolfe as epitomizing "Radical Chic," self-serving indulgence of fashionable causes by guilt-ridden wealthy liberals. Bernstein was understandably displeased with the criticism and Wolfe succeeded in implanting the term "radical chic" into the culture for several decades. However, the criticism failed to diminish either Bernstein's artistic or civic reputation.

Bernstein's final full original musical for Broadway was the anticlimactic election-year flop *1600 Pennsylvania Avenue* (1976), which he wrote with *My Fair Lady* lyricist, **Alan Jay Lerner**. Yet Bernstein remained an unmistakable presence on Broadway long after his musical composing career had effectively ended. Revivals and tours of his shows abound, and his songs frequently reappear in special Broadway events and retrospective runs, such as *Side by Side by Sondheim* (1977), *Jerome Robbins' Broadway* (1989), and *Barbara Cook's Broadway* (2004). Bernstein died of heart failure on October 14, 1990, in New York City.

Felicia J. Ruff

Further Reading

Bernstein, Burton, and Barbara Haws. *Leonard Bernstein: American Original.* New York: HarperCollins, 2008.

Oja, Carol J. *Leonard Bernstein.* New Haven, CT: Yale University Press, 2007.

THE BLACK CROOK

Broadway Run: Niblo's Garden
Opening: September 12, 1866
Closing: January 4, 1868
Total Performances: 475
Book/libretto: Charles M. Barras
Lyricist: Theodore Kennick
Composer: George Bickwell
Directors: William Wheatley and Leon Vincent
Producer: William Wheatley in association with Harry Palmer and Henry C. Jarrett
Lead Performers: George Boniface, Pauline Markham, Marie Bonfanti, and Milly Cavendish

The Black Crook, so named for the arts of black magic practiced by one of the show's villains, enjoys a secure place in Broadway history as America's first long-running, million-dollar-grossing hit musical (approximately 475 performances over nearly 16 months). Its astonishing popularity for its time and its historical milestone status belie the fact that the show presented a haphazard combination (perhaps, more accurately, an overblown hodgepodge) of theatrical elements already familiar to American theater audiences of the day—although not necessarily on the same stage on the same night. These included lavish sets and backdrops (from opera and **operetta**), a bevy of young ballerinas (from formal ballet)—alluringly and suggestively attired (from lowbrow burlesque and "bodily display" shows), a hackneyed love story combined with European intrigue and exotica (from melodrama and, again, opera and operetta), and songs interspersed throughout the evening (from operetta, revues, and **vaudeville**). Historians disagree as to whether *The Black Crook* represented an artistic breakthrough in its blending of disparate theatrical elements into a then distinctive and new American theatrical form, a prescient example of overspending on spectacle, or simply the first time a New York producer paraded dozens of scantily clad young women in a legitimate theater production and got away with it. But the unprecedented public response reestablished the boundaries of what the American **musical** could, and did, become.

In 1866 William Wheatley managed the famous Niblo's Garden, one of New York's largest and most prestigious legitimate theatrical venues. Wheatley and the theater had made their reputations with productions that underscored the upscale "bigness" of a night out on Broadway—principally operas and operettas that called for elaborate sets and full orchestrations. Wheatley had secured the rights to a nonmusical melodrama, the original *The Black Crook* by Charles Barras, with which to open his fall season. But Wheatley's stock and trade was musical productions on a grand scale, and he was eager to open his season with a grabber of a show. To make Barras's script suitable for Niblo's Garden's traditional audience, Wheatley hired a composer, a lyricist, and a choreographer to create a far more expansive production than the play script could generate on its own. (Wholesale reconstruction of a script by a **producer** without a writer's approval, although not unheard of in modern theater, was far more common prior to the founding of the American Society of Composers, Authors and Publishers [ASCAP] in 1914, which strengthened enforcement of copyright laws.)

Wheatley was also in possession of several elaborate sets and backdrops from an opera that had fallen through prior to production. In a decision almost certainly borne of financial expedience rather than artistic judgment, he decided to use them in his new show. In addition, he had the odd good fortune to secure the services of a French ballet company stranded in New York without a gig when the theater in which they were to appear burned to the ground. Into Wheatley's opening night mix they went.

Caught up in the growing size of it all—and unknowingly anticipating the history-making production extravagances of producer/director **David Belasco** by some 20 years—Wheatley also introduced elaborate scene transitions, expansive props, and lavish exterior sets into the money-burning production. In addition, likely influenced by recent successful, albeit controversial, bodily display stage performances of new female stage stars like Adah Isaacs Menken as well as the long-standing success of "girlie show" numbers in burlesque, Wheatley adorned his ballerinas with formfitting, leg-enhancing costumes.

Wheatley's sprawling mix of nearly everything theatrical opened in September to overwhelming audience reaction, jaw-dropping revues, and great-for-business protests from religious groups. Running approximately twice the length of a typical show (5 hours instead of 2-1/2 hours) and having cost upwards of twice the production investment of typical musicals of the time, the show was unlike anything Broadway had ever seen, even as it presented so much of what Broadway had already experienced in other productions of various stripes.

Audiences flocked to the show and kept it on the boards for an unprecedented run of almost 16 months. In mid-nineteenth century Broadway was principally drawing its audiences from the New York City area and a handful of business travelers; it was still more than half a century away from supporting its largest hits with tourists from across the nation and around the world. Thus, a run of any show for more than a few weeks was atypical and a run of several months was genuinely noteworthy. *The Black Crook*'s run was simply unheard of. The gross receipts for the 1866–1868 Broadway run reached a then mind-boggling $1 million (approximately 1 percent of the pre–Civil War 1860 national debt). Tours and revivals followed for years. Wheatley, in his early thirties, retired on his profits from the show. Marie Bonfanti, principal ballerina of the stranded French ballet company, remained in America for years as a star with *The Black Crook* in New York and across the country on tour.

Broadway eventually saw Wheatley's savant-like inspiration in *The Black Crook* manifested in the spectacular stagings of Belasco in the 1880s through the 1920s and the *Ziegfeld Follies* leg-show franchise that ran almost annually from 1907 into the early 1930s. But *The Black Crook* lacked the basics—good acting, good singing, a good script, and a good score. It was eventually eclipsed in public memory by the stature and success of **Victor Herbert**'s American operettas, Belasco's ability to wed spectacle to quality dramatization, and the better-written musicals of the 1920s and 1930s by the likes of **Cole Porter**, **Jerome Kern**, and the **Gershwins**. But *The Black Crook* gave the American musical its first financial runaway success, establishing forever a place on Broadway for the producer willing to throw all caution and budgetary constraint to the wind in order to overwhelm an audience.

Thomas A. Greenfield

Further Reading

Kenrick, John. "History of the Musical Stage 1860s: *The Black Crook*." Musicals 101. com. Copyright 1996 & 2003. http://www.musicals101.com/1860to79.htm (accessed February 28, 2009).

Smith, Cecil A. *Musical Comedy in America: From The Black Crook to South Pacific, From The King & I to Sweeney Todd.* New York: Theatre Arts Book, 1987.

BOOTH, EDWIN (1833–1893)
ACTOR, PRODUCER, THEATER OWNER

Edwin Booth was one of the most famous and prominent American actors of the nineteenth century as well as a leading theater owner and manager. Toward the end of his life, he became an important patron of New York's theater community as principal founder of the famous private club The Players. Although his fame is overshadowed by the infamy of his brother, President Abraham Lincoln's assassin John Wilkes Booth, theater historians generally consider Booth to be the first truly world-class American Shakespearean actor and an early prototype for the dashing American male "matinee idol" and celebrity star. His refined, subtle approach to dramatic roles, especially *Hamlet*, eventually won him critical and popular favor at the expense of **Edwin Forrest**, the leading American dramatic actor during the mid-nineteenth century. Booth was 27 years Forrest's junior but a professional competitor at the beginning of his career and, ultimately, Forrest's vanquisher in their rivalry for acclaim.

Booth was born in Bel Air, Maryland, to actor Junius Brutus Booth and Mary Booth. He began touring with his father while in his teens, first sharing the stage with him in a Boston production of *Richard III*. For the next few years, Booth continued his acting career filling small roles in plays in which his father was acting. He eventually replaced his father in **touring productions** of *Richard III*. Booth made his first appearance in New York City in *The Iron Chest* (1850), but spent most of the early 1850s touring in the western United States, Hawaii, and Australia.

When Booth returned to the East Coast, he began in earnest the stage career for which he would be remembered. His first Broadway appearance was in a contemporary drama, *The Fool's Revenge* (1864) by English **playwright** Tom Taylor (author of *Our American Cousin*, the play Lincoln was attending in Washington on the night of his assassination). Technically, Booth made his initial Broadway appearance in a **Shakespeare** play on November 25 of that same year in a one-night-only benefit production at the Winter Garden Theatre. He played Brutus in *Julius Caesar*, opposite his brothers John Wilkes and Junius Brutus Jr. The next night, however, he opened at the Winter Garden in the title role of *Hamlet*, which ran for a then unprecedented 100 performances (now famously "the 100 nights of Hamlet") for a classical drama on Broadway. Reviewers swooned over Booth's interpretation of the character as well as his commanding presence and good looks. Despite serious financial and other career setbacks following Lincoln's assassination, Booth would play the leads in Broadway productions of *Othello* (1865), *Macbeth* (1870), and *Hamlet* two additional times, including his final appearance in 1891. He also toured the country throughout his career, most often as Hamlet, cementing his reputation as both a national heartthrob and America's premiere Shakespearean actor. With the exception of an 1870 performance in *A New Way to Pay Old Debts* by Shakespeare's contemporary Phillip Massinger, Booth never appeared on Broadway in a non-Shakespearean role after 1864.

Although acting accounted for the majority of his career activity and fame, Booth also became a theater manager and producer—a common career expansion for leading actors and actresses in the mid to late nineteenth century. He assumed management of the Winter Garden Theatre in 1864 in the hopes of making the venue a centerpiece for prestige legitimate theater. In 1864 he managed and produced his own starring appearances in *Julius Caesar* and *Othello* but took a five-year hiatus from performing after Lincoln's assassination. He continued to manage Winter Garden productions until the theater burned down in 1867. In 1869 Booth opened his own theater in lower midtown Manhattan (Booth Theatre), which had been designed to his very expensive specifications. As owner and manager he hosted his own starring turn in *Hamlet* (1870)—ending his post-assassination performing hiatus—as well as numerous other productions in which he did not perform. Owing to the expense of operating the theater, Booth faced bankruptcy in 1873. He surrendered control of the theater and began an extensive series of tours. As he proceeded to regain his wealth through the lucrative and pampered life of an established touring star, he withdrew from most theatrical production in New York for the remainder of his life. However, he did invest in an 1878 production of *Richard II* and, appropriately, offered his Broadway swan song with an 1891 performance of *Hamlet*. This performance was heralded by **critics** as being every bit as good as his historic debut in the role 27 years earlier.

A leader and larger-than-life figure within the Broadway community even during his less active later years, Booth and several other luminaries—including Mark Twain and General William Tecumseh Sherman—founded a private club for actors, The Players, in 1888. The association, housed in a large lower Manhattan mansion owned by Booth, was established to help theater professionals maintain social and business contact with New York's leading intellectuals, industrialists, artists, and leaders in other fields. Active to this day, The Players is credited with helping professional stage actors shake off the last vestiges of Puritan or Victorian era stigmatization and lay claim to a place of respect in American intellectual life and culture.

Edwin Booth died in New York in 1893 at the age of 59 after a long bout with a respiratory illness. His life has been the subject of several biographies as well as a 1958 Broadway play (Milton Geiger's *Edwin Booth*). The Booth Theatre on 45th Street, built and posthumously named for Edwin Booth in 1913, is one of Broadway's busier theaters and immortalizes his legacy to this day.

Thomas A. Greenfield and Caitlin Klein

Further Reading

"Edwin Booth in London." *New York Times*, January 2, 1881. Archive nytimes.com, September 29, 2009.

Oggel, L. Terry. *Edwin Booth: A Bio-bibliography*. Westport, CT: Greenwood Press, 1992.

Shattuck, Charles Harlen. *Shakespeare on the American Stage: From the Hallams to Edwin Booth*, edition 2. Washington, DC: Folger Shakespeare Library, 1976.

BRANDO, MARLON (1924–2004)
ACTOR

Although overshadowed by his accomplishments in Hollywood, Marlon Brando's whirlwind New York theatrical career left an indelible stamp on post–World War II Broadway. In only a handful of stage performances during the mid to late 1940s, particularly as Stanley Kowalski in **Tennessee Williams**'s *A Streetcar Named Desire* (1947), Brando pointed the way to a revolution in acting—

especially for males—that still exerts its influence on acting and actor training from New York to Hollywood.

Marlon Brando Jr. was born in Omaha, Nebraska. His family moved frequently during his youth, eventually settling in Libertyville, Illinois. A discipline problem to his parents and teachers, Brando was sent to military school, but physical ailments kept him out of military service during World War II. He was eventually expelled from military school in 1943 and moved to New York where his two older sisters were living.

His sister Jocelyn was taking acting classes with Stella Adler at the New School for Social Research Dramatic Workshop. Adler was one of New York's leading instructors of Russian director Konstantin Stanislavsky's

Marlon Brando in 1949. (AP Photo)

System (which came to be commonly known in America as "Method Acting" or "the Method"). Brando began taking classes with Adler, who almost immediately saw in his rebellious spirit a startling intuitive theatrical intelligence that she accurately predicted would soon make him America's premiere actor.

After working in summer stock and becoming a familiar presence in both the New School workshop and the **Actors Studio** (New York's other citadel of Method Acting instruction), Brando debuted on Broadway in 1944 in **Richard Rodgers and Oscar Hammerstein II**'s *I Remember Mama.* The play was a hit but Brando, in a minor role, generally went unnoticed by **critics**. However, playing a 14-year-old boy in the first act who returns later in the play as a dashing 20-year-old, Brando reportedly caused women in the audience to gasp audibly upon his reentry as a man his own age—a harbinger of things to come (Fiore 32).

During the run of *I Remember Mama,* Brando befriended **Elia Kazan** and **Harold Clurman**, two of Broadway's leading producer/directors and veterans of the **Group Theatre** of the 1930s, admirers of Stanislavsky's teachings. They offered Brando a role as a returning war veteran in **Maxwell Anderson**'s *Truckline Café,* which Kazan co-produced and Clurman directed. Although the play had dreadful reviews and closed in two weeks, it retains a curious place in Broadway history for two reasons. First, Clurman and Kazan took the unusual step of placing a large ad in the *New York Times* condemning critics for causing the play to close. Second, Brando, as a veteran torn apart by the stresses of the war and his wife's unfaithfulness, stopped the show for several minutes every night with a soul-tortured lengthy speech that sent the audience into paroxysms of applause and shouts.

Brando next starred in **George Bernard Shaw**'s *Candida* (1946), which closed in a month after mixed reviews. In Ben Hecht's *A Flag Is Born* (1947), a fund-raising production to help the cause of establishing a free Palestine for Jewish refugees, he had a secondary role. The production ran for 120 performances largely on the strength of its charitable intentions. Neither performance was particularly notable, but the momentum of his earlier work kept alive Brando's fame as a major new Broadway actor during this relatively slow period. The slow period ended abruptly in 1947.

Brando landed the role of Stanley Kowalski in Tennessee Williams's *A Streetcar Named Desire* when Group Theatre alumnus John Garfield was released from his contract after several disputes with director Elia Kazan. At Kazan's request, Brando auditioned in front of the author, who was enraptured by Brando's reading. Williams and Kazan gave Brando the part on the spot. Critics raved about the play, identifying the production itself as well as the performances of Brando and Jessica Tandy as landmark accomplishments. However, over time Brando became bored and restless with the long run of the show. He eventually began diverging away from Kazan's original direction, ad-libbing lines, missing cues, and startling his co-stars with unanticipated changes to his character. Nonetheless, he continued to apply the acting techniques he had observed and developed with Adler and others, and the impact of his performance as the brutish Kowalski suffered little for his apparent inability to discipline himself during the run. His internalized emotions and the depth of his character—trademarks of Method Acting—astonished audiences, who were unaccustomed to the level of emotional intensity and complexity Brando brought to the role.

Leaving Broadway forever after *Streetcar*, Brando moved to Hollywood at the urging of Kazan and other admirers of his acting. He immediately launched what would become one of the most storied **film** careers of the twentieth century. Brando recreated the role of Stanley in the 1951 movie version of *Streetcar*, which Kazan also directed. Brando and Kazan successfully recaptured the power of the stage performance on **film**, significantly enhancing the legacy of the Broadway production. Brando and Kazan also collaborated on *Viva Zapata!* (1952) and *On the Waterfront* (1954), for which Brando won the first of his two Best Actor Academy Awards.

Brando's stage and film portrayals of Stanley Kowalski and his performance in *On the Waterfront* as would-be boxing "contender" turned longshoreman Terry Malloy gave both a cultural and commercial legitimacy to Method Acting. Although teachers like **Lee Strasberg** and Adler had been teaching Stanislavsky's theories for 20 years, Brando's Broadway career and early films heralded the incontrovertible ascent of Method Acting in Hollywood and Broadway. Brando's ability to balance his "classical" good looks and hypermasculine swagger with subtle and complex expressions of internalized emotions became the inspiration for a new generation of leading Broadway and Hollywood men, including Al Pacino, Dustin Hoffman, Robert Duval, Harvey Keitel, Robert DeNiro, and Kevin Spacey.

Marlon Brando died at the age of 80 in 2004 from pulmonary fibrosis.

Thomas A. Greenfield and Brian Balduzzi

Further Reading

Downing, David. *Marlon Brando*. New York: Stein and Day, 1984.

Fiore, Carlo. *Bud: The Brando I Knew; The Untold Story of Brando's Private Life*. New York: Delacorte, 1974.

Manso, Peter. *Brando: The Biography*. New York: Hyperion, 1995.

BRICE, FANNY (1891–1951)
COMEDIAN, SINGER, ACTRESS

A fixture in the legendary *Ziegfeld Follies* revues from 1910 until her final Broadway performance in 1936, Fanny Brice was one of the few female burlesque-style performers to make a lasting impact on Broadway as a comic star. Her slapstick, rubber-faced spoofs of ballet dancers, chanteuses, glamour girls, and stewbrained "goilfriends" endeared her to two generations of Broadway audiences. Producer **Florenz ("Flo") Ziegfeld** cultivated her as a performer and star, rewarding her over time with large salaries and high-profile billing. Her relatively few forays into **film** were generally unsuccessful but earned her the distinction of being the first woman to star in a "talkie" (*My Man*, 1928). In her mid-forties, Brice made a very successful transition from stage to **radio** comedy, one of the few female performers to do so.

Born Fanny Borach in the Lower East Side of New York, Brice's parents were saloon and club owners. The family business afforded the schoolgirl singer and jokester easy access to her parents' customers who served as unwitting and willing audiences for her routines. Brice entered amateur singing competitions and local shows throughout her childhood, eventually dropping out of school as a teenager to pursue a singing career in the flourishing burlesque scene of pre–World War I New York. Inauspiciously dismissed from the chorus of her first major stage show by an unimpressed **George M. Cohan**, Brice caught Ziegfeld's attention during an amateur show performance when she was 19. Ziegfeld put her in his 1910 production of *The Follies*—a relatively early edition of the recurring hit revue shows. By 1916 Brice had established herself as one of the *Follies*' top stars and would remain so for

Fanny Brice (undated). (AP Photo)

20 years. Although she performed in a handful of other Broadway shows throughout her career—including a featured appearance in then husband Billy Rose's 1931 revue *Billy Rose's Crazy Quilt*—Brice's stage successes are generally associated with Ziegfeld and the *Follies*. While performing with the *Follies* Brice became famous for the exaggerated Yiddish accents and "Jewish mannerisms" of her comic characters, which she transported to Broadway from the Vaudeville Jewish stage comedy she had seen in her youth. Owing to her ability to charm audiences even as she prodded them as well as a general lack of public self-consciousness about ethnic humor prior to World War II, Brice's bald-faced, overplayed ethnic stereotypes generated no significant opposition or protest during her career with the *Follies*. Beloved by *Follies* audiences for her comedy skits and routines, Brice was also a first-rate torch song and cabaret-style singer. Her *Follies* appearances generally featured one or more singing performances, some of which she later transformed into recording and sheet music hits. The most notable of her singing successes was the tormented, bluesy "My Man" from the 1921 *Follies*, for which she was awarded a posthumous "Hall of Fame" Grammy Award in 1999.

Brice was a well-established Broadway star in the 1930s when the fledgling radio networks were broadcasting numerous variety and comedy programs to their rapidly expanding national audience. Veteran music hall, **vaudeville**, and Broadway performers were drawn to the big salaries and national fame they could garner on radio without having to endure the rigors of touring. For their part, radio networks were only too happy to employ the talents of established, well-known experienced singers and comics. Brice was among the most successful in making the transition; her mastery of voice comedy and stage antics made her a natural fit for the new, live, aural medium. Brice's transition was made that much easier by the fact that by 1932 Ziegfeld was airing a radio version of his *Follies* on CBS with Brice appearing regularly. Reviving for the Ziegfeld broadcasts a child character she had developed in her early stage career, Brice—now in her forties—began appearing in the recurring role of an impish preschooler named Baby Snooks. Baby Snooks became such a hit with radio audiences and sponsors that in 1944 Brice, now well into her fifties, was given her own CBS radio show for the character. *The Baby Snooks Show* ran for a remarkable seven years and was still a CBS hit when Brice died of a cerebral hemorrhage in 1951.

In 1964 composer **Jule Styne** and lyricist Bob Merrill consecrated Brice's Broadway legacy with a highly successful musical based on her life. *Funny Girl*, which starred Barbra Streisand as Brice, ran for three years, and produced two of Streisand's biggest hit songs of her career: her trademark "People" and the self-declarative "Don't Rain on My Parade."

Thomas A. Greenfield

Further Reading

Goldman, Herbert G. *Fanny Brice: The Original Funny Girl*. New York: Oxford, 1993.
Grossman, Barbara W. *Funny Woman: The Life and Times of Fanny Brice*. Bloomington: University of Indiana Press, 1992.

BROADWAY (LOCATION)

Broadway is a diagonal street running generally north-south (uptown-downtown) in Manhattan. It was given its current name by the English in the seventeenth century. In theatrical terms, lower Broadway was the street around which many of New York's first major theaters were clustered during the early to mid-nineteenth century. As new immigrants poured into lower Manhattan, the New York "theater district" migrated, generally following Broadway's trajectory uptown and giving Broadway its cache as a synonym for New York professional theater. In the late nineteenth and early twentieth century, as New York became the undisputed center of American professional theater, Broadway assumed the luster of theater's national home. At the turn of the century, theater owner Oscar Hammerstein I and other impresarios developed the theater district around Times Square's triple intersection of Broadway, 7th Avenue, and 42nd Street (until 1904 known as Long Acre Square). Broadway's historic importance as a street soon gave way to its status as the icon for American theater in all its glamour, brilliance, decadence, creativity, perils, excitement, and frenetic energy. Today the Broadway League, the professional association for commercial theater producers, and the major theatrical unions recognize 40 venues as official Broadway theaters (see below). In all cases these theaters have seating for at least 500. With the exception of the Vivian Beaumont Theater, located in Lincoln Center on West 65th Street, all are located in the midtown Manhattan theater district between 41st Street to 54th Street within three blocks east or west of Broadway. The enigmatic quality of the word "Broadway" provides an impetus for many of the books written about it, including this one.

Broadway Theaters

Please refer to the map that appears on p. xxx.

1. Al Hirschfeld Theater
2. Ambassador Theater
3. American Airlines Theater
4. August Wilson Theater
5. Belasco Theater
6. Bernard B. Jacobs Theater
7. Biltmore Theater
8. Booth Theater
9. Broadhurst Theater
10. Broadway Theater
11. Brooks Atkinson Theater

12. Circle in the Square
13. Cort Theater
14. Ethel Barrymore Theater
15. Eugene O'Neill Theater
16. Gerald Schoenfeld Theater
17. Gershwin Theater
18. Helen Hayes Theater
19. Henry Miller's Theatre
20. Hilton Theater
21. Imperial Theater
22. John Golden Theater
23. Longacre Theater
24. Lunt-Fontanne Theater
25. Lyceum Theater
26. Majestic Theater
27. Marquis Theater
28. Minskoff Theater
29. Music Box Theater
30. Nederlander Theater
31. Neil Simon Theater
32. New Amsterdam Theater
33. Palace Theater
34. Richard Rodgers Theater
35. Shubert Theater
36. St. James Theater
37. Studio 54
38. Vivian Beaumont Theater
39. Walter Kerr Theater
40. Cadillac Winter Garden Theater

Thomas A. Greenfield

Further Reading

Henderson, Mary C. *The City and the Theatre*. New York: Backstage Books, 2004.
Morrison, William. *Broadway Theatres: History and Architecture*. Mineola, NY: Dover Publications, 1999.

BROADWAY'S THEATERS AND THEATER DISTRICT

New York City was not the first city in the United States, before or after independence from England, to have a thriving theater community. It was only in the nineteenth century that New York grew to prominence as a theater center. What we know of as the theater district on Broadway began far downtown from Times Square in Lower Manhattan and gradually migrated uptown with the wealthier population. It arrived in the Times Square area around 1900.

Broadway was a trail used by the Lenape Indians before any colonists from Europe arrived. The Dutch traders who first settled Manhattan (or New Amsterdam, as it was named) used the trail, naming it *Heerestraat*. It ended near Wall Street then split into two roads that continued up the east and west sides of Manhattan. When the English took over peacefully in 1664 they renamed the road Broadway. Not until near the end of the nineteenth century did Broadway become the extended thoroughfare that it is now, running diagonally northwest up the entire island of Manhattan and continuing through the Bronx and into Westchester County. Theater was not a part of the Dutch trading settlement, which boasted people of many nationalities, languages, and religions. Their entertainment would have consisted of church celebrations and amateur entertainment at taverns. The English took over New York immediately after the Restoration, which explains the slow rise of theater. The English generation raised during the 18 years of the Commonwealth (1642–1660) had no direct experience with theater because virtually all theaters had been closed down by the Puritan-dominated government. (Theater activity resumed and flourished in England after 1660 with the restoration of the monarchy under Charles II.)

Eighteenth Century

Theatrical activity in New York grew slowly throughout the eighteenth century. Unlike other northern seaboard colonial cities, which were mostly settled by Puritans with an extreme antipathy to the theater, the merchant town of New York was more hospitable toward players. Early maps of New York identify two theaters as early as 1732: the New Theatre on Nassau Street and the Theatre on Broadway. Both were in existing buildings refitted as theaters. Still there is little known about any specific performances in these venues although itinerant troupes' repertoire, amateur performances of plays and music, Punch and Judy shows, and other variety acts would have been the likely fare.

By 1753 Lewis Hallam's London Company of Comedians arrived in New York, having heard of other actors' success there. Hallam built another theater in Nassau Street on the site of the former and played for about six months. When touring, the Hallam Company played three nights a week, performing a repertoire of plays fashionable in London by such authors as **Shakespeare**, Cibber, Addison, and Fielding, but often in forms heavily edited by the company. David Douglass assumed leadership of the troupe after Hallam's death (c. 1756). He took the company back to New York in 1758, 1761, and finally in 1767, each time building a theater to house the company's performances. The final one, the Theatre on John Street, built just east of Broadway, was to begin the tradition of permanent theatrical performances in the city and last the rest of the eighteenth century.

Douglass's company, now renamed the American Company of Comedians owing to the colonists' growing antipathy to the British, remained in New York until war broke out. From August 1776 until 1783 (when General George Washington returned in triumph) the Theatre in John Street was used by amateur performers to entertain English military personnel. When Douglass died, Lewis Hallam, son of the original company manager, took over the company and brought it back to the old John Street theater in New York in 1785.

Hallam prospered there as did New York City in general when it rebuilt after the war. A group of well-to-do citizens banded together and hired French architect Marc Brunel to build a new large theater, which was to be called the Park Theatre, adjacent to what was to become City Hall Park at the intersection of Park and Broadway. The Park was an ornate Greek Revival building. The interior had a U-shaped auditorium with three tiers of boxes, a gallery above, and bench seating in the pit below. Newspaper accounts of its opening reported that the theater seated 2,000 people, had excellent acoustics, and presented a masterful display of scenery. At last, New York had a theater to rival the great halls in Europe.

The opening of the Park Theatre marks the beginning of the gradual migration of New York's theater district uptown. The American Company, now under William Dunlap, moved into the Park Theatre in 1798. By the turn of the century, the Park was the only theater in New York to offer a full season of plays in repertory by a permanent, professional ensemble.

1800–1850

In the first half of the nineteenth century, New York City saw enormous growth in its population, from approximately 35,000 to over half a million. Theater construction boomed in kind, from one active theater building to two dozen. Immigration was completely unregulated and waves of Irish and German newcomers flooded into New York. The city's expansion began where land was easiest to access, up the east side of Manhattan Island. In 1811 a planned expansion, the Randel plan, was adopted by the state legislature, calling for leveling topographic features, filling in swamps and streams, and, importantly, building Manhattan's avenues and streets to uniform size, all at right angles. Broadway itself, a diagonal thoroughfare, was one of the few notable exceptions to the tidiness of the street plan, but it was slated to stop at 14th Street. Broadway remained the city's most fashionable residential street at its lower end, while entertainment venues filled its northern end. The street itself continued stretching northward uptown: eventually streetlamps, paving, gas pipes, and omnibuses made Broadway accessible and easy to traverse. Two train lines and ferries also appeared, but in 1850 the majority of New Yorkers were still able to walk everywhere they went for work or pleasure.

In the mid-nineteenth century, while new immigrants generally crowded into tenements with others from the same homeland and the wealthiest New Yorkers still owned single-family homes, increasingly large numbers of people lived in boarding houses, which varied greatly in degree of comfort. As it had been in colonial times, New York was still governed by the Common Council, which levied the first tax on theaters in 1829. While city government and religious figures publicly associated the theatrical entertainment with vice and corruption throughout the nineteenth century, the City's leading families supported theaters, attended concerts, and sponsored balls at the new hotels that sprang up replacing the older pubs. By mid-century, theaters that specialized in specific forms of entertainment (like minstrelsy or German language theater) had replaced the older repertory system used by the American Company in 1800.

Among the dozens of venues that flourished in New York in the first half of the nineteenth century, the fortunes and travails of four of the most famous are particularly reflective of the time: The Park Theatre, the African Grove, the Bowery Theatre, and Niblo's Garden.

From its opening at the turn of the century through 1848 the Park sustained itself under various management arrangements. The Park's managers tended to lease the theater to different companies once competition among strong rival producers and troupes became a routine part of the New York theater business. From 1825 until its demise in 1848 the Park became a leading New York theatrical venue featuring touring stars from abroad, blackface shows, melodrama, and novelty acts. When it burned down in 1848, investors chose not to rebuild because the population that supported the theater had, again, moved farther uptown.

The African Grove was a particularly important pleasure garden in the predominantly African American neighborhoods east of Broadway. New York had had a substantial black population since the mid-1600s, when slaves were brought to the city for building projects like the wall in lower Manhattan for which Wall Street is named. The Dutch had relatively liberal laws by which slaves could secure their freedom, so New York had a sizable population of free African Americans even before the state made slavery illegal in 1827. The African Company, which played at the African Grove, was founded by James Hewlett (of Jamaican birth) and William Alexander Brown (from the West Indies), both of whom had been ships' stewards. Brown owned the land on which the African Grove was built and wrote what is believed to be the first professional play by an African American: *King Shotaway*. Hewlett played leading roles at the Grove like *Richard III*. The African Grove also launched the career of Ira Aldridge, the first U.S. African American international star. Often harassed or shut down by the police, the company shifted venues often, including playing for a while at the Pantheon Theatre next door to the Park. By 1826 the Company had disappeared completely.

The Bowery Theatre was both the largest and longest-lasting theater in American history. Intending to compete with the Park, investors built the Bowery on a larger and grander scale, holding 3,500 patrons in a lavishly appointed, neoclassically designed house. Charles Gilfert, the first manager, opened the theater in 1826 as the New York Theatre and programmed seasons of dramas, operas, and ballets to appeal to an upper-class clientele. But within five years the character of the area had changed completely due to immigration. When the theater burned down, Thomas Hamblin rebuilt it as the American Theatre, Bowery. He changed the offerings to new shows, largely melodramas, often by or starring unknown Americans. However, headline performers appeared there as well, including blackface pioneer Thomas D. Rice, **Edwin Forrest**, and Louisa Lane Drew. Hamblin introduced gas-lighting and chose shows for their spectacle and appeal to working-class, often immigrant, audiences, eventually earning the theater the nickname "the slaughterhouse." When the theater burned again in the 1840s, Hamblin rebuilt it to hold 4,000 and included a massive stage to house the spectacles for which the theater had become famous. These measures enabled Hamblin to continue to compete effectively even as rivals were building new theaters across the city. After Hamblin's death in 1853, the theater's management continued to present similar fare until its Lower East Side neighborhood became dominated by successive waves of various immigrant groups. The Bowery became, in turn, an Irish, then German, then Yiddish theater. In the early years of the twentieth century it housed Italian and then Chinese vaudeville companies. The theater finally closed permanently after another fire in 1929.

In 1828 William Niblo opened a summer theater called Sans Souci located uptown from the Bowery district. Niblo's Garden, as it became known, was a success until it burned down in 1846. Niblo rebuilt the theater and, a few years later, put up the Metropolitan Hotel on adjacent land. Niblo's attracted a fashionable clientele for decades. The theater held 3,200 patrons and had a stage capable of impressive spectacle. Its offerings varied from minstrel shows and acrobats to dramas and Italian opera. Niblo's most famous and longest-running show was *The Black Crook* (1866), widely considered to be the first American contemporary musical comedy. Niblo's was torn down in 1895 to make room for an office building.

During this period other kinds of entertainments began to cluster around lower Broadway in addition to theater. Some minstrel companies took long-term leases on city music halls. P. T. Barnum founded his American Museum, showcasing odd and exotic humans, animals, and performances in a theater-like setting. Some fledgling opera companies sought, unsuccessfully, to establish permanent resident companies. An economic recession during the late 1830s resulted in the demise of many new and established theatrical ventures. However, those catering to the poor thrived, as masses of New Yorkers sought distraction from their economic hardships. By 1850 New York City was the largest U.S. city and boasted the most theaters; New York was well on its way to becoming the theatrical capital of the country.

1850–1900

New York at midcentury was a city of social and cultural extremes, a situation encapsulated in theater history by the Astor Place Riots of May 10, 1849. Initiated by supporters of American actor Edwin Forrest, the riots brought to the streets a quarrel of dubious origin between Forrest and English actor/manager William Charles Macready. Macready was touring the United States in *Macbeth* and was scheduled to perform that night at the Astor Place Opera House. The battle lines were ostensibly drawn over who was the better actor. Forrest's mostly immigrant, working-class supporters liked what he represented as an image of America and disliked with intensity what Macready represented by contrast. While the imbroglio raged over the relative merits of two actors, it also clearly exposed long-standing tensions between the egalitarian, democratic values of American culture and English traditions of class privilege and inherited wealth. Incited by posters bearing slogans like "Workingmen, shall Americans or English rule in this city?" several theatergoers rioted upon Macready's entrance as Macbeth. A mob that had gathered outside in the street echoed the riot in the theater. The melee was finally stopped by the National Guard, which fired several rounds into the crowd and killed approximately two dozen people.

It was clear by 1850 that the city needed reform in its government, municipal services, and charities to better serve its poor, largely immigrant, population. New groups of immigrants continued to flood the city, now arriving primarily from central and eastern Europe. Manhattan's mobile middle class left in large numbers for better living conditions in Brooklyn, New Jersey, and Long Island, to which the

A Currier and Ives engraving of the riot between working-class demonstrators who protested the appearance at the Astor Place Opera House of the British actor William Charles Macready as Macbeth, and his upper-class supporters. At least 22 people were killed and more wounded during the riot of May 10, 1849. (Library of Congress LC-USZC2-2532 [color film copy slide] LC-USZ62-42326 [b&w film copy neg.])

ferries ran every five minutes. For those who stayed in Manhattan, the "French flat" began to replace boardinghouses and the rich built elaborate homes ever farther uptown, finally settling on Fifth Avenue from Thirtieth Street to Central Park.

The city also became increasingly divided into districts for residences, work, and entertainment, as various trades and entertainment styles clustered together in certain streets or regions. As publishing, garment, banking, and shipping districts grew, so too did Broadway as a recognizable theater district. In the second half of the nineteenth century, the center of theatrical activity moved steadily uptown from the Washington Square region, to Union Square, to Herald Square, finally breaking into Times Square with the new century. Public transportation expanded to move New Yorkers from home, to work, to shopping, to the theater. Horse streetcars and trains gave way to elevated lines, and the Brooklyn Bridge opened in 1883.

The late nineteenth century saw New York develop the new amenities of emerging modern urban life. The city built or improved numerous museums, monuments, and parks. It filled land all around Manhattan Island. Skyscrapers sprang up as older buildings came down. Broadway had evolved into its own district for shopping, hotels, and entertainment. As theaters themselves moved uptown, Union Square remained the center of the industry that sustained them, housing numerous costume shops, theater bookstores, and theatrical agents.

The dominant theatrical form in New York City during the middle of the nineteenth century was minstrelsy, starting in 1847 when Christy's Minstrels opened in Mechanics Hall downtown from Washington Square. Most minstrel shows featured white men in blackface, portraying stereotypical comic portraits of African Americans. (After the Civil War black minstrel troupes, also in blackface, would become popular touring attractions.) Minstrel shows involved music, dance, and comic banter. In the late nineteenth century and thereafter, blackface minstrelsy would come under increasing social scrutiny as racist denigration of African Americans, but at the time it was widely accepted as clean family fun. Other minstrel troupes besides Christy's succeeded during this period as touring acts that often made stops or had extended runs in New York. However, variety theaters like those housing minstrel shows were hurt by the Concert Hall act of 1862 that banned alcohol sales in theaters. After the Civil War, New York's fascination with minstrelsy waned, but it was just catching on in the rest of the country and abroad.

Among the storied Broadway theaters of the latter half of the nineteenth century, the fortunes and misfortunes of the Metropolitan Theatre, the Academy of Music, the Germania Theatre, Wallack's Lyceum, and the Fifth Avenue Theatre illustrate the tempestuousness business of theatrical management at the time.

The Metropolitan Theatre was originally built to house Swedish opera star Jenny Lind's New York debut in 1850, but it was not ready on schedule and, instead, opened with a minstrel company. It passed to producer/actress **Laura Keene**, then William Burton who hoped to move his theater company uptown from Chambers Street, and then Dion Boucicault, the European writer/actor of popular melodramas like *The Octoroon*. Boucicault filled it with tropical plants and renamed it the Winter Garden. **Edwin Booth** then leased it and put on a

Broadway in approximately 1920, looking north from 38th Street, showing the Winter Garden, Maxine Elliott's, Casino, and Knickerbocker Theatres. (Library of Congress LC-USZ62-66615)

performance of *Julius Caesar* with his brothers Junius Brutus Jr. and John Wilkes. When it burned in 1867, Booth designed and built his own theater farther uptown at 23rd Street and Sixth Avenue.

The Academy of Music, built on Union Square in 1854, represented yet another of the numerous attempts in the nineteenth century to find a permanent home for opera in Manhattan. This venture lasted longer than previous efforts. The Academy supported seasons of opera and legitimate drama, with and without big name starring performers, until 1888. Then, suffering the fate of many late nineteenth and early twentieth century theaters, it became a **vaudeville** house, then a movie theater, and then a demolition project to be cleared for skyscraper construction in 1926.

A block south of the Academy was Wallack's Lyceum Theatre in its second incarnation, having moved uptown from Broome Street in 1861. James Wallack ran an exceptionally successful company, producing mostly comedies, in an unusually attractive space. James's son Lester took over the company and moved it farther uptown, leaving the old Union Square theater to become a combination house (a theater that books individual shows for the length of a profitable run only).

Tony Pastor is the most famous name associated with the origins of vaudeville, which became the next huge Broadway vogue after minstrelsy. A minstrel performer and variety songwriter before becoming a manager, he was producing a variety show in the Bowery when, in 1881, he moved the show uptown to the Germania Theatre on 14th Street. He began alternating **operettas** and variety shows, but soon became known for his brand of variety, dubbed vaudeville. Vaudeville specialized in ethnic humor, dance and specialty acts, and musical numbers, often popularizing new styles like ragtime music. American legends like Lillian Russell and **George M. Cohan** began in vaudeville at Tony Pastor's. Producers B. F. Keith and **Edward F. Albee** soon joined Pastor's vaudeville company in Union Square. By the end of the century New York vaudeville houses were offering up to five shows a day to accommodate demand. Vaudeville spread throughout the United States, and many cities had their own prestigious vaudeville halls for hosting touring acts, but none had the caché of the top New York City vaudeville houses.

The Fifth Avenue Theatre was built adjacent to a hotel, a popular pattern. It briefly housed Christy's Minstrels but became one of New York's most popular theaters when Augustin Daly ran it from 1869 with a repertoire of high quality comedies. Daly then joined the movement uptown, installing his company at the New Fifth Avenue Theatre, located at 28th Street and Broadway. He moved it one more time to 30th Street. When Steele MacKaye rebuilt the first Fifth Avenue Theatre after a fire, he opened it as the Madison Square. The Madison Square enjoyed another burst of success due to MacKaye's technological experiments, which included air conditioning (blowing air over ice in the basement then up throughout the house), the folding chair that is now standard in theaters, a double stage that allowed a full scene to be set above the main stage before it was needed, and many innovations in gas-lighting. After MacKaye moved uptown, the theater's management changed hands several times before closing in 1908; its location was now too far downtown to attract audiences.

MacKaye built another theater at 23rd Street and Fourth Avenue in 1885, named the Lyceum. Thomas Edison, MacKaye's friend, supervised the electrical installation personally, and the Lyceum was the first theater in the world lit with electricity. In spite of excellent reviews of the theater and its repertoire, it was located off the beaten path and lasted only until 1902. At that time, the theater district was centered around Madison Square (23rd to 26th Streets, Fifth Avenue, and Broadway) and was gravitating uptown quickly.

In the 1890s, most new theaters were built in Herald Square (34th Street, Sixth Avenue, and Broadway). Ned Harrigan's Theatre, built in 1890, then renamed the Garrick by actor/producer Richard Mansfield, had many famous managers and tenants. Charles Frohman, leading executive of the **Theatrical Syndicate**, used it as a booking house. Philanthropist Otto Kahn leased it to the Théâtre du Vieux

Colombier, an innovative French company that played in New York in the 1910s, and then the **Theatre Guild**. The **Provincetown Players** booked it for some of their shows as well. The Garrick was pulled down in 1932.

Frohman built the Empire Theatre just below 41st Street in 1893. Unlike at the Garrick, where he booked shows on a long run basis, Frohman ran a stock company at the Empire, filling the acting company with the biggest names he could afford. **Ethel Barrymore** debuted on Broadway at the Empire in 1895 and Maude Adams starred in James M. Barrie's *Peter Pan* (1905). Frohman was still at the height of his theatrical influence when he went down on the *Lusitania* in 1915. Since the Empire was at the south edge of Long Acre Square, soon to be renamed Times Square, it enjoyed a long life. Lindsay and Crouse's *Life with Father* ran there throughout World War II, from 1939 to 1947, still the longest run of any non-musical play on Broadway. In 1953 the Empire was torn down.

By 1900 the business of Broadway was booming; vaudeville, classic plays, new comedies, French and German drama, English high comedy, operetta, and grand opera all played on Broadway in specialized houses. Because of the size and scope of its offerings, theater had become a major tourist attraction in New York City. In addition to the performance houses, the business of theater was centered around Broadway as well. Drama newspapers and magazines, costume houses, scenic studios, managers' offices, clubs, and restaurants flourished in the shadows of the theaters. The long run system, which offered greatest profits for investors, had replaced almost all stock companies. The combination company that sent Broadway hits touring the country was designed to maximize investment in New York theater. On the down side, organizations like the Theatrical Syndicate and the United Bookings Office took increasing advantage of small-time managers and talent in order to maximize profits for the larger entertainment corporations like themselves.

The Times Square Theater District

At the turn of the twentieth century New Yorkers basked in optimism over their city's steady growth. In 1898 the city boundaries were extended to contain the current five boroughs. By 1899 the population topped two million. The ground was broken for New York's first subway tunnel in 1900, which opened under a long stretch of Broadway in 1904. New bridges and tunnels opened over the next two decades as automobiles became affordable to the middle class. Skyscrapers continued to replace older buildings, creating the beginnings of the skyline we recognize today, and major public buildings like Penn Station and the Public Library at 42nd Street were completed. In 1916, new zoning laws governed the growth of the city and limited the migration of businesses. This development had a salutary effect on the theaters. Although Fifth Avenue became the main retail center and hotels spread throughout the fashionable areas of the city, theater stayed on Broadway.

As theater became the main business of midtown Broadway around 1900, a theatrical building boom began where Broadway crossed Seventh Avenue around

An aerial view of Times Square in 1942, looking north from the New York Times *building at 42nd Street, during a dimout in midtown Manhattan during World War II. The large signs illuminating Broadway, the street on the left, are out in addition to the marquee lights above the theaters and restaurants along Seventh Avenue, on the right. (AP Photo)*

45th Street. The square was called Long Acre Square until the *New York Times* built its towered office building in 1904, after which New Yorkers began to call it Times Square. Eighty theaters were built within the region before the 1929 stock market crash and the motion picture industry began to chip away at the live theater. (In the 1927–1928 season, generally considered to be the historical high-water mark for Broadway openings, 71 theaters in the Times Square area opened a combined 257 shows.)

By 1905, the Theatrical Syndicate's business practices had steadily driven out smaller theater owners. When six men joined to form the Theatrical Syndicate in 1896, they jointly controlled 33 theaters in the United States. At the height of their influence they controlled over 700 theaters, including most theaters in Times Square, and at least one in every city in the United States with a population over 5,000. The Syndicate was eventually broken by Frohman's death and the rise of the **Shubert Brothers**, whose monopolistic practices beat the Syndicate on their own terms.

Both the Syndicate and the Shuberts built many theaters in Times Square and across the nation, but other investors were also eager to try the theatrical business. The profits could be enormous. An investor in the 1920s could build a theater for

A night scene of Shubert Alley, showing the Shubert Theatre, between 44th and 45th Streets near Broadway in September 1967. (AP Photo/ Marty Lederhandler)

approximately a million dollars and earn it back in a couple of years with a hit show. Yet it was also a risky business; approximately 70 percent of shows failed to earn back their initial investment.

The oldest standing theater in the Times Square area is the New Victory on West 42nd Street. It was built in 1900 by Oscar Hammerstein I, who sold it to **David Belasco** in 1902. Belasco's most successful production there was *Abie's Irish Rose*, which ran for five years in the 1920s. Throughout the Depression years it was a burlesque house, and then a movie theater renamed Victory during World War II. By the 1970s it had become a porn theater. It was totally restored at a cost of $11.4 million in the famous 1990s cleanup of Times Square ("The New Forty

Second Street" project), to look as it did in Belasco's day, and is now dedicated to producing children's theater.

The current Winter Garden Theatre at Broadway and 50th Street opened in 1911 on the site of an old horse exchange owned by the Vanderbilt family. The Shuberts built it and the **Shubert Organization** still runs it. The Winter Garden seats 1,500 and faces directly onto Broadway. Since World War II, it has been a musical theater house. Long-running musicals at the Winter Garden include *Wonderful Town* (1953), ***West Side Story*** (1957), *Funny Girl* (1964), *Follies* (1971), *42nd Street* (1980), ***Cats*** (1982), and *Mamma Mia!* (2001). The stage and auditorium were completely rebuilt to house *Cats* whose giant-sized junkyard encompassed the audience. When *Cats* finally closed, architects restored the Winter Garden to look as it did in the 1920s. It remains one of very few independently owned and operated Broadway theaters today.

The Little Theatre on West 44th Street, now known as the Helen Hayes, is the smallest existing Broadway house, with 597 seats. It was built by Winthrop Ames in 1912, who named the theater in honor of Europe's little theater movement, which was just about to hit the United States. Ames operated the theater until 1931, when he sold it to the *New York Times* located directly next door. Ames management was marked by several critical successes, such as **George Bernard Shaw's** *The Philanderer* (1913) and Arthur Schnitzler's *Anatol* (1931), but little financial return. The *Times* used it for lectures and concerts, then leased it to **television** and **radio** studios. It was returned briefly to a theater during the 1960s, then permanently in the 1970s. It was named for **Helen Hayes** in 1983 when the Marriott Corporation razed three theaters, including the older theater to bear Hayes's name, to make way for their flagship hotel, the Marriott Marquis on Times Square. Successful shows there include *Torch Song Trilogy* (1982), *Prelude to a Kiss* (1990), *By Jeeves* (2001), and *The 39 Steps* (2009).

The Palace Theatre opened in 1913, at Broadway and West 47th Street, as the prime theater of the Keith-Albee vaudeville circuit during the height of vaudeville's popularity. The phrase "play the Palace" was synonymous throughout the century with success as a performer, and many who appeared there are still household names: Lillian Russell, Ethel Barrymore, Will Rogers, Bill "Bojangles" Robinson, W. C. Fields, **Fanny Brice**, Sarah Bernhardt, and Bob Hope. It remained a variety house until 1935, adding shows and lowering prices in response to the Great Depression. In the 1940s it served briefly as a movie house and showed the premiere of *Citizen Kane* in 1941. RKO, a Hollywood studio with financial interests in Broadway, tried unsuccessfully to revive vaudeville at the Palace in the 1950s with big name stars like Judy Garland and Frank Sinatra. The **Nederlander Organization** bought the Palace in 1965 and rebuilt it to be more suitable for traditional theater. Since then the Palace has mostly housed musicals, such as *Sweet Charity* (1966), *George M.* (1968), *Man of La Mancha* (1977), *La Cage aux Folles* (1983), *Beauty and the Beast* (1994), and the recent revival of *West Side Story* (2009).

The New Victory, the Winter Garden, the Little Theatre, and the Palace are but four examples of some 80 theaters that were built during the period in which Times

Billboards for Broadway musicals line Times Square, 2007. (AP Photos/Bebeto Matthews)

Square became New York's theater district. All four are still running, each having taken a different trajectory to its present state of operation.

Few theaters have been built since 1930 and many have been torn down or repurposed. Although today Broadway is still centered at Times Square, after World War II small **Off-Broadway** and then Off-off-Broadway companies provided more financially accessible venues for new or risky theater. As their names suggest, many such theaters are located all around New York City, although some are located in midtown. From the 1950s through the 1980s Times Square infamously shared its territory with drug traffickers, prostitution operations, and pornography shops. Helped substantially by the boom years of the 1990s and motivated by many New Yorkers (including people in the theater industry) clamoring for the government "to do something about Times Square," the City and state combined forces to clean up the area. The project eventually made the district highly accommodating to tourists, especially families and school groups who had avoided Times Square for years. The nonprofit corporation The New Forty-Second Street has overseen the revitalization of seven theaters in the heart of Times Square. In addition, the corporation built the New Forty-Second Street Studios, a ten-story complex of rehearsal halls for theater and dance, offices, and a small theater (The Duke). Two producing corporations, Livent and Clear Channel, refurbished and combined the Lyric and Apollo theaters into the large complex of

---

"CHURCH AND STAGE"

Of the houses of worship associated with New York's theater district as it has evolved, two merit particular attention. The Episcopal Church of the Transfiguration—familiarly, "The Little Church Around the Corner"—was founded in 1848 and has been located since 1849 at 1 East 29th Street. Its nickname and association with the theater date from 1870, when it conducted a funeral service for actor George Holland. The rector of a nearby church had refused to do so because of the deceased's profession and recommended "a little church around the corner." The church continues to serve as the venue for theatrical weddings and funerals. In 1923, the Episcopal Actors' Guild held its first meeting there.

St. Malachy's Roman Catholic Church (239 West 49th Street, between Broadway and 8th Avenue) was founded in 1902. From the early decades of the century, it increasingly ministered to the spiritual needs of Catholic performers and others in show business as the theater district moved north from Union Square to Long Acre (Times) Square. The Actors' Chapel was constructed below the main church in 1920. The church remains an integral, dynamic member of the theater community, with a special commitment to the neighborhood's elderly since the 1970s.

—John Spalding Gatton

---

the Ford Center for the Performing Arts on West 42nd Street. The **Disney** Corporation remodeled the New Amsterdam Theatre and ventured assertively into musical theater production in the 1990s.

Having come almost full circle in the past 100 years, Broadway now thrives commercially on revivals, long-running **musicals**, and Disney's adaptations from its film catalog, drawing the same kind of crowds that made minstrelsy and vaudeville popular in their day. The Times Square Redevelopment Project is attracting the kind of retail and chain restaurants that this audience looks for: Toys 'R' Us, a three-story M&M candy store, and popular "neighborhood" family chain restaurants, like TGI Friday's, and McDonald's. Some purists claim to miss the "authentic" New York grittiness of the pre-cleanup days. However, the commercial theater industry—the cultural heirs to Time Square—has happily sung so long, farewell, auf wiedershein, and good-bye to the old mean streets of midtown while bidding waves of new visitors a warm wilkommen, bien venue, and welcome to the redeveloped family-friendly Great White Way.

Melanie N. Blood

Further Reading

Henderson, Mary C. *The City and the Theater: New York Playhouses from Bowling Green to Times Square.* Clifton, NJ: James T. White & Co., 1973.

Hornblow, Arther. *A History of the Theater in America from Its Beginnings to the Present Time*. Vols. 1 and 2. New York: J. B. Lippincott & Co., 1919.

http://www.nypl.org/research/chss/lhg/nyc2.cfm.

Morrison, William. *Broadway Theaters: History and Architecture*. Mineola, NY: Dover Publications, Inc., 1999.

Van Hoogstraten, Nicholas. *Lost Broadway Theaters*. Rev. ed. New York: Princeton Architectural Press, 1997.

Witham, Barry B., ed. *Theater in the United States: A Documentary History*, vol. 1 1750–1915. Cambridge, U.K.: Cambridge University Press, 1996.

Brown, Jason Robert (1970–)
Composer

Despite few Broadway credits and no long-running hits, Jason Robert Brown is widely viewed as the most influential musical theater composer born after the 1960s. Brown's distinctive songwriting style marries pop and rock-influenced melodies with theatrical lyrics, reflecting a remarkable ability to craft melodic lines to the intonation of naturalistic speech. His best-known songs are often substantially longer than conventional **show tunes**, taking his characters on complex emotional journeys that add extraordinary depth to story lines and character development.

Within the musical theater community Brown is widely assumed to be the heir to **Stephen Sondheim**'s tradition of writing small, intimate, sophisticated shows (often called "chamber **musicals**") that counterbalance the grand **European megamusicals** and **Disney** spectacles that dominate contemporary Broadway. He has acquired a devoted fan base—much of it quite young despite the fact that he first came to prominence in his late thirties. Yet, Brown's career both symbolizes and promotes the overlapping of Broadway and **Off-Broadway** sensibilities that has characterized New York professional theater in the past two decades.

Brown was born in Ossining, New York. He studied piano and composition at Eastman School of Music in Rochester, New York, but left before graduating to start his career in New York City as a freelance club pianist. His breakthrough as a musical theater composer came Off-Broadway in 1995 with his song cycle show *Songs for a New World*. The show produced a significant hit, "Stars and the Moon," which has become a contemporary cabaret standard covered by numerous recording artists. The show itself is a favorite of clubs and small theaters around the country.

Brown premiered on Broadway in 1998 writing music and lyrics for a traditional book musical, *Parade*, directed by **Harold Prince**. *Parade* earned Brown the Tony Award for Best Original Musical Score. His next significant work, *The Last Five Years*, opened Off-Broadway in 2002. *The Last Five Years* is a two-character romance tale, based largely upon Brown's own first marriage. As with *Songs for a New World*, the show has become a favorite of small theaters, largely on the strength of memorable songs like "Shiksa Goddess" and "I'm Still Hurting" that showcase Brown's gift for lyrical exposition.

Between various other projects in and out of theater—ranging from show pit pianist, to solo recording artist, to musical arranger for other recording artists, to chorale composer—Brown ventured back to Broadway in 2003 as orchestrator, musical director, and one of several songwriters for the ill-fated stage adaptation of the **film** *Urban Cowboy.* However, Brown made a noteworthy contribution to contemporary Broadway culture with *13* (2008), a teenage-centered musical, which for the first time in Broadway history was performed entirely by actors and musicians under the age of 18. Although it drew inevitable and not always flattering comparisons with Disney's franchise *High School Musical* shows (which have never been staged on Broadway), *13* solidified Brown's place as a leading innovator in contemporary musical theater, especially among younger artists and audiences.

Marisa Fratto

Further Reading

Jackson, R. Bryer, and Richard Allan Davison. *The Art of the American Musical: Conversations with the Creators.* New Brunswick, NJ: Rutgers University Press, 2005.

Singer, Barry. *Ever After: The Last Years of Musical Theater and Beyond.* Milwaukee: Hal Leonard, 2004.

BURROWS, ABE (1910–1985)
LIBRETTIST, DIRECTOR, PRODUCER

If Abe Burrows had done nothing more than create pungently witty libretti filled with razor-sharp dialogue, his Broadway legacy would have been considerable. But in addition to writing the award-winning musical comedies *Guys and Dolls* (1950) and *How to Succeed in Business Without Really Trying* (1961) among others, he was one of the most successful and influential **producers** and directors of Broadway **musicals** during the 1950s, the height of the Golden Age of the American musical. He was a master at adapting preexisting material for Broadway and was one of the few people ever to preside as both librettist and director of hit Broadway shows.

Burrows was born in Manhattan's Lower East Side on December 18, 1910. Shortly after his birth, his family relocated to the Bronx and then Brooklyn. After completing high school in Brooklyn, Burrows enrolled at City College of New York but dropped out to enter the workforce as a runner in the Wall Street business district. He worked his way up on Wall Street for a few years, even into the early years of the Depression, until stock brokerage opportunities exhausted themselves. (His Wall Street experiences would stand him in good stead 30 years later when he wrote the libretto for *How to Succeed in Business Without Really Trying*.) In the mid-1930s he began writing jokes for comics who were performing on network **radio**, one of the few New York–based industries that prospered during the Depression. The witty, wisecracking Burrows proved particularly adept at helping **vaudeville** comics add sparkle to their preexisting routines for their transition to radio. By 1940 Burrows was working full time as a writer for New York radio shows. In 1941, he began what would become a five-year stint writing for the enormously popular radio series *Duffy's Tavern*.

In the 1940s New York–based network radio had very close ties to Broadway as many singers, actors, comics, and writers happily developed careers in both media. During his years as a radio writer, Burrows made many important contacts in the New York theater community, including **Eddie Cantor**, **Alan J. Lerner**, Danny Kaye, Tallulah Bankhead, and, significantly, **Frank Loesser**, with whom he co-wrote the theme song for *Duffy's Tavern*. After leaving *Duffy's Tavern*, Burrows continued to develop and write new shows for radio and even tried touring the American nightclub circuit as a stand-up comedian. In 1949, he signed a contract with CBS as a writer and occasional on-air personality. One of his contract duties was to serve on a panel of a radio program titled *This Is Show Business*. Burrows met and befriended fellow panelist **George S. Kaufman**, Broadway's most prolific and successful **playwright**. The association with Kaufman effectively launched Burrow's Broadway career.

Kaufman was director of a developing show that was inspired by Damon Runyon's short story "The Idyll of Sarah Brown." Kaufman felt the existing book by Jo Swerling to be largely unusable, so he invited Burrows to bring his gift for sizzling adult comic dialogue to the work. Burrows's efforts did much to salvage the show, which is much better known by its final title *Guys and Dolls*. Burrows's success with *Guys and Dolls* represents one of the most auspicious writing debuts in Broadway history. The musical won the Tony Award for Best Musical and ran for 1,200 performances. It is widely viewed as a masterpiece of musical comedy and, for its form and content, is often cited as evidence that the Broadway "book musical" was evolving into a distinctly American art form during the middle of the twentieth century.

Burrows was immediately invited to work on the libretto for the show *Make a Wish* and direct a revue titled *Two on the Aisle* (both 1951). While neither was a major hit, *Make a Wish* earned respectable notices and *Two on the Aisle* ran 276 performances, a solid showing for a production in this now nostalgia-laden Broadway format. With three solid Broadway credits under his belt, Burrows was offered the director-librettist position for producer Cy Feuer's newest show: the 1953 hit *Can-Can,* which ran for two years and launched actress/dancer **Gwen Verdon** to stardom. *Can-Can* created for Burrows the rare position in Broadway musical theater of a librettist/director. Two years later, he had another success with the well-received *Silk Stockings*, co-written with former radio colleague George S. Kaufman. At the close of the 1950s Burrows busily helped mount the London West End productions of his biggest Broadway successes, wrote the Hollywood screenplay of the play *The Solid Gold Cadillac*, and directed **Ethel Merman** on

Broadway in the 1957 star vehicle *Happy Hunting*. In 1961, Burrows would climax his career as a librettist/director of musicals with *How to Succeed in Business Without Really Trying*. Not only would this show bring him two Tony Awards and the Pulitzer Prize for Drama, it would bring full circle his talent for working with a preexisting literary source.

While *Guys and Dolls* and *How to Succeed in Business* secured Burrows's place in Broadway history, he continued to write and direct original productions through the 1960s and 1970s—even as he frequently directed or supervised revivals of his past shows. Among his post *How to Succeed* hits were musicals *What Makes Sammy Run?* (1965), *Cactus Flower* (1965)—which at 1,234 performances ran longer than the original *Guys and Dolls*—and the stage comedy *Forty Carats* (1968). Hardly infallible, Burrows had his share of failures, including a disappointing 1981 Broadway swan song at age 70 as director of a dismally received revival of *Can-Can*.

Burrows was married twice and had two children. His son James Burrows is a leading **television** comedy writer/director in Hollywood, with *Taxi, Cheers, Frasier,* and *Will & Grace* among his more noteworthy credits.

Burrows died in 1985 in New York City after struggling with Alzheimer's disease.

Darryl Kent Clark

Further Reading

Burrows, Abe. *Honest, Abe: Is There Really No Business Like Show Business?* Boston: Little, Brown, 1980.

Ostrow, Stuart. *Present at the Creation, Leaping in the Dark, and Going Against the Grain: 1776, Pippin, M. Butterfly, La Bête, and Other Broadway Adventures.* Milwaukee, WI: Hal Leonard, 2005.

Riis, Thomas Laurence, and Geoffrey Block. *Frank Loesser.* New Haven, CT: Yale University Press, 2008.

CANTOR, EDDIE (1892–1964)
COMEDIAN

To the extent that he is remembered today at all, Eddie Cantor is often perceived as a caricature figure who appears in old cartoons, popping his eyes, singing, and prancing back and forth while clapping his hands. However, during his heyday in the late 1910s and the 1920s, he was one of the biggest names on Broadway and in all of show business, straddling the worlds of theater, motion pictures, broadcasting, and even politics.

Cantor was born Israel Iskowitz in New York City in 1892. He was orphaned early and raised by his maternal grandmother, Esther Kantrowitz. As a boy he was accidentally assigned his grandmother's surname by a school registrar. His childhood on the Lower East Side was very difficult. He was small, scrawny, poor, and frequently victimized by larger boys, but he soon discovered that his gift for mimicry could turn hostility to laughter.

As a teenager he entered small-time talent shows. One of his early jobs was singing comic songs in a Coney Island saloon accompanied by a teenage pianist named Jimmy Durante. Israel Kantrowitz—now "Eddie Cantor"—became a seasoned performer touring in **vaudeville** with various partners. His Broadway breakthrough came in 1916 when he was signed by **Florenz ("Flo") Ziegfeld** to appear in his *Midnight Frolic* revue on the roof of the New Amsterdam Theatre.

The following year Cantor signed a contract to appear in Ziegfeld's *Follies.* Cantor's appearances as a featured comedian in several editions of the *Follies* between 1917 and 1927 marked his arrival as a top star. Audiences adored him for his high-energy delivery, sassy attitude, and "groaner" punch lines. During these years he also introduced and recorded hit songs, including "You'd Be

Comedian Eddie Cantor is shown in blackface as his character from the Broadway musical Banjo Eyes, *playing at the Hollywood Theatre, in New York City in 1942. Cantor's ensemble included a straw hat, white-rimmed glasses, cotton gloves, ribbon tie, silken coat, white-spatted shoes, and blackface, which originated in his first Broadway appearance in* Ziegfeld Follies *of 1917. (AP Photo)*

Surprised" and "If You Knew Susie." At the peak of his fame Cantor starred in three Broadway **musical** comedies contrived solely to showcase his talents: *Make It Snappy* (1922), *Kid Boots* (1923), and *Whoopee!* (1928), the last two produced by Ziegfeld. Other well-known comedians were featured in *Follies*, but when *Kid Boots* opened Cantor was the first male star to headline one of Ziegfeld's Broadway shows. In 1927 he became the only male star to receive top billing in the *Follies*.

During the 1930s Cantor became less involved with Broadway, concentrating instead on a **film** career and lucrative weekly **radio** shows. He also became active in public life, speaking out against Adolf Hitler and fascism when doing so was considered risky. Cantor starred in one last Broadway show in 1941, *Banjo Eyes*, a musical version of **George Abbott**'s 1935 comedy *Three Men on a Horse*. It was not a great success, and when Cantor was forced to withdraw for health reasons the show closed.

Eddie Cantor's once great renown was already fading during his later years. Like colleagues Jack Benny, Durante, and George Burns, Cantor was among a number of Broadway and vaudeville performers who had made a successful transition to early radio. However, unlike these men, he never starred in a **television** series that could keep his fame alive in the postwar television eras. His hit Broadway shows of the 1920s were flimsy star vehicles that are never revived. Unlike the Marx Brothers' movies, which are perpetually rediscovered and celebrated by successive generations of film buffs, Cantor's films enjoy no such currency. However, in the 1920s, when vaudeville, follies, and revues ruled musical Broadway, Cantor was a superstar among stars.

Cantor died of a heart attack in 1964 in Beverly Hills, California, at the age of 72.

William Charles Morrow

Further Reading

Epstein, Lawrence J. *The Haunted Smile: The Story of Jewish Comedians in America.* New York: Public Affairs Press, 2002.

Goldman, Herbert G. *Banjo Eyes: Eddie Cantor and the Birth of Modern Stardom.* New York: Oxford University Press, 1997.

CATS

Broadway Run: Winter Garden Theatre
Opening: October 7, 1982
Closing: September 10, 2000
Total Performances: 7,485
Composer: Andrew Lloyd Webber
Lyricist: T. S. Eliot; Additional Lyrics by Trevor Nunn and Richard Stilgoe
Choreographer: Gillian Lynne
Director: Trevor Nunn
Producers: Cameron Mackintosh, The Really Useful Theatre Company Ltd., David Geffen, and the Shubert Organization
Lead Performers: Ken Page (Old Deuteronomy), Betty Buckley (Grizabella), Terrence Mann (Rum Tum Tugger)

Andrew Lloyd Webber's musical *Cats* left an indelible mark on Broadway in innumerable ways. The first of the **European megamusicals** to successfully transfer from London's West End to Broadway, *Cats* was beloved by children and adults alike for its sheer spectacle, including its gargantuan junkyard unit set, meticulous costumes and makeup, and daring choreography. The simplistic framework plot of

Cats was accessible to a wide audience and reflective of the concept musical trend that had preceded it on Broadway in the 1960s and 1970s. Between its enormous fan base and a stellar marketing campaign conceived by producer **Cameron Mackintosh**, *Cats* surpassed *A Chorus Line* (1975) as the longest-running **musical** in Broadway history—only to be outdone by Lloyd Webber's other monstrous success, *The Phantom of the Opera* (1988). *Cats'* unprecedented success and popularity not only energized the **Broadway theater district**, but also revolutionized the Broadway touring business as cities across America clamored to become part of this Broadway hit turned cultural phenomenon.

Prior to composing *Cats*, Lloyd Webber had already achieved considerable success in musical theater through collaborations with lyricist Tim Rice on *Joseph and the Amazing Technicolor Dreamcoat* (1968), *Jesus Christ Superstar* (1970), and *Evita* (1979). However, the relationship between Lloyd Webber and Rice was rife with conflict, and Lloyd Webber started working on *Cats* without a lyricist. He composed music to the set poetry of T. S. Eliot's 1939 children's book *Old Possum's Book of Practical Cats*, which the composer had read in his youth. Inasmuch as it was based upon a book of poetry that lacked narrative structure, the show was originally conceived as a concert anthology by Lloyd Webber, which he showcased with a small cast in 1980 to an enthusiastic private audience at

Actress-singer Betty Buckley performs in the role of Grizabella in the Broadway musical Cats *at the 37th Annual Tony Awards ceremony, 1983. Based on the late T. S. Eliot's feline poetry,* Cats *won seven awards, and Buckley won best featured actress in a musical. (AP Photo/Richard Drew)*

Sydmonton, his London estate. However, to maintain audience interest and conform to some of the conventions of musical theater, he integrated a story line in which the show's many cats compete for the chance to ascend to the not so subtly allegorical "Heaviside Layer." Following the positive response he received at Sydmonton, Lloyd Webber made the decision to meet with director Trevor Nunn to work on shaping his song-cycle into something more theatrical.

The vision concocted by Lloyd Webber, Nunn, and their creative team soon became something far larger than Lloyd Webber originally imagined for his feline-inspired song set. They would require a very large theatrical space to accommodate the lofty ambitions of what was turning into a highly experimental and elaborate project. Once conceived, the show represented a huge financial risk for any potential backer because of its unconventional structure and subject matter, and, in fact, the team initially had difficulty finding backers to mount the project. However, Cameron Mackintosh, a then little-known West End producer, became involved with the show and would prove to be instrumental in its success.

Cats opened to generally positive reviews on May 11, 1981, at the New London Theatre in the West End. Mackintosh arranged for a Broadway transfer a year later, establishing a trend that other European megamusicals would follow thereafter. *Cats* opened in Broadway's Winter Garden Theatre on October 7, 1982, to a tepid critical reception. While **critics** praised the technical aspects of the production, they made disparaging remarks about the flimsy narrative. Despite these criticisms, Frank Rich, theater critic for the *New York Times* (who would later become one of the megamusical genre's more vocal detractors), predicted a long run for the show on the basis of its ability to make the audience suspend their disbelief and become engulfed in the "complete fantasy world" that *Cats* provided.

The spectacle of *Cats* was, by far, the most impressive and innovative aspect of the musical as a whole. Designer John Napier's colossal junkyard set required the demolition of the Winter Garden's proscenium arch and a radical adjustment of its stage. His slinky costume and makeup designs were highly praised by critics and audiences alike. So too was Gillian Lynne's acrobatic high energy choreography that overflowed from the stage into the theater, breaking the fourth wall to the delight of audience members. Adding to all this, the climactic (and very loud) ascent heavenward of a gigantic hydraulic-powered tire, *Cats* embued Broadway audiences with a new fascination for "over the top" visual splendor (or, to detractors, gimmickry) that has influenced commercial musical theater production ever since: from staging to marketing, from budgeting to scheduling, from touring to product licensing.

Notwithstanding its overwhelming visual and technical qualities, *Cats* also triumphed in more traditional musical theater terms. Lloyd Webber's eclectic score, a pastiche of swing, rock and roll, and more traditional composition hearkening back to **Rodgers and Hammerstein** musicals, earned the composer considerable praise. Betty Buckley's Tony-winning performance as Grizabella, the Glamour Cat, won acclaim from reviewers, and her haunting rendition of the show's most famous song, "Memory," made it one of the biggest hit **show tunes** of the decade. *Cats*' multilayered appeal was reflected in its seven total Tony Awards, including

Best Musical, Best Original Score (for Lloyd Webber), Best Costume Design (for Napier), Best Lighting Design (to David Hershey), and Best Director of a Musical (to Nunn) as well as Buckley's Tony award.

Cats also had a lasting impact on the Broadway touring business. Owing to the unprecedented nationwide demand for the show and Mackintosh's promotional ingenuity, *Cats* became a hot touring property almost immediately after it started to attract Broadway crowds. Local presenters and theater managers, often wary of how well even successful Broadway shows might play in their hometowns, were besieged by their local communities to book a *Cats* tour—even if older, smaller local venues could barely handle the logistical demands of getting the set in and out the door much less up and running. Moreover, after *Cats'* first national tours, Mackintosh insisted that, regardless of venue size or technical capacity, all subsequent **touring productions** must replicate every aspect of the Broadway show. Many theater owners and local presenters, motivated by the success of the early *Cats* tours and fearful of missing out on future bounty, expanded and upgraded their theater venues in anticipation of hot ticket touring spectacles to come. Thanks principally to Mackintosh and, later, **Disney Theatrical Productions**, they were not disappointed.

The popularity of *Cats* on tour also led to expanded touring runs, lasting weeks or even months at a time in any given city instead of the traditional one week or ten day local run of a touring show. This concept for expanded scheduling in local venues, once unimaginable, is now part of the Broadway tour booking business. **Producers** and local presenters will often happily book extended stays even for non-megamusical touring hits like *Jersey Boys* (2005) or *Legally Blonde* (2007).

On June 19, 1997, *Cats* became the longest-running show in Broadway history, surpassing *A Chorus Line* with 6,138 performances. It closed in 2002 after 7,485 shows. *Cats'* longevity record remained unbeaten until 2006, when *The Phantom of the Opera* surpassed it. *Cats* now ranks number two. However, *Cats* is the first of the megamusical spectacles, whose numbers include not only the European musicals *Les Misérables* (1987), *The Phantom of the Opera* (1988), and *Miss Saigon* (1991), but also Disney Theatrical Productions shows like *Beauty and the Beast* (1994) and *The Lion King* (1997).

Not everyone is pleased with what *Cats* hath wrought. American critics often excoriate the megamusical for its lack of subtlety in staging, acting, and writing as well as for a formulaic gaudiness that seems at once too easy and too expensive. Yet for countless audiences, whether sitting in a Broadway theater or attending a **touring production** in their hometowns, the British-born megamusical, as embodied by *Cats*, represents the apex of American musical theater.

Thomas A. Greenfield and Mary Hanrahan

Further Reading

Snelson, John, and Geoffrey Holden Block. *Andrew Lloyd Webber.* New Haven, CT: Yale University Press, 2004.

Walsh, Michael. *Andrew Lloyd Webber: His Life and Works.* New York: Abrams, 1989.

CHAMPION, GOWER (1919–1980)
CHOREOGRAPHER, DANCER, DIRECTOR

Gower Champion was a unique and rare musical theater dance artist. His dances were often based on storied vignettes, making him an important innovator in the application of dance to advance plot and the use of props and set pieces to reveal character. He was also a visionary conceiver of **musicals**, capable of viewing a show as a large movement piece with choreography added as an important element that built on the strengths of his performers.

Champion was born in Illinois but raised in Los Angeles. He took dance lessons from childhood and at age 13 studied at acclaimed dance teacher Ernest Belcher's Los Angeles dance studio. Taking quickly to ballroom dancing, by age 16 Champion was winning ballroom competitions, choreographing much of his own material, and receiving professional offers to tour in nightclubs and theaters across the country. He developed an early mastery for "story" ballroom dancing, creating short narratives that avoided ballroom clichés. He soon caught the eye of Broadway choreographer Robert Alton, who quickly put Champion and partner Jeanne Tyler in a revue, *Streets of Paris* (1939). The following year, at 21, he and Tyler were featured performers at both the Radio City Music Hall and New York's famous Rainbow Room. After appearances in two lackluster musicals, *The Lady Comes Across* and *Count Me Later* (both 1942), Champion enrolled in the Coast Guard, returning to dance at the end of the war. Champion replaced Tyler with Marge Belcher, daughter of his former teacher Ernest Belcher. They married in 1947 and the famous Gower and Marge Champion dance duet was born.

By his late twenties, Champion had developed a passion for choreography and

Gower Champion, dancer turned producer, in 1967. (AP Photo)

directing. After a false start with the revue *Small Wonder* (1948), his choreography for the musical *Lend an Ear* (1948) earned him a Tony and a *Dance Magazine* award for choreography. He also appeared regularly in Sid Caesar's pioneering **television** program, *Your Show of Shows*, creating and directing two new dance routines every week—a grueling pace. Through the rest of the 1950s, the Champions earned fame primarily in movie musicals (including as co-stars in 1952's *Everything I Have Is Yours*) and television (especially a 1953 CBS special, *The Marge and Gower Champion Story*). Champion staged two unsuccessful Broadway shows in the 1950s, *Make a Wish* (1951) and *3 For Tonight* (1955), but during the 1950s the Champions were **film** and television stars.

Champion's first Broadway success as director and choreographer was the musical *Bye Bye Birdie* (1960). While he regarded rock and roll as a passing fad, he approached this improbable tale of a teen idol's visit to a small town with an openness to experiment in form and style to tell the story as creatively as he could. While he developed many appealing dances for the show, Chita Rivera's performance in the "Shriner's Ballet" is appreciated, discussed, and analyzed to this day. *Birdie* is widely viewed as having articulated and defined Champion's trademark mix of imaginative brilliance and measured taste to give his shows dynamism and coherence (Gilvey 2005, 88).

While Champion directed and choreographed Broadway musicals that ranged from the conventional to the experimental, his shows were characterized by new ideas, a keen appreciation for the collaborative nature of musical theater, and high professional expectations for all concerned—including himself. He would have some weak Broadway shows after *Birdie*, including the play *My Mother, My Father, and Me* (1963) and *Rockabye Hamlet* (1976), but most were at least moderately successful and several were big hits. Four shows in particular demonstrate the range of his contributions to musical theater and dance.

Champion followed *Bye Bye Birdie* with producer **David Merrick**'s *Carnival!* (1961). Sensitive to the fact that female dancers had dominated Broadway musicals over the last 20 years (*West Side Story* being the obvious anomaly), Champion as director/choreographer developed the dance aspect of the leading male role, Marco, and encouraged his male dancers to become a prominent force in the musical. He also conceived eliminating the act curtain, replacing it in the prologue with the building of a circus, which would not be taken down until the end of the show. This device cleverly allowed him to convey a narrative within a theatricalized circus world, justifying unexpected interruptions or surprises. Puppets came alive, acrobats danced, and the scenography contributed to the continuous movement flow from prologue to finale. Champion's meticulous care in directing the show earned him rave reviews and enormous respect within the Broadway community

Champion's career megahit was *Hello, Dolly!* (1964), which ran for 2,844 performances and garnered 10 Tony Awards (including two for Champion, one each for direction and choreography). It became a star vehicle for some of musical theater's most prominent women, including original star **Carol Channing**, Ginger Rogers, and Pearl Bailey. Based on **Thornton Wilder**'s play *The Matchmaker*, this musical has a unique combination of story, music, lyrics, staging, scenic elements, and themes that came together in a way that enthralled its audience.

Again, Champion came up with a device-as-metaphor that established a continuous flow of movement for the show and made a kinesthetic connection with the audience; he constructed a ramp around the orchestra pit that connected the stage with the audience. From "Before the Parade Passes By" to "The Waiters Gallop" to the title song "Hello, Dolly!" Champion created a musical whose staging seemed to continually top itself. If *Carnival!* was one continual movement punctuated by dance, *Hello, Dolly!* was one extended musical dance punctuated by character, narrative, and song. With *Hello, Dolly!* Champion brought to fruition a seamless combination of dance as narration and style combined with old-fashioned American optimism (that would soon be tested by the assassination of President John F. Kennedy, the Vietnam War, and more). He drew upon his years in Hollywood musicals by employing cinematic staging to move the show effortlessly from one scene to the next. Calling on his experiences in developing story dances for nightclub shows, he created detailed choreography and stage movements that reflected subtleties in character and supported his directorial vision of a fully cohesive musical. It was a grand success for Champion and a hallmark in musical theater.

As large and brassy as *Hello, Dolly!* was, Champion's next hit, based on the play *The Fourposter* (1951), was small and intimate. The musical *I Do! I Do!* (1966) starring two of the best musical leads of the time, **Mary Martin** and Robert Preston, allowed Champion to elaborate on the intimacy that dance can convey between two married people over a lifetime. What was so often unexpressed verbally in Champion's own story duets with Marge could now be explored with text, song, minimum scenery, and props. With the orchestra onstage and actors performing on an extension built over the pit, Champion created a familiarity with the audience that allowed them access to the actors' smallest and simplest movements. Champion worked intricately with props, costumes, lights and set designs, blending movement, color, and shape to reveal character and story—and to move it all along with the music. *I Do! I Do!* is generally acknowledged to be one of Champion's finest shows.

Champion's final Broadway musical, *42nd Street* (1980), earned Champion his fifth career Tony for choreography (he also had won three for directing). Based on Busby Berkeley's 1933 film of the same name, this backstage musical put tap dance front and center, capitalizing on the then nostalgic appeal of old-time Broadway musicals. From the moment the curtain rises on 40 pairs of tap-dancing legs auditioning for a musical, *42nd Street* builds continuously one number at a time. Champion had created dances for such Broadway standards as "We're in the Money," "Lullaby of Broadway," and "Forty-Second Street." Interspersed with the love story of a director-choreographer played by Jerry Orbach and the small town chorine-turned-star played by Wanda Richert, Champion capitalized on a lifetime of experience to consecrate musical theater dance as a metaphor for possibility, optimism, and, indeed, love.

Champion died in New York on opening day of this show—a show that in many respects best summarized the best of his contribution to musical theater dance.

Ray Miller

Further Reading

Gilvey, John Anthony. *Before the Parade Passes By: Gower Champion and the Glorious American Musical.* New York: St. Martin's Press, 2005.

Payne-Carter, David, Brooks McNamara, and Stephen Nelson. *Gower Champion: Dance and American Musical Theatre.* Westport, CT: Greenwood Press, 1999.

CHANNING, CAROL (1921–)
ACTRESS

Carol Channing fashioned a rich career by performing numerous roles in a diversity of genres and media, and was blessed with a distinctive, husky voice and wide smile. However, she became an icon in American culture through one of them: Dolly Levi, the irrepressible matchmaker in **Jerry Herman**'s *Hello, Dolly!* She has played the role at least 5,000 times over a span of five decades on Broadway and in major national and international tours. More than escaping the common pitfalls of being typecast or overly identified with one role, Channing has triumphed as Dolly. She has captivated multiple generations in a role that, by all odds, should have devolved into a quaint or painful nostalgia turn in the era of *Sweeney Todd*, **Rent**, and **The Phantom of the Opera**. Yet, like the character she embodies so thoroughly, Channing refused to allow anything so trivial as the seemingly impossible stand in the way of what she ultimately accomplished

Carol Channing was born January 31, 1921, in Seattle, Washington, to George and Adelaide (Glaser) Channing. In her autobiography, Channing revealed that her father was a light-skinned African American who concealed his racial identity to work as a prominent newspaper editor. She credits him with teaching her to sing, to overcome stage fright, and to connect with an audience. The family spent most of Channing's childhood in San Francisco where Channing graduated from the well-known Lowell High School. A natural mimic, Channing was preoccupied in high school with dramatics and debate. Although she began studying at Bennington College in Vermont, the sight of a magazine audition notice for a minor role in a Broadway play prompted her to move to Manhattan. Within a year she was understudying for Eve Arden in **Cole Porter**'s *Let's Face It* (1941).

The show ran through 1943, but further engagements were scarce. She developed a nightclub act impersonating show business celebrities, but got few bookings. In March 1946, Channing acceded to her father's pleas to return home to California. After a year of intermittent stand-up work in Los Angeles, Channing was cast in a revue, *Lend an Ear*, directed by **Gower Champion**. The show was

Carol Channing, during her curtain call after the matinee performance of Hello, Dolly! *at Broadway's Lunt-Fontanne Theater in New York, 1996. Channing was celebrating her 4,500th performance of the legendary show. (AP Photo/Aubrey Reuben)*

a hit, running for five months in Los Angeles and then for over a year on Broadway starting in December 1948. Critics singled out Channing for her strong performance in numerous sketches and musical numbers. Her standout performance and glowing notices convinced **playwright** Anita Loos to cast her as Lorelei Lee in the musical production based on her book *Gentlemen Prefer Blondes*. Opening in 1949 to rave reviews, Channing as Lorelei was embraced as a new comic talent. The play ran for almost two years on Broadway and then toured for a year. Channing's songs in the show, particularly "Diamonds Are a Girl's Best Friend," became overnight hits.

In 1953 Channing replaced Rosalind Russell as Ruth in **Leonard Bernstein**'s *Wonderful Town*, playing six months on Broadway and two years on tour. She began her next play in the title role of *The Vamp* (1955) immediately thereafter. Based on the life of Theda Bara, the script was faulted by **critics** who felt that even Channing could not turn it into lively theater. The show closed after 60 performances. After a brief, unhappy experience in Hollywood that yielded no **film** successes, she created a nightclub act that opened at the Tropicana Hotel in Las Vegas in July 1957. She toured with the act for the next three years. Much of the act was incorporated into a musical revue, *Show Girl*, which she took to Broadway in

1961. *Show Girl* ran for 100 performances, after which Channing returned to the nightclub circuit.

In 1963, producer **David Merrick** offered Channing the title role in *Hello, Dolly!*, Jerry Herman's **musical** adaptation of **Thornton Wilder**'s *The Matchmaker*. Opening in January 1964 to ecstatic reviews, the show won an astounding ten Tony Awards (including Best Actress in a Musical for Channing) and ran for seven years—the second longest run for any Broadway show that opened in the 1960s (*Fiddler on the Roof*, also opening in 1964, ran longer).

Touring with the show at various times over the next three decades, Channing as Dolly became a particular favorite with local theater presenters and audiences, as one of the few Broadway headliners still willing to do national tours in roles they originated on Broadway.

Channing did not limit herself to Dolly performances, although she certainly could have if she so chose. In 1971, she appeared in *Four on a Garden*, an evening of one-act plays adapted and directed by **Abe Burrows**. A 1974 sequel to *Gentleman Prefer Blondes*, entitled *Lorelei, or Gentlemen Still Prefer Blondes* ran for a year, earned her a Tony nomination, and toured successfully for an additional season. In 1985, she toured with **Mary Martin** in *Legends*, the durable two-woman road comedy about a pair of feuding elder stateswomen of the silver screen. But two Broadway revivals of *Hello, Dolly!* and several tours have kept Dolly Levi, as local reviewers like to say when Channing comes to town, glowin', crowin', and goin' strong.

Apart from her Tony Award for *Dolly!* Channing has won two additional Tonys: a Special Award in 1965 and a Lifetime Achievement Award in 1995 among many other honors. But her singular distinction among her peers is that for as long as most people can remember, or care to, Channing is the last remaining original star from the Golden Age of Musicals who can still hit the boards in her historic role. The original *Oklahoma!*'s Curly and Laurie, *My Fair Lady*'s Higgins and Eliza, *West Side Story*'s Tony and Maria, and *Fiddler*'s Tevye are long gone. But 40+ years after she ceremoniously introduced herself, the original Dolly Levi might still be descending a staircase at a theater near you.

James A. Kaser

Further Reading

Channing, Carol. *Just Lucky I Guess: A Memoir of Sorts*. New York: Simon & Schuster, 2002.

Martin, Linda, and Kerry Segrave. *Women in Comedy*. Secaucus, NJ: Citadel Press, 1986.

A CHORUS LINE

Broadway Run: Shubert Theatre
Opening: July 25, 1975

Closing: April 28, 1990
Total Performances: 6,137
Co-Choreographer: Bob Avian
Composer: Marvin Hamlisch
Lyricist: Edward Kleban
Book: James Kirkwood, Nicholas Dante
Director/Choreographer: Michael Bennett
Producer: Joseph Papp, in association with Plum Productions, Inc.
Lead Performers: Donna McKechnie (Cassie), Priscilla Lopez (Diana), Sammy
Williams (Paul), and Baayork Lee (Connie).

In 1974 frustration was widespread among Broadway "gypsies," the show dancers
who eke out a living going from audition to audition and chorus to chorus. Two of
these dancers, Tony Stevens and Michon Peacock, decided to take action. They
gathered a group of friends and colleagues to talk about their lives and their art
in hopes of finding a way to speak back to the larger industry that, in the view of
many dancers and nondancers alike, devalued their creativity and talent. They also
hoped to come up with a new project, something to give them work during one of
Broadway's periodic lean times. The pair invited director-choreographer **Michael
Bennett** to be a part of the evening, and eventually decided to sell him full rights
(for the sum of one dollar each) to the tapes made of the night's discussions. From
those tapes, Bennett and some collaborators created *A Chorus Line*, which went on

Cast members of A Chorus Line, *New York's longest-running musical on Broadway at the
time, dance in the final scene of the show, at Shubert Theatre, New York City, on August 11,
1987. (AP Photo)*

to become one of the longest-running shows in the history of Broadway. In the process of staging *A Chorus Line*, Bennett and company reimagined what a successful **musical** could be—and how it could be made.

The history of *A Chorus Line* and the career of its principal creator, Michael Bennett, are inextricably entwined. Bennett started his career as a dancer, although he moved quickly into the ranks of Broadway's choreographers and directors. During his first professional role as a dancer in a **touring production** of *West Side Story*, he worked under the great director-choreographer **Jerome Robbins**. He also met Bob Avian, his lifelong creative partner who would become his co-choreographer for *A Chorus Line*. On Broadway, Bennett danced in just three shows before becoming a choreographer. After choreographing a few unsuccessful shows during the mid and late 1960s, he joined composer/lyricist **Stephen Sondheim** and producer/director **Hal Prince** on the seminal concept musical *Company* (1970). He earned his first Broadway directing credit working again with Prince and Sondheim on *Follies* (1971), doing the choreography as well. Bennett won two Tony Awards for *Follies*, one each for choreography and direction, thereafter becoming a Broadway star director-choreographer and a well-known "show doctor" who could improve other people's struggling musicals.

It was at this point in his career that he attended the session organized by Peacock and Stevens. His participation in the session included the creation of questions for each of the dancers to discuss, ranging from their real names and hometowns, to how they came to New York, to why they danced. The evening was taped (Broadway legend has it that Bennett himself did the taping) and those tapes, along with the tapes of another similar meeting a few weeks later, provided the raw material that became the concept, book, and lyrics of *A Chorus Line*.

A Chorus Line resembles a form of documentary theater, as the words of actual people become the source material for a production. The musical was not, as some Broadway urban legends suggest, simply transcribed from those tapes. Some of the lines in the show come directly from what the dancers said; however, book writers Nicholas Dante and James Kirkwood and lyricist Edward Kleban wrote original material as well. Many characters in the show are composites, blending elements of different dancers' stories.

The actual text of the show—written and performed—came into being in a way that was also totally new to Broadway. Up until this point, the model for developing a musical was fairly straightforward. A creative team would come together and write a show, cast it, and rehearse it before taking it to another city or two for "tryouts." Changes would be made based on audience and critical response (often with the assistance of a "show doctor" like Bennett), and then the show would come to Broadway. *A Chorus Line* took a different path. Bennett formed an agreement with **Joseph Papp**'s heralded **Off-Broadway** theater company, the Public Theater, to workshop the show, with Papp paying the creative team and a cast to work the ideas out, literally, on their feet. The initial team included Bennett and Avian, as well as Dante, who had participated in the taped sessions and whose story became the character Paul's climactic monologue about dancing in the *Jewel Box Revue* (a famous upscale drag show). As workshops began, composer Marvin Hamlisch and

Kleban joined the group. The cast was composed of dancers who had been at the tape sessions, as well as some who had not. Everyone auditioned, and some whose stories became part of the show were not chosen to perform in it. The cast continued to evolve throughout the initial workshop, as well as during a second workshop and the rehearsal period that followed. Among the more notable original cast members who were part of the initial workshops were Donna McKechnie (Cassie), Priscilla Lopez (Diana), Sammy Williams (Paul), and Baayork Lee (Connie). The first performances were done Off-Broadway, at the Public's Newman Theatre. The show then moved to Broadway, opening on July 25, 1975, at the Shubert Theatre.

As it evolved throughout the workshop process and emerged on Broadway, *A Chorus Line* shared the dancers' stories through the lens of a Broadway audition for dancers, run by a director named Zach. Zach demands that the dancers tell him about their lives as part of his casting process, and the characters' complicated histories and stories emerge in dialogue, monologue, and song. At the end, of the 17 dancers on the line, Zach chooses four women and four men, and dismisses the rest. *A Chorus Line* has no intermission and no blackouts; each moment flows into the next through a complex and subtle integration of movement, music, and text. The set is extraordinarily simple and sparse—as, indeed, actual dance audition spaces generally are—and encourages the seamless, almost cinematic quality of movement for which Bennett's work was known.

The show takes place on an empty stage, with a white line painted downstage and a row of three-sided set pieces upstage, allowing the background to shift from a black expanse, to mirrors, to a sunburst. The sunburst appears only at the end, as the show concludes with a giant production number, "One," with all the dancers now dressed identically in shiny lamé suits, top hats, and canes backing an invisible star—the nameless "singular sensation." In this moment, we see the loss of individuality demanded of most successful Broadway chorus dancers. The unique individuals the audience has come to know become a nameless, faceless mass. It is a beautiful moment, but within the context of the show, heartbreaking as well, and represents another way in which *A Chorus Line* challenged Broadway traditions.

The show was overwhelmingly successful. From the specificity of the dancers' lives, a universal story emerged and captivated audiences and critics alike. *A Chorus Line* won numerous awards, including the Pulitzer Prize for Drama and the 1976 Tony Award for Best Musical (one of nine Tony Awards it received that year). It went on to break the record for the longest-running show on Broadway, and Bennett restaged the record-breaking performance (No. 3,389) to include company members from around the world, as well as various incarnations of the Broadway cast. Touring productions have continued to proliferate, carefully staged—often by original cast member Baayork Lee—to replicate the original production as closely as possible. And in 2006, 16 years after the original production closed, a Broadway revival helmed by Bob Avian and Lee brought *A Chorus Line* to a new generation of theatergoers.

In the end, *A Chorus Line*, for all its success, was a mixed blessing for those involved. The show, designed to highlight the individuality of dancers who were typically members of the chorus, gave enormous success to the performers involved for the length of their run. Outside *A Chorus Line*, though, most were unable to maintain careers as leading or featured actors. While the show could not change all these dancers' lives, it did create work for dancers around the world—and continues to do so to this day.

A Chorus Line changed the nature of the development process for a Broadway musical, offering the new option of an off-Broadway workshop model where the creation of the text and score could happen in conjunction with staging and in conversation with performers—paving the way for shows like **Rent** (1996). On the technical side, the Broadway production brought the first computerized lighting board to Broadway, as designer Tharon Musser required computerized technology to handle the complicated lighting design she had created. And, perhaps most importantly, *A Chorus Line* showed that a simple story, stripped down to its theatrical essentials, about the lives of dancers could be the stuff of which musical theater history was made.

Michelle Dvoskin

Further Reading

Sheward, David. *It's a Hit: The Backstage Book of Longest-Running Broadway Shows, 1884 to the Present.* New York: Watson, Guptill Publications, 1994.

Viagas, Robert, Baayork Lee, and Thommie Walsh. *On the Line: The Creation of* A Chorus Line. Milwaukee: Hal Leonard Corporation, 2006.

CLURMAN, HAROLD (1901–1980)
DIRECTOR, PRODUCER, CRITIC

Harold Edgar Clurman was one of three co-founders of the **Group Theatre**, the Depression-era collective that established social drama about working-class Americans' daily lives as a vital part of New York theater. Clurman's Group Theatre introduced American actors to Russian director Konstantin Stanislavsky's Method Acting techniques, which exerted a profound influence on future generations of actors and the way they are trained. Clurman himself directed and staged over 35 plays on **Broadway** and numerous **Off-Broadway** productions, becoming one of New York's most sought-after drama directors from the 1930s through the mid-1960s. In addition, Clurman was a distinguished theater **critic** whose erudition and impassioned advocacy for artistically and socially significant drama elevated the stature of theater and theater criticism in twentieth-century American culture.

Born and raised in New York City, Clurman began attending theater productions with his parents during childhood. As a teenager, he organized amateur theatrical ventures in his Lower East Side neighborhood. After receiving his education in New York City's public schools, he studied at Columbia University and the

Sorbonne in Paris. International study and travel gave him an erudition about world culture, and European culture in particular, that would inform many of his theatrical productions and writings.

Clurman returned to America in 1924 to work in theater. He took various jobs in the 1920s, including a few minor acting roles both on and Off-Broadway. However, the major turning point in his professional career came not so much from his early roles but from his tenure in the mid and late 1920s as a journeyman member of the **Theatre Guild**, where he did stage managing, script reading, and occasional acting. While at the Guild he met the two people with whom he would establish the Group Theatre, Cheryl Crawford and **Lee Stras-**

Critic and director Harold Clurman, 1968. (AP Photo)

berg. He also started developing interests in producing and directing which, rather than acting, would prove to be his fortes. A lifetime believer in the power of theater to impact people's daily lives, Clurman and some like-minded young Guild members (including Strasberg and Crawford) pressed the more conservative, pragmatic Guild establishment to support production of a few low-cost, decidedly noncommercial "studio" productions. In 1929, Clurman, Strasberg, and Crawford produced some of these small plays (most notably an adaptation of a contemporary Russian drama *Red Rust*) with an eye toward forming an independent, more avant-garde theater company of their own. In the summer of 1931, the trio rented a barn in Connecticut and persuaded 25 other young theater artists to join the core of their new Group Theatre, so named to reflect their commitment to ensemble-driven rather than star-driven approaches to productions. In the Group's first few years, Clurman concentrated on producing, raising money (a chronic problem for the Group Theatre, even in its best years), and providing intellectual leadership to the aesthetic and philosophy-driven collective. In the Group's earlier years, Strasberg and Crawford were more involved with directing and staging, and Strasberg also served as the chief acting instructor.

The Group's first production, Paul Green's *The House of Connelly* (1931), was a critical success. After two flops, their fourth production, John Howard Lawson's *Success Story* (1932) also won some respectable notices. In 1933, Sidney Kingsley's *Men in White* won the Pulitzer Prize and ushered in a four-year peak period of success for the Group, highlighted by the unlikely discovery of **playwright**

Clifford Odets within the ranks of its actors. At this point Clurman became more involved in directing plays for the Group. He did the staging for Odets's *Awake and Sing* (1935), ultimately the most successful and highly regarded play the Group ever produced. He went on to become the principal director for the Group, staging or directing seven other productions on Broadway—including the Group's last play, Irwin Shaw's *Retreat to Pleasure* (1940). By 1941 the Group Theatre collapsed under the weight of financial stress and internal squabbles. However, by virtue of their work with the Group, Clurman and many of his colleagues had established sterling reputations as actors and directors, and moved readily into successful theater and film careers.

Clurman spent some time working in Hollywood in the 1940s, but his first love remained New York theater. Between 1940 and 1946, he directed a handful of Broadway plays, including works by Irwin Shaw and **Maxwell Anderson**, but did not have "a hit" until he co-produced **Arthur Miller**'s *All My Sons* (1947) with Group alumnus **Elia Kazan**. (Kazan also directed the play.) A prolific risk taker, Clurman became a fixture on Broadway in the 1950s and 1960s choosing projects for their artistic merit rather than potential for profit and long runs. Nevertheless, he managed to create commercial successes out of several seemingly "noncommercial" works, including Carson McCullers's *The Member of the Wedding* (1950), which ran for over 500 performances and launched actress **Julie Harris** into stardom. He also found success with **William Inge**'s longest-running play *Bus Stop* (1955), French existentialist writer Jean Giraudoux's *Tiger at the Gates* (1955), **Eugene O'Neill**'s *A Touch of the Poet* (1958), and a stage farce, *A Shot in the Dark* (1961), based upon French playwright Marcel Achard's bumbling French detective characters. Clurman retired from theater production in the 1960s.

Although he worked primarily "behind the scenes," Clurman was a New York and national celebrity: a noted raconteur, fashion plate, speaker, interview subject, editor, and author. His 1972 book *On Directing* is still considered to be a major work in the field. His 1975 autobiographical history of the Group Theatre, *The Fervent Years*, is one of the fundamental resources in the history of American theater. The numerous play volumes he edited and annotated played a major role in bringing American playwrights into high school and college curricula.

Clurman died of cancer in Manhattan on September 9, 1980. A small Off-Broadway theater bears his name and operates in the spirit of his own love of avant-garde, progressive drama.

Thomas A. Greenfield and Nicholas J. Ponterio

Further Reading

Clurman, Harold. *The Fervent Years: The Group Theatre and the Thirties*. New York: Da Capo, 1983. (Original 1975.)

Smith, Wendy. *Real Life Drama: The Group Theatre and America*. New York: Knopf, 1990.

COBB, LEE J. (1911–1976)
ACTOR

Lee J. Cobb was a well-respected character actor who, although having done more acting in **television** and movies than on Broadway, is best remembered for creating the broad-shouldered, lumbering archetype of Willy Loman in **Arthur Miller**'s *Death of a Salesman* (1949). Largely through Cobb's performance, the character of Willy Loman gained instant status as a twentieth-century American icon, symbolizing the pitfalls of misdirected ambition, the false promise of appearances, and the tragic existence of "the common man."

Born Leo Jacoby in New York City, Cobb's father was a compositor for a foreign-language newspaper in Manhattan. Upon graduating high school Cobb left New York to pursue an acting career in Hollywood. After shuttling back and forth between New York and Hollywood for a few years, Cobb landed a relatively steady position as an actor and director for the Pasadena Playhouse in Los Angeles from 1931 to 1933. He did not "catch on" in the **film** industry during this time and by 1935 he had returned to New York to become a member of the **Group Theatre**. Cobb played character roles in some of the Group Theatre's most important productions, including **Clifford Odets**'s *Waiting for Lefty* (1935), *Till the Day I Die* (1935), and *Golden Boy* (1937). Outside of the Group Theatre, Cobb acted in other stage work including the 1935 Broadway production of Bertolt Brecht's *Mother.*

Cobb's work with the Group Theatre, ironically, would allow him to realize his previous ambition to become a Hollywood actor. The Group's production of *Golden Boy*, with Cobb playing Father Bonaparte, was so successful that it became one of the Group Theatre's few productions to be adapted as a Hollywood movie. Cobb was cast in the movie version, giving him his long-sought breakthrough role in film. Thereafter he fashioned a moderately successful bicoastal career as an actor both in Hollywood and on Broadway.

Except for a brief term of military service, Cobb worked in film through most of the 1940s, although in 1949 he was ready to return to the stage. *Salesman*'s director and fellow Group Theatre alumnus **Elia Kazan** invited Cobb to take the lead role, although the director did have to persuade Miller, who envisioned Willy as a smaller man. Kazan's instincts proved to be correct. Critics and audiences thrilled to the play and were captivated by Cobb's performance in particular. The image of Cobb's slow-moving, ungainly Willy Loman became the play's defining visual symbol, appearing on covers of the book editions and cast recordings as well as guiding the casting of Willy in countless regional and stock productions for years to come.

In an intriguing counterpoint to Cobb's landmark portrayal, noted film actor Dustin Hoffman, a lifelong admirer of Miller and *Death of a Salesman*, played Willy Loman in a 1984 Broadway revival of the play. The short, agile Hoffman deliberately set out to alter Cobb's interpretation, substituting nervous exhaustion and, at times, even comic fidgeting and befuddlement for Cobb's hulkishness.

Playwright Miller openly preferred Hoffman's portrayal but Cobb's Willy Loman is still widely viewed as the definitive interpretation of this seminal role in American theater.

The rest of Cobb's major work would mainly be in film, including his Oscar-nominated role in Elia Kazan's film *On the Waterfront* (1954). Cobb's reputation in the artistic community became marred in the 1950s when he, along with a number of other notables in the entertainment industry (including Kazan), was subpoenaed by Congress's House Un-American Activities Committee (HUAC) and "named names" of people whom the Committee suspected of disloyalty to America. Cobb continued to act in television and film until his death in 1976. However, with the exception of a three-month run in 1968 in a Lincoln Center production of *King Lear*, he never again performed on Broadway after 1954.

Cobb died of a heart attack in Woodland Hills, California.

Thomas A. Greenfield and Nicholas J. Ponterio

Further Reading

Brater, Enoch. *Arthur Miller's America: Theater & Culture in a Time of Change.* Ann Arbor, MI: University of Michigan Press, 2005.

Murphy, Brenda. *Miller: Death of a Salesman.* Cambridge, England: Cambridge University Press, 1995.

COHAN, GEORGE M. (1878–1942)
ACTOR, SONGWRITER, PRODUCER, DIRECTOR

Modern American theater owes much of its American character and identity to George M. Cohan. "The Man Who Owned Broadway" was a captivating performer as well as a prodigious composer, producer, director, librettist, and lyricist. In songs like "Yankee Doodle Dandy," "You're a Grand Old Flag," and "Over There," Cohan infused his high-energy shows with equally energetic songs of American pride and nationalism. In so doing, he married the values of American optimism, charming naiveté, and "can-do" spirit to the brassy extroversion of up-tempo showstopping Broadway production numbers. Though reportedly arrogant, egotistical, and overbearing to family, friends, and co-workers, his hard work and determination brought forth pioneering works of theater in the early twentieth century.

Cohan was born in July 1878 in Providence, Rhode Island, to a pair of **vaudeville** entertainers, Jerry and Helen Cohan. (Notwithstanding his proud boast in the song "Yankee Doodle Dandy" that he was born on the Fourth of July, there is some historical dispute as to whether he was actually born on July 3 or July 4.) Cohan began his theatrical career touring with his vaudevillian parents and younger sister Josie during the 1880s and 1890s in an act popularly known as The

Four Cohans. The road substituted for Cohan's formal education with the family's variety act serving as a hands-on residency for learning song composition, stage writing, show dancing, theatrical production, and audience control. Although primarily a vaudeville music and comedy act, the Cohans occasionally performed in plays. In 1891, at age 13, Cohan starred in a stage adaptation of *Peck's Bad Boy*, based on a popular series of stories by George W. Peck. Cohan was so effective in playing the mischievous, tough teenager Hennery Peck that he sometimes found himself accosted after performances by young boys from the audience waiting outside the theater to take him on. The fictitious Peck's orneriness was all too close to Cohan's own, and as he grew older his contentiousness and self-centeredness made him difficult

George M. Cohan in a 1935 photo by Carl Van Vechten. (Library of Congress, Prints & Photographs Division, Carl Van Vechten Collection, LC-USZ62-137278.)

to work with. Over time the family lost some bookings but soldiered on through the 1890s, negotiating the double bind of young George's remarkable creative talent and off-putting personality.

By his middle teens Cohan was writing skits and songs for his family to perform, casting himself as the lead role in each, and often writing of patriotic themes and ideals. Cohan began publishing his songs in 1893 in order to earn money. Cohan married vaudevillian actress Ethel Levey in 1899 who, though generally disliked by the rest of the family, used her talents effectively in their road act and, later, in George's early Broadway productions.

Toward the end of the 1890s George, whose role as both performer and leader of the family act had been growing steadily, formally took over as manager. He immediately started looking for opportunities to play Broadway music halls and theaters in addition to road tours. His 1901 Broadway debut, a musical farce entitled *The Governor's Son* for which he wrote the book, music, and lyrics, starred Cohan with his family in supporting roles. *The Governor's Son* opened in the Savoy Theatre to poor reviews, and it closed in a month. However, the show proved successful on the road as part of the family's touring repertoire.

Cohan's next Broadway show, *Running for Office* (1903), based on one of the family's old vaudeville sketches, was more successful and launched Cohan's Broadway career. Cohan's next show, *Little Johnny Jones* (1904), was his first true triumph on Broadway. The show introduced two musical standards, "Give My Regards to Broadway" (to this day Broadway's unofficial anthem) and "The Yankee Doodle Boy," more commonly known as "Yankee Doodle Dandy." Though some **critics** found the thin plot and loud, talky songs grating, audiences loved the musical comedy about the brash American jockey of the title. Cohan took the play on tour and revived an updated version of it on Broadway twice in 1905. It was after the success of *Little Johnny Jones* that Cohan began turning his attention away from the family touring act to focus on writing, producing, and starring on Broadway. He formed a partnership with Sam Harris, the producer for *Little Johnny Jones*, with whom he would produce over three dozen shows from 1906 to 1926—many with his family members in the cast.

Forty-Five Minutes from Broadway (1906) was Cohan's next Broadway success. It introduced the popular hit "Mary Is a Grand Old Name" and starred vaudeville legend Fay Templeton. The show ran 90 performances, at the time a healthy Broadway run for a new **musical**. Cohan went on to produce, write, and star in more musicals whose simple and similar plots, characters, and sentiments delighted audiences even as they left some critics cold. Cohan followed *Forty-Five Minutes* with *George Washington, Jr.* (1906), another hit that introduced yet another patriotic classic song, "You're a Grand Old Flag." Over the next ten years Cohan would produce, direct, write, and/or star in numerous vehicles for Broadway, including musicals, revues, minstrel shows, and straight plays. His most successful productions during this period included the musical satire *The Yankee Prince* (1908), the musical farce *The Little Millionaire* (1911), and a remarkably successful straightforward nonmusical comedic play, *Seven Keys to Baldpate* (1913), which ran for 320 performances. (Cohan wrote and co-produced the play but did not perform in it.)

Returning constantly to his familiar themes of boyishly enthusiastic national pride, Cohan also continued to develop popular self-referential Broadway songs and shows that lionized Broadway itself. Musicals such as *The Man Who Owns Broadway* (1909), *Broadway Jones* (1912), and *Hello, Broadway!* (1914) along with songs like "Give My Regards to Broadway" and "(It's a Long Way) From Broadway to Edinboro Town" from *The Cohan Revue of 1916* helped establish unselfconscious worship of Broadway as a recurring theme in American musicals. Even relatively recent shows, such as **A Chorus Line** (1975), *42nd Street* (1980), and Disney's omnipresent *High School Musical* franchise, owe much of their self-referential Broadway allure to Cohan's affable if unmitigated nerve.

When World War I broke out in 1917, Cohan was inspired to write his famous patriotic anthem "Over There," which became popular with the American public and remains a popular brass band patriotic rouser to this day. In the 1920s, with changes in audience taste and more sophisticated writers and composers coming to the fore, Cohan lost his position of primacy in Broadway musical theater. Nevertheless, he remained productive and even scored a few hits during the era of **Rodgers** and Hart and **Jerome Kern**. Cohan's final hit musical, *The Merry Malones* (1928), which he produced, wrote, and starred in, played 216 times. The last successful original production in which Cohan served as writer, producer, and star was a straightforward play, *Gambling* (1929), which ran for 152 performances.

Cohan died of cancer in New York in 1942. The nation's efforts to honor his legacy have been myriad yet have met with mixed results. James Cagney played Cohan in a film biography, *Yankee Doodle Dandy* (1942), which Cohan viewed shortly before he died and reportedly did not like. In 1968, a biographical Broadway musical revue, *George M!*, opened to tepid reviews but ran for a full year on the strength of **Joel Grey**'s performance as Cohan. Cohan's first major hit, *Little Johnny Jones*, was revived in 1982 with Donny Osmond as Cohan but closed on opening night owing to bad reviews.

The most successful and arguably most fitting tribute was initiated by lyricist Oscar Hammerstein II who headed a movement to erect a bronze statue of Cohan in the center of Times Square. The statue, unveiled in 1959, is the only statue of a Broadway performer to be erected in New York's theater district. Appropriately, almost everyone going to or from a Broadway theater on any given evening will walk by the statue beneath George M. Cohan's knowing gaze.

Thomas A. Greenfield and Mary Hanrahan

Further Reading

Deffa, Chip, and George Michael Cohan. *George M. Cohan in His Own Words.* New York: Samuel French, Inc., 2004.

McCabe, John. *George M. Cohan: The Man Who Owned Broadway.* Garden City, NY: Doubleday, 1973.

COMDEN, BETTY (1915–2006),
AND GREEN, ADOLPH (1914–2002)
LYRICISTS, LIBRETTISTS

No creative team for the Broadway **musical** collaborated longer than Betty Comden and Adolph Green—more than 60 years. In addition to song lyrics, they wrote books for more than two dozen Broadway and Hollywood musicals from *On the Town* (1944), to *Singin' in the Rain* (**film**, 1952; musical, 1985), to *The Will Rogers Follies* (1991). They worked with numerous composers, but neither of them ever wrote a single word without the other. Sophisticated, witty, and in love with parody and burlesque, their sensibility, like their humor, was strictly New York.

Betty Comden was born Elizabeth Cohen in Brooklyn on May 13, 1915 (although some sources say that she was born four years later), the daughter of an attorney and a schoolteacher. Adolph Green was born in the Bronx on December 2, 1914, to Hungarian immigrants of modest means. Both were first drawn to the theater in school, Comden at New York University and Green at the various public schools he attended. Eventually, they formed an act with comedienne Judy Holliday called The Revuers. Encouraged by Green's roommate, **Leonard Bernstein**, they wrote their own sketches and songs, and eventually made their way to fashionable uptown clubs like the Rainbow Room.

In 1944, Bernstein was asked to turn his recent ballet, *Fancy Free*, into a Broadway musical. He and choreographer **Jerome Robbins** requested Comden and Green as lyricists. When the show opened later that year as *On the Town*, they had written book and lyrics for a story about three sailors on a 24-hour pass in New York City. (They were also in the cast, Comden as a man-chasing anthropologist and Green as one of the three sailors.) The critics raved about the show's dramatic use of dance sequences, its youthfully romantic story, its robust music, and its inventively wisecracking lyrics.

Surprisingly, their next two shows did not succeed. In 1945, they collaborated with Morton Gould on *Billion Dollar Baby*, a nonsensical take on the 1920s. It ran for six months and produced no songs that survived the run. Two years later, they wrote *Bonanza Bound* with composer Saul Chaplin, but it folded before its Broadway opening.

With things not going well in New York, Comden and Green tried Hollywood, where they signed on with Metro-Goldwyn-Mayer. They wrote screenplays for seven important movie musicals between 1947 and 1954, including *The Barkleys of Broadway* (1949), which reunited Fred Astaire and Ginger Rogers in their last movie together, *Take Me Out to the Ballgame* (1949), and *Singin' in the Rain* (1952).

As in their theater songs, their movie lyrics were witty and inventive but only rarely conventionally romantic. They were earning a reputation for youthful exuberance but had not yet written a memorable love song despite the tender "Lonely Town" in *On the Town*. Because they were fond of comic word play and gentle satire, and because they began as performers, their songs often felt rooted in **vaudeville** and revue rather than Broadway's more romantic forms. Many of their plots are about people in show business, on Broadway from *Wonderful Town* (1953) about an aspiring actress to *The Will Rogers Follies* (1991) about a great Broadway star, and in Hollywood from *Singin' in the Rain* (1952) about a silent movie star.

They returned to New York once during their movie years, in 1951, to write a revue, *Two on the Aisle*, with composer **Jule Styne**. He would become their most frequent collaborator. The show featured a fine example of Comden and Green's easy mastery of patter songs, "If You Hadn't, but You Did." Two years later, they wrote the sparkling *Wonderful Town*, a musical comedy adapted from Joseph Fields and Jerome Chodorov's successful 1940 play *My Sister Eileen*. With Edie Adams as the naïve Eileen and Rosalind Russell as her tougher older sister Ruth, its story of two young Ohioans who come to New York in the 1930s to find fame and fortune was ready-made for Comden and Green's take on the city: it terrified newcomers but by the final curtain had made them feel at home and let them find true love. The city was demanding but never dangerous, frenzied but never grotesque. The score included the comic lyricism of "Ohio"; "One Hundred Easy Ways to Lose a Man," a comic star turn for Rosalind Russell that was limited to her range of exactly four notes; and two ballads, "It's Love" and "A Quiet Girl," that demonstrated the pair's growing ease with ballads. By the time they wrote *Wonderful Town*, Comden and Green had their own way of working. The form and structure of their work came from Betty, as did style and sensibility. Green provided the madness: outlandish, surreal, weird, and goofy. The twosome wrote an additional seven scores with Styne, beginning with *Peter Pan* in 1954 and concluding with *Hallelujah, Baby!* in 1967. The shows included one major hit, *Bells*

Are Ringing (1956), along with a number of entertaining, moderately successful shows, including *Say, Darling* (1958), *Do Re Mi* (1960), and *Subways Are for Sleeping* (1961).

Comden and Green were most at home on Broadway, where songs usually propelled plot or revealed character. That helps to explain why relatively few of their songs became popular hits or standards; they were woven into the fabric of the show that produced them. The exception was *Bells Are Ringing* (1956) written for Judy Holliday, their old friend from The Revuers. It tells the story of Ella Peterson, an answering service operator who loves one of her customers, a successful but unhappy playwright. The show yielded "Just in Time" and "The Party's Over," two of Comden and Green's most important standards. Among their other important songs are "Make Someone Happy" from *Do Re Mi* and "Comes Once in a Lifetime" from *Subways Are for Sleeping*.

Their contribution to the 1954 Broadway musical adaptation of James M. Barrie's *Peter Pan* is unusual in that the show had already played around the country with a score by composer Moose Charlap and lyricist Carolyn Leigh. When producer Richard Halliday decided to bring it to Broadway, he hired Styne, Comden, and Green to write additional songs, including the lilting "Neverland" and the comic masterpiece "Hook's Waltz." Although the show has become a classic, the original production ran for only 152 performances; since then, it has had five Broadway revivals, the most recent in 1999. In 1974, Comden and Green also contributed songs to *Lorelei*, an unsuccessful attempt to revise Styne and Leo Robin's successful *Gentlemen Prefer Blondes* (1949) even though Carol Channing recreated her part as Lorelei Lee. Their most innovative show was *Hallelujah, Baby!* in 1967, in the midst of the Civil Rights Movement. Starring Leslie Uggams, it chronicled the struggle of African Americans for equality by following one woman, Georgina, over four decades. In 1970, they contributed the book only to the musical, *Applause*, starring Lauren Bacall, with a score by Charles Strouse and Lee Adams.

Their last successes on Broadway were *On the Twentieth Century* (1978) and *The Will Rogers Follies*, both with music by Cy Coleman. *Century*, starring John Cullum, Madeline Kahn, Imogene Coca, and Kevin Kline, is an adaptation of the 1934 screwball comedy *The Twentieth Century*. A desperate movie director takes the 20th Century Limited train to New York to convince a star—his former wife —to appear in his new movie. The score borders on opera *bouffe*, with trios, duets, and comic arias galore. *Follies*, a loose biography of Will Rogers, ran for 981 performances despite mixed revues. Loosely structured and often performed directly to the audience, it starred Keith Carradine as Rogers, and it enabled Comden and Green to write typically witty, brash songs, most memorably "Will a Mania," written for a "hand dance" by a line of seated sexy chorus girls. In 1982, the team had its worst flop, *A Doll's Life*, an attempt to follow the life of Nora from Henrik Ibsen's *A Doll's House* after she leaves her husband at the final curtain. It ran for five performances.

Comden and Green won Tony Awards in 1953 for *Wonderful Town* (Best Musical), 1966 for *Hallelujah, Baby!* (Best Musical and Best Score), 1970 for *Applause*

(Best Musical), 1978 for *On the Twentieth Century* (Best Score and Best Book), and 1991 for *The Will Rogers Follies* (Best Score). They received Oscar nominations for Best Screenplay for *The Band Wagon* in 1953 and *It's Always Fair Weather* in 1955. They were inducted into the Songwriters Hall of Fame in 1980, and received Kennedy Center Honors in 1991.

Green died in New York on October 23, 2002, at the age of 87, and Comden, also in New York, on November 23, 2006, at the age of 89.

Michael Lasser

Further Reading

Furia, Philip, and Michael L. Lasser. *America's Songs: The Stories Behind the Songs of Broadway, Hollywood, and Tin Pan Alley.* New York: Routledge, 2006.

Robinson, Alice M. *Betty Comden and Adolph Green: A Bio-Bibliography.* Westport CT: Greenwood Press, 1994.

COMIC STRIPS

From its inception the American comic strip has provided source material for Broadway and American theater productions. The traditional comic strip panel, like the movie screen, creates a near identical image frame to that of the theater's stage. The basic conventions of the comic strip: the sequential organization of panels to propel the story or gag and the synthesis of visual images and text, function in a similar fashion to that of a storyboard. Within each comic strip panel the comic dialog balloon provides dialog while the visual comic image provides the setting and scenery. These various elements have made the comic strip a medium ripe for adaptation to the theater stage.

Early Theatrical Adaptations of Comic Strips

The comic strip entered the public's popular consciousness as an art form during the 1890s as newspaper publishers Joseph Pulitzer and William Randolph Hearst challenged each other for supremacy of the New York City market. Pulitzer's *New York World* introduced the Sunday comics section in 1889, the four-color printing process in 1894, and the character of "the Yellow Kid," created by Richard Outcault, to the Sunday funnies in 1895. Hearst's purchase of the *New York Morning Journal* the same year led to a bitter circulation war between the two papers as Hearst raided *The World*'s staff for writers and artists, including Outcault. Hearst viewed the popular success of "the Yellow Kid" and the comic strip that spawned him, *Hogan's Alley*, as a key component in making the *Morning Journal* the dominant paper in New York City. Hearst would spare no expense to succeed. Richard Outcault's "the Yellow Kid" debuted in Hearst's *Morning*

Journal in October 1896. In a cross-market media blitz, a theatrical version of *Hogan's Alley* opened at the People's Theater in the same month. Charles Edward Schulz's comic strip *Foxy Grandpa* would receive a similar treatment when it joined Hearst's stable of comic strips in the *New York American* (formerly the *Journal-American*) in 1902 as a theatrical version of the strip and its stage sets did double duty for a series of one-reel *Foxy Grandpa* shorts filmed during the stage play's run.

The success of *Hogan's Alley*, which eventually moved to Weber and Fields's Broadway Music Hall, led to the adaptation of other comic strips created by Richard Outcault. *Kelly's Kindergarten*, a comic strip Outcault produced for the *New York World*, briefly made it to Broadway in 1898. In 1902 Outcault premiered *Buster Brown* in the *New York Herald*. Buster, "the mischievous son of prosperous parents," proved to be a cultural phenomenon. Outcault licensed the image and name of Buster Brown to a series of companies, most notably a shoe manufacturer, making Buster Brown a nationally known commodity. In 1905 a stage show based upon the character and titled *Buster Brown* debuted at the Majestic Theatre. While the Broadway farce lasted only 95 performances, *Buster Brown* would have a long successful run as a stock-touring show helping to promote a variety of *Buster Brown* products. The success of *Buster Brown* as a touring show led Richard Outcault to use the characters from the comic strip in his speaking tours of theaters across the United States. For Richard Outcault and other successful creators of comic strips, the Broadway farce became another means of selling and promoting their characters.

Shortly thereafter, Winsor McCay followed Outcault's lead. McCay's comic strip *Little Nemo in Slumberland* debuted in the *New York Herald* in 1905. Almost immediately theater producer **David Belasco** optioned the strip. By 1908 *Little Nemo* reached the New Amsterdam Theatre in New York with music by **Victor Herbert** and lyrics and book by Harry B. Smith. Master Gabriel, an over-30-year-old midget who had previously starred as Buster Brown, returned to the New York stage as the lead, Little Nemo. The **musical** played before 250,000 patrons over a 15-week engagement before going on the road for another two years. McCay followed the touring show of *Little Nemo*, appearing in local **vaudeville** theaters giving "chalk talks" on how he created his animations while, concurrently, the stage production of *Little Nemo* played the town or city's main theater. To further cross-promote *Little Nemo*, McCay often had his son, dressed as "Little Nemo," greet theatergoers in the lobby of the vaudeville theater where the elder McCay was appearing. Despite the popularity of *Little Nemo*, the staggeringly expensive cost of re-creating the surrealistic fantasy elements of the comic strip onto the stage limited the production's profitability. McCay found the medium of the cinema to be a more expressive canvas for his work as well as a more profitable one. Many comic strip artists and their syndicates would follow McCay's lead, choosing to focus on **film** rather than the stage for adapting their comic strips.

George McManus was an exception. In 1912 the musical *Let George Do It*, based on McManus's published drawings, appeared for two one-week engagements at the West End Theatre and Manhattan Opera House. The next year

McManus created what became his most popular comic strip, *Bringing Up Father*, featuring the characters Miggs and Jiggs. A musical version of *Bringing Up Father* flopped on Broadway in 1925, leaving the Broadway and New York stage lights dark on comic strip–inspired productions for the next 30 years.

Li'l Abner and the Modern Broadway Musical

The comic strip returned to the Broadway stage in 1956 with a musical production of *Li'l Abner*. The Al Capp–penned strip made its debut in American newspapers during the height of the Great Depression in 1934 and quickly became one of the most popular syndicated comic strips in the country. *Li'l Abner* joined the expanding ranks of continuity strips, both comedic and dramatic, which had become increasingly popular from the 1920s onward. Readers followed the daily adventures of Li'l Abner, Daisy Mae, and the other residents of Dogpatch as Al Capp used his resident "hillbillies" to delve into political and social commentary as well as satire. By the time *Li'l Abner* reached the Broadway stage, the comic strip had brought Sadie Hawkins Day into the popular American lexicon and consciousness, and the 1952 marriage of Li'l Abner to Daisy Mae received national media coverage from both *Time* and *Life* magazines.

Unlike earlier initial stage productions of comic strips, which were either contemporaneous to the debut of the comic strip itself or followed soon thereafter, *Li'l Abner* reached Broadway with a devoted following over two decades in the making. Thus the creators of *Li'l Abner* faced a daunting dilemma. On the one hand, so as not to lose the core fan of the strip they had to create a musical that was true to the basic plot of the strip without merely repeating it. At the same time, the musical adaptation could not require the audience to have prior knowledge of the comic strip's plots so as not to alienate the theatergoers unfamiliar with the source material. Later comic strips adapted for the stage (or film) would face the same dilemma.

Li'l Abner successfully made the transition to Broadway musical, running for 693 performances over two seasons. Though the political and social satire that made the comic strip a forerunner to *Pogo* and *Doonesbury* was deemphasized, the Broadway musical re-created Dogpatch and its denizens using the setting and characters as a springboard for strong musical numbers and comedy with broad appeal. Michael Kidd's choreography received a Tony Award as did Edith Adams's portrayal of Daisy Mae. A 1959 film version of *Li'l Abner* re-created much of the look of the original Broadway musical.

Charles Schulz's comic strip *Peanuts* would receive its musical adaptation a decade after *Li'l Abner*. *Peanuts* the comic strip debuted in October 1950. The strip differed from comic strips of previous eras. Like many strips before it, *Peanuts* contained a large cast of characters whose personalities continued to develop over time like continuity strips. However, *Peanuts* took a new approach to the traditional gag comic strip, using a variety of situations and routines to produce a punch line at the end of each strip that was sarcastic, slyly ironic, or even philosophic rather than "funny." The immense popularity of the comic strip and Schulz's use of a series of set pieces that lent themselves to constant reinterpretation made *Peanuts* ripe for adaptation.

Musician Clark Gesner used the *Peanuts* characters to create a series of songs that eventually evolved into the musical *You're a Good Man, Charlie Brown*. The musical debuted Off-Broadway in Greenwich Village in March 1967 starring Gary Burghoff, who would later earn fame as "Radar" O'Reilly in the *M*A*S*H* film and television series. The **Off-Broadway** production featured a small cast, limited stage design, and musical composition that fit the intimate confines of its small venue. *You're a Good Man, Charlie Brown* had a successful four-year Off-Broadway run of 1,597 performances and produced numerous touring companies before attempting to make the jump to Broadway in 1971. Though its Broadway run was surprisingly brief, lasting only one month, *You're a Good Man, Charlie Brown* is one of the most performed musicals in American theater history, having become over the years a staple for school and community theater productions in America and abroad. The original theatrical production was faithfully restaged for television in 1973 as a *Hallmark* presentation and adapted for an animated television special in 1985. It also spawned a musical sequel, *Snoopy: The Musical*, for the London stage. In 1999 *You're a Good Man, Charlie Brown* returned to Broadway for four months as a revival featuring Kristin Chenoweth as Charlie Brown's sister Sally, a character added for the revival, and Roger Bart as Snoopy, both of whom won Tony awards for their performances.

The success of *You're a Good Man, Charlie Brown*, like *Li'l Abner*, was fueled in part by the broad popularity of the comic strip. *Annie*, based on the Harold Gray comic strip *Little Orphan Annie*, was produced in 1976 at the Goodspeed Opera House in Connecticut eight years after Gray's death. *Little Orphan Annie*, a melodramatic continuity strip, had debuted in 1924 and achieved widespread popularity by the 1930s, spawning hit songs, films, movie serials, and a radio show sponsored by Ovaltine chocolate drink. By the 1970s the strip's popularity had waned, and *Little Orphan Annie* was viewed as more of a relic of a bygone era than part of current popular culture. The musical *Annie* focused itself not on the *Little Orphan Annie* of the 1970s but went back to *Little Orphan Annie* of the 1930s without Harold Gray's conservative political subtext. *Annie* debuted on Broadway at the Alvin Theatre in April 1977 with Andrea McArdle as the title character. *Annie* proved to be a critical and popular smash hit. The musical received eleven Tony nominations and won seven, including Best Choreography, Score, Book, Scenic and Costume Designers, and Best Musical. Its featured song, "Tomorrow," became one of the top Broadway show hit songs of the decade. *Annie* ran on Broadway until 1983 after 2,377 performances. In 1997 *Annie* returned to Broadway for another 239 performances and captured the Tony for Best Revival. Two attempted musical sequels, *Annie 2* and *Annie Warbucks*, failed to reach Broadway.

Annie's success was not limited to the stage. A film version of *Annie*, featuring Carol Burnett, Albert Finney, and Aileen Quinn in the title role, appeared in 1982. The success of the *Annie* musical and film led the comic strip *Little Orphan Annie* to be recast and retitled based on the musical. *Annie* the comic strip was relaunched in American papers in 1980.

The phenomenal financial and artistic success of *Annie* failed to be repeated by the last major original Broadway production to be based upon a popular comic strip. *Doonesbury*, a musical based on Garry Trudeau's comic strip of the same name, opened in November 1983. Trudeau's strip, like Schulz's *Peanuts*, featured a large cast and a variety of routines and situations to produce a punch line. However, unlike the broadly popular *Peanuts*, which focused on the irony of life, *Doonesbury* tackled the political issues of the day. *Doonesbury* became the first comic strip to earn its creator a Pulitzer Prize in Cartooning, an award usually reserved for editorial cartoonists. Its topicality and controversial subject matter resulted in the strip constantly being voted "best" and "worst" strip in newspaper reader surveys. Either loved or loathed, *Doonesbury* the comic strip was difficult to ignore. Like *You're a Good Man, Charlie Brown*, *Doonesbury* featured a small cast for a musical, only ten characters. However, unlike the successful stage adaptations of comic strips that had preceded it, *Doonesbury* had not been successfully adapted to other mediums, or marketed to the broader public via merchandise. *Doonesbury*, at its core, was a comic strip of political commentary. Unlike *Li'l Abner*, *You're a Good Man, Charlie Brown*, or *Annie*, all of which were readapted to multiple mediums a variety of times bringing their cast of characters to new audiences while retaining the core fan base from the comic strip, *Doonesbury* proved difficult to adapt to a broader audience while retaining the elements that made the comic strip successful in the first place. Lacking star power in its cast, a hit song in its score, or any other means of appealing to an audience beyond its fan base, *Doonesbury* the musical lasted 104 performances before closing in February 1984.

Throughout American theater history comic strips have provided source material for Broadway and Off-Broadway productions. Those adaptations that have been successful contain certain similar elements. The comic strips these productions have been based upon have been very popular and readily adapted to other mediums, especially film (*Foxy Grandpa, Little Orphan Annie*) and television (*Peanuts*). They also have been cross-marketed, tying themselves to a variety of products used and consumed by the public at-large (*Buster Brown, Li'l Abner*). Finally, successful theatrical adaptations of comic strips have been able to be true to the essential core of the strip while making the new production accessible to new audiences unfamiliar with the continuing plotlines or settings of the comic strip itself.

Francis Rexford Cooley

Further Reading

Canemaker, John. *Winsor McCay: His Life and Art*. New York: Abbeville Press, 1987.
Conperie, Pierre, and Maurice C. Horn. *A History of the Comic Strip*. New York: Crown Publishers Inc., 1968.

Ganzl, Kurt. *Ganzl's Book of the Broadway Musical: 75 Favorite Shows, From H.M.S. Pinafore to Sunset Boulevard.* New York: Schirmer Books, 1995.

Harvey, Robert C. *The Art of the Funnies: An Aesthetic History.* Jackson: University of Mississippi Press, 1994.

Horn, Maurice, ed. *The World Encyclopedia of Comics.* New York: Chelsea House Publishers, 1976.

Johnson, Rheta Grimsley. *Good Grief: The Story of Charles M. Schulz.* New York: Pharos Books, 1989.

Laufe, Abe. *Broadway's Greatest Musicals.* New York: Funk & Wagnalls, 1977.

Mandelbaum, Ken. *Not Since Carrie: Forty Years of Broadway Musical Flops.* New York: St. Martin's Press, 1991.

Marschall, Richard. *America's Great Comic Strip Artists.* New York: Albeville Press, 1989.

Mordden, Ethan. *Better Foot Forward: The History of American Musical Theater.* New York: Grossman Publishers, 1976.

O'Sullivan, Judith. *The Great American Comic Strip: One Hundred Years of Cartoon Art.* Boston: Bulfinch Press Book, 1990.

Stevenson, Isabella, and Roy A. Somlyo, eds. *The Tony Award: A Complete Listing of Winners and Nominees of the American Theater Wing's Tony Award.* Portsmouth, NH: Heinemann, 2001.

COMPANY

Broadway Run: Alvin Theatre
Opening: April 26, 1970
Closing: January 1, 1972
Total Performances: 705
Composer: Stephen Sondheim
Lyricist: Stephen Sondheim
Book: George Furth
Choreographer: Michael Bennett
Director: Harold Prince
Producer: Harold Prince; in association with Ruth Mitchell
Lead Performers: Barbara Barrie (Sarah), Charles Braswell (Larry), Susan Browning (April), George Coe (David), John Cunningham (Peter), Steve Elmore (Paul), Beth Howland (Amy), Dean Jones (Robert), Charles Kimbrough (Harry), Merle Louise (Susan), Donna McKechnie (Kathy), Pamela Myers (Marta), Teri Ralston (Jenny), and Elaine Stritch (Joanne)

With the 1970 premiere of *Company*, American audiences witnessed an outstanding foray into the frequently tried, frequently unsuccessful genre of the concept **musical**—an approach to theater that focuses on a central theme or idea rather than a linear story. *Company* (billed as a "musical comedy") was by no means the first concept musical to appear on Broadway, but it was the first profitable production of this type in a long time. Two of the most prominent earlier examples—*Allegro* (1947) and *Love Life* (1948)—had both lost money. *Company*, however, presented a series of contemporary scenarios, using modern language and a wide range of musical approaches, as the backdrop for the mid-1930s central character's dilemma: should he or should he not get married?

The timing of the production was fortuitous. Various social changes, especially the feminist movement of the preceding decade, had challenged the traditional assumption that marriage was for everyone. Among the most significant of these changes had occurred in 1960 when the Federal Drug Administration approved the birth control pill. "The Pill" gave women who chose to take it an unprecedented amount of reproductive and sexual freedom, which often affected their marital and relationship choices. A second social trend was the growing belief that court requirements for getting a divorce were often unduly onerous, and that a legal "no-fault" option could be a welcome alternative for desperately unhappy couples. The legislation for the first of the no-fault divorce laws was signed in 1969.

Into this shifting environment came *Company*, which grew out of a series of 11 one-act plays by George Furth, a respected character actor who was turning his hand to playwriting at the time. Furth intended to feature the same actress in each play but experienced difficulties in getting his concept produced. His friend **Stephen Sondheim** suggested that Furth seek advice on the project from **Hal Prince**, who by the late 1960s had become one of Broadway's most prolific and successful **producers** and directors. Prince suggested that the project could become a musical rather than a play. Surprised, Sondheim explained that the characters did not seem to "sing," but Prince argued that that was what was interesting about the notion.

Gradually, the show's premise gained a new focus: the axis of *Company* would be Robert, a bachelor, who is approaching his thirty-fifth birthday and is struggling to decide if he wants to marry. The show then presents vignettes from the romantic relationships of five couples—all friends of Robert, but not well acquainted with each other. By observing and interacting with these couples, Robert gathers evidence about marriage to guide him in his decision. He is the third wheel in each of their partnerships, which suggests that one nuance of the show's title may be an allusion to the old saying "two's company, three's a crowd." Complicating matters is the fact that all the couples have, to greater or lesser degrees, dysfunctional partnerships. Besides the examination of marriage, *Company*'s creators sought to convey a second theme: that "looking at it" is not the same thing as "living it"—a message that Robert must also come to understand.

Because there is no chronological story line to cement the show, various motifs hold *Company* together: the friends gather several times to celebrate Robert's birthday (although this may be the same birthday party each time, viewed from different perspectives). Visually, set designer Boris Aronson let two onstage elevators function in multiple ways: they suggested the high-rise apartments that characterize New York, they evoked the rise and fall of emotions, and they symbolized isolation—people in different elevators will never meet. Sondheim contributed an aural motif—a repetitive "buzz-buzz-buzz" that resembled a telephone's busy signal—representing the frustrating inability to "get through" to another person in a harried environment.

Sondheim's music, partnered with various aspects of the staging, enhanced both the subtexts and the ambivalence of Robert's situation. Sondheim used the sultry sound of a bossa nova—a Brazilian jazz style newly popular in chic urban American supper clubs—to suggest the nightclub in which one of the wives makes a pass at Robert. On other occasions, though, the music and **Michael Bennett**'s choreography resembled some of the high-energy dance routines of the **vaudeville** era— another meaning to the "company" of the title. Bennett also uses a tap-dance routine to underscore the show's central marital theme: each man dances a simple four-beat pattern, and each woman responds with a four-beat "answer." When it is bachelor Robert's turn, however, only silence follows his dance pattern until the other couples all rush to fill in the gap. The three women whom Robert is dating join together in the trio "You Could Drive a Person Crazy," their tight-knit, Andrews Sisters–style harmony suggesting that there is no real difference among the three of them.

No character is truly fleshed out in the course of the show, and the most ambiguous of them all is Robert himself. For this reason, perhaps, the creators struggled to find the right closing number for the production; four different songs were tried. They ran the gamut from bitterness to optimism, and Sondheim later said he liked each of them for different reasons. Ultimately, the choice was "Being Alive," in which Robert moves from ambivalence to decisiveness; by the end of the tune he is asking, "Somebody, hold me too close."

Critical response to *Company* was very favorable, some calling it a "landmark" after opening night. Others complained that many of the characters were not really likeable, but recognized that it still was compelling theater. They admired its sophistication and brilliant polish. It was not a show that appealed to the heartstrings, but it had intelligence, wit, and—some felt—a refreshing cynicism. Quite a few individual songs from *Company* have also developed lives of their own as parts of revues and even as popular audition numbers. *Company*'s overall success, despite its unconventional format and dearth of "feel-good" qualities, opened the door to a host of other experimental productions, including several by Sondheim himself. Some of the concept shows that followed did well (sometimes astonishingly well, such as Michael Bennett's *A Chorus Line* [1975] or **Andrew Lloyd Webber**'s *Cats* [1982]), while others quickly failed. For Sondheim himself, however, *Company* stood at an important juncture.

The show brought Sondheim to the Tony Awards podium for the first time in his career; he won the Best Score and Best Lyrics awards. The show itself took the Best Musical prize. *Company* launched a three-year stretch of consecutive awards for Sondheim; he would win the Best Score Tony again the following year for *Follies*, and again the year after that for *A Little Night Music*. After this extended stretch of recognition, Sondheim was well and truly launched as America's most acclaimed musical theater composer of his time.

Alyson McLamore

Further Reading

McLamore, Alyson. *Musical Theatre: An Appreciation*. Upper Saddle River, NJ: Prentice-Hall, 2004.

Secrest, Meryle. *Stephen Sondheim: A Life*. New York: Knopf, 1998.

THE CRADLE WILL ROCK

Broadway Run: Windsor Theatre
Original Scheduled Opening: June 16, 1937
Opening: January 3, 1938
Closing: April 1938
Total Performances: 108
Composer: Marc Blitzstein
Lyricist: Marc Blitzstein
Book: Marc Blitzstein
Director: Orson Welles
Producer: Sam H. Grisman and John Houseman (The Mercury Theatre); A Federal Theatre Project
Lead Performers: Marc Blitzstein (Clerk, First Report), Howard DaSilva (Larry Foreman), Will Geer (Mr. Mister), John Hoysradt, Hiram Sherman, and Olive Stanton (Moll)

Current events and political commentary have been staples of Broadway productions, both serious and light, since the beginnings of American theater. However, *The Cradle Will Rock* was the first fully formed Broadway **musical** to draw its central action and tone from contemporary social and political unrest—in this case the tumult of the 1930s. The show also reflected an artistic maturation point in American musical theater as composer, lyricist, and author Marc Blitzstein became the first American to integrate German avant-garde dramatist Bertolt Brecht's radical theater philosophies into a bound-for-Broadway musical. In addition to its groundbreaking artistic innovations, *The Cradle Will Rock*'s premiere marked the first and only time in history that federal law enforcement agents tried to shut down a Broadway show on opening night. However, the triumphant defiance of the producer, director, writer, cast, and audience—who marched to another theater that very same night to save the show—has become the stuff of Broadway legend.

The Cradle Will Rock was written during a period of great unrest, internationally and domestically. At the height of the Great Depression, Americans were

The original cast of The Cradle Will Rock, *rehearsing with Marc Blitzstein in 1938. (Courtesy of Photofest)*

doing whatever they could to find work. Unionism and socialism were fiercely debated at the dinner tables, and Italy and Germany were turning into expansionist dictatorships. With *The Cradle Will Rock*, writer and composer Marc Blitzstein sought to capture the political intensity of the times and make it the central focus of a musical.

Blitzstein was born in Philadelphia. A classically trained pianist, he had studied music at Philadelphia's famed Curtis Institute. He later studied piano in Europe during the 1920s, where he befriended Bertolt Brecht and became a disciple of the **playwright**'s politically and artistically radical approaches to theater. While there he met writer Eva Goldbeck, who returned to the United States with him. They married in 1933. During the 1930s, Blitzstein worked as a musician and composer, occasionally contributing songs to traditional Broadway revues such as *Garrick Gaeities* (revival 1930) and *Parade* (1935). In 1936, spurred on by his left-wing political beliefs, his frustration with the irrelevance of American music and theater to the social crises of the times, and the sudden illness and death of his young wife that same year, Blitzstein began to write what would become a groundbreaking, self-consciously political "mainstream" musical.

The Cradle Will Rock features the song "The Nickel Under the Foot" and an idea: A prostitute, selling her body for food, sees a nickel on the floor, but there is no nickel at all. It was Brecht, upon hearing the song while Blitzstein was writing the musical, who suggested that the song become the centerpiece for the entire show. Set in Steeltown, USA, *Cradle* focuses on the prostitute, Moll, as she compares her profession to more socially acceptable professions such as artist, journalist, religious leader, doctor, and educator. A second plotline details the struggle and eventual victory of union organizer Larry Foreman battling against the very powerful and corrupt Mr. Mister, who owns everyone and everything in the town.

The Cradle Will Rock is almost entirely sung-through, and is often referred to as an opera written in American popular song idioms. Orson Welles and John Houseman, **producers** and directors for the **Federal Theatre Project** (FTP) in New York, heard Blitzstein sing through the show, liked its politically and artistically radical vision (which coincided with their own), and wanted to include it in their 1937 season. Blitzstein then played it through for Federal Theatre Project head Hallie Flanagan, who approved it—radical themes and all. The original production of *Cradle* was set to open June 16, 1937, at Maxine Elliott's Theatre on 39th Street. Welles intended the show to be a spectacle (typical for a Welles production) with a full orchestra, hundreds of lighting cues, elaborate glass sets, and a rocking stage for the final number.

The rehearsal period, however, reflected the strife depicted in the play, as various unions in New York repeatedly clashed with police, and President Franklin Roosevelt's political opponents fought to undercut several New Deal activities—the FTP among them. While *Cradle* was in rehearsal, the House Un-American Activities Committee (HUAC) pressured the Roosevelt administration to cut the Federal Theatre Project's budget by 30 percent; 1,700 workers were dismissed. A seemingly crucial dress rehearsal scheduled shortly after the firings did not go well, as Welles and Houseman struggled to save the now threatened show. Knowing it might not open, the pair had invited prominent theater professionals to view a final dress rehearsal in the hopes of rallying support for the show. However, Blitzstein's score and message were lost amid failed cues, falling scenery, and countless technical glitches.

When the performers, crew, and production staff arrived at the Maxine Elliott for opening night the following evening, they were met by armed guards and padlocked doors—there, ostensibly, to prevent the theft of props, costumes, and scenery, which were all now considered property of the U.S. government. The federal government had shut down its first and, so far, only performance on Broadway. Predictably, government officials claimed the shutdown was strictly a consequence of funding cutoffs, while the creators of the show attributed the rough tactics to reaction against the pro-union, left-wing slant of the show itself.

Welles and Houseman, however, were determined to open the show in another theater without props, costumes, or sets. Having anticipated a confrontation at Maxine Elliott's, they had also secured for the night (for $100) the use of the Venice Theatre on 59th Street, complete with a piano. Welles and Houseman announced to the gathering crowd outside of the guarded Maxine Elliott's Theatre that Blitzstein would perform the entire show himself at the Venice 20 blocks uptown. A now legendary march began, growing to a thousand patrons joining the cast, crew, producers, and press. By the time everyone had settled into the Venice Theatre none of the 1,500-plus seats was empty.

The performers, although forbidden by Actors' Equity rules from speaking their lines in this *ad hoc* "production" and venue, were encouraged by Blitzstein to exercise their freedom of speech and deliver their lines from the audience. Lead actress Olive Stanton joined Blitzstein singing her role from her seat inspiring several others to follow suit; Blitzstein filled in as necessary. Broadway lore holds that many in attendance claimed it was the most moving theatrical experience of their life inasmuch as the production itself triumphed over the very same kinds of struggles it had fictionalized. To this day performances of *Cradle* are usually staged with minimal use of set or orchestra in what has come to be, consciously or not, a collective historical tribute to the scaled-down, defiant one-night performance. The stir over the production helped inspire Welles and Houseman to create the New Mercury Theatre Company, which mounted a 108-performance run of *Cradle* in 1938 at Broadway's Windsor Theatre.

As a pioneering foray into *avant-garde* staging and radical politics as well as a symbolic monument to freedom of expression, *The Cradle Will Rock* is a rare example of an American Broadway musical that made a historical impact without making much of a profit. Although revived only once on Broadway and performed professionally only occasionally, the show maintains a place of high regard in musical theater literature as early evidence that Broadway musicals can, even if under duress, move beyond the strictures of artistic convention and popular belief.

Carissa Cordes

Further Reading

Flanagan, Hallie. *Arena, The Story of the Federal Theatre.* New York: Duell, Sloan & Pearce, 1940.

Gordon, Eric A. *Mark the Music: The Life and Work of Marc Blitzstein.* New York: St. Martin's Press, 2000.

CRITICS

American drama criticism is the product of mass-market journalism techniques perfected after the turn of the nineteenth century. Through much of the nineteenth century the ethics of newspaper critics were notoriously lax due to the practice of using writers to review shows and solicit advertising from theater managers. Literary figures who briefly took up drama criticism, such as Washington Irving, Edgar Allan Poe, and Walt Whitman, fought against contemporary critical corruption. Nevertheless, such practices continued into the early twentieth century, although the better newspapers had stopped using their reviewers to solicit advertising before then. Nevertheless, to this day many American newspapers regard the opening of a play as primarily a news event and are less concerned with criticism so much as they are with description.

The year 1917 is a watershed for drama criticism in American newspapers for two reasons. The most powerful producing organization, the **Shubert Brothers**, lifted their two-year-old ban on the drama critic of the *New York Times*, Alexander Woollcott (1887–1943). Woollcott had been kept out of Shubert theaters since 1915 for declaring *Taking Chances*, one of their shows, to be "not vastly amusing." The *Times* decided to fight this, but lost in court. The court declared that theater owners had the right to keep out anyone as long as it was not done so on the basis of race, creed, or color. Faced with this defeat, the *Times* refused advertising from the Shuberts. However, within two years the Shuberts gave in and invited Woollcott back. All of this was widely reported in the press. The second important development of 1917 was that producers started using extracts from reviews in their advertising. Critics now vied with stars for space on marquees and frequently had their names up in lights. This was fine with Alexander Woollcott. In the three years since his appointment to the position of drama critic for the *New York Times* he had become as famous for his antics between the acts as for anything he wrote. The celebrity newspaper critic with a distinct personality who signed his reviews was born.

Magazine critics had achieved such individuality earlier. Magazine writer and editor George Jean Nathan (1882–1958) was the most important and influential drama critic of his time. He had been writing for magazines since 1908. By 1917 he was co-editor of *The Smart Set*, the most iconoclastic intellectual magazine in the country, and was firmly established as a preeminent cultural commentator. Active from 1905 to 1958, he published 34 books on the theater, co-edited *The Smart Set* and *The American Mercury* with H. L. Mencken, and zealously practiced "destructive" (i.e., exquisitely harsh) theater criticism. More than the most feared first-night theatergoer in New York, Nathan was a renowned man-about-town (and the model for the acerbic critic Addison De Witt in the film *All About Eve*). He had his own table at Broadway's famed 21 Club and was a regular at the fashionable east Manhattan Stork Club, where even the omnipotent columnist Walter Winchell deferred to him.

Among Nathan's contemporaries, the best known is Stark Young (1881–1963). He is the most important critic to make his mark after Nathan began his career. His descriptions of acting are generally considered the best ever written by an American critic. He began his career in 1921 writing for *Theatre Arts* and the *New Republic*, two highly regarded magazines. He made an ill-advised transfer to daily reviewing for the *Times* from 1924 to 1925, and his stint there was quite unhappy. He returned to the weekly *New Republic* and remained there until 1947, when he resigned in a dispute over editorial policy. Young remains one of the most respected reviewers of the American theater. He brought erudition untinged by pedantry to drama criticism. A polished stylist particularly skilled in describing acting, Young is still almost universally respected and admired.

Young and Woollcott were Nathan's major rivals for different reasons. Young's background and learning challenged Nathan's status as the best-read critic. Woollcott's grandstanding could crowd anyone's limelight, and he demanded attention constantly. These three reviewers were the most important critics of the 1920s, yet each lived something of a hidden life. Nathan kept his Jewishness secret. Young was a homosexual determined to remain in the closet. Woollcott's sexual ambiguity and pervasive emotional insecurities were completely masked by a bizarrely magnetic public persona. The choices each of these men made did not necessarily harm their criticism, but their public functioning is emblematic of mainstream American culture and its demands. Their decisions about the conduct of their lives inform us about the twentieth-century conceptions of the "man of letters" and the "man about town." Certain eccentricities of manner and demeanor were appropriate because they made good copy. Superficial flamboyance was welcomed; more intimate departures from accepted norms of conduct were not. This is hardly a revelation; but the 1920s is a particularly important decade in this regard. For this was the era when critics themselves became celebrities. And while Nathan and Woollcott embraced fame, Young shied away from it. Ironically, today Young is the best remembered of the three and is the critic most respected by historians. Nathan is attended to mainly by **Eugene O'Neill** or Mencken scholars. Woollcott survives as a stage character in a **George S. Kaufman** and Moss Hart comedy. Nonetheless, the ambiguous relationship each one of these critics developed with American culture is compelling; each chose to play the part of the critic, while being to his own self untrue.

Another important critic was John Mason Brown (1900–1963), who reviewed for the *New York Evening Post* (1929–1941) and the *Saturday Review* (1944–1953) among other publications, and diligently educated himself to become a drama critic. All through his years at Harvard, where he worked with George Pierce Baker, he studied the history of the theater and its literature with one purpose: that he might one day criticize it professionally. Brown's use of his knowledge of theatrical history and stage conventions as applied in his whimsical, yet pointed, series of "letters from green room ghosts" exemplifies his high-minded yet humorous style. What is more, Brown's editing, with Montrose J. Moses, of *The American Theatre as Seen by Its Critics 1752–1934* is a testament to the strong place secured by serious criticism in American culture by the mid-1930s.

The most influential critic to emerge after Nathan's maturity was the most important of Woollcott's successors at the *Times*, **Brooks Atkinson** (1894–1984). Like Brown, Atkinson had been educated at Harvard and had enrolled in George Pierce Baker's "Drama 47 Workshop." Then, after being graduated, he was an English professor at Dartmouth College for a year, a reporter on the *Springfield Daily News* in western Massachusetts, and the assistant drama critic on the *Boston Evening Transcript*. Atkinson's apprenticeship under the legendary H. T. Parker, known as "H. T. P" or "Hell-to-Pay," gave him lasting admiration for the craft of newspaper reviewing as well as respect for his readers' intelligence.

Atkinson remains the most beloved American drama critic of all time, a genial pipe smoker reduced to tears by the umbrellas-in-the-rain finale of ***Our Town*** (1938). He wrote for the general public and its casual theater enthusiasts. Dubbed "Manhattan's Thoreau" by John Mason Brown, Atkinson's New England nostalgia and liberal convictions were central to his criticism. When the United States entered World War II, he went abroad as a war correspondent, and was awarded the Pulitzer Prize for his reports from Russia. After the war he returned to the drama desk, His four decades of reviewing won him the admiration of everyone in the theatrical community. When he retired in 1960, the Mansfield Theatre on 47th Street was renamed the Brooks Atkinson Theatre.

Atkinson's reviews when reread today stand in sharp contrast to Nathan's. They are relaxed and detached. Atkinson's reviews reveal that the *Times* had become the paper of record for the New York theater. Their tone is authoritative without being assertive. Given Atkinson's great reputation one might expect more from his reviews, but they offer little substantive commentary compared to Nathan's. Atkinson's concentration on keeping his temper and in maintaining the perspective of the average theatergoer broadened his perspective in a way that limited his critical effectiveness.

Thus through the first decades of the twentieth century the stature of drama criticism as a profession rose steadily. In 1935, under Nathan's leadership, the New York Drama Critics' Circle was founded. This was the high point for American drama criticism. For a few years the award given by the Critics' Circle was more prestigious than the Pulitzer Prize for drama. The early years of the New York Drama Critics' Circle best indicate the prestige critics held at that time. Helen Deutsch, a prominent New York press agent, instigated the Critics' Circle and served as its first executive secretary. In 1936 she sent a letter to the 12 leading critics in New York suggesting that they ought to confer an award of their own in response to the Pulitzer Prize committee's awarding "best play" to Zoë Akins's adaptation of Edith Wharton's novel *The Old Maid*. Nathan's voice had long been loudest in protest against the Pulitzer committee's choices. Nathan never forgave the Pulitzer committee's shameless about-face of 1923 when it awarded Hatcher Hughes, a lecturer at Columbia University, the prize for *Hell-bent fer Heaven*, a hyperreligious, pseudofolk drama. Determined that his Columbia colleague should win the prize, Brander Matthews browbeat the committee into reversing its initial, unanimous vote for George Kelly's *The Show-off*. In 1925 Nathan assailed the choice of Sidney Howard's *They Knew What They Wanted* and protested the following year when the prize was given to George Kelly for *Craig's Wife*.

Nathan's antipathy to the Pulitzer committee continued after the Critics' Circle was formed. In 1943, John Anderson, critic for the *Journal-American*, told Helen Deutsch that Nathan had sought redress for the Pulitzer blunders for "a long time before you came along." Anderson was helping Deutsch fend off attacks that she had organized the Circle strictly as a boon for her clients. Such a suspicion had been aroused the first year when her client and neighbor, **Maxwell Anderson**, was awarded the first Critics' Circle Prize for the verse drama *Winterset* (1935). Nathan was elected the second president of the Circle and served from 1937 to 1939. Nathan's determination to ensure that dramatic standards, rather than political, social, or personal agendas, were followed in granting the award helped maintain the Critics' Circle award as the predominant accolade for playwriting. Eventually the pressures of war fever, social crusading, and the inherently fractious nature of drama criticism itself began compromising the award in the 1940s.

During much of the twentieth century, for the purposes of the commercial theater, the American theater had the right critics at the right time and in the right place. And as long as theater was a profitable venture, critics and **producers** coexisted, however uneasily. Through much of the first half of the twentieth century there were more than a dozen newspapers serving New Yorkers and there were usually more than 100 openings in a season. (On the night of December 26, 1927, alone, there were 11 openings. During the entire 1926–1927 season there were 269 openings. By 1950 a busy season would have less than 50 openings.) Theater advertising contributed substantially to newspaper profits and attracted many other advertisers—not only those for productions. As noted, the "powerful" position that critics assumed through these decades had been consolidated during the war years (1914–1918) and was able to sustain a level of seriousness through the late 1940s.

In 1950 Walter Kerr began his career writing for the Catholic monthly *Commonweal*. A year later he joined *The New York Herald Tribune* where he remained until the moderate Republican newspaper's demise in 1966. Transferring to the *Times* troubled drama desk (he was their third critic in a year), he became best known for his weekly essays thereafter. Kerr remained with the *Times* for 17 years. Widely read and even revered until his death in 1996, Kerr had a theater named for him in 1990. He despised the Theater of the Absurd movement that emerged **Off-Broadway** (and occasionally on **Broadway**) in the 1960s and castigated Anton Chekhov for having a disastrous influence on American playwriting, positions that put Kerr's legacy at odds with much of contemporary dramatic scholarship and criticism.

Howard Taubman took over from Atkinson in 1960 and immediately came under fire from producer **David Merrick**, who also feuded with Kerr. Perhaps the last time the old-time Broadway critical grit was tested was Merrick's war on the critics; he even attempted to bar them from his shows. He infamously hoodwinked the public to promote his slipping **musical** *Subways Are for Sleeping* in 1961 by placing a full-page advertisement in the *Herald-Tribune* quoting rave reviews from "Howard Taubman," "Walter Kerr," and four other major critics. It was bunk: Merrick had found New Yorkers with the same names as the critics and suborned them. The ad ran in only one late edition, but was subsequently reprinted in newspapers all over the world. Taubman and his colleagues were outraged, but the stunt paid off at the box office.

Taubman lasted only six seasons, and his replacement, Stanley Kauffman, barely one. The newspaper strikes of the 1960s killed off six of the nine New York daily papers. **Radio** and **television** began broadcasting news as never before—including on-air theater reviews. But these capsule critiques could never be what the daily and weekly columns had been.

Many historians and observers of American theater assert that drama criticism has been in a steady decline through the second half of the twentieth century, owing in large measure to the relentless downturning of the newspaper business and the increasing precariousness of the theater business as a viable commercial enterprise. The disappearance of newspapers has been dramatic. There is only one daily broadsheet in New York today, the *Times*. Its companions are two tabloids, the *New York Post* and the *Daily News*. (One could argue that another daily, *Newsday*, lies somewhere between the tabloids and the *Times*.)

Not surprisingly, as the last remaining major daily newspaper in New York, the *Times* has been a focal point for controversies surrounding Broadway theater criticism for the past few decades. Detractors contend that the paper takes essentially the same approach to theater that it did in 1917, namely that theater is primarily a news event and the average upper-middle-class reader needs only to have criticism that appeals to his or her average sensibilities. In short, they charge that the times have changed but the *Times* has not.

Frank Rich, the so-called "Butcher of Broadway," reigned at the *Times* from 1980 to 1993. A serious admirer of **Stephen Sondheim**'s musicals since his Harvard days and a devotee of the **Rodgers and Hammerstein** book musical tradition, Rich decried the splurge of megamusicals that flooded Broadway during his tenure. On the other hand, he praised the historical sweep of **August Wilson**'s plays and the AIDS extravaganza *Angels in America*. Nonetheless, his consistent polemic rejecting the idea that his reviews had any power to close or "butcher" shows was much derided. Rich left reviewing to become a *Times* op-ed political columnist in 1994. His successor at the *Times* drama desk, Ben Brantley, is decidedly less controversial. Probably the most hated critic of all time, John Simon wrote for *New York Magazine* from 1968 until he was fired without warning in 2005. Born in what is now Serbia and holding three Harvard degrees, Simon's persona of continental erudition, acidic opinions on theater and culture, and a fondness for appearing on national television made him better known than most of his rivals as well as the publication for which he wrote. Simon was infamous for attacking actors and actresses for their appearance as well as their performances (he once dismissed the relative civility of his fellow critics as weakness that stood in contrast to his "Balkan" strength). Simon had his partisans, but Broadway's reaction to his sudden dismissal from *New York* was summed up by **playwright** David Mamet, "(Simon) has finally done something for the American Theater."

In spite of relentless attempts by the theater community to blame critics for their insidious influence, today critics function largely in suspension from the hurly-burly of theatrical production. The closest most critics get to the production process nowadays is a pre-opening interview, which is likely to appear in print as a celebrity interview or human-interest feature rather than anything resembling serious criticism. By contrast, theater critics and editors of the 1930s steered clear of writing show business feature stories. However, current newspaper and magazine practice is far more accommodating to the blending of criticism and "entertainment reporting," notwithstanding the obvious potential of compromising genuine criticism through conflict of interest. Recently the *New Yorker* drama critic John Lahr has been the subject of controversy due to his technique of mixing interview, feature article, and criticism. Lahr's attempts at defending his technique on the basis that he *is* involving himself in the theatrical process did not satisfy those who believe that criticism must stand apart as much as possible from social networking, media relations, and celebrity reporting.

The current shrunken states of both commercial theater and the newspaper industry are ill suited to fostering meaningful drama criticism, and the turn-of-the-millennium critic functions largely as a consumer guide. There are obvious reasons for this. Outside of New York City, where producers attempt to attract busloads of tourists to fill the theaters in which megamusicals play year after year, serious theater is viewed as a coterie art. The day-to-day critical situation is aesthetically grim. Most newspapers do not even have a regular theater critic; they have some sort of arts reporter who is expected to write about all of the arts and do interviews as well. Perhaps unavoidably contemporary theater criticism, to the extent that it exists at all, has become an adjunct of feature writing.

Thomas F. Connolly

Further Reading

Brown, John Mason, and Montrose J. Moses. *The American Theatre as Seen by Its Critics.* New York: Norton, 1934.

Connolly, Thomas F. *George Jean Nathan and the Making of the Modern American Theatre.* Madison, NJ: Fairleigh-Dickinson University Press, 2000.

Lehman, Engel. *The Critics.* New York: Macmillan, 1976.

CRONYN, HUME (1911–2003)
ACTOR, DIRECTOR, PRODUCER, WRITER, LYRICIST

Hume Cronyn, a Canadian American, was one of the great Renaissance men of Broadway from the 1940s to the 1970s, succeeding primarily as an actor but making his mark as a director, producer, writer, and discoverer of new stage talent. He often teamed up on stage with his wife, actress **Jessica Tandy**. The two became unparalleled masters of the two-character marriage play and eventually succeeded 1920s–1930s stars **Alfred Lunt and Lynn Fontanne** as Broadway's premiere acting couple.

Born in London, Ontario, in 1911 to a prominent political family, Cronyn fell in love with theater while a university student. He graduated from McGill University with a degree in drama. In 1931 he immigrated to the United States, where he continued his studies at New York's American Academy of Dramatic Arts. After understudying and performing in minor theatrical projects he was cast in producer **George Abbott**'s *Three Men on a Horse* (1935), an enormous hit that is still revived frequently in regional and community theaters. Cronyn remained with Abbott throughout the 1930s, performing in *Boy Meets Girl* (1936) and *Room Service* (1938). The two plays firmly established the 26-year-old Cronyn as a bankable, versatile Broadway actor. In the 1940s he added **film** work to his expanding career, striking up a particularly fruitful relationship with mystery director Alfred Hitchcock. Cronyn appeared in Hitchcock's *Shadow of a Doubt* (1943) and

Hume Cronyn, shown with wife Jessica Tandy, in Edward Albee's A Delicate Balance *in 1967. (AP Photo/HO)*

Lifeboat (1944). In subsequent years he would adapt texts for Hitchcock's films *Rope* (1948) and *Under Capricorn* (1949).

A major success by age 40, Cronyn's career ascended to new levels when he began co-starring with his third wife, Jessica Tandy (they were married in 1942). They first co-starred on Broadway in Jan de Hartog's sophisticated two-character marriage comedy *The Fourposter* (1951). The play was a sensation, running 632 performances over 18 months. The team followed up with a string of Broadway successes: an evening of short plays (*Triple Play* [1959]), Hugh Wheeler's *Big Fish, Little Fish* (1962), and a highly regarded production of *Hamlet* (1963), for which Cronyn as Polonius won a Tony Award for Best Supporting Actor. **Critics** and audiences were thrilled by their onstage chemistry, their mastery of both comedy and tragedy, and the unassuming elegance of their stage presence. Cronyn and Tandy continued to work individually both on stage and in film throughout the 1960s and 1970s, with Cronyn adding Broadway **producer** to his resumé. The two also toured frequently throughout North America.

In 1977 they consecrated their position as Broadway's premiere acting couple in D. L. Coburn's Pulitzer Prize–winning two-character drama *The Gin Game*. Cronyn would close out his Broadway career, appropriately enough, opposite Tandy in *Petition* (1986), another two-character marriage play. Tandy died in 1994.

Cronyn did not work on Broadway again, although he made occasional appearances in **television** and films throughout the 1990s.

Cronyn died of prostate cancer in Fairfield, Connecticut, on June 15, 2003.

Thomas A. Greenfield and Laura Lonski

Further Reading

Bryer, Jackson R., and Richard Allan Davison. *The Actor's Art: Conversations with Contemporary American Stage Performers*. New Brunswick, NJ: Rutgers University Press, 2001.

Cronyn, Hume. *A Terrible Liar: A Memoir*. New York: Morrow, 1991.

CROTHERS, RACHEL (1878–1958)
PLAYWRIGHT, DIRECTOR, PRODUCER, PERFORMER

Rachel Crothers was the predominant American female **playwright** of the first half of the twentieth century and by far the most prodigious female Broadway dramatist in history. The first American woman to sustain a lifelong career in playwriting, Crothers left an astonishing legacy of 24 original Broadway plays, with numerous hits among them. Crothers's body of work, developed with remarkable consistency from 1906 through the late 1930s, places her with the likes of **Neil Simon** and **George S. Kaufmann** as one of America's most prolific commercial playwrights. Casually acknowledging that writing plays came easily to her, Crothers also became a successful **producer** and director—principally of her own works—as well as a distinguished leader on behalf of theater industry charities and philanthropies. A pioneer in modern American feminist literature, many of her plays focus on women contending with the seemingly irreconcilable tensions of economic survival, personal independence, and family life.

Crothers was born in Bloomington, Illinois. Her parents were both successful physicians. She attributed her penchant for playwriting to her childhood hobby of creating elaborate story lines for her dolls. Crothers claimed that at age 12 she had written a full five-act play; the characters were British (except for one "wicked French woman") notwithstanding the fact that she knew nothing of British culture other than it was generally considered to be more elegant than America's. As a young Sunday school teacher in Bloomington, she directed her students in Bible skits and scenes as a regular part of her pedagogy.

Moving to the East Coast in the hopes of becoming a professional actress, she spent her early twenties studying acting and landing the occasional professional role in New York and surrounding areas. She also continued to write and, as plum acting roles eluded her through her mid-twenties, she decided to market herself as a playwright. She attracted the interest of a veteran theater producer, Walter N. Lawrence, with a frontier mining town family drama, *The Three of Us*. The

Rachel Crothers. Date unknown. (George Grantham Bain Collection, Library of Congress)

play, which ushered in the female-centered dramas and comedies that would become the predominating focus of her work, opened in October 1906 and ran a very impressive five months and 227 performances. It was the biggest success of Lawrence's producing career and gave the 27-year-old Crothers a foothold in Broadway she would never relinquish.

A follow-up play produced by Lawrence was unsuccessful, but over the next two years Crothers saw Maxine Elliott, one of the most influential female actress-producers of the day, produce *Myself–Bettina* (1908) and the inimitable **Shubert Brothers** produce *A Man's World* (1910). For the next decade Crothers wrote at an approximate rate of one produced play per year, working with some of the most important producers of the time: the Shuberts, John Cort, and **George M. Cohan** among them. Not all of her plays were hits, but productions such as *Old Lady 31* (1916), *A Little Journey* (1918), and *39 East* (1919) each enjoyed 150+ performance runs.

By 1920 Crothers was sufficiently well established in New York theater circles to branch into directing her own plays. She debuted as a director-author for producer Sam Harris, formerly George M. Cohan's producing partner, with *Nice People*, a sophisticated New York comedy. Audience reaction was excellent and the play ran a very respectable 120 performances. She would go on to direct and/or produce almost all of her own original Broadway plays as well as a few works by other playwrights. As writer-director, her most successful shows included *A Lady's Virtue* (1925), *Let Us Be Gay* (1929), *When Ladies Meet* (1932), and her last original play *Susan and God* (1937), which was the first Broadway play ever televised with an original cast.

Crothers's plays tended to feature characters and themes that challenged traditional, Victorian-era restrictions on women's social roles while stopping short of alienating her mainstream audiences. Her commercial successes helped open the door for women playwrights who followed shortly after her, including Edna

Ferber, Anita Loos, and **Lillian Hellman**. A major force in supporting the theatrical community as well as working in it, Crothers founded a theater women's relief fundraising organization during World War I. She was a co-founder of the Stage Relief Fund, which provided assistance for out of work actors during the Depression. In 1939 she was a driving force behind the establishment of the **American Theatre Wing**, a mainstay of theater industry philanthropy and professional support to this day (but best known as presenters of the annual **Tony Awards**).

Crothers died of natural causes in her home in Danbury, Connecticut, on July 6, 1958.

Thomas A. Greenfield

Further Reading

Gottlieb, Lois. "Looking to Women: Rachel Crothers and the Feminist Heroine." *Women in American Theatre*, edition 3 revised. Helen Krich Chinoy and Linda Walsh Jenkins, eds. New York: Theatre Communications Group, 2006.

Lindroth, Colette, and James R. Lindroth. *Rachel Crothers: A Research and Production Sourcebook*. Westport, CT: Greenwood Press, 1995.

THE CRUCIBLE

Broadway Run: Martin Beck Theatre
Opening: January 22, 1953
Closing: July 11, 1953
Total Performances: 197
Playwright: Arthur Miller
Director: Jed Harris
Producer: Kermit Bloomgarden
Lead Performers: Arthur Kennedy (John Proctor), Beatrice Straight (Elizabeth Proctor), Madeline Sherwood (Abigail Williams), and E. G. Marshall (the Reverend John Hale)

Arthur Miller's *The Crucible* premiered on Broadway in 1953 to rather tepid reviews from **critics**, yet the play holds an enduring place as one of the two or three most revered—and most performed—dramas ever written by an American **playwright**. The plot centers on the famous witch trials of Salem, Massachusetts, in the late seventeenth century. However, the play also serves as an allegory condemning Senator Joseph McCarthy and the House Un-American Activities Committee (HUAC) for their ruthless and often reckless attempts to root out communist activity in the United States during the late 1940s and early 1950s. For Miller, the job of the playwright was always to speak to issues of morality in the context of identifiable social forces. *The Crucible* was Miller's attempt to warn

A scene from The Crucible *by Arthur Miller, from the 1953 production staged by Jed Harris. Among the actors were Jenny Egan, E. G. Marshall, Arthur Kennedy, and Walter Hempden. (AP Photo/Fred Fehl)*

Broadway and the nation of the insidiousness of McCarthyism and the consequences of acquiescing to it.

Over 50 years after its Broadway premiere, the play is a staple of college and high school English reading lists. Moreover, with an uncommonly large number of young characters for a nonmusical—particularly Abigail and the Salem girls whom she controls—*The Crucible* is a perennial favorite for school drama and community theaters as well as regional professional and semiprofessional theater companies.

Despite the lukewarm initial response, in the years immediately following its premiere Miller received a great deal of correspondence from friends, admirers, and detractors expressing their opinions of the play's meaning and engaging the play's themes of personal integrity, community, citizenship, and loyalty. One such letter came from a representative of the American Bar Association, protesting *The Crucible*'s decidedly unflattering portrayal of lawyers and requesting that the harsher aspects of those criticisms be removed from the play. (In response to the offended attorney Miller pointedly declined.)

Miller wrote *The Crucible* largely as an allegorical representation of HUAC, which was investigating the **film**, theater, and communications industries for purported infiltration by communists and their "follow travelers." Miller had considered other titles for the play, including *The Men's Conversation, Conversation of*

Men, *Inside and Outside*, *If We Could Speak*, and *The Reserved Crime*. Yet none captured the insular, incendiary nature of the trials as effectively as his ultimate choice, *The Crucible*.

The play also became famously associated with a rift between Miller and his closest friend in the theater world, **Elia Kazan**. Kazan had directed Miller's first two Broadway successes, *All My Sons* (1947) and ***Death of a Salesman*** (1949), and by 1950 the two friends were anticipating working together on future projects in both New York and Hollywood. But the relationship soured after Kazan testified before HUAC in 1952 and chose to give the committee the names of those he knew or thought to be communists—including some theater and film colleagues. Many believe that Kazan's decision to "name names," which deeply offended Miller, influenced the playwright's decision to write *The Crucible*.

The Crucible tells the story of Salem, a small Puritan community caught up in the furor of witch trials. Following an affair, farmer John Proctor and his wife, Elizabeth, are accused of witchcraft by Abigail Williams, Proctor's young mistress who is jealous of Elizabeth and enraged at Proctor for ending their affair. The Proctors are just two of many community members accused by the town's young girls (under Abigail's tyrannical control) of consorting with the devil. Esteemed religious and judicial authorities are summoned from afar. They immediately identify the source of the town's travails as being rooted in its citizens' supposed witchcraft and act swiftly to purge the community of its evildoers. Caught up in the frenzy of accusation, the town tries and condemns "the guilty" to death by hanging. Proctor maintains his innocence until the end and, despite threat of execution, refuses to confess to witchcraft or, significantly, bear any witness against neighbors already under suspicion.

The immediate impact of the play helped establish Miller as a major American artist and, along with his own *Death of a Salesman* and early major works by **Tennessee Williams** (*The Glass Menagerie* [1945] and ***A Streetcar Named Desire*** [1947]) and those of other dramatists, staked a claim for serious, literate drama on Broadway in the years immediately following World War II. In the decades following *The Crucible*'s premiere, Miller's masterful treatment of the play's universal themes has resonated with successive generations of Americans and international audiences, to whom the 1950s McCarthyism and the HUAC controversies are an increasingly remote or even unknown phenomenon. *The Crucible* has seen four Broadway revivals (the most successful of these staged in 2002—nearly 50 years after the Broadway premiere). Miller also adapted the play for a highly regarded 1996 film, starring his son-in-law Daniel Day-Lewis, for which Miller received an Academy Award nomination for writing ("Best Screenplay Based on Material from another Medium"). The play is also a popular revival piece for companies in Europe and Canada. In the minds of many observers of American theater, *The Crucible* is the finest American play written in the last half of the twentieth century and, by virtually all accounts, one of the most important works in all of modern American literature.

Chase Bringardner

Further Reading

Bigsby, C. W. E. *Arthur Miller: A Critical Study.* Cambridge, England: Cambridge University Press, 2005.

Bloom, Harold. *Arthur Miller's* The Crucible. New York: Chelsea House Publishers, 1996.

Dance and Choreography

As many historians have noted, American culture's combination of democratic emphasis on individualism combined with capitalism's emphasis on realizing one's "pursuit of happiness" in materialistic terms proved a strong basis for the development of commercial theater and entertainment in America. Colonial and pre-Revolutionary live song and dance entertainment eventually evolved into what we now call the Broadway **musical**. This unique form of American musical theater has a tradition theater historians date from the production of *The Black Crook* in 1866 in Lower Manhattan. A musical extravaganza based on a melodrama, *The Black Crook* ran for a then unprecedented 474 performances and remained popular late into the century. In many ways, the unexpected success of this show set the stage not only for the development of the Broadway musical as its own genre but also for the role of dance in musical theater performance.

Eighteenth- and Nineteenth-Century Background

Dance in colonial America enjoyed a symbiotic relationship between social dance forms and theater dance forms. The dancing master was an important member of society in many cities and towns throughout America. He (the nineteenth-century dancing master was invariably male) brought with him the latest social dances and taught them to young people as a part of their courtship rituals. The dancing master also choreographed and performed in theatrical entertainments throughout the colonies, teaching a variety of dances that included everything from formal minuets to folk dances like the hornpipe.

147

While there were many popular dancers and choreographers throughout the Colonial period, the first American musical theater dance star was John Durang (1768–1822). When he first auditioned for the famous Hallam Theatre Company (a London-based company that toured America), he performed the wildly popular hornpipe dance in a sailor outfit. Illustrations and reports of Durang's performance style seem to anticipate those of the twentieth-century dance stars **George M. Cohan** and Gene Kelly: a strong sense of brashness, clear masculine identity, and infectious energy. Durang performed with all of the major theater companies of his day.

The antecedents to the musical theater dance that coalesced in *The Black Crook* included many other dance styles and genres, such as French and Italian ballet pantomimes performed in America by touring dance troops between the late 1700s and the mid-1800s. The ballet star of the mid-nineteenth century was Austrian-born Fanny Elssler. Her 1840 appearance in the United States created such a phenomenon that when her tour came to Washington, D.C., Congress adjourned so they could see her perform. Consequently, European ballet joined with competitive dances like the hornpipe and the jig to become regular parts of nineteenth-century musical theater.

The culmination of these influences reached their peak with *The Black Crook*. In addition to the show's interpolated popular songs, melodramatic acting, and special effects scenography, it was the elaborate choreography of David Costa and the performance of trained ballet dancers from Europe (performing with 50 additional American dancers) that captivated audiences. Two dancers in particular rose to stardom from this production—Marie Bonfanti and Rita Sangalli. It was clear that as the musical developed as a theater genre, dance would have a vital role to play in its development.

The end of the nineteenth century witnessed the early beginnings of what would come to dominate dance in musical theater. This was the period in which ragtime music was making an impact on musical theater, particularly on the **vaudeville** circuit. Ragtime music encouraged the development of soft shoe and tap dance as fixtures in vaudeville. It would later have an impact on the musicals and revues of **George Gershwin** and Eubie Blake. What had originally begun in the minstrel show tradition of tap dance artists like William Henry Lane (better known as Master Juba) and John Diamond in the nineteenth century was being perfected on the Broadway stage by early director-choreographers like Julian Mitchell in elaborate productions like *The Wizard of Oz* (1903), *Babes in Toyland* (1903), and the *Ziegfeld Follies* (1907–1915).

In addition to the ballet performers, tap dancers, special acts, and others, musical theater was a draw for social dance enthusiasts as well. While many ballroom-dancing couples performed on Broadway during the 1910s, none was as important as Vernon and Irene Castle. They entranced Broadway audiences with their version of the Turkey Trot, the Maxixe, and their famous Castle Walk. **Irving Berlin**'s debut musical *Watch Your Step* (1914) was the most popular of the Castles' Broadway shows.

Between the Wars

Dance on the Broadway musical stage developed quickly in the two decades between World War I and World War II. Rather than dance sequences being interpolated by performers, **producers**, and stage directors, the "dance director" emerged as the prevailing force in coordinating the efforts of chorus dancers with those of star performers with specialty acts. Ned Wayburn, George White, Sammy Lee, David Bennett, and Seymour Felix dominated the Broadway musical of the 1920s and 1930s. Busby Berkeley, before establishing himself as the preeminent Hollywood musical choreographer of kaleidoscopic images of chorus girls, enjoyed a career as one of the most sought after Broadway musical choreographers of the 1920s with such productions as *A Connecticut Yankee* (1927) and *Earl Carroll's Vanities of 1927.*

Many dances introduced or adapted to Broadway shows by dance directors became national dance crazes as a result of exposure on Broadway. Bobby Connolly, one of **Florenz Ziegfeld**'s favorite *Follies* choreographers, was the dance director on several major Broadway musicals. His *Good News!* (1927) introduced the song and dance "The Varsity Drag," which succeeded the highly popular Charleston. The Charleston had been introduced in the musical, *Runnin' Wild* (1923). The Black Bottom, a popular dance in southern African American communities, became a "mainstream" hit when performed by dancer Ann Pennington in *The George White Scandals* (1926).

While the dance director dominated Broadway throughout the 1920s and 1930s, another movement began during this period that strongly advanced the integration of dance and dance concepts with musicals: modern concert dance. American modern concert dance got its start in the work of the dancer-choreographers Ruth St. Denis, Doris Humphrey, Charles Weidman, and Martha Graham. Many of them performed in Broadway shows and in vaudeville as well as on the concert stage. In addition, many former Russian ballet dancers relocated to the United States to perform, choreograph, and teach. The most significant among them was **George Balanchine**.

Balanchine immigrated to New York in 1933 at the invitation of Lincoln Kirstein, a dance impresario who wanted Balanchine to develop ballet for American audiences. While doing so, Balanchine also contributed to Broadway musicals, bringing a concert dance sensibility to the construction of dance. He was the first Broadway choreographer to insist that he be listed in programs as choreographer, not as dance director. For Balanchine, choreography could be about much more than exhibiting the latest dance craze or dazzling an audience with the performer's personality or technique. One of his most innovative contributions came early in his career when he choreographed the **Richard Rodgers** and **Lorenz Hart** musical *On Your Toes* (1936), starring Ray Bolger and Tamara Geva. The musical tells the story of the attraction between a tap dancer and a Russian ballerina. The musical concludes with a 20-minute ballet, "Slaughter on Tenth Avenue," in which a gangster shoots the ballerina and Bolger's character seeks revenge by defeating his adversary through tap dance. Balanchine went on to choreograph many other

JACK COLE AND MODERN MUSICAL THEATER DANCE VOCABULARY

Many musical theater historians acknowledge the invaluable influence of Jack Cole (1919–1974) on dance vocabulary—the manner by which discrete positions and steps convey particular meanings and emotions. Cole performed, directed, and choreographed on Broadway periodically from the 1930s to the 1970s. However, the significance of his Broadway legacy belies his relatively modest number of musical theater credits. His approach to working with dancers bore similarities to that of the revolutionary Stanislavsky method of acting—getting dancers to internalize and even personalize the emotions of the dances they were to learn and perform. He was also a pioneer in opening Broadway choreography to cultural and artistic diversity, bringing new influences and traditions that are now familiar to Broadway audiences—thanks to disciples such as **Bob Fosse**, **Jerome Robbins**, **Michael Bennett**, and Peter Gennaro, who are far better known than he.

Cole began his training and early performing career in modern dance with the Denis Hawn Dance Company and later the Doris Humphrey (1895–1958) and Charles Weidman (1901–1975) Dance Companies. His interest in dance from a wide variety of world cultures was well known. He knew how to capitalize on these varied dance traditions and to marry them with jazz and popular music in unique, interesting, and challenging ways. Some of his musical theater credits include the dances for *Kismet* (1953), *A Funny Thing Happened on the Way to the Forum* (1962), *Kean* (1961), and *Man of La Mancha* (1965). Among his many films is the now classic 1953 Marilyn Monroe comedy *Gentlemen Prefer Blondes* (1953).

musicals including *Cabin in the Sky* (1940) in which he collaborated with African American dancer-choreographer Katherine Dunham.

Show Boat and Oklahoma!

As early as the production of **Show Boat** (1927), Broadway began a movement toward a thorough integration of book, lyrics, and music. The influence of a "new stagecraft" movement created richer visual statements for musicals. Moreover, the influence of **Group Theatre** and Stanislavsky's "Method Acting" theory as well as the accompanying sophistication of new directorial approaches gave the musical increasing complexity of performance. The musical was moving from an exclusively popular entertainment genre to a commercial art form with fine art aspirations. The maturation of that development occurred in 1943 with the opening of *Oklahoma!*

Agnes de Mille in conjunction with composer **Richard Rodgers**, lyricist/librettist **Oscar Hammerstein II**, and director Rouben Mamoulian saw the potential to integrate dance into the narrative of the musical more fully than had earlier shows. Through de Mille's dances, the audience would come to understand otherwise inexpressible aspects in the development of the three principal characters and subtleties of the central conflict between the ranchers and farmers. Primarily through Balanchine and de Mille dance and choreography on the Broadway stage had now been elevated from conspicuous "showstopper" to an artistically integral part of an entire production.

Broadway was ready for this change, and a few choreographers had even anticipated it. Robert Alton had established himself as a well-respected choreographer since the early 1930s. One of his many shows, Cole Porter's musical *Anything Goes* (1934) has been described as the quintessential 1930s musical. Alton is credited for eliminating old-style precision "one-size-fits-all" choreography for chorus numbers and replacing it with choreography that accented the individuality of each chorus dancer within his dances. He anticipated de Mille's later accomplishment by choreographing tap routines that reflected the disintegration of the lead character in *Pal Joey* (1940), played by Gene Kelly.

Soon after, imitators built upon the breakthrough developments of de Mille and Alton. Two of the most successful in their own right were Michael Kidd and Hanya Holm. Kidd began his career performing in ballet with **Jerome Robbins** in the New York Ballet Theater among other companies. He is best known for his athletic electrifying choreography for the film musical *Seven Brides for Seven Brothers* (1954). However, Kidd enjoyed a substantial career as Broadway choreographer on such important musicals as *Finian's Rainbow* (1947), *Can-Can* (1953), *Li'l Abner* (1956) but most notably for *Guys and Dolls* (1950). Like de Mille, he was able to effortlessly integrate small and large group dances into the lives of *Guys and Dolls'* broadly comic characters while adding choreography that introduced a strong sense of athletic competitiveness and humor into the characters' actions and interrelationships.

Whereas Kidd came to Broadway from the American ballet world, Hanya Holm was an American disciple of European modern dance. Along with Martha Graham, Doris Humphrey, and Charles Weidman, she was on the forefront of developing an American modern dance tradition and brought a "modern" sensibility to Broadway choreography. Rather than stamp a particular style on her work, she researched the background for each show. She worked with the dancers as individuals and often used improvisation as a choreographic tool to develop a unique movement vocabulary for each show she choreographed. Among her most well-known shows are *Kiss Me, Kate* (1948), *My Fair Lady* (1956), and *Camelot* (1960).

By the late 1950s, it was inevitable that some of the choreographers would want to direct entire shows as well as create dances for them. Musicals were becoming more complicated and required an increasingly strong directorial vision. Dance was becoming a prominent and popular art form, both on Broadway and on concert stages. George Balanchine was developing at the New York City Ballet a classical yet "American" style that had international appeal. It brought a prominence to ballet in America that had not been realized before. In addition, beginning with the defection of several Russian dancers—from Rudolph Nureyev in 1961 to Mikhail Baryshnikov in 1974—"American" ballet achieved wide popular appeal beyond the traditional ballet audience into the wider audience of musicals and **television**.

At the same time, the modern dance concert stage was exploding with new work and new ideas about dance and choreography. The larger-than-life appeal of Martha Graham, the avant-garde dynamism of Merce Cunningham, and the eclectic youthful exuberance of Paul Taylor created what has become known as "America's dance boom." In the 1950s and 1960s modern dance was "cool," manly, "with it." Dance's new high standing in American culture was mirrored not only in the success of the Hollywood musicals, but it was also reflected on Broadway too.

West Side Story

West Side Story (1957) created a seismic change in the way the Broadway musical was conceived, constructed, and performed—due primarily to the contribution of dance from director-choreographer Jerome Robbins. Broadway had seen musicals in the past in which dance was integral to the production. However, this was the first time that the concept of the musical was envisioned in dance terms with the narrative and music developed from that central idea. Robbins saw in strong visual, kinesthetic, and musical terms how **Shakespeare**'s *Romeo and Juliet* could be placed within contemporary America, which had been slowly coming to terms with ethnic tensions stemming from immigration. For this show, Robbins chose tensions between whites and the newly arrived Puerto Rican community of New York.

Musical comedy, dance, and song have had a long tradition of accommodating new immigrants as they assimilated into American society. While that was generally executed in a lighthearted and satirical way in vaudeville and musical theater, Robbins wanted to address the underbelly of that experience and use dance as its primary vehicle to do so. Robbins, like Gene Kelly, understood that dance had the potential to extend what the musical had to say about romance, masculinity, humor, violence, and a widening emotional range for each character. He accomplished this with collaborators **Leonard Bernstein** (composer), **Stephen Sondheim** (lyricist), and **Arthur Laurents** (book writer). The now familiar story of the Jets and Sharks and how they tease each other in dance ("Dance in the Gym"), poke fun at authority figures in dance ("Gee, Officer Krupke"), define what it is to "be cool" in dance ("Cool"), and fight to the death in dance ("The Rumble") required Robbins to cast "triple threats"; he needed performers who could dance, sing, and act equally well. The success of this ambitious, new kind of musical secured for dance a central rather than a peripheral position in Broadway musicals from then to today.

Another advance occurring at this time—again, reflecting Robbins's considerable influence—was the evolutionary rise of the director-choreographer, one person who fused the two heretofore separate functions. The creation of this position came about for several reasons. Performance of modern musicals now transcended the old model of actors, singers, dancers, and specialty acts performing as separate entities alongside each other in "parallel play." Many new musicals now required performers who could act, sing, and dance seamlessly. The director-choreographer emerged to address this new reality on stage. Moreover, the introduction of more complex scenographic possibilities required a leader who could realize a total visual statement by bringing together narration with music, visual technology, and the performer into one unified whole. The musical itself was also reaching a new level of potential to combine popular appeal with artistic aspiration, taking the musical from mere popular entertainment for a wide audience to an art to be measured alongside the best in theater, dance, music, and film of its day. Robbins continued to set the standard for director-choreographers with shows like **Gypsy** (1959), *A Funny Thing Happened on the Way to the Forum* (1962), and *Fiddler on the Roof* (1964), but there were other innovative choreographers also working at the time.

From his now famous Act II opening number "Steam Heat" from *The Pajama Game* (1954) though his last original Broadway show *Big Deal* (1986), Bob Fosse was a powerful force as director-choreographer for three decades. Fosse developed a signature dance-choreography style: a hunched-over back, unexpected syncopation with different body parts, a keen sensuality, and costumes accentuated with a bowler hat and white gloves. His hit musicals such as *Sweet Charity* (1966), *Pippin* (1972), and *Chicago* (1975) are often characterized by a hard-edged realism along with a self-deprecating style. Other director-choreographers also contributed to the post–*West Side Story* maturity of dance on the Broadway stage. Michael Bennett is best known for conceiving, directing, and choreographing the phenomenally successful **A Chorus Line** (1975). Bennett and his collaborators placed the chorus dancer at the center of the narrative for the musical and, in the process, created a powerful metaphor for the audience by which they could self-identify with having "a role to play" in something larger than themselves, even if that something was to dance in a chorus line. *A Chorus Line* represented the ultimate democratization of the Broadway musical. The longest-running Broadway musical originating in the United States, the show continues to enjoy revivals and nationwide performances. Bennett had other major Broadway successes including his choreography for the Sondheim and **Harold Prince** musical **Company** (1970), which some historians claim as the first successful Broadway "concept" musical. Bennett was also director-choreographer for the hit *Dreamgirls* (1981), in which he choreographed mobile light towers to tell the story of an ostensibly fictitious pop girl trio (although comparisons to the legendary 1960s Motown group The Supremes remain part of the show's legend).

Gower Champion was a director-choreographer who came to the Broadway stage as one-half of the famous ballroom dance team of Marge and Gower Champion. He was unique in that he had established a celebrity status as a dancer in films and on television before beginning his career as a Broadway director-choreographer. Champion perfected a kind of old-style wholesome approach in his choreography. Nonetheless, he was a meticulous craftsman at coordinating all of the elements to create a musical. His biggest successes include *Bye Bye Birdie* (1960), *Carnival!* (1961), and the hugely popular *Hello, Dolly!* (1964). Champion died on opening night of his last and ultimately most successful Broadway show— *42nd Street* (1980).

Tommy Tune is another unique Broadway director-choreographer. He started as a dancer in Broadway shows, including two that had been choreographed by Michael Bennett: *A Joyful Noise* (1966) and *Seesaw* (1973). *The Best Little Whorehouse in Texas* (1978) marked his first Broadway choreographic credit. He went on to direct and choreograph musicals like *A Day in Hollywood/A Night in the Ukraine* (1980), *Grand Hotel* (1989), and *The Will Rodgers Follies* (1991). Tune brings to his direction and choreography a quirky yet highly theatrical sense of movement combined with strong visual imagery. Like Champion, Tune invokes in much of his work a sense of nostalgia for a Broadway of a mythical bygone era.

Toward the Twenty-first Century

Dance on the Broadway stage over the past few decades has been vibrant, eclectic, and central to most musicals. By the late 1960s and early 1970s, dance in musical theater had become more and more individualistic—based increasingly on the needs of a particular show and the individual characters and scenes within the show. The cat-like choreography of London ballet veteran Gillian Lynne for **Cats** (1982) relies more on developing a feline movement vocabulary peculiar to the nature of that show than to a standard musical theater dance vocabulary. Patricia Birch, a student of de Mille and Martha Graham, used Kabuki-style choreography for *Pacific Overtures* (1976), a musical about the opening up of Japan by the United States in 1873. Her choreography required a highly eclectic training for its cast. **Julie Taymor**'s hit musical *The Lion King* (1997), among others, signaled an openness on the part of producers to explore new ways of conceiving musicals. Taymor revamped *The Lion King*, based on the animated Disney film, by rethinking it in terms of strong moving visual imagery. In this case, Taymor brought her background in Indonesian theater and a fascination with **puppetry** arts to collaborate with modern dance choreographer Garth Fagan to create a phantasmagoria of cartoon-like characters in a children's vision of the jungle.

Since the 1990s most Broadway choreographers have come with backgrounds founded on ballet and modern concert dance and now an almost pro forma understanding that each show requires its own theatrical language. Some of the more successful of this more recent generation include Lar Lubovitch, who choreographed the dances for the hits *Into the Woods* (1987), *The Red Shoes* (1993), and the 1996 revival of *The King and I*. Another would be Twyla Tharp, who in addition to her Broadway choreographic credits such as *Singin' in the Rain* (1985) and the Billy Joel jukebox musical *Movin' Out* (2004), would be recognized by film audiences for her dances in such popular films as *Hair*, *Ragtime*, and *Amadeus*. Most recently, concert dance veterans Mark Morris directed and choreographed Paul Simon's *The Capeman* (1998), Bill T. Jones won the Tony Award for his choreography for *Spring Awakening* (2007), and the choreographer known as the "punk ballerina" Karole Armitage created the dances for the rock club–style musical *Passing Strange* (2008). These choreographers create original choreographic approaches to the musicals that they work on, deliberately refraining from recycling Broadway musical theater movement from the past unless to do so directly suits the needs of a specific show.

While not all musicals require a director-choreographer in the same person, this role continues to inform contemporary musical theater. Today, however, that role is not exclusively held by men. Two women director-choreographers have enjoyed considerable success in recent years: **Susan Stroman** and Graciela Daniele. Stroman started as a Broadway dancer and **Off-Broadway** choreographer in the 1980s. Her first significant Broadway choreographic credit was the thoroughly researched, cleverly staged dances for Hal Prince's revival of *Show Boat* in 1994. Her first Broadway director-choreographer production was the dance suite *Contact* (2000), which earned her the Tony Award for Best Musical and accompanying awards for her direction and choreography. The following year, she received the Tony Award for Best Musical, Best Direction of a Musical, and Best Choreography for her Herculean efforts on the Mel Brooks hit, ***The Producers*** (2001). Stroman tends to choreograph performers and scenery in the style that is appropriate to the period of the musical she is working on. Daniele came to Broadway from her native Argentina. She studied modern dance with Martha Graham and Merce Cunningham and performed in the chorus of several Broadway musicals in the 1960s. By the 1980s, she was choreographing and receiving awards for musicals, including *The Pirates of Penzance* (1981), *The Rink* (1984), and *The Mystery of Edwin Drood* (1986). Her first director-choreographer Broadway credit was *Once on This Island* (1990). She has continued to direct and choreograph innovative, avant-garde Broadway musicals including *Chronicle of a Death Foretold* (1995) and *Marie Christine* (1999) as well as the more commercially appealing *Chita Rivera: The Dancer's Life* (2005). She often chooses potentially noncommercial musicals to explore unusual subject matter and unique choreographic structures.

If it is true, as Confucius observed centuries ago, that "a nation's character is typified by its dancers," then Broadway choreographers have reflected an American culture that is diverse, vital, electric, and innovative. There is a dynamic quality that informed Broadway musical dance from its inception. There is also an assumed optimism that characterizes much of the dance on the Broadway musical theater stage. This does not mean that the subject matter is superficial. Looking at dance on the Broadway stage during the half century between *West Side Story* and *Spring Awakening* confirms that serious subject matter can inspire life-affirming choreography and performance. Fundamentally, the Broadway musical is romantic in the sense that it affirms our past while invoking a forward affirmation into our uncertain future. Dance is the keystone where they meet in our present.

Ray Miller

Further Reading

Grody, Svetlana Mclee, and Lister, Dorothy Daniels. *Conversations with Choreographers*. Portsmouth, NH: Heinemann, 1996.

Kislan, Richard. *Hoofing on Broadway: A History of Show Dancing*. New York: Prentice-Hall Press, 1987.

Long, Robert Emmet. *Broadway the Golden Years: Jerome Robbins and the Great Choreographer-Directors 1940 to the Present*. New York: Continuum, 2001.

Society of Stage Directors and Choreographers. http://ssdc.org.

Stearns, Marshall and Jean. *Jazz Dance: The Story of American Vernacular Dance*. New York: Schirmer Books, 1968.

DAVIS, OSSIE (1917–2005)
ACTOR, WRITER, DIRECTOR

Ossie Davis figured prominently in the advances made by African Americans in theater and film throughout the latter half of the twentieth century. In a performing and writing career that spanned six decades, his distinguished and complex performances helped elevate African American actors from stereotyped roles to sophisticated dramatic parts—particularly in theater. Davis's lifelong commitment to civil rights, which he saw as inextricably linked to his career as an artist, placed him literally at the sides of Martin Luther King Jr. and Malcolm X and made him a noteworthy historical figure within the Civil Rights Movement over and above his celebrity status.

Davis was born and raised in Cogdell, Georgia. Originally named Raiford Chatman, Davis was inadvertently renamed Ossie when a courthouse clerk misheard his mother pronounce "R.C." while filing her son's birth certificate. He attended college at Howard University in Washington, D.C., where he developed a lifelong love of playwriting. While at Howard, Davis studied under Professor Alain Locke, one of the intellectual spearheads of the Harlem Renaissance. Locke introduced Davis to the works of Harlem Renaissance authors and encouraged him to pursue theater. The influence of Locke's mentorship had a lasting impact on Davis as he committed himself to a life of theater and activism for racial justice more or less simultaneously.

Davis left Howard after his junior year to begin his professional theater career in New York. On Locke's recommendation he joined the **Rose McClendon** Players, a Harlem-based theater group named for the then recently deceased Harlem Renaissance actress and director. The Players staged their productions almost exclusively in neighborhood buildings. Davis's experiences in these venues solidified his belief in the importance of community-based artistic outlets to the social development of African American urban neighborhoods. He remained active in African American community-based theater, both professional and amateur, throughout his career.

Davis continued to work with the McClendon Players until the start of World War II, when he served overseas in the army. After Davis completed military service, Richard Campbell, a director with the McClendon Players with Broadway connections, arranged for him try out for the title role in *Jeb* (1946), a new play by Robert Ardrey. Davis won the part and made his Broadway debut. Although the play ran only a week, Davis impressed critics and producer/director Herman Shumlin, who had directed Broadway plays by **Lillian Hellman**, **Thornton Wilder**, and James Thurber. *Jeb* was also significant in that Davis met and eventually married Ruby Dee, a young actress in the cast. Their marriage evolved into an enduring

Ossie Davis in the title role, as Purlie Victorious Judson in Purlie Victorious. *The play, written by Ossie Davis and directed by Howard Da Silva, ran on Broadway from 1961 to 1962. (Courtesy of Photofest)*

theatrical and personal partnership that lasted from 1948 until Davis's death in 2005.

In the five years following *Jeb*, Davis performed regularly on Broadway. His reputation grew as he turned in winning performances while working with many of the leading theater artists of the day: Garson Kanin and Ruth Gordon (in *The Leading Lady*, 1948), **Joshua Logan** and **Helen Hayes** (in *The Wisteria Trees*, 1950), and **George S. Kaufman** (in *The Royal Family*, 1951). Although he worked occasionally in **television** and **film**, including the title role in a 1955 *Kraft Television Theatre* production of **Eugene O'Neill**'s *The Emperor Jones*, Davis concentrated on stage work during the 1950s.

Davis's first role in a genuine Broadway hit came in the Harold Arlen and E. Y. Harburg **musical** *Jamaica* (1957). The show ran 555 performances over 18 months. The visibility of *Jamaica* led to Davis's leading role on Broadway—replacing Sidney Poitier as Walter Lee Younger in the original production of Lorraine Hansberry's *A Raisin in the Sun* (1959). Sharing the stage with him was Ruby Dee as his wife, Ruth Younger.

Even as Davis found increasing success onstage, he maintained the commitment to playwriting he had cultivated at Howard. In 1953, his one-act play *Alice in*

Wonder was produced in Harlem. The play addressed governmental oppression during the McCarthy era. Davis's ambitions to write for Broadway were realized with the opening of his *Purlie Victorious* (1961), a satire on racial stereotyping. **Critics** and audiences loved *Purlie Victorious*, especially co-stars Davis and Dee. The show ran for 261 performances, giving Davis the greatest commercial writing and acting successes of his career. He reprised his lead role in the 1963 film adaptation of the play, entitled *Gone Are the Days.* (Initially unsuccessful, a re-release of the film under the title of the original play fared better.) In 1970 a musical adaptation of the play, *Purlie*, became a hit, running for nearly 700 performances and earning Davis a Tony nomination as co-author for the book. Davis would achieve his last Broadway success replacing Cleavon Little as Midge in Herb Gardiner's *I'm Not Rappaport* (1985). Davis particularly admired the play's presentation of an African American character whose fate and dialog are not centered upon racial issues.

Throughout his career, and during the 1960s in particular, Davis worked tenaciously for civil rights. In August 1963, Davis and Dee helped organize the historic civil rights march and demonstration at the Lincoln Memorial in Washington, D.C. (best known as the site of Martin Luther King Jr.'s "I Have a Dream" speech). The two also served as master and mistress of ceremonies. Davis's own considerable skills as an orator and his close association with the Civil Rights Movement later led to family invitations for him to deliver eulogies at the funerals of King and Malcolm X.

Davis also worked steadily in television and film throughout his career, principally as an actor but also, occasionally, as a writer. Although he never won a top-level industry film or television award, he and Dee earned multiple honors within the black entertainment community for their artistic work and social activism. Davis won a Screenwriter's Guild Award in 1983 as co-author of *For Us the Living: The Medgar Evers Story*, a televised biography of the young Mississippi civil rights worker who was murdered by Ku Klux Klan members in 1963. The Screen Actors Guild presented both Davis and Dee with lifetime achievement awards in 2001, and the two received the Kennedy Center Honors in 2004.

Davis was still making television, stage, and personal appearances up until his death. He died in Miami, Florida, on February 5, 2005, shortly after battling pneumonia.

Thomas A. Greenfield and Nicholas J. Ponterio

Further Reading

Davis, Ossie, and Ruby Dee. *With Ossie and Ruby: In This Life Together.* New York: W. Morrow, 1998.

Donalson, Melvin Burke. *Black Directors in Hollywood.* Austin: University of Texas Press, 2003.

DE MILLE, AGNES (1905–1993)
DANCER, CHOREOGRAPHER

Agnes de Mille ushered in the choreography of the postwar Golden Age of **musicals**, beginning with her revolutionary work in **Rodgers and Hammerstein**'s *Oklahoma!* (1943). Over the next eight years, she pioneered choreography for the "book" musical, adapting the psychological, emotive, and storytelling powers of ballet and modern dance to musical theater. Her choreography for *Oklahoma!*, *Carousel* (1945), *Gentleman Prefer Blondes* (1949), *Brigadoon* (1950), and *Paint Your Wagon* (1951) collectively set new standards of complexity and depth of expression for Broadway show dancing. Younger colleagues and competitors, such as **Jerome Robbins** and **Bob Fosse**, would soon thereafter expand upon her pioneering vision and significantly elevate the role of choreographer and choreography in the modern musical.

De Mille was born in 1905 in Harlem, New York, to a family of artists, her father, **playwright** William de Mille, and her uncle, **film** producer/director Cecil B. De Mille, being the most notable among them. Her family moved to Hollywood when she was a child, and she grew up in the company of artists, writers, and filmmakers. She developed and sustained a childhood interest in ballet, despite family disapproval of what they considered to be a dubious career pursuit. She persuaded her parents to let her take dance lessons as a teenager and continued studying dance as a student at UCLA. By all accounts, including her own, she showed little promise for her chosen profession but remained undeterred.

After college she moved back to New York City, then as now the capital of the American dance world. Early professional jobs included a well-reviewed solo choreography piece entitled "Stage Fright" (1928) and a stint as a dancer and choreographer in a 1929 revival of the nineteenth-century musical melodrama *The Black Crook* in New Jersey. In 1932 she worked and studied in Europe with leading ballet choreographers of the day, including Marie Rambert and Anthony Tudor. Intermittently she returned to the states to take various jobs, including a minor acting role in her

Dancer and choreographer Agnes de Mille poses in New York City, 1944. (AP Photo)

uncle's film *Cleopatra* (1934) and an assignment as choreographer for MGM Studio's film version of *Romeo and Juliet* (1936).

In 1939, de Mille joined the in New York Ballet Theater (later renamed American Ballet Theatre), from which she began her rapid ascent in the world of dance. The following year she choreographed her first ballet, *Black Ritual* (1940), the first of the Ballet Theatre's dances to use black dancers. The success of *Black Ritual* led to more offers—including one from the world-renowned Ballet Russe de Monte Carlo, for whom she would choreograph "Rodeo" in 1942. This American Western-themed piece helped establish her as an important new talent in New York dance circles and served as preparation for *Oklahoma!*

De Mille did not specifically aspire to choreograph for Broadway and, in 1943, had virtually no musical theater track record. However, by that time the two Manhattan-based worlds of musical theater and concert dance had been interconnected for years. Dance masters **George Balanchine** and Charles Weidman had each enhanced their reputations (and income) with several popular Broadway musicals and revues. Richard Rodgers, the composer of *Oklahoma!*, had worked with ballet-trained choreographers before, including Balanchine, and was familiar with de Mille's recent work. Accounts vary somewhat over the degree to which the choreographer pursued the composer and **producers** to get the job or vice versa, but the historical verdict on de Mille's contribution to *Oklahoma!* is unanimous.

De Mille's choreography for *Oklahoma!* is universally heralded as one of the splendors of the show and a breakthrough in Broadway dancing. Most famously the extended "dream sequence," in which de Mille opens up the unspoken inner thoughts and desires of the main female character, Laurie, brought interpretive dance to a mass audience in a way they would understand and thrill to. De Mille immediately became Broadway's most important and most imitated choreographer. (Many believe she still is.) Her work in *Oklahoma!* and her other hit shows (*Carousel* and *Brigadoon* in particular) permanently elevated the public stature and industry clout of the Broadway choreographer.

Although she received high praise for adapting her original stage choreography for the 1955 film of *Oklahoma!*, de Mille would soon surrender her preeminence on Broadway to the likes of Jerome Robbins, Robert Fosse, and later, **Tommy Tune**. She continued to work in musical theater, often on revivals of her masterpieces as well as new shows (including *Goldilocks* [1958] and *110 in the Shade* [1963]). But she never matched the achievement of her earlier years. However, de Mille prospered through the 1960s and 1970s as a prolific choreographer for the American Ballet Theatre as well as her own dance companies. She was still participating in the creation of new dance works into the 1980s and even the early 1990s.

De Mille was also a highly regarded author, who wrote over ten books. *To a Young Dancer* (1962) is widely considered to be an indispensable work for dance initiates, and her 1992 biography of friend and colleague Martha Graham, *Martha: The Life and Work of Martha Graham*, is a valuable contribution to modern dance history. De Mille won virtually every award her Broadway and concert dance careers had to offer, including the Tony Award (for choreography in *Brigadoon*) and the Kennedy Center Career Achievement Award.

De Mille died of a stroke in New York City in 1993.

Thomas A. Greenfield and Nicole Katz

Further Reading

Hasday, Judy L. *Agnes De Mille*. New York: Chelsea House, 2003.

Hischak, Thomas. *The Rodgers and Hammerstein Encyclopedia*. Westport, CT: Greenwood, 2007.

DEATH OF A SALESMAN

Broadway Run: Morosco Theatre
Opening: February 10, 1949
Closing: November 18, 1950
Total Performances: 742
Author: Arthur Miller
Director: Elia Kazan
Producer: Kermit Bloomgarden and Walter Fried
Lead Performers: Lee J. Cobb (Willy Loman); Mildred Dunnock (Linda Loman); Arthur Kennedy (Biff); and Cameron Mitchell (Happy)

When **Brooks Atkinson** reviewed the original Broadway production of **Arthur Miller**'s *Death of a Salesman* in the *New York Times* (February 10, 1949), he gave the impression that he was seeing two dramas playing out at once. On the one hand he was deeply moved by Miller's tale of Willy Loman's Sophoclean march to self-destruction being played out masterfully and achingly upon the stage. But no less telling was Atkinson's thrall at the cast members' unmistakable self-consciousness that "for once in their lives they (were) participating in a rare event in the theatre."

The "rare event" turned out to be an epiphany in American theater and culture. *Death of a Salesman* leapt almost immediately from Broadway into the fabric of modern literature, world theater, American education, and national culture. By most observations and calculations, it is one of the two or three most widely read or seen plays ever written by an American. Even 60 years after its Broadway premiere, a plethora of *Salesman* productions, production reviews, books, academic papers, and articles emerge every year.

For shear literary merit, it is routinely ranked along with **Eugene O'Neill**'s *Long Day's Journey into Night* (1956) and **Tennessee Williams**'s *A Streetcar Named Desire* (1947) as among America's finest achievements in dramatic writing. In 1995 the Modern Language Association (MLA), the influential professional

Death of a Salesman, *from its original run on Broadway, 1949–1950. Shown from left: Mildred Dunnock as Linda Loman, Lee J. Cobb as Willy Loman, Arthur Kennedy as Biff Loman, and Cameron Mitchell as Happy Loman.* (Courtesy of Photofest)

association for the nation's English professors, speculated that *Salesman* is the most commonly taught play in America and, on the strength of that assumption, produced an extensive book-length study on the teaching of the play.

Miller was a 33-year-old, promising new voice in American theater when Broadway's leading director of serious drama, **Elia Kazan**, agreed to direct and co-produce *Death of a Salesman*. The two had just collaborated on Miller's first Broadway success, *All My Sons* (1947), for which each man had won a Tony Award—for best play and best director, respectively. (Miller had made an inauspicious Broadway debut three years earlier with *The Man That Had All the Luck*; the show closed in three days.)

Although Kazan enjoyed a successful career as a Hollywood filmmaker—having recently directed his critically acclaimed *A Tree Grows in Brooklyn* and his Oscar-winning *A Gentleman's Agreement* (both 1945)—he had plenty of reason for staying in New York to direct Miller's next project. Over and above his previous success with *All My Sons*, Kazan coveted his emerging reputation as America's premiere director of both film and stage. In addition, although he had directed the original Broadway production of Williams's *Streetcar* immediately after staging *All My Sons*, his next two Broadway productions were decidedly less successful. Moreover, during the production of *All My Sons*, Miller and Kazan (Miller's senior by nine years of age and 15 years of professional experience) had formed an intensely close friendship that they themselves would describe as that of kindred spirits and brothers.

This friendship—from its numerous artistic collaborations, to the shared interest in famous women (most notably Marilyn Monroe), to its eventual dissolution in the wake of the House Un-American Activities Commission hearings on alleged communist infiltration of the entertainment industry—would itself become a real-life show business drama of loyalty, integrity, and betrayal. However, in 1948, at the height of their friendship, Kazan and Miller set about developing a modern tragedy based upon the world of struggling salesmen that Miller knew all too well growing up in New York during the Depression.

During casting for the play, Miller and Kazan expressed different visions for how the main character, Willy Loman, should be played and what kind of actor should play him. Miller wanted an actor who was short in stature and could bring a comedic quality to the role. But relatively early on Kazan had in mind **Lee J. Cobb**, a friend and colleague from his Depression-era days in the **Group Theatre**. The barrel-chested, broad-shouldered, growly voiced Cobb presented little of the "shrimp" of a man Miller had originally conceived, but after Cobb auditioned Miller deferred to Kazan's wishes. From opening night Lee J. Cobb's exhausted, elephantine Willy Loman became the face and body of the character and the iconic image of the play itself (even though Fredric March would play Willy in the 1951 film). Miller would complain decades later that Cobb's lumbering performance trampled essential comic subtleties out of the role. But the American public—including the professional, amateur, and educational theater communities that quickly absorbed the play into its standard repertoire—had embraced Cobb's stage performance and, by extension, Kazan's rather than Miller's original vision of the character.

At 742 performances, *Death of a Salesman* did not come anywhere near setting box-office or longevity records for its time—even when compared with other Broadway dramas. Jack Kirkland's *Tobacco Road* (1933), Patrick Hamilton's *Angel Street* (1931), Philip Yadoff's *Anna Lucasta* (1944), and Jerome Lawrence and Robert Lee's *Inherit the Wind* (1955) all had longer runs. But none has had a comparable impact upon Broadway or American culture.

In the ensuing years, numerous artists, including actor Dustin Hoffman and **playwright** Adrienne Kennedy, would cite *Death of a Salesman* as a critical influence and inspiration in their decision to work in professional theater. (To Miller's delight, the athletic, agile, short Hoffman gave a subtly tragic-comedic performance as Willy in a 1984 Broadway revival of *Salesman* and a widely praised **television** staging of the play. Miller, at long last seeing the comedic undertones of the character come to life in production, hailed Hoffman's performance as better than Cobb's.) Countless scholars and teachers of dramatic literature also point to their youthful encounters with the play as milestone events in their careers. But perhaps the greatest testimony to *Death of a Salesman*'s timelessness is that in the 60 years since its Broadway premiere, audiences from New York, to Wyoming, to Hawaii, to Dublin, to Paris, to Beijing, have embraced the play as a penetrating examination of their own lives, their own cultures, and their own times.

Thomas A. Greenfield

Further Reading

Kazan, Elia. *Elia Kazan: A Life*. Cambridge. MA: Da Capo, 1997.
Miller, Arthur. *Timebends: A Life*. London: Methuen, 1999.

DISNEY THEATRICAL PRODUCTIONS
PRODUCER

The Walt Disney Company, a corporate titan in the field of family entertainment since the 1930s, brought its iconic brand to Broadway with the opening of *Beauty and the Beast* (1994), an adaptation of their 1991 animated **film**. The show featured music by Alan Menken and lyrics by Howard Ashman and Tim Rice. What ultimately became the Broadway **musical** had started out as a rather modest 20-minute stage show unveiled at one of the Disney theme parks shortly after the film's release. Disney then developed the full musical, which tried out in Houston in 1993 under the auspices of the newly formed Walt Disney Theatrical Productions. The mission of Disney Theatricals, as it is commonly known, was to bring the Disney brand to Broadway theater, which had been newly revitalized by successful spectacles from Europe, such as *Les Misérables* (1987) and ***The Phantom of the Opera*** (1988).

Beauty and the Beast proved to be an auspicious beginning for Disney Theatricals. It was nominated for nine Tony Awards, winning one for its innovative and extravagant costume designs. The show ran for 13 years, making it at the time of its closing in 2007 the sixth longest-running show in Broadway history. Worldwide it has earned over $1 billion. With its first hit, Disney Theatricals emerged quickly as a major force on Broadway.

Disney's early success in adapting its animated films to Broadway is due in large measure to the work of Menken and Ashman. The pair had established themselves as a successful songwriting team with *Little Shop of Horrors*, which became a long-running hit **Off-Broadway** in 1982. Several years later they would provide a distinctly Broadway sound to the 1989 animated film *The Little Mermaid*, whose success launched a new era in animation for Disney Studios. The films *Beauty and the Beast* and *Aladdin* (1992) followed, both with songs by Menken and Ashman. Disney's next major animated film, *The Lion King* (1994), won two Academy Awards for music by Elton John and Tim Rice and became the world's most successful traditional animated feature. **Julie Taymor**, a highly respected designer, director, and puppeteer who had worked primarily in New York experimental theater, was selected to design and direct *The Lion King* for Broadway.

The Lion King premiered in November 1997. For the opening number, "Circle of Life," a pageant of masked actors and puppets representing giraffes, elephants, birds, lions, and all manner of beasts astonished the audience and **critics** with magical, uplifting innovative design and staging. The adaptation included an infusion of African sounds with additional music and chants. The show was another triumph for Disney. It won six Tony Awards, including Best Musical and Best Director for Julie Taymor, making her the first woman ever to win a Tony for directing a musical.

Reflecting confidence earned from their previous successes, Disney Theatricals' next project was not cartoon based. *Aida* (2000), with music and lyrics by Elton John and Tim Rice, played on Broadway for four years. *Tarzan* (2006), another adaptation of a Disney animated film, was the first Disney Theatricals venture to fall short of genuine hit status. It received negative reviews but still ran a respectable 14 months. The much-loved score of the 1964 Disney film *Mary Poppins* made it a prime candidate for the stage. The musical of *Mary Poppins*, which opened in London in 2004, arrived on Broadway in 2006, where it still enjoys a successful run. (New songs have been added to the original score, but the film's hits "A Spoonful of Sugar" and "Supercalifragilisticexpialidocious" are the production's showstoppers.) Nineteen years after the release of the film, *The Little Mermaid* opened on Broadway in 2008 with great fanfare (mixed with skepticism) owing to its elaborately staged representation of life beneath the sea.

Disney's influence on Broadway has extended far beyond the considerable impact of its musical productions. Since the 1990s Disney has become increasingly involved in theater restoration as well as the famous (and occasionally controversial) "cleaning up" of the Times Square theater district toward the end of the twentieth century. Disney began its restoration interests by announcing plans to restore Broadway's New Amsterdam Theatre. Built in 1903, the New Amsterdam was the home of the *Ziegfeld Follies* until 1937. The historic but crumbling theater had been taken over in 1992 by the City of New York, who turned over renovation to Disney in 1993. The $34 million renovation of the theater was completed in 1997.

The arrival of Disney in the theater district sent an important signal to the theatergoing public that Times Square at night had changed from the seedy haven for pornography, drugs, and prostitution it had been for decades to a family-friendly tourist attraction. While the effort to turn Times Square into a safe commercial center required enormous investments from numerous public and private concerns, Disney's brand has become closely identified with the project. The transformation of Times Square is widely hailed as a success, although some New Yorkers lament that the theater district has taken on the pointedly non–New York appearance and the feel of a Disney theme park.

Because Disney's corporate history is unique among Broadway producers, Disney Theatricals functions in ways that are uniquely its own—at times to the dismay of Broadway traditionalists. Disney stage shows sometimes completely bypass Broadway. *The Hunchback of Notre Dame* opened in Berlin in 1999. The staged revue of Disney tunes, *On The Record* (2004), has toured to several cities nationally without a Broadway appearance. Ironically, Disney's *High School Musical* (2006)—based on American high schools' long-standing love affair with Broadway musicals—premiered as a made-for-TV production. With three sequels, an ice show, video games, and numerous local productions, *High School Musical* has generated enormous income, with licensed local productions and national touring versions. However, to date it has not played on Broadway. The show has been criticized for being formulaic, but it has created new stars and kindled dreams of musical theater stardom in countless twenty-first-century teenagers.

Disney Theatricals, which does not belong to the Broadway League (the official professional association of Broadway producers), negotiates its own contracts with the theatrical unions. Disney resources include the rights to its catalog of audience-pleasing titles and characters going back over 80 years. Since the 1950s Disney has been a pioneer in cross-marketing (using the company's films, television, theatrical productions, merchandising, theme parks, etc., to promote and support each other). Thus, Disney can cross-promote its Broadway shows on a scale far exceeding the capabilities of most other Broadway producers. Walt Disney Theatrical Productions has also helped change the profile of the Broadway audience over the past 20 years to include millions of children, ages 5 to 15. For most of the post–World War II period children had been a limited market for Broadway, especially prior to the reclamation of Times Square. However, today, instead of looking and waiting for the rare "suitable" show, parents and grandparents can now choose from many family-friendly theater selections—whether produced by Disney Theatricals or other producers tapping into what can fairly be called Disney's market.

Steve Abrams

Further Reading

Griffin, Sean. *Tinker Belles and Evil Queens: The Walt Disney Company from the Inside Out.* New York: New York University Press, 2000.
Taymor, Julie, and Eileen Blumenthal. *Playing with Fire.* New York: Harry Abrams, 1999.

DRAKE, ALFRED (1914–1992)
ACTOR

Alfred Drake was the most successful of the robust, hardy "matinee idol" baritone actor/singers who were mainstays on Broadway during the Golden Age of **musicals** from 1943 to the mid-1960s. Heading an impressive list of dashing young leading men that included **John Raitt**, Richard Kiley, Robert Goulet, Robert Preston, and Robert Alda, Drake possessed charm, good looks, and charisma reminiscent of Hollywood's traditional romantic male movie stars. A skilled dramatic actor, Drake's ability to sing movingly while remaining in character made him a critical asset to the hit original productions of *Oklahoma!* (1943) and *Kiss Me*

Kate (1948), as well as *Kismet* (1953) for which he won a Tony Award for Best Actor in a Musical. His performance of "Oh What a Beautiful Morning," the solo number that opens *Oklahoma!*, was in and of itself a landmark performance in modern musical theater.

Born Alfred Capurro, Drake was raised in Brooklyn, New York, and began singing seriously in childhood. Drawn early on to opera and the **operettas** of **Gilbert and Sullivan**, he attended Brooklyn College where he joined the glee club and performed light opera and choral music. Drake made his first Broadway appearance in the ensemble of a 1935 revival of the operetta *The Mikado*. For the next eight years he would work almost continuously in numerous short or limited-run Broadway productions, starting with Gilbert and Sullivan operettas such as *The Pirates of Penzance*, *The Yeomen of the Guard*, and *H.M.S. Pinafore* (all in repertory in 1935). He later expanded into comedies, revues, and musicals, including holding down two small parts in **Richard Rodgers** and **Lorenz Hart**'s hit musical *Babes in Arms* (1937). By the time he won the lead role of the affable, winsome Curly in **Rodgers and Hammerstein**'s *Oklahoma!*, Drake, at 28, while virtually unknown to the public, had established himself within the theater community as a versatile, capable young actor and singer.

The longest-running musical up to that time, *Oklahoma!* ran for over five years and revolutionized almost every aspect of Broadway musical theater, including the way musicals are written, composed, staged, choreographed, and marketed. Drake's performance in particular created a new demand in musicals for young, energetic romantic Hollywood-type leading men. The next 20 years saw a plethora of such roles emerging on Broadway. While Drake picked up his share of these roles in the years following *Oklahoma!*, including *Kiss Me Kate* and *Kismet*, other young leading actors found success originating memorable brawny-yet-sensitive characters whose voices could project emotively to the upper balcony. Raitt starred as Billy Bigelow in *Carousel* (1945) and Sid Sorokin in *The Pajama Game* (1954). Robert Alda won a Tony Award as Sky Masterson in *Guys and Dolls* (1950). Goulet starred as Lancelot in *Camelot* (1960), Preston starred as Harold Hill in *The Music Man* (1957), and Kiley starred as Don Quixote in *Man of La Mancha* (1965).

To be sure, some hit musicals of this period went off-trend and presented older "exotic" romantic leading men whose age, appearance, and national origins contrasted sharply with those of the Drake/Curly prototype. London theater star **Rex Harrison** became a Broadway legend as the fiftyish linguistics Professor Henry Higgins in ***My Fair Lady*** (1956). Italian actor Ezio Pinza triumphed as a love-struck, middle-aged, French landowner in *South Pacific* (1949). At the height of the Cold War, Russian-born actor Yul Brynner became an unlikely American icon as the bald, widowed father and autocratic monarch in *The King and I* (1951). But the hale, white, broad-shouldered, rich-voiced "common man" that Alfred Drake, *Oklahoma!*, and Curly ushered onto the Broadway stage in 1943 represented the predominating musical hero of the times.

When the Broadway musical began to outgrow its golden era during the mid-1960s, new kinds of musicals came to the fore and different kinds of leading roles emerged. As Broadway responded to the increasing social tensions of the 1960s, the charismatic young heterosexual, leading man began to fall from prominence. The new social debates over political freedom, feminism, civil rights, antimilitarism, and gay/lesbian rights all served to make characters like Curly seem cloyingly quaint and culturally irrelevant. However, Drake was able to utilize his versatility when both his age and the changing face of Broadway meant he would no longer be getting lucrative, long-running leading roles in musicals. Unlike some of his contemporaries, Drake worked regularly on Broadway well into the 1970s, moving easily out of the romantic leading prototype he had helped create into lesser dramatic roles and other theatrical endeavors. Of Drake's last five Broadway appearances, only one was a musical: the 1973 **Lerner and Loewe** adaptation of *Gigi* in which Drake, approaching 60, played the decidedly nonromantic role of Uncle Honore. He also performed in a successful revival of *Hamlet* (1964) and a short-lived revival of **Thornton Wilder**'s *The Skin of Our Teeth* (1975). Along the way he also directed and adapted scripts for production and even translated an Italian musical into English for a Broadway run (*Rugantino*, 1964).

Sporadically throughout his career Drake worked on **television**, usually participating in prestige drama productions on such programs as *The Hallmark Hall of Fame* or network special presentations of a theatrical production. Despite his "Hollywood" good looks, Drake did very little **film** work.

In 1990 the **American Theatre Wing** presented Drake with a special Tony Honor of Excellence in Theater Award. The award recognized his achievements throughout his 40-plus-year career, even though Drake had made his mark in the 1940s and 1950s as Broadway's leading man among leading men.

Drake died on July 25, 1992, from cancer in New York City.

Thomas A. Greenfield and Sean Roche

Further Reading

Mordden, Ethan. *Broadway Babies: The People Who Made the American Musical.* New York: Oxford University Press, 1988.

Carter, Tim. *Oklahoma!: The Making of an American Musical.* New Haven, CT: Yale University Press, 2007.

European "Megamusicals"

The Broadway **musical** traces its roots to both American and European traditions, the music-and-story mix of **operetta** being principal among the latter. However, ever since *Show Boat* in 1927 it has been widely viewed as a distinctively American art form. Musical story lines are often steeped in American myths (*Oklahoma!*) and imbued with American sensibilities of innocence and optimism even if some of the musicals themselves were not set in the United States (*Fiddler on the Roof*). However, over the past 30 years, two Englishmen have proved that there is nothing essentially American about the musical genre that could not be duplicated abroad. **Andrew Lloyd Webber**, a composer and **producer**, and **Cameron Mackintosh**, a producer, have been responsible for the majority of the greatest financial successes among Broadway musicals since the late 1970s, and their shows share many similar aesthetic elements, most importantly the use of popular music. The enormity of Lloyd Webber and Mackintosh's commercial success and their flare for onstage spectacle begat the begrudgingly flattering term "European megamusical" as journalistic and industry shorthand for their shows or any Broadway "import" from Europe produced and marketed in their grand fashion.

Certainly there had been notable musicals on Broadway imported from the London stage throughout the twentieth century. In addition to his straight comedies, Noël Coward's musicals appeared sporadically on Broadway from the 1920s through the 1960s. Lionel Bart's *Oliver* (1963) was an enormous Broadway hit. The comic operettas of **Gilbert and Sullivan** have also appeared on Broadway stages regularly since the 1920s and are still frequently revived. But prior to the 1970s, financially and artistically successful English musicals on Broadway had been relatively few and far between. What has made the work of Lloyd Webber and Mackintosh stand out on Broadway from the European imports of the past is the scale on which their shows are produced. Lloyd Webber/Mackintosh presales continually break their own revenue records. They brand their shows and sell show-related merchandise on an unprecedented scale and, in the process, reap enormous profits for investors in the risky business of theater producing.

Between them, Lloyd Webber and Mackintosh currently hold the top three spots for the longest-running shows on Broadway: **The Phantom of the Opera** (1988, with music by Lloyd Webber and produced by Mackintosh) surpassed **Cats** (1982) in January 2006 and is still running, presenting its 8,700th performance in January 2009. *Cats*, also with music by Lloyd Webber and produced by Mackintosh, still holds the second position. *Les Misérables* (2003), which was produced by Mackintosh, is in third place. Lloyd Webber is not only the most popular musical theater composer living but he also has a strong business sense. Under the name of his producing organization, the Really Useful Group, he has coproduced most of his own musicals and some by other composers, *Bombay Dreams* (2004) or the 2006 London revival of *The Sound of Music*. He also owns seven West End theaters. Likewise, it is the combination of artistic and business practices that has led to the tremendous success of Lloyd Webber and Mackintosh's style of musical theater on Broadway.

Andrew Lloyd Webber has nearly single-handedly brought popular music and the Broadway stage back together, restoring Broadway to the kind of popularity it had before the advent of rock and roll in the 1950s. His music reflects many styles, but most critics agree it is rock and roll, nineteenth-century Romantic music (operas in particular), and the musicals of **Richard Rodgers** that have had the greatest influence on him as a composer. Like Rodgers before him, Lloyd Webber purposefully composes one or more hit songs for each of his scores. However, he pioneered the strategy of recording and marketing those hit songs in advance of any theatrical production. It is this generation of hits on the popular airwaves, from *Jesus Christ Superstar*'s "I Don't Know How to Love Him" to *Cats*' "Memory," followed by intensive marketing, which has driven his advance Broadway ticket sales to unprecedented levels.

Lloyd Webber's first Broadway show, *Jesus Christ Superstar* (1972), with lyricist Tim Rice, was a modest success at best. The show's soundtrack recording, released over a year before a stage production of the show had been produced, had generated plenty of radio airplay and healthy record sales, making the 23-year-old composer prosperous (if not yet genuinely wealthy) and famous on two continents. However, in the hands of director Tom O'Horgan the flamboyant Broadway production earned mixed reviews at best.

Lloyd Webber's first genuine Broadway triumph, again with lyricist Rice, was *Evita* (1979), directed by Broadway veteran **Hal Prince**. The advance ticket sales followed the release of the hit song "Don't Cry for Me Argentina," and the show ran nearly four years. A loosely biographical retelling of real-life Argentinean actress and First Lady Eva Peron's rise to power in the 1940s, *Evita* set a pattern for even greater successes to come. Like his earlier works, but unlike most Broadway shows of the time, *Evita* was sung throughout. The character Che sang the necessary exposition, setting up scenes and offering ironic commentary on Evita and husband/ruler Juan's political fortunes. The score includes several reprised melodies associated with characters or emotional moments and identifiable motifs that return repeatedly until even relatively unsophisticated theatergoers can hear them. The staging along with the music provide the main foci of the show, while plot and characterization are less fully developed than they had been in most other successful musicals up to that time. Prince's staging included military-style formations for the Argentinean military, a game of musical chairs among would-be dictators that leaves Juan Peron alone onstage at the end, and rousingly chaotic scenes of Evita's devoted poor, the *descamisados*, who want her sainted. The signature song "Don't Cry for Me Argentina" is strategically placed just after intermission, and in it Eva trumps her husband's speech and has Argentina's oppressed populace eating out of her hand. The drama onstage matches the power of the music.

Cats (1982) marked the first collaboration of Lloyd Webber and Mackintosh on both sides of the Atlantic. Lloyd Webber had been setting T. S. Eliot's poems in *Old Possums Book of Practical Cats* to music for fun as a personal challenge, before it occurred to him that he had the makings of a show. He chose Trevor Nunn to direct, a seemingly risky choice inasmuch as Nunn was the artistic director of England's Royal Shakespeare Company and had virtually no experience with modern musical theater. He also asked Cameron Mackintosh, then an obscure, small-time London theater producer, to produce it. "Memory" was the song that sold the show, and throughout its run stars were recruited to play the role of Grizabella (who sings "Memory") in an otherwise ensemble-based show. Lloyd Webber and company created a loose thread through the disconnected poems by comparing cats to humans, perhaps inspired by Eliot's numerous personifications and anthropomorphic allusions in his cat poems. Another thread in the show is provided by the elderly Grizabella, who, at the end of her nine lives and the climax of the show, ascends to the Heaviside layer atop the central spectacle of the production—a gigantic tire on a hydraulic lifts her from the junkyard to the afterlife. This scene required substantial modification to Broadway's Winter Garden Theatre, which hosted *Cats* for 18 years from 1982 to 2000, and wreaked havoc for many local theaters when the show went on national tours.

Claude-Michel Schönberg and Alain Boublil

The most famous of the European megamusicals not associated with Lloyd Webber or, for that matter, any other British composer is *Les Misérables* (1987), which is quite similar to Lloyd Webber's work in both theatrical and musical style. The show was produced by Mackintosh, and the American theatergoing public—which adores the show—has tended to equate it with Lloyd Webber and British musicals. The show was actually written by the French team of Claude-Michel Schönberg and Alain Boublil (although Lloyd Webber did take a share in the profits, since his Really Useful Group owned the theater where it played in London). *Les Miz*, as it is commonly called, holds third place for longest-running Broadway shows. It is a through-sung musical that uses a variety of musical styles, including many numbers that hearken back to older musical comedy: aria-like solos for its principals, and pop tunes like the hit "On My Own," sung in the show by Eponine. Very much in the mold of the Lloyd Webber "megamusical," *Les Miz* features a central staging conceit by Trevor Nunn and designer John Napier: a massive turntable that at the dramatic height of the youthful revolution accepts two piles of broken wooden furniture from opposite sides of the stage that rotate and fit into place around one another as a giant barricade. So central is the turntable and the barricade to the show that it is hard to imagine *Les Miz* separately from the brilliantly executed staging and design. The story pits Jean Valjean, as a romantic hero, against Javert, the rigid representative of law and order. At the top of the story Valjean has been imprisoned for stealing bread. Valjean escapes and dedicates his life to one good deed after another, but he is ruthlessly hunted by Javert, who still calls him by his prison number. The supporting characters are involved in one melodramatic incident after another; in scene after scene we are introduced to a good character who then dies. The emotions evoked in the episodes are supported by the music; the political backdrop of the failed revolution of 1830 and Hugo's thematic exploration of law versus justice are downplayed in the musical version.

The second Schönberg/Boublil musical, nearly as successful as the first, and also produced by Mackintosh, was *Miss Saigon*. Set in 1975 during the U.S. evacuation of Saigon as it falls to the North Vietnamese, this story highlights a love affair between an American soldier, Chris, and a Vietnamese girl, Kim. The writers were inspired by Puccini's *Madame Butterfly* and by a photo of a Vietnamese woman handing her child to be taken by American soldiers in hopes of finding his father who could give him a better life, an act that Schönberg called "The Ultimate Sacrifice." It is another through-sung pop opera full of melodramatic moments, soaring music, and huge spectacle. *Miss Saigon* features perhaps the most ambitious feat in the history of musical comedy—landing a helicopter on the stage. *Miss Saigon* ran for ten years and is the tenth longest-running Broadway show, as of March 2009.

The Phantom

The Phantom of the Opera, now the longest-running show in Broadway history, brought Lloyd Webber and Mackintosh back together. Lloyd Webber conceived of developing a musical from the Gaston Leroux novel about the deformed composer living in the Paris Opera, as a vehicle for his second wife, singer Sarah Brightman, who had a functional range of nearly three octaves. The show was coproduced by Mackintosh and Lloyd Webber's Really Useful Group. Richard Stilgoe was brought in as lyricist after legendary American lyricist **Alan Jay Lerner (*My Fair Lady*)** fell ill and could not complete the score. Hal Prince was brought in to direct. The story turns around the deformed composer, the Phantom, and the object of his love, a young performer named Christine for whom he composes. It is clear why this story would attract Lloyd Webber: he could create opera scenes for each act and still tell the novel's story in the through-sung style with his usual use of themes and leitmotifs. The score had four hit songs, including "Music of the

Night" and "All I Ask of You," and garnered Lloyd Webber the best critical notices of his career. (One of the surprising aspects about Lloyd Webber's Broadway productions is that they consistently have tremendous popular appeal in spite of receiving mediocre critical notices. For decades it has been a "truism" of Broadway folklore that a handful of New York newspaper **critics** can, on the strength of their opening-night reviews, determine whether a show survives or dies. Lloyd Webber's popular musical style and intense marketing campaigns have largely inoculated him against the skewers of American critics.)

In spite of the hit song "Love Changes Everything," Lloyd Webber's next show after *Phantom, Aspects of Love* (1990), was neither a critical nor a popular success. But his next project was to be his greatest critical success to date. *Sunset Boulevard* (1994), was adapted from the brilliant 1950 film noir classic by Billy Wilder, starring Gloria Swanson as silent film star Norma Desmond. Both Lloyd Webber and director Hal Prince had been thinking of adapting the film for years. Lloyd Webber judiciously chose Los Angeles for the American debut, hoping to do an end run around the generally harsh Broadway reviewers while appealing to the "local" audience's adoration of Hollywood lore. Trevor Nunn directed and screen luminary Glenn Close was signed to perform Norma Desmond, both key features of the original production's success. In addition, though the full score was not released prior to the show's opening—differing from Lloyd Webber's past practice—Barbra Streisand recorded two of the songs including the *tour de force* "With One Look," before its American debut. In another break with past practice *Sunset Boulevard* contains dialogue; it is not through-sung. The characters of Norma, Max, and Joe are better developed than the principal characters in most Lloyd Webber musicals, with Max being given some particularly haunting music, full of tritones or augmented fourths, to bring his complex character as the man who once directed, then married, and now serves Norma fully into the musical drama. The show swept the Tony Awards for Andrew Lloyd Webber and his creative team, winning Best Score, Best Book, Best Musical, Best Set and Lighting, Best Actress (Close as Norma), and Best Featured Actor (George Hearn as Max).

Lloyd Webber and Mackintosh have also had their share of failures, many of them fairly recently. Lloyd Webber's *Woman in White* (2005) led some critics to state that his work belongs to the 1980s. Perhaps this is true of their artistic innovations in the musical form and of their producing tactics—including heavy-handed marketing. However, the Lloyd Webber/Mackintosh approach to art and business still dominates Broadway, as demonstrated by the number of their musicals still running and by their influence on other would-be producers and composers.

By the end of the twentieth century, very few shows, even musicals, were produced on Broadway as profit-seeking ventures. Even though he is the acknowledged American master of the musical theater, all of **Stephen Sondheim**'s shows, except *A Little Night Music* and *Into the Woods*, failed to recoup their initial investments. Investing in a Sondheim show is akin to philanthropy; one does not expect a return but is proud to support the acknowledged American master of the genre. Most young composers are writing smaller scale musicals, which can be produced in **Off-Broadway** or even tinier venues, in a clear acknowledgment that new or innovative work, or any work by an unknown artist, is unlikely to survive in the economic climate of Broadway in the twenty-first century. The only American producer to rival the successes of Lloyd Webber and Mackintosh is **Disney Theatrical Productions**. Disney's successes are more recent, beginning with *Beauty and the Beast* (1994) followed by the still-running *The Lion King* (1997) and *The Little Mermaid* (2008). Like Lloyd Webber and Mackintosh, Disney is an innovative marketer of Broadway shows. In Disney's case, the company tends to rely on name recognition from popular Disney movies, such as the three mentioned above. Mackintosh's most recent musical on Broadway, *Mary Poppins*, is a coproduction with Disney, an obvious linking of high-level promotional philosophies.

Along with the unprecedented financial prosperity of the European megamusical on Broadway has come considerable production clout for the Lloyd Webber/Mackintosh team. When *Phantom* first transferred to Broadway after opening in London, Lloyd Webber pressed Actors' Equity, America's strong stage actors' union, to allow his wife Sarah Brightman to star in the Broadway production. Equity objected on the grounds that she was not an American Equity actress and not essential to the success of the show (a potentially mitigating factor for which Equity might have granted an exception). Lloyd Webber won, but promised to feature an unknown American performer in his next London opening. Another conflict with Actors' Equity concerning *Miss Saigon*'s transfer to Broadway ended with similar results in 1990. Actors' Equity argued vociferously that the role of the engineer in *Miss Saigon* should go to an American, preferably Asian American, actor rather than the Caucasian British actor Jonathan Pryce, who originated the role in London. Part of the battle concerned Pryce's makeup as a Eurasian character, which Actors' Equity viewed as an insult to America's **Asian and Asian American** communities. Mackintosh and Lloyd Webber threatened to cancel the show if Pryce were not allowed to perform. He eventually won this battle as well, offering a concession on casting and use of makeup in Pryce's replacement if Pryce left the show before it closed. (Pryce, in fact, did leave while the show was running on Broadway, and they made good on their agreement.)

The economic and artistic success of Lloyd Webber and Mackintosh has transformed the face of 42nd Street and, as much as any single factor, ensured the economic viability of Broadway theater. However, it has done so at the price of intense commodification of the Broadway show and to the considerable detriment of new artistic talents. When *Phantom* celebrated its 7,486th show in January 2006, director Hal Prince was quick to note that the show had employed 6,850 people in the United States. Perhaps this is the most important contribution of Andrew Lloyd Webber, Cameron Mackintosh, and the European megamusical: it has kept Broadway economically viable, returning it to national popularity while employing tens of thousands of artists and technicians over the past three decades.

Melanie N. Blood

Further Reading

Citron, Stephen. *Sondheim and Lloyd Webber: The New Musical*. Oxford, U.K.: Oxford University Press, 2001.

McKiley, Jesse. " 'Phantom' Breaks Record With 7,486th Show." *New York Times* (Late Edition [East Coast]), January 10, 2006.

Snelson, John. *Andrew Lloyd Webber*. Yale Broadway Masters, no. 2. New Haven, CT: Yale University Press, 2004

Witchel, Alex. "Actors' Equity Attacks Casting of 'Miss Saigon.' " *New York Times*, July 26, 1990.

The Federal Theatre Project

Founded in 1935 as part of President Franklin Roosevelt's Works Progress Administration, the Federal Theatre Project (FTP or "Federal Theatre") was developed to employ thousands of theater professionals unable to find work in theater during the Depression. Designed as a regionally based federally funded "national" theater, the FTP oversaw the building and refurbishing of new theater venues, the mounting of over 1,200 professional productions, and the underwriting of low-cost and free admission tickets for the general public from Broadway to California ("The Work Program," 1–4). The FTP's pinchpenny productions and socially conscious management philosophy bore little resemblance to the high end "show biz" glamour associated with today's Broadway. However, the Federal Theatre Project left a deep imprint on modern commercial theater. It salvaged and/or launched the careers of numerous theater artists, it brought professional African American theater to the fore in commercial theater, and it laid the groundwork for the **regional theater** movement that later emerged as an essential part of Broadway's artistic and economic survival.

Hallie Flanagan, whose background lies in academic and experimental theater rather than commercial theater, was appointed director of the Federal Theatre by Harry Hopkins, Roosevelt's director of the WPA. Flanagan developed a regionally based organization for the FTP in order to foster the development of experimental, nonprofit theater based on the needs and interests of local communities. It was her hope that the FTP would both sustain professional theater in communities that had a history of theatrical activity and bring professional theater to new communities and audiences that had never been exposed to it. She and Hopkins also intended the Federal Theatre to be completely free from censorship, an aspiration that from a contemporary perspective seems naïve and unrealistic. And, indeed, it was.

Though the FTP was the first and only theater program to be supported solely by the U.S. government, it sought significantly different purposes than the national theaters of Europe. The FTP's primary goal was to employ the thousands of skilled theater people on relief rolls. Using a minimum of 90 percent of each production's money toward workers' salaries, the FTP employed approximately 10,000 men and women a year. To accommodate the wide scope of this plan, the FTP split the country into several regions, each headed by a director, who in turn reported to Flanagan.

While early criticism of the program focused on FTP as a potential competitor with the struggling commercial theater **producers** still operating in the late 1930s, the program diligently and purposefully experimented in forms of theater rarely seen on commercial stages at the time, including children's and marionette theater, **vaudeville**, and circus. Flanagan encouraged theater artists in the Federal Theatre's employ to experiment in form and style, include original natively produced works, and maintain relevancy for their audiences. Despite initial, and largely justified, skepticism over FTP's ability to produce quality or popular productions, Flanagan and her charges eventually found their footing. One innovative type of production, the Living Newspapers (new plays based on up-to-the-minute social and political issues) proved to be particularly effective in accommodating both the FTP's financial limitations and ambitious programmatic goals. Living Newspapers required a large cast and demanded little scenery. More significantly, Flanagan hoped Living Newspapers would serve as a catalyst for social change by dramatizing average people finding solutions to contemporary economic and social problems. Details for productions were researched from current newspapers and magazines; political cartoons, graphs, and direct quotations from newspapers and magazines often found their way into Living Newspaper performances. Though many productions drew acclaim, such as *Power* in 1937 (an exposé of monopolistic practices of utility companies), the Living Newspaper quickly came under attack as communist propaganda, providing fodder for political opponents of the FTP and the Roosevelt administration's New Deal as a whole.

The widespread inclusion of African Americans into FTP productions and theater unions represented one of the most important components of the Federal Theatre's legacy. Decades before the Civil Rights era, the FTP created "Negro Units" throughout the country. The Negro Units allowed African Americans to assume major leadership roles, both on and off stage, that heretofore all-but-exclusively went to whites. Under the leadership of **Rose McClendon** and John Houseman, the Units became well known for productions such as *Voodoo Macbeth* (1936), *Little Black Sambo* (1937), and *The Swing Mikado* (1938). *Voodoo Macbeth*, performed by the New York City unit and directed by 21-year-old Orson Welles, represented a particularly important breakthrough in African American theater. An adaptation of Shakespeare's play, *Voodoo Macbeth* earned praise from white and black critics alike. The production displayed a wide range of African American artists' talents and helped cement the FTP's reputation for innovation and quality. Other productions that earned the FTP credibility with theater professionals and critics included Sinclair Lewis and John Moffitt's *It Can't Happen Here*

(1936), *Revolt of the Beavers* (1937), Arthur Arent's *One Third of a Nation* (1938), and W. E. B. Du Bois's *Haiti* (1938).

FTP's most famous, or infamous, production was the heralded "banned" opening night performance on Broadway of Marc Blitzstein's ***The Cradle Will Rock***, directed by Orson Welles and produced by John Houseman. Although officially a consequence of budget cuts, the government-ordered lock-down of the theater on opening night was widely understood as an attempt to censor the uncompromisingly left-wing musical. In response to the government's action, Welles and company paraded the performers and the opening night audience to a new venue that Welles had secured in case of such an emergency. Company and audience settled into the theater seats, and Blitzstein played piano while cast members, contractually banned from performing their roles "onstage," performed from the audience.

The Federal Theatre also salvaged, advanced, or launched the careers of many artists who would become active on Broadway during its recovery in the years following World War II, including **Arthur Miller**, **Elia Kazan**, actors Howard DaSilva, Will Lee, Will Geer, Canada Lee, and, of course, actor/director Houseman (and to a lesser extent, Welles).

By the time *The Cradle Will Rock* had literally marched its way into Broadway history, the FTP was on the defensive against critics angered over its use of public funds for producing left-wing propaganda and the alleged subversive political affiliations of some people in its employ. A Congressional committee known as the "Dies Committee" (a forerunner of what was to become the House Un-American Activities Committee, named for chair Representative Martin Dies of Texas) conducted extensive hearings on the FTP beginning in 1938. Committee tactics included a strategic delay of several months before calling Flanagan to testify in rebuttal to the mounting accusations of anti-Americanism and malfeasance that had piled up in the course of the hearings. Although by all accounts Flanagan gave an eloquent defense of herself and the FTP when she was finally called to testify, the Federal Theatre Project had become so controversial that even politicians sympathetic to the program could no longer be counted on to defend it. Congress officially terminated the Federal Theatre Project on June 30, 1939.

To this day detractors of the Federal Theatre Project point to Flanagan's unflinching use of public money and public office to advance left-wing political propaganda as a serious fault in her leadership and a root cause of the FTP's well-merited demise. But many, especially within the theater profession, believe that the FTP saved American professional theater from complete extinction in the face of America's economic collapse and the onset of "talking" motion pictures as a lucrative alternative by which theater owners could fill their auditoriums. Among supporters Flanagan's record enjoys high praise and even heroic stature for imbuing modern commercial theater with an enhanced sensitivity to racial diversity, creating a legacy of politically and socially relevant American theater, and instilling in New York City's consciousness an enduring awareness that excellent American theater can be found several blocks, miles, and time zones west of 8th Avenue.

Thomas A. Greenfield and Kaitlin Snyder

Further Reading

Bigsby, C. W. E. *A Critical Introduction to Twentieth Century American Drama: Vol. I, 1900–1940.* Cambridge, England: Cambridge University Press, 1982.

Flanagan, Hallie. *Arena: The Story of the Federal Theatre.* New York: Limelight Editions, 1985.

"The Work Program." Report from Works Progress Administration, Federal Theatre Project for New York City. Undated (c. 1937). Original document scanned on *The New Deal Stage: Selections from the Federal Theatre Project, 1935–1939.* Washington, D.C.: Library of Congress. Retrieved August 15, 2009, from http://lcweb2.loc.gov/cgibin/ampage?collId=ftscript&fileName=farbf/00010012/ftscript.db&recNum=0.

FERRER, JOSÉ (1912c.–1992)
ACTOR, DIRECTOR

Famed as a theatrical jack-of-all-trades and master of practically all of them, José Ferrer established himself as one of Broadway's leading comedic actors, dramatic actors, and stage directors from the 1940s through the mid-1960s. He also performed in opera periodically and even starred in **musicals** toward the end of his career. He was the first person ever to win a Tony and Oscar for the same role (*Cyrano de Bergerac*, Broadway 1946; film 1950), having co-won the first ever Tony for Best Actor (along with Fredric March) for that role. Playing Cyrano hundreds of times in Broadway revivals, on film, on television, and in national tours, Ferrer essentially assumed ownership of that iconic role for the last half of the twentieth century. Yet owing to his extraordinary versatility he escaped typecasting and pigeonholing throughout his prodigious career.

Ferrer was born José Vicente Ferrer de Otero y Cintrón in San Juan, Puerto Rico. After World War I, his family moved to New York. A talented singer and musician in his youth, Ferrer attended Princeton University where, among other activities, he formed his own professional show band. In 1935, two years after graduating from Princeton, he began working on Broadway. For a year and a half he played small roles in forgettable comedies but found himself working with some of Broadway's leading directors, including Howard Lindsay and Jed Harris. In 1936, **producer**/director **George Abbott** cast him as the second male lead to Eddie Albert in the military school comedy *Brother Rat*. The play was a huge hit, running 577 performances over 18 months and giving Ferrer solid footing in the business. He subsequently had moderate success with roles in Dorothy Heyward and DuBose Heyward's play *Mamba's Daughters* and **Maxwell Anderson**'s *Key Largo* (both 1939). However, in 1940 he triumphed in a revival of the nineteenth-century "drag" farce *Charley's Aunt* and had **critics** and audiences singing his praises for his controlled yet hilarious command of the show's exquisite nonsense.

After *Charley's Aunt*, Ferrer made his Broadway directorial debut (while also starring) in a short-lived farce, *Vickie* (1942). He also appeared briefly in Cole Porter's *Let's Face It* (1941) at the end of its run. In 1943, director Margaret Webster cast him as Iago opposite **Paul Robeson** in what is now known as the "Robeson *Othello*." The longest-running American **Shakespeare** production in history and the first major New York Shakespeare play anchored by an African American in an otherwise predominantly white cast, the production was so widely admired that it enhanced the stature of virtually everyone connected with it—including Ferrer and then wife **Uta Hagen** as Desdemona.

By 1946 with two vastly different star-making performances under his belt (*Char-*

José Ferrer in the title role of Cyrano De Bergerac, shown here in the 1950 Hollywood adaptation of a seventeenth-century French poet with an oversized nose. Ferrer was the first person ever to win a Tony (in 1946 for the Broadway production) and an Oscar for the same role. (AP Photo)

ley's Aunt and *Othello*), Ferrer took on the role that would trump all of his prior performances. Edmond Rostand's *Cyrano de Bergerac* was an unlikely career-making turn for Ferrer. The play had been produced on Broadway nearly a dozen times with famed actor Richard Mansfield laying principal claim to the role prior to World War I and the now generally forgotten, physically towering William Hampden marshaling the part through five Broadway revivals and triumphant national tours in the 1920s and 1930s. Ferrer admitted that he took on the play because there was nothing better in front of him at the time. If Ferrer was looking for a mere stopgap in his career with Cyrano, he certainly surprised himself. Between adoring notices, audience thrall, and the historic cache of co-winning the first Best Actor Tony Award, Ferrer effectively seized the role from Hampden and held it as his own for the remainder of the twentieth century.

Ferrer went on to revive the role in 1953 in a self-directed version of the play, continuing his reputation as the paragon of the large-nosed romantic hero. Thanks to his accumulated clout in the 1950s by virtue of Cyrano, *Othello*, and *Charley's*

Aunt, there was little stopping Ferrer from doing whatever he wanted on Broadway, and he took full advantage of his position. In 1951–1952 Ferrer had one of the most remarkable seasons any dramatic actor or director has ever had on Broadway. He directed and/or produced the hits *Stalag 17*, *The Fourposter* (both 1951), and *The Shrike* (1952), winning the Tony as Best Director (collectively for all three) as well as a second Tony as Best Actor in *The Shrike.*

Cyrano also helped Ferrer make a transition into movies and **television**. He played Cyrano in the 1946 movie *Cyrano et d'Artagnan*, the 1950 Oscar-winning **film** version, and two television versions of the play (making Ferrer the only person ever to receive Tony, Oscar, and Emmy nominations for the same role). By the end of his career he had acted in nearly 20 films, including *Lawrence of Arabia* (1962) and Henry (*Gideon's Trumpet* 1980), and directed another four, including a movie version of *The Shrike* (film 1955), which he had produced, directed, and starred in on Broadway.

After reviving his famous roles in *Charley's Aunt* and *The Shrike* (both 1953), Ferrer did relatively little Broadway stage acting for the remainder of his career. Filmmaking, television acting and directing, and some directing on Broadway began to occupy his time. He directed George C. Scott in the successful drama *The Andersonville Trial* (1959), although the musical *Oh, Captain* (1958) was disappointing and another musical *Juno* (1959) flopped badly. Ferrer's last notable stage performance brought him back to his music roots as Don Quixote in *Man of La Mancha* (1965). He replaced Richard Kiley on Broadway and toured the show to great acclaim in 1967.

Younger and middle-aged audiences know Ferrer best through his work on television, where he acted regularly in an extraordinary range of parts from the 1970s until shortly before his death in 1992. He had recurring roles in the sitcom *Newhart* and the soap opera *Another World* and made dozens of appearances in network series and made for television movies. However, even on television, his stage-filling voice and commanding presence routinely made him stand out among the "TV" actors who surrounded him, often to remarkable comic or dramatic effect.

Even on the small screen, Ferrer brought with him the powerful if unseen legacy of Cyrano, Iago, and *Charley's Aunt*.

Ferrer died in Coral Gables, Florida, in 1992.

Thomas A. Greenfield and Michael Radi

Further Reading

Mendez, Serafin Mendez, Gail Cueto, and Neysa Rodríguez Deynes. *Notable Caribbeans and Caribbean Americans: A Biographical Dictionary.* Westport, CT: Greenwood Press, 2003.

Shipman, David. *The Great Movie Stars: The Golden Years.* New York: Hill and Wang, 1979.

FIELDS, LEW (1867–1941)
PRODUCER, ACTOR, WRITER

Born Moses Schoenfeld, the son of Jewish and Polish immigrants from the Bowery neighborhood of Lower Manhattan, Lew Fields was one-half of the renowned Weber and Fields **vaudeville** comedy team and an important theatrical **producer** in the period between the end of the vaudeville era and the beginning of modern Broadway. From the late 1880s through 1905, the Weber and Fields team was the most famous comedy team in America. Later Fields, working as an independent producer, evolved into one of Broadway's leading impresarios. In the process he became a key figure in the transition of the American **musical** from vaudeville "schtick" and musical farce to early jazz-era maturity.

Schoolmates and childhood friends, Joe Weber (1867–1942) and Fields were performing comedy routines professionally in Bowery neighborhood theaters before they were in their teens. By 1882, the adolescents were working as "juvenile comedians" at Bunnell's New Museum on Broadway. In the late 1880s they toured with various vaudeville companies, gaining fame and sharpening their ethnic characters, broad physical comedy, and stage patter. By 1890 they had established their own touring vaudeville troop produced by and starring themselves. As a touring act, Fields and Weber routinely set house records for the venues in which they performed and quickly became the highest paid comedy team in the country. Audiences particularly loved their "Mike & Meyer" skits—exaggerated comic stereotypes of new European immigrants struggling and bumbling toward their dreams of a better life in America.

In 1893, a few days after Fields's twenty-sixth birthday, the company opened on Broadway at the Park Theatre—known more for staging legitimate theater and mainstream productions than vaudeville shows. The pair triumphed in this prestigious venue, gaining sufficient clout, popularity, and self-confidence to "get off the road" and work in New York on a more or less permanent basis. Among their more significant New York appearances in the years that followed was a yearlong engagement in 1895 at Oscar Hammerstein I's new Olympia Theatre on Broadway at 44th Street. Working steadily in New York brought Fields in contact with the major figures in all aspects of theater, not just vaudeville, and enabled him to expand his interest in theatrical production and management.

Immediately following their stint at the Olympia, Weber and Fields took over their first self-managed venue: the Weber and Fields' Broadway Music Hall between 29th and 30th Streets near what was then the center of Manhattan's mainstream theater district. They began to produce more contemporary burlesque shows aimed at more adult audiences. Between 1897 and 1903 they specialized in writing and producing high-energy romping musical farces that combined vaudeville road energy with big time Broadway production values. *Whirl-i-gig* (1899), *Fiddle-dee-dee* (1900), *Hoity Toity* (1901), and *Twirly Whirly* (1902) were among their most popular shows of this period.

Weber and Fields' fortunes began to decline in 1903, sending the two veterans, only in their mid-thirties, back to touring to keep their name alive and money coming in. In 1904, shortly after the completion of their tour, they separated as business partners, having grown apart under the stress of their longevity and recent reversal of fortune. They would reunite later for various projects, but at this point each man struck out on his own .

Fields threw himself into producing while still remaining active as a writer and performer for his own productions and those of others. Between 1906 and 1930, Fields produced over 40 Broadway shows. While his earliest productions tended toward the musical farce traditions he had grown up with, he gradually expanded into the more subtle, urbane, hit-song vehicles that would become the trademark of modern Broadway musicals in the 1920s and 1930s.

By 1906, no longer viewed as a vaudeville novelty, Fields was producing (as well as writing and performing) with the most important talents on Broadway and generating some of the best press notices of any producer working in New York. He continued to work with Hammerstein, securing and refurbishing theatrical venues in which he would stage his shows—particularly the Herald Square Theatre, which housed a number of Fields's productions. In collaboration with the **Shubert Brothers**, Fields coproduced and starred in several successful shows, including a smart English-American romantic comedy, *The Girl Behind the Counter* (1907). *The Girl Behind the Counter* ran at the Herald for 16 months and 282 performances. Fields produced musicals and **operettas** by **Victor Herbert**, America's leading composer of operetta and popular songs at the time. His works with Herbert included *The Rose of Algeria* (1909) and *Old Dutch* (1909). (This latter play marked the Broadway debut of nine-year-old Fields's discovery, **Helen Hayes**, who would become the premiere American stage actress of the 1930s.) For his musical revue *Hokey Pokey* (1912), Fields enlisted the songwriting talent of a young newcomer, **Irving Berlin**.

During World War I, Fields's theatrical productivity slowed considerably. With theaters to maintain and cast and crew to pay, he soon found himself struggling financially. He made a few forays to Hollywood in the hopes of establishing a lucrative **film** career, principally through a reunion of convenience with Weber in an effort to bring their Mike & Meyer routines to the silent screen. A few undistinguished short films briefly sustained this effort. However, Fields soon returned to New York and, in 1921, declared bankruptcy.

Ever resourceful, persistent, and adaptable, Fields rebounded as a Broadway producer in the 1920s, making a remarkable transition from vaudeville and farce to newly emerging more sophisticated jazz-age musicals. Most notably, he produced four of the early hits for the new team of **Richard Rodgers** and **Lorenz Hart**: *The Girl Friend* (1926), *Peggy-Ann* (1926), *A Connecticut Yankee* (1927), and *Present Arms* (1928). While these shows had elements of Fields's old vaudeville silliness, as a producer he understood that the well-crafted popular song was coming into its own on Broadway.

After the stock market crash in 1929, Fields struggled to produce another hit. He had a successful one-year run as producer and star of *Hello, Daddy* (1930), written for him by his son Herbert Fields and daughter Dorothy Fields. However, approaching his mid-sixties, he effectively retired from active theater production and stage performing in 1931, believing the business and audience tastes had grown beyond him. He reunited with Weber in 1932 as part of a one-night special for the opening of Radio City Music Hall, and the two would work occasionally in cameo stage and film appearances over the next nine years.

Fields died of pneumonia in 1941 in Beverly Hills, California, leaving a unique legacy as a highly successful producer in both the "old Broadway" of vaudeville and the "new Broadway" of the jazz-age musical.

Thomas A. Greenfield and Brian Balduzzi

Further Reading

Bordman, Gerald Martin. *American Musical Theatre: A Chronicle*. Edition 2, revised. New York: Oxford University Press, 1992. Digitized December 29, 2006.

Fields, Armond, and L. Marc. *From the Bowery to Broadway: Lew Fields and the Roots of American Popular Theatre*. New York: Oxford University Press, 1993.

FIERSTEIN, HARVEY (1954–)
ACTOR, PLAYWRIGHT

A pioneer in expanding and destigmatizing gay themes in commercial theater and film, Harvey Fierstein is one of the most versatile talents working in the American arts. The only person ever to have won two Tony Awards as Best Actor and author for the same play (*Torch Song Trilogy*, 1982), Fierstein is one of American theater's most venerated talents, despite abandoning Broadway for 14 years to pursue careers in **film** and **television**.

Fierstein was born in Brooklyn, New York, and took to performing from childhood. He worked in drag shows at local bars while still in his teens but actually aspired to be a painter. In the early 1970s he attended Brooklyn's Pratt Institute, studying painting while maintaining connections with New York's avant-garde arts and theater community. While in his teens and early twenties he appeared in numerous **Off-Broadway** productions, several with the heralded La MaMa Experimental Theater Club. During this period he wrote one-act plays and short stage performances about gay love affairs and friendships. Among the earliest was 1972's *The International Stud*, premised on a breakup between a gay man and a bisexual man. He continued to develop other pieces until he had the makings of *The Torch Song Trilogy*, which debuted Off-Broadway in 1981 and transferred to Broadway the following year.

A three-play/three-act odyssey about the loves and losses of a bisexual Jewish drag performer, *Torch Song*'s superb writing and moving performances overwhelmed prurient or distracting concern about its decidedly nonmainstream content. The show ran for three years, eventually becoming the second longest-running Broadway play to open in the 1980s (behind **Neil Simon**'s *Brighton Beach Memoirs*, 1983). It now ranks among the most important gay-themed American plays ever written. Fierstein followed this success by writing the book for the musical, *La Cage aux Folles* (1983), which he adapted from a popular French play of the same title. Broadway veteran **Jerry Herman** wrote the music and lyrics. Essentially a domestic comedy with a gay father/drag club manager as the improbable patriarch, *La Cage* further acclimated mainstream Broadway audiences to gay life and vice versa. *La Cage* swept the Tony awards winning for Best Musical, Book (for Fierstein), Actor in a Musical, Original Score, Director of a Musical, and Costumes.

After his initial forays in theater, Fierstein left Broadway from 1988 to 2002 to perform in film and television. He landed some small roles at first and provided a signature gravelly voice-over narration for the Oscar-winning documentary, *The Life and Times of Harvey Milk* (1984). In 1988, he wrote the screenplay adaptation and acted in *Torch Song Trilogy*, which, despite success on Broadway, flopped as a movie. Eventually Fierstein found work in some Hollywood successes including *Mrs. Doubtfire* (1993) and *Independence Day* (1996) as well as numerous **television** appearances, but never achieved in Hollywood the stature he has earned in theater.

Fierstein returned to Broadway in 2002, portraying Edna Turnblad in the hit *Hairspray* (2002). His scene-stealing performance is credited with being a major factor in the show's success. *Hairspray* won Fierstein the Tony for Best Actor in a Musical, placing him among the elite theater artists who have won four Tony Awards in different categories. Subsequently he has played Tevye in a 2005 revival of *A Fiddler on the Roof* and both wrote and acted in a poignant limited run play-with-music, *A Catered Affair* (2008), for which he received strong reviews.

Fierstein lives in the New York area and is considered one of the city's beloved "characters," whether he is performing occasionally in local drag clubs or dressing up as Mrs. Claus for a civic parade. Yet despite his campy persona, Fierstein is an iconic elder statesmen in one of Broadway's more notable acts of cultural diplomacy—championing open recognition and respect for gay life.

Thomas A. Greenfield and Nicole Katz

Further Reading

Nelson, Emmanuel Sampath. *Contemporary Gay American Poets and Playwrights: An A-to-Z Guide.* Westport, CT: Greenwood Publishing Group, 2003.

Shewey, Don, and Susan Shacter. *Caught in the Act: New York Actors Face to Face.* New York: New American Library, 1986.

FILM

As the motion picture industry grew throughout the twentieth century, it inspired countless screen adaptations of plays and **musicals** originally popularized on the

Broadway stage. From the earliest days of the Hollywood studio system, **producers** purchased the film rights to successful Broadway stage shows in the hopes of transforming them into successful movies. The mass distribution of these filmed adaptations exposed "the Broadway show" to a wide audience, often bringing national and international attention to lesser-known stories, scripts, songs, songwriters, performers, and authors as well as the shows themselves.

Film versions often differ considerably from their Broadway sources. Scenes or characters may be altered and added. Original dialogue and musical numbers are routinely eliminated or shortened to account for a commercial film's standard running time, which is generally shorter than that of a major Broadway stage show. The practice of "opening up" a filmed version of a play by moving the action to more locations than are feasible to mount on stage has also become common. For theater purists, film versions of plays often stand as pale imitations of the original, failing to replicate the intimate experience of a live performance even when the adaptation is relatively faithful to the original stage production. Nevertheless, the commercial and critical success of such Broadway-to-film hits as *West Side Story* (1961), *Amadeus* (1984), *Chicago* (2002), *Dreamgirls* (2006), and *Mamma Mia!* (2008) suggests that film audiences and even film critics are relatively unfazed by the vicissitudes of adaptation. (Unless otherwise noted, dates in parentheses indicate the year in which the film was released.)

Film Adaptations of Stage Dramas and Comedies

The history of film adaptation of theatrical productions is almost as old as the film industry itself. Short films of **Shakespeare** plays, often featuring only a scene or two, date back as early as the silent-film era. The advent of sound technology in the late 1920s allowed films to feature spoken dialogue, and by the 1930s film versions of popular Broadway hits of the time, such as **George S. Kaufman** and Moss Hart comedies, were available to movie audiences. Of the stage productions optioned for the screen in the late 1930s and 1940s, most were musicals, comedies, or melodramas that had already proven successful with Broadway audiences, such as Kaufman and Hart's *You Can't Take It With You* (1938) and Philip Barry's witty high-society comedy *The Philadelphia Story* (1940). **George Bernard Shaw** adapted his London and Broadway comedy hit *Pygmalion* into the most critically successful of the numerous screen adaptations of his plays. Following the film's U.S. release in 1938, Shaw won the Academy Award as screenwriter for the film. (*Pygmalion* was also the main source for the 1956 **Lerner and Loewe** hit musical *My Fair Lady*, which, in turn, was adapted for the screen in 1964.) From the 1960s into the 1990s, playwright **Neil Simon** became almost as famous as a screenwriter for his numerous film adaptations of his stage comedies as he did for having written them as plays in the first place. His most successful film adaptations of his Broadway hits included *Barefoot in the Park* (1967), *The Odd Couple* (1968, which thereafter became a successful television series), *Plaza Suite* (1971), *The Prisoner of Second Avenue* (1975), *Brighton Beach Memoirs* (1986), and *Lost in Yonkers* (1993).

Marlon Brando and Vivien Leigh are shown in a scene from the 1951 film version of A Streetcar Named Desire. *(AP Photo)*

Highly charged dramas were often used to showcase virtuoso acting performances. Inasmuch as plays adapted to film prior to 1960 rarely offered spectacular action scenes or breathtaking scenery, the actors themselves were often touted as the main attraction. Thus Broadway star Shirley Booth's reprisal of her acclaimed 1950 stage role in **William Inge**'s *Come Back Little Sheba* became the reason to see Daniel Mann's 1952 film adaptation, and the electrifying, sexually charged performances of Vivien Leigh and **Marlon Brando** helped to sell **Elia Kazan**'s film of **Tennessee Williams**'s *A Streetcar Named Desire* (1951). Stepping into a challenging stage role also became a means by which some Hollywood actors, who were often dismissed by **critics** and the public as glamour goddesses or sex symbols, attempted to prove their talent. By doing so, many actors also went on to earn critical acclaim and even Academy Awards for performances that often seemed to trump those found in "ordinary" Hollywood films not based on plays. Elizabeth Taylor was so rewarded for her decidedly unglamorous turn as Martha in **Mike Nichols**'s 1966 film of **Edward Albee**'s play *Who's Afraid of Virginia Woolf?*

Although Hollywood studios continue to option Broadway hits in the hope that the show's popularity with theater audiences will translate to success with moviegoers, the growing independent film movement of the 1990s allowed lesser-known **playwrights** to bring their own less conventional work to a larger audience. Playwrights-turned-filmmakers such as Neil LaBute, David Mamet, and Kenneth Lonergan have adapted their own work from stage to screen, thereby ensuring themselves a significant degree of creative control over film production.

Independent or art-house film versions of other plays that explore controversial issues of harassment, sexuality, incest, and transgender identity, such as Mamet's *Oleanna* (1994), Wendy MacLeod's *The House of Yes* (1996), **Terrence McNally**'s *Love! Valour! Compassion!* (1997), and John Cameron Mitchell's defiantly unconventional *Hedwig and the Angry Inch* (2001), have made no attempt to conform to the tastes of mainstream audiences in the way that Hollywood productions generally do. While these films are unlikely to ever generate the financial return of a studio blockbuster, the playwrights accept the reduced compensation in return for control over production. On television, HBO Films has found success mounting a series of thoughtfully conceived, expertly cast productions of contemporary plays, including Margaret Edson's *Wit* (2001) and Moises Kaufman's *The Laramie Project* (2002). In 2003, HBO Films launched a massive six-hour-long film of **Tony Kushner**'s *Angels in America*, directed by Mike Nichols and starring Al Pacino and Meryl Streep. The film retained the entirety of Kushner's text and was presented as a two-part miniseries; it went on to win 11 Emmy Awards. HBO Films has allowed directors, playwrights, and actors more creative flexibility than they would likely have working in the Hollywood studio system. As a result, HBO Films' adaptations of plays have generally remained faithful to their source material, featured A-list performers, and attracted large audiences of home viewers.

Yet even well into the age of the independent film producer and the small play, major film producers and "big name" plays still found big name Hollywood stars to try their hand at translating a successful Broadway role to film. Gwyneth Paltrow and Anthony Hopkins took the leads for Miramax Films in David Auburn's *Proof* (2005), the Tony Award and Pulitzer Prize winning play about a disturbed young woman who is a mathematical genius. Reviews were mixed and box-office receipts were very disappointing. Oscar winners Meryl Streep and Phillip Seymour Hoffman successfully brought a claustrophobic, small stage tension to Scott Rudin Productions' adaptation of *Doubt* (2008), playwright John Patrick Shanley's 2005 test-of-wills drama about a nun, as head of a small Catholic school, who persecutes a priest on the basis of her suspicions that he has molested one of the school's children.

Film Adaptations of Musicals

Early Hollywood musicals consisted mainly of revue-style numbers, gags, and insubstantial plots, which bore the influence of **vaudeville**. Other early films featured heavily truncated versions of Broadway shows in which songs were cut or rearranged and plotlines edited. Metro-Goldwyn-Mayer's *Broadway Melody* series (1929, 1935, 1937, 1940) and Warner Brothers' similar *Gold Diggers* series (1929, 1933, 1935, 1936, 1938) used film to showcase a string of theatrical song-and-dance numbers. In these films (all but the 1929 edition), choreographer Busby Berkeley attempted to reconceptualize the musical number by experimenting with overhead shots of his dancers, releasing them from the visually dull constraints of the chorus line. Improvements in sound technology and the advent of three-strip

Technicolor (a film technology enhancement that expanded the spectrum of colors that could be contained within a single image) in 1932 helped boost popularity of musical films, though they were often viewed as being conventional and stagy. Studio executives perceptively saw musicals as a convenient and appealing means of capitalizing on popular songs by such songwriters as **Cole Porter** and **Richard Rodgers** and **Lorenz Hart** while dazzling audiences with flashy costumes and star performances. They were often rewarded for their foresight with hit films that enjoyed both commercial and critical success.

By the 1950s, the Broadway musical had evolved into a complete, self-contained work with developed characters, a complex plot, and a more integrated use of music and song than those found in musicals of the 1930s. Consequently, a Hollywood film could no longer get away with substituting a whole new plot or an entirely different set of songs when filming an adaptation of a Broadway musical, nor could it simply tack the hit music of a Broadway show onto a different film —a common practice in film adaptation of musicals prior to 1950. This new trend of crafting the film as a replication of the original stage musical resulted in faithful, if sometimes bland, adaptations of such Broadway hits as *Annie Get Your Gun* (1950), *Kiss Me Kate* (1953), *Oklahoma!* (1955), *Guys and Dolls* (1955), and *Carousel* (1956). While popular with audiences, the films were seen by many critics as uninteresting.

Although music and plot offered little flexibility or room for alteration, filmmakers learned to take advantage of the camera's mobility by "opening up" the action of a musical from single to multiple settings and by showcasing location shooting. Fred Zinnemann shot 20th Century Fox's film of *Oklahoma!* in Arizona. The film's song-and-dance scenes take place in real cornfields and apple orchards, and the hero Curly (Gordon MacRae) sings the opening number "Oh, What a Beautiful Morning" on horseback. (In the original 1943 Broadway production, Alfred Drake as Curly famously strides up to his sweetheart Laurie's front porch, *sans* horse.) Similarly, **Joshua Logan** filmed *South Pacific* (1958) in the Pacific Islands. In the 1950s studio executives also found the musical to be an excellent vehicle for experimenting with newly developed wide-screen technology, giving big dance numbers and choral scenes expanded space and an enlarged visual presence.

When casting a musical, Hollywood filmmakers often replace the stars of the original Broadway casts with established Hollywood actors whose name recognition might better appeal to a nationwide audience only marginally familiar with Broadway celebrities. The film of *Annie Get Your Gun* starred Hollywood comedienne Betty Hutton as Annie Oakley rather than **Ethel Merman**, who made the original show a hit on Broadway. The film of *Guys and Dolls* featured **Marlon Brando** and Frank Sinatra, iconic figures of male toughness who were widely viewed as having been miscast as song-and-dance caricature tough guys Sky Masterson and Nathan Detroit, respectively. Sound technology allowed filmmakers to cast nonsinging stars in leading musical roles, later dubbing them in postproduction (to mixed results) with more trained vocal performers. In the 1950s and 1960s vocalist Marni Nixon became a much sought-after dubbing artist, providing the on-screen singing voices of Deborah Kerr in *The King and I* (1956), Natalie Wood in **West Side Story** (1961), and Audrey Hepburn in **My Fair Lady** (1964).

If the 1940s through the mid-1960s were the Golden Age of the Broadway musical, the 1960s stand as the golden age of Hollywood musicals, as studios commissioned lavish, big-budget adaptations of such Broadway hits as *West Side Story* (1961), *The Music Man* (1962), *My Fair Lady*, *The Sound of Music* (1965), and *Oliver!* (1968)—all of which enjoyed success at the box office and generally favorable critical attention. The films offered hit songs, popular film stars, and literate subject matter that nevertheless remained appropriate for family audiences. Some adaptations attempted to re-create the look and feel of a stage production, relying on painted backdrops and studio sets, while others attempted to dazzle movie audiences with location settings to inconsistent effect. For example, many critics argued that the musical numbers in the film adaptation of *West Side Story* simply felt out-of-place when set against the very real asphalt and grime of New York's Hell's Kitchen.

Contemporary musicals, which often revive the conventions of 1940s and 1950s musicals, can pose new challenges for filmmakers hoping to adapt them for the screen. Since the release of the film adaptation of the musical *Chicago* (2002), the Hollywood musical has enjoyed renewed interest, although the response from audiences and critics has been lukewarm at times. An onstage hit cannot guarantee success on screen as film versions of **The Phantom of the Opera** (2004), **Rent** (2005), and **The Producers** (2005) have proven. The long-awaited film version of **Andrew Lloyd Webber**'s *Phantom* was widely panned by critics. **Susan Stroman**'s faithful adaptation of Mel Brooks's highly successful musical *The Producers* enjoyed only moderate success with critics and audiences, and Chris Columbus's film version of the Pulitzer Prize–winning *Rent* failed to meet critical and commercial expectations. Nevertheless, Hollywood studios and producers remain undaunted. DreamWorks Studios' much-hyped film of the musical *Dreamgirls*, featuring Beyoncé Knowles and former *American Idol* television contestant Jennifer Hudson, premiered in 2006 to modest acclaim but excellent box-office response. Hudson's performance and impressive rendition of the torch song "And I Am Telling You I Am Not Going" garnered considerable press attention; she went on to win an Academy Award for the role. The studio soon followed with a gory, gloomy film of **Stephen Sondheim**'s horror-comedy *Sweeney Todd* (2007), directed by Tim Burton. The film featured a cast of performers with little vocal training, led by Johnny Depp in the title role. Nevertheless, the film received an enthusiastic reception from critics and Depp's star power—as well as that of Burton—helped ensure a healthy return at the box office. In true Hollywood tradition, first-rate singers rarely guarantee a successful film musical, nor do second-rate singers guarantee a ruinous one, as the film versions of *Dreamgirls* and *Sweeney Todd* (and *Chicago*, the stars of which were also actors first and singers second) prove. The Hollywood star power of veterans Meryl Streep and Pierce Brosnan (filmdom's James Bond from 1995 to 2002) delivered huge audiences and charmed critics in Universal Studios' *Mamma Mia!* (2008), although neither lead performer was overly impressive as on-screen musical singers. (That the two stars actually did their own singing became part of the film's successful promotion campaign.)

From Film to Broadway

Although most musicals have originated on the stage before moving to the screen, others that were originally produced as Hollywood films have eventually made a transition to Broadway. *Meet Me in St. Louis* (1944) and *Singin' in the Rain* (1952), two of Hollywood's most beloved original musicals, were transformed with limited success into Broadway stage productions in the 1980s. Broadway producers found the process of converting a successful film musical into a theatrical hit as difficult as Hollywood had found the reverse process. Just as a successful stage production does not always guarantee a hit film, a hit film is no guarantee of a successful stage production.

In addition, the transformation of many nonmusical films into stage musicals has become a recent phenomenon. In 1972, the Academy Award–winning *All About Eve* (1950), a film about Broadway acting careers, became *Applause*, a musical about Broadway acting careers. In 1994, Andrew Lloyd Webber adapted *Sunset Boulevard* (1950), Billy Wilder's Gothic satire of the Hollywood star system. As the cross-promotion of well-known films and well-known stage shows has become increasingly appealing to producers, the reciprocal relationships between Hollywood and Broadway have grown increasingly complex. In 2005, Universal released its big-budget musical film of Mel Brooks's *The Producers*, based on the 2001 musical stage production, which was itself based on Brooks's 1968 comedy film of the same title. (Brooks's follow-up Hollywood-to-Broadway 2008 adaptation of his hit film *Young Frankenstein* was much less successful than the musical *The Producers*, although several critics felt it was every bit as funny and entertaining.)

Following Brooks's lead, the campy John Waters's comedy *Hairspray* (1988) arrived on Broadway in 2002 and back on the screen in 2007, with John Travolta donning drag for the lead role of Edna Turnblad. The nonmusical films *Sweet Smell of Success* (1957), *Footloose* (1984), and *The Full Monty* (1998) all inspired Broadway musicals in the 1990s and early 2000s. More recently, Broadway has seen musical productions of the 2000 film comedy *High Fidelity* (2006) and, more strangely, of the 1975 cult documentary *Grey Gardens* (2006), a portrait of two eccentric, reclusive cousins of the late Jacqueline Kennedy Onassis. In the early 2000s the Walt Disney Company capitalized on the success of its many musical films by converting them to wildly successful stage shows, including *Mary Poppins* (2006) and the animated musical features *Beauty and the Beast* (1991) and *The Lion King* (1994). A "small" British film, *Billy Elliot* (2000), became the toast of the 2008–2009 season as *Billy Elliot: The Musical*, winning the Tony Award for Best Musical and numerous other honors.

While strong film adaptations of Broadway comedies and dramas provide an occasional enrichment of the American film scene, the film musical has proven its staying power as an indestructible American art form. Having adapted over the past century to various changes in film technology, to commercial and critical tastes, and to the changing face of Broadway itself, the musical genre promises to remain a strong presence well into the twenty-first century. The symbiotic relationship of Broadway to Hollywood—always present, but recently intensified—suggests that musical films and stage musicals will continue looking to each other for creative inspiration.

Ian Scott Todd

Further Reading

Altman, Rick. *The American Film Musical*. Bloomington: Indiana University Press, 1987.

Cohan, Steven, ed. *Hollywood Musicals: The Film Reader*. In Focus: Routledge Film Readers. New York: Routledge, 2002.

Denkert, Darcie. *A Fine Romance*. New York: Watson-Guptill, 2005.

Dunne, Michael. *American Film Musical Themes and Forms*. Jefferson, NC: McFarland, 2004.

Everett, William A. *The Musical: A Research Guide to Musical Theater and Film*. Routledge Music Bibliographics. New York: Routledge, 2004.

Feuer, Jane. *The Hollywood Musical*. Bloomington: Indiana University Press, 1982.

Hischak, Thomas S. *Through the Screen Door: What Happened to the Broadway Musical When It Went to Hollywood*. Lanham, MD: Scarecrow, 2004.

Internet Broadway Database. www.ibdb.com.

Internet Movie Database. www.imdb.com.

Kantor, Michael, and Laurence Maslon. *Broadway: The American Musical*. New York: Bulfinch, 2004.

Roberts, Jerry. *The Great American Playwrights on the Screen*. New York: Applause, 2003.

Sennett, Ted. *Hollywood Musicals*. New York: Abrams, 1981.

FISKE, MINNIE MADDERN (1865–1932)
ACTRESS, DIRECTOR, WRITER, PRODUCER

Minnie Maddern Fiske (born Mary Augusta Davey) or Mrs. Fiske, as she was known professionally throughout her adult life, was one of the earliest and most forceful advocates for the advancement of women in commercial theater: as serious actresses, writers, directors, and **producers**. Using the fame and stature she earned as a brilliant lead actress and producer for such challenging productions as Henrik Ibsen's *A Doll's House* (1894) and *Hedda Gabler* (1903), Fiske rallied women to the causes of suffragism with speeches both on and off stage. A formidable negotiator and organizer, she also helped mobilize fellow producers and actors to fight the exploitative business practices of the **Theatrical Syndicate**, which controlled virtually every aspect of American commercial theater at the turn of the century.

The daughter of a successful theater manager and producer in New Orleans, Mary Davey began appearing on stage as a young child, eventually substituting her mother's surname of Maddern for her father's. She actually began her acting career at age three, when her father put her on the stage as the little Duke of York in *King Richard III*. While she was still in her teens, plays were being written specifically for her talent. Although educated in convents in the Midwest, Mary Maddern continued to act in both amateur and professional productions throughout her youth. In 1889 she married theatrical writer, producer, and editor, Harrison Grey Fiske. Her marriage prompted a turn to playwriting, which supplemented her lifelong interest in acting.

In 1901 Fiske and her husband opened the Manhattan Theatre under Mrs. Fiske's direction and management. Her goal as a director and theater manager was to bridge the gap between popular (anti-intellectual) entertainment and serious drama of the kind emerging in late nineteenth-century Europe. Fiske demanded complex roles such as Ibsen's Nora and, in so doing, persuaded audiences and **critics** to view her offstage in connection with such characters: sharp, independent, and intelligent—qualities seen as more masculine than feminine at the time. Yet her effectiveness at playing women onstage, regardless of the characters' complexity, inspired critics to also deem her appropriately feminine and ladylike.

Fiske became a proponent of Ibsen plays because of their strong female characters, an unusual feature for plays of the time. She first starred in Ibsen's *A Doll's House* and later undertook other Ibsen roles such as the female leads in Ibsen's *Hedda Gabler*, *Rosmerholm* (1907), and *Pillars of Society* (1910). Fiske's determination to find this rare commodity of psychologically complex and intellectually active female roles evidenced her belief that plays provided an opportunity for women to project intellectually complex and autonomous identities. Although she starred in and/or produced plays on Broadway by numerous other writers, she focused her career almost entirely upon women who transgressed social expectations for women: *Becky Sharp* (1899) by Langdon Mitchell, *Tess of the D'Urbervilles* (1899) by Lorimer Stoddard, *Mary of Magdala* (1902) by Paul Heyse, and *Leah Kleschna* (1904) by C. M. S. McLellan

The courage and leadership Fiske admired in the characters she staged led her to the defining event of her career, her battle with the Theatrical Syndicate. The Syndicate, as it was known, was the commercial effort of six businessmen—Abraham Ehrlanger, Charles Frohman, Alfred Hayman, Marc Klaw, Samuel F. Nixon, and Fred Zimmerman—who in 1896 moved toward controlling all commercial theaters in the country. As a controlling monopoly, the Theatrical Syndicate was anathema to Fiske, and she frequently spoke out against them. The very fact of her public opposition to the six men, which began in earnest around 1910, represented a serious challenge to gender stereotypes and a singularly courageous act of defiance in an industry that had virtually knuckled under to the Syndicate's power.

Fiske took an aggressive stance against the Syndicate, not only speaking against its members but also organizing with other theater professionals willing to stand in opposition to them. Fiske and some anti-Syndicate colleagues refused to act in any theater controlled by the Syndicate, which effectively exiled Fiske from all

Broadway theater. Fiske took her fight to the public. Because of her popularity as an actress and director/producer, she became a popular figure whose voice took a central role in a public debate about the Syndicate. Then, as now, industry-wide conflict in commercial theater was major news in New York, and the New York press generally lauded Fiske's open, courageous defiance of the all-male monopoly. Owing to her skill in creating fictional strong women on stage, Fiske's own words were given particular weight and attention. Many of her speeches were widely quoted in the press or even published whole.

By the mid-1910s the Syndicate had lost its hold on commercial theater, a fact owing more to competition with younger rivals, the **Shubert Brothers**, than Mrs. Fiske herself. However, Fiske's prominence and accomplishments during the controversy laid important groundwork for women theater artists and producers of the future. Mrs. Fiske did not produce or direct plays after 1916 but continued to perform in dramas and light comedies both in New York and on tour until 1930.

Mrs. Fiske was rehearsing for another Broadway appearance in 1932 when she died of a heart attack in New York City.

Pamela Cobrin

Further Reading

Auster, Alibert. *Actresses and Suffragists: Women in the American Theater 1890–1920.* New York: Praeger Publishers, 1984.

Glenn, Susan A. *Female Spectacle: The Roots of Modern Feminism.* Cambridge, MA: Harvard University Press, 2000.

FITCH, CLYDE (1865–1909)
PLAYWRIGHT, DIRECTOR

William Clyde Fitch was the first American author to cultivate a long-term, lucrative playwriting career in New York commercial theater. Drawing extensively on American-based themes, Fitch provided early momentum in pointing American drama toward a national self-identity. Perhaps more notable for his longevity and productivity than his craftsmanship, Fitch's body of work—including 33 produced plays and 22 additional adaptations—helped establish the American **playwright** as a pivotal force in the collaborative enterprise of making commercial theater.

Born in Elmira, New York, Fitch was a self-admitted "sissy" and spent much of his youth isolating himself from other boys. Even in childhood he enjoyed the solitude of writing to the company of male playmates, penning numerous love notes on perfumed paper to female classmates. As he entered adolescence, Fitch maintained an overt theatricality and public effeminacy that, for its time, would have bordered on social deviance. His disinclination to conform to societal roles prescribed for males allowed him a significant flexibility in his perspective on theatrical roles, a characteristic that delighted his female contemporaries at Amherst College. Fitch's youthful experiments with gender identity anticipated his later success in writing successful romantic roles for some of Broadway's leading actresses of the day.

After college, Fitch moved to New York City in the hopes of working in architecture or interior design. However, he continued to write plays and, through friendships cultivated in Manhattan as well as assertive self-promotion, soon saw his plays produced in New York's premiere theaters starring major actors and actresses. His first genuine hit was *Beau Brummel* (1890), which he wrote for Richard Mansfield, one of the rising actors of the day. Critical praise and audience enthusiasm helped make celebrities of both writer and actor. Mansfield would play the nineteenth-century English dandy throughout his career, including five Broadway revivals. His *The Masked Ball* (1892), staged at the famed Lyceum Theatre, starred the popular English actress Mrs. Thomas Wiffen. For the remainder of the 1890s most of Fitch's plays had short and uncelebrated stagings in New York. Yet his interest in American themes and his ability to write appealing star vehicles for leading actresses made him a well-known if not altogether venerated Broadway figure in the closing years of the nineteenth century. His *Gossip* (1895) starred British actress and international femme fatale Lillie Langtry as well as American star Effie Shannon. In *Nathan Hale* (1898) and *Barbara Frietchie* (1899), the latter starring the celebrated English Shakespearean actress Julia Marlowe, he intertwined a fictional love story around the biographies of real life historic American figures.

With the new century Fitch achieved critical acclaim once again with *The Climbers* and *Captain Jinx of the Horse Marines* (both 1901). Each was commercially successful and each brought Fitch in contact with two of the most important women in American theater. *The Climbers* represented the first of several collaborations between Fitch and producer/actress Amelia Bingham, a popular female star and one of Broadway's first women theater managers. *Captain Jinks of the Horse Marines* marked the auspicious debut of **Ethel Barrymore**, who would become the premiere American dramatic actress of the World War I era.

These two successive hits elevated Fitch's reputation to the point that, while he suffered the occasional flop, he was able to sustain his reputation as both a commercial success and a respected artist for the remainder of his career. His late career successes included *The Girl With the Green Eyes* (1902), *The Truth* (1907), and *The City* (1909). He also saw numerous revivals of earlier works, most notably *Beau Brummel* and *Captain Jinks of the Horse Marines*.

Now viewed as theatrical artifacts, Fitch's plays are rarely performed and only occasionally studied outside of the narrow confines of academic theater history. However, Fitch created an early prototype for the career Broadway playwright, who writes skillfully and prolifically in response to commercial demand and persists doggedly in the face of repeated critical and even commercial setbacks.

Fitch died in 1909 from complications of a lifelong condition of appendicitis.

Thomas A. Greenfield and Megan Lee

Further Reading

Hapgood, Norman. *The Stage in America, 1897–1900.* New York: Macmillan Company, 1901. Original digitized from Harvard University. Digitized July 16, 2006.

Moses, Montrose Jonas. *The American Dramatist.* Edition 2. New York: Little, Brown, and Company, 1917. Original digitalized from the University of California. Digitized November 30, 2007.

Turney, Wayne S. "Clyde Fitch." *A Glimpse of Theater History.* Wayne S. Turney Theater Page. Retrieved May 14, 2009, from http://www.wayneturney.20m.com/fitchclyde.htm.

FONTANNE, LYNN

See **Lunt, Alfred, and Fontanne, Lynn**.

FOR COLORED GIRLS WHO HAVE CONSIDERED SUICIDE/
WHEN THE RAINBOW IS ENUF

Broadway Run: Booth Theatre
Opening: September 15, 1976
Closing: July 16, 1978
Total Performances: 742
Writer: Ntozake Shange
Choreographer: Paula Moss
Arranger and Director: Oz Scott
Producers: Joseph Papp and Woodie King Jr.; in association with Henry Street Settlement's New Federal Theatre; Associate Producer: Bernard Gersten
Cast: Trazana Beverley (Lady in Red), Laurie Carlos (Lady in Blue), Risë Collins (Lady in Purple), Aku Kadogo (Lady in Yellow), Janet League (Lady in Brown), Paula Moss (Lady in Green), and Ntozake Shange (Lady in Orange)

Ntozake Shange's play, *for colored girls who have considered suicide/when the rainbow is enuf,* brought the often-unheard voice of African American women to mainstream American theater. Shange's innovative hybrid of drama, dance, and poetry, which she labeled a "choreopoem," presented an intensely emotional and controversial exploration of contemporary African American women's self-identity. The 1976 Broadway production enjoyed immediate critical and commercial success. Although not a "straight play" script in the strictest sense, *for colored girls . . .* went on to become the longest-running Broadway play ever written by an African American and one of the top-ten longest-running dramatic Broadway productions of the 1970s. In the decades following its nearly two-year Broadway run, the play has become a canonical work of twentieth-century African American and

Poet, playwright, and actress Ntozake Shange, New York City, 1976. (AP Photo)

feminist literatures and a ubiquitous school and college production choice, particularly among African American students.

Shange was born Paulette Williams in Trenton, New Jersey. She was married for a short time while attending Barnard College in New York in the late 1960s. After her marriage failed, Shange spiraled into a severe depression that led to several suicide attempts. Her intense feelings of alienation during this period would eventually serve as the emotional core of *for colored girls . . .* She adopted her African name (Ntozake meaning "she who comes with her own things," and Shange—"she who walks like a lion") in 1971 while attending graduate school at the University of Southern California in Los Angeles.

Upon receiving her master's degree, Shange remained in California during the early 1970s, teaching humanities courses in various colleges while writing poetry and performing with professional dance companies. Her writing became increasingly influenced by the burgeoning feminist literary movement of the 1970s and especially by the numerous California feminist writers and artists with whom she was associated. Eventually, Shange began her own dance company along with a fellow dancer, Paula Moss, who would eventually join Shange in the **Off-Broadway** and Broadway productions of *for colored girls . . .* With this new dance company Shange and Moss began creating the **choreography** that would appear in *for colored girls . . .* In the mid-1970s, Shange and Moss moved to New York. Shange began working as a poet, dancer, and performing artist throughout the city, performing material that would also later make its way into the play.

The full play *for colored girls . . .* evolved gradually during the early 1970s through Shange's continuous writing, choreographing, and dance performances in California and New York. Much like the 1970s hit musicals *Company* (1970) and *A Chorus Line* (1975), *for colored girls . . .* is a conceptual piece structured upon thematically interrelated vignettes rather than a conventional story line. A rare (for the time) dramatic foray into African American feminism, *for colored girls . . .* represented Shange's purposeful effort to fill a void in theater and literature with respect to stories of black women. Shange sought to address black women's ostracization by white patriarchal society while also shining a light on black women's diminished self-esteem resulting from abuse by black men.

While performing in New York, Shange caught the attention of **Joseph Papp**'s production team, best known then as now for their highly successful New York Shakespeare Festival and the Public Theater Off-Broadway venue. Shange, with Papp as producer and Moss as choreographer, mounted an Off-Broadway production of *for colored girls* . . . in the summer of 1976. Both Shange and Moss, apart from, respectively, writing and choreographing the show, performed in the cast. The summer production drew rave reviews for its power and ingenuity—including numerous favorable comparisons with *A Chorus Line*, which Papp had produced Off-Broadway and brought to Broadway only a year before. *For colored girls* . . . won the Obie Award for Best Play, and Papp moved the show to Broadway's Booth Theatre in September. Notwithstanding its frank exploration of abortion, racial tensions, and other themes normally deemed too controversial for mainstream Broadway audiences, the show generated overwhelmingly favorable critical and audience responses.

The play's straightforward confrontation of problems plaguing the intimate relationships between black men and women proved to be highly controversial, particularly among African Americans. Against the prevailing calls for black unity in contemporary black politics and artistic expression, the play seemed to many to be a counterproductive and even irresponsible attack against the black man. On the other hand, many others felt that Shange's story of seven black women, each representing a different color of the rainbow, who eventually overcome self-loathing to declare love and dignity for themselves, was long overdue.

For colored girls . . . is now viewed as a central work of modern African American drama and literature. Although it is her only Broadway credit, Shange has written several other dramatic works (including other choreopoems), novels, and volumes of poetry. Literary critics and scholars consider *for colored girls* . . . to be Shange's signature work, which places her securely in the ranks of major African American female writers.

Kristen Gentry

Further Reading

Beaulieu, Elizabeth Ann. *Writing African American Women*. Westport, CT: Greenwood Publishing Group, 2006.

Nelson, Emmanuel Sampath. *African American Dramatists: An A-to-Z Guide*. Westport, CT: Greenwood Publishing Group, 2004.

FORREST, EDWIN (1806–1872)
ACTOR

Edwin Forrest was the most acclaimed American actor from the 1820s through the 1850s. During the course of his career, he won over audiences as a "blackface" comic, a Shakespearean tragedian, and a nobly sentimentalized native American chieftain. The first American-born actor to translate his success at home to substantial critical acceptance in London, Forrest helped American theater gain its first vestiges of international respect. In so doing, he paved the way for future American actors and **playwrights** to develop international followings. Possessed of a rugged stage presence and rough hewn personal demeanor, Forrest's often extravagant performances enthralled audiences, even as sophisticated **critics** frequently took him to task for his theatrical excesses.

Edwin Forrest was born in 1806, in Philadelphia, Pennsylvania, a major American theater capital at the time. He made his stage debut in Philadelphia at age 11 and worked his way up to his first professional lead role in John Home's *Douglas* while still in his early teens. In the early 1820s, he began a Western tour of the United States, developing a reputation for his rugged good looks and skills as a blackface comic performer. Forrest made his first appearance in New York theater starring as *Othello* (1826) at the Park Theatre. He revived the role later that same year at the Bowery Theatre. His *Othello* was a triumph, bringing him acclaim and wealth and eventually emboldening him to perform in Europe.

In the late 1820s, trading on his growing reputation as a leading man, Forrest began to sponsor playwriting contests, offering cash and promise of production (with Forrest as star) for new, original American plays with American themes. One winning entry was John Augustus Stone's *Metamora: or, The Last of the Wampanoags*, which Forrest did, indeed, produce for himself. It became one of his most popular roles, and he performed it numerous times in New York and on tour throughout his career.

In 1836, Forrest succeeded in landing a significant part in London's prestigious Drury Lane Theatre. He made his international debut as Sparticus in American writer Robert Montgomery Bird's *The Gladiator*. (This rare London staging of an American play—another product of one of Forrest's playwriting contests—reflected Forrest's influence and stature during this period.) London critics praised Forrest's performance although, not surprisingly, they were ungenerous to the play.

Forrest remained in England for several months thereafter, starring successfully in productions of *King Lear*, *Macbeth*, and *Othello*—a previously unheard of accomplishment for an American actor. He became a popular figure in London high society and fell in love with Catherine Norton Sinclair, the daughter of a famous English singer. They married in 1837, and she returned to the United States with him.

Back on the American stage in the late 1830s, Forrest had successful New York star turns in *The Lady of Lyons* (1838) and *Richelieu* (1839), both by the contemporary British playwright Sir Edward Bulwer-Lytton. He also capitalized on his fame by touring successfully in some of his popular roles. In 1845, Forrest returned to England to play *Macbeth*, but this time audience response was decidedly negative. Forrest and his friends attributed audience dissatisfaction to nationalistic antagonisms. Forrest was particularly peeved at what he took to be chauvinistic loyalty to English Shakespearean actor William Charles Macready, who had toured the United States successfully the year before. The feud simmered over time—largely through Forrest's jealous provocations—and came to a head in 1849 when Macready returned to New York to play *Macbeth* at the Astor Place Opera House. Supporters of Forrest attended opening night intending to riot in protest of Macready's presence. Police called in to quell what is now known as the Astor Place Riots ended up killing upwards of 20 people. Forrest's reputation, already laced with tales of excessive social behavior, suffered in the aftermath. No less damaging to his career and public favor was his highly publicized, scandalous 1851 divorce from wife Catherine, wherein each publicly accused the other of infidelity. The riot and the divorce scandal quickly took their toll on his career. By 1855 Forrest had virtually retired as a headline actor, but became a major collector of dramatic literature and theater memorabilia. He died in Philadelphia in 1872.

Forrest's legacy is among the most significant in all of nineteenth-century American theater. His accomplishments as a singularly successful performer of comedy and tragedy, an internationally recognized American Shakespearean actor, and a promoter of new American plays elevated the stature of American theater arts both in the United States and across the Atlantic.

Thomas A. Greenfield and Caitlin Klein

Further Reading

Rees, James. *The Life of Edwin Forrest. With Reminiscences and Personal Recollections.* Michigan Historical Reprint Series. Ann Arbor: Scholarly Publishing Office, University of Michigan Library, 2005.

Shaw, Dale. *Titans of the American Stage; Edwin Forrest, the Booths, the O'Neills.* Philadelphia: Westminster Press, 1971.

FOSSE, BOB (1927–1987)
CHOREOGRAPHER, DIRECTOR, PERFORMER, WRITER

Renowned for his distinct choreography featuring shoulder and hip rolls, snapping fingers in white gloves, and riveting isolated hand movements, Bob Fosse brought a new jazz-influenced physical edginess to Broadway show dancing. He was among the central figures in the post-1950s evolution of Broadway choreographers from dance specialists to production *auteurs* and helped usher in the ascendance of dance and spectacle over "the book" as the prevailing element in Broadway **musicals** after 1970. No less an innovator in **film**, his choreography for movie musicals anticipated the signature screen-filling, high-energy group choreography of rock music videos in the 1980s and 1990s.

Born in Chicago into a family of **vaudeville** performers, Fosse himself performed professionally even as he was attending classes in children's dance academies. He choreographed his first professional night club show at age 15. After

Bob Fosse, center, leads the cast through an energetic dance number during a rehearsal of his musical Big Deal *at the Minskoff Rehearsal Studios on Broadway in New York, 1986. (AP Photo/Suzanne Vlamis)*

graduation from high school, Fosse enlisted in the navy, getting himself assigned to entertainment units where he continued to practice his craft. Shortly after leaving the navy, he moved to New York and began auditioning as a show dancer. In 1950 he landed a part as a dancer and singer in an undistinguished revue, *Dance Me a Song*. Nevertheless, it was a bona fide Broadway debut, and Fosse worked steadily as a Broadway and Hollywood dancer, choreographer, actor, and director for the next 36 years.

After understudying the lead in the 1952 revival of ***Pal Joey*** (1940), he starred in the role during the show's successful tour. Still in his mid-twenties, he signed with MGM studios in 1953 and performed in a few Hollywood musical films over the next year—most notably in *Kiss Me Kate*. He returned to New York in 1954 to choreograph *The Pajama Game*, a new musical for producer **Hal Prince** and directors **George Abbott** and **Jerome Robbins**. The show was a tremendous success, earning Fosse his first Tony Award. The number "Steam Heat," in which Fosse choreographed singers' movements to complement the onomatopoetic hissing and clanging of a furnace, represents a classic demonstration of Fosse's innovative infusion of hip jazz dance into mainstream 1950s musicals. Abbott worked with Fosse again in *Damn Yankees* (1958), which starred dancer **Gwen Verdon**. Verdon would become Fosse's lover, wife, dance partner, and the definitive interpreter of his idiosyncratic choreography. She starred in most of Fosse's works through the mid-1970s.

Fosse began his career as a Broadway director in 1959 for *Redhead*, which won the Tony for Best Musical. Verdon again starred and won a Tony for Best Actress. In 1966 Fosse created, directed, and choreographed *Sweet Charity* specifically for Verdon. His choreography for "Big Spender" is considered a masterpiece of comic sexuality as the chorus of "working girls" greets their gentlemen clients for the evening. Fosse won a Tony for his choreography. He then directed Shirley MacLaine in the 1969 film adaptation. He scored a second directing assignment for the 1972 film adaptation of *Cabaret* (1966), the stylish Broadway hit about the rise of the Nazis in Germany. Fosse, who had no creative involvement with the original Broadway production, scored an unqualified triumph with the film, which won eight Oscars (including one for Fosse as Best Director).

Even with the remarkable success he earned in Hollywood with these two films, Fosse returned to Broadway in 1972 and embarked upon the most successful phase of his career. In 1972, he choreographed and directed the musical *Pippin*, for which he won two Tony Awards. He followed *Pippin* with *Chicago* (1975), which ran for two years and toured successfully. A posthumous 1996 revival of *Chicago*, choreographed "in the style of Bob Fosse" by former Fosse disciple and paramour Ann Reinking, has been running on Broadway for over 12 years. (Reinking also starred in the original cast of the 1996 revival.) The most successful revival in Broadway history, the 1996 *Chicago* won Tony Awards for Best Revival of a Musical and for Reinking's choreography—which she designed as an unabashed tribute to Fosse's sexy jazz-textured artistry.

Fosse's last successful original production was *Dancin'* (1978), which gained critical attention for its innovative diminishment of story line and construction of plotline through dance. The show ran for four years, earning Fosse yet another Tony for choreography. He continued to do some film and television direction in the mid and late 1970s, most notably as director and co-author of his autobiographical 1979 film, *All That Jazz*. In addition to being commercially successful, the film drew attention for Fosse's frankness in presenting his idiosyncrasies, infidelities, and failings.

At the peak of his success in the 1970s Fosse, a chain smoker, began to suffer the ill effects of a decidedly immoderate life. In 1975, at age 48, he had a heart attack. Although he recovered sufficiently to keep working, his career soon began to falter. His last Broadway show, *Big Deal* (1986), flopped, closing in two months.

Fosse died from a second heart attack on September 23, 1987, in Washington, D.C., while working on a local staging of *Sweet Charity*. In 1999, Reinking led a creative team to mount *Fosse* on Broadway, a successful anthology of highlight scenes from Fosse's major shows and films. The show, which ran for over 1,000 performances in a span of two and a half years, won a Tony Award for Best Musical and featured re-creations or inspired adaptations of Fosse's choreography. The quick hand and body movements, athleticism, and jazzy sexiness that characterized Fosse's best work remain an enduring influence on the overall look of modern musicals as well as musical films and videos.

Thomas A. Greenfield and Nicole Katz

Further Reading

Cutcher, Jenai. *Bob Fosse*. New York: Rosen Central, 2006.

McWaters, Deborah. *The Fosse Style*. Gainesville: University Press of Florida, 2008.

GAY CULTURE

Across periods and cultures, the theater has embraced imagination, dress-up, fun, abundance, escape, and exaggeration while establishing community among those often marginalized in other areas of civic life—a phenomenon particularly applicable to modern American gay culture. As scores of gay artists contributed to the content of the American theater canon and its execution on the commercial stage, the lure, excitement, and escapism of Broadway, especially its **musicals**, have become an integral part of gay culture, and, in turn, gay culture has had a profound influence upon American theater on Broadway and beyond.

Homosexuals have participated in the art form since its inception, but documenting and legitimizing that participation is a relatively recent endeavor, coinciding with the rise of American gay political activism and a corresponding tide of theater professionals and scholars coming out of the closet to give light and context to their place in American theater and society at large. Gay culture around Broadway has tended to encompass stage, screen, and **film** dramas, especially musicals, as well as other products of popular culture. However, the work of gay artists that reached official Broadway theaters, which need to reach a wide audience for their success and legitimacy, is particularly instructive for assessing the impact of gay culture on modern Broadway.

Until recent decades homosexuals working on Broadway kept their private lives out of the public sphere and out of their art. This "closet" extended to homosexuals in the audience and produced the cultural phenomenon—and stereotype—of the "show queen": the gay man who religiously attends musicals, worships divas, collects cast recordings, scrutinizes lyrics for subtle "queer messages" (coded references to homosexuality likely to be missed by listeners unfamiliar with gay culture), and memorizes Broadway trivia with an obsession matched only by sports fans' obsession with baseball or football statistics. Of course, not all homosexuals match the stereotypical behavior of loving musicals, or even theater, and millions of women and heterosexuals are musical fans. Nonetheless, for nearly a century Broadway has been an integral and enriching part of American gay culture and a professional home for scores of legendary American theater artists who happen to be gay.

Closets and Codes before Stonewall

The birth of Broadway coincided with that of modern gay culture: ***The Black Crook*** (1866), widely considered to be the first piece of American musical theater and a progenitor of the book musical, premiered just a few years before the German sexologist Karl-Maria Kertbeny coined the term *homosexual* in a pamphlet arguing against a Prussian anti-sodomy law. Since it would be many decades into the twentieth century before homosexuality ceased to be considered a mental illness, the stigma of "sexual deviance" persisted, keeping gay artists in the closet and influencing the portrayal of gay characters, often to comic effect. Spoofing sexually ambiguous European aesthetes such as English **playwright** Oscar Wilde and painter James Whistler, **Gilbert and Sullivan** created an over-the-top dandy in Reginald Bunthorne from their **operetta** *Patience* (1881). Although no representation of gayness that outrageous would be seen on Broadway for a hundred years, the "Pansy" act found its place in **vaudeville** among the staple gender, racial, and ethnic stereotypes that privileged, white, straight men could ridicule for entertainment.

New York homosexuals of the "Roaring '20s" were able to find welcoming social outlets at bohemian balls and wild parties. Still, hundreds were arrested for "perverted" sexual behavior and many were committed to asylums to treat their "deviancy." In this climate, the Shuberts, legendary theater producers who hired more gay designers and chorus boys ("nances") than anyone in the industry, would not deign to give a leading role to an effeminate man. In the 1930s, homosexuals remained invisible in Broadway musicals, coinciding with the Hays Code in Hollywood, which in 1934 began to prescribe "morally acceptable" content and prohibited any cinematic depiction of "sexual perversion," which, of course, included homosexuality.

With the Code and the closet firmly in place for the next three decades, homosexuals found creative ways to communicate, with wit and wordplay becoming staples. The homosexual code embedded in Broadway musicals was obvious to those who created it and received it. The more one knew, the more one would be shown. Songwriter **Cole Porter** was born into a life of privilege and in adulthood entered a marriage of convenience with socialite Linda Lee Thomas, both factors enabling him to maintain a successful career as a Broadway entertainer, writing scores for many popular musical comedies—including *Gay Divorce* (1932), *Anything Goes* (1934), *Red, Hot and Blue* (1936), and *Kiss Me, Kate* (1948)—without suffering consequences from the open secret of his sexual orientation within the industry. Those "in the know" could read Porter's lyrics, especially for female characters, as an expression of male homosexual desire.

An Englishman without the material wealth of Cole Porter, songwriter Noël Coward had to depend often on his own performances to make a living in both London and New York. But like Porter, Coward led a joyful, extravagant life when he could, and his popularity as a songwriter, playwright, performer, director, and **producer** allowed those who would otherwise stand in the way of his success to "look the other way" when it came to his homosexuality. Among Coward's many and enduring hits were *Private Lives* (1931), *Design for Living* (1933), *Blithe Spirit* (1941), and *Present Laughter* (1946). *Design for Living*, a comedy about a threesome of neurotic and campy artists—Gilda, Otto, and Leo—was written for married stars **Lynn Fontanne** and the bisexual **Alfred Lunt**, with Coward himself in the role of Leo. The Broadway poster depicted the three dressed for bed in a strongly hinted *ménage à trois*: Lunt cradles Coward's head in his lap while Fontanne holds both men's hands. Unsurprisingly, the pre–Hays Code film of *Design for Living*, directed and produced by Ernst Lubitsch, has become part of the "camp canon" in gay movie libraries.

Not all gay Broadway writers of the period were as flamboyantly well adjusted as Porter and Coward. The first major writing partner of composer **Richard Rodgers** was tortured lyricist **Lorenz Hart**. Unable to come to terms with his homosexuality, Hart resorted to alcohol abuse and unfulfilling sexual liaisons. An informed reading of his lyrics, despite their wit and technical sophistication, often reveals self-hate, an unrequited desire for caddish men, and a cynical view of sexual mores. Before his death in 1943 at age 48, Hart's work found success on Broadway for over two decades, including the hits *Babes in Arms* (1936), *The Boys from Syracuse* (1937), and *Pal Joey* (1940).

Rodgers and his next collaborator, **Oscar Hammerstein II**—both straight men —firmly established themselves as masters of the book musical and Broadway's chief purveyors of American heteronormative values and stories. Under their lead, the ideological trajectory of midcentury musical theater became a journey of the heterosexual couple from enemies to lovers, representing the unification of various dichotomies in American culture: city/country, work/play, whites/nonwhites, "us"/"them." It is no surprise, then, that **Stephen Sondheim**, the premier Broadway composer/lyricist of the post–Rodgers and Hammerstein era, an acolyte of Hammerstein, and a homosexual, would struggle to address sexuality in his writing.

While still in his twenties, Sondheim was encouraged by Hammerstein to contribute lyrics to two shows that would become enduring hits. *West Side Story* (1957) was created by four gay or bisexual Jews: composer **Leonard Bernstein**, book writer **Arthur Laurents**, director **Jerome Robbins**, and Sondheim, the least experienced of the group. At that time, with America's gay closet remaining tightly closed in the waning years of McCarthyism, commercial success depended on, among other factors, not being openly gay. As a result, the creative team's shared Judaism played a greater role in their collaboration on a musical about ethnic strife than did their sexual orientation. Still, gay adults coming of age in the 1960s, before the birth of the modern gay liberation movement, found the romance and danger of the show's original cast album reflective of their life experiences.

The lyrics of the song "Somewhere," with its hopeful if distant vision of a future place for "us," carried particular resonance. While Sondheim's homosexuality may have posed artistic challenges for him, it may also have enabled him to more easily break the conventions of his straight predecessors and encouraged continued collaboration with other gay artists. Laurents, for example, enlisted Sondheim to write the lyrics for *Gypsy* (1959) which, with **Ethel Merman** as the irrepressible Mama Rose, became one of the biggest diva musicals ever created.

If Broadway is a cornerstone of gay culture, diva worship is another. Hallmarks of a diva are feminine assertiveness and survival, the latter being a core element of the gay experience. The first musical diva idol was Judy Garland, beginning with her turn as Dorothy in the 1939 film classic *The Wizard of Oz*, which garnered her many "friends" in the gay community. On Broadway in the 1950s, **Mary Martin** and Ethel Merman became divas, while coincidentally battling rumors about their own homosexuality. Their toughness came out in performance, often a triumph over personal limitations or disaster. Later decades welcomed a long line of leading ladies revered by gay men: **Julie Andrews**, **Gwen Verdon**, Barbara Cook, Betty Buckley, Liza Minnelli, Bernadette Peters, **Patti LuPone**, along with Barbra Streisand and Bette Midler, primarily in other media. A contemporary of Sondheim's whose work more directly reflected his own homosexuality was composer/lyricist **Jerry Herman**. Herman created two hit diva musicals—*Hello, Dolly!* (1964) and *Mame* (1966)—that catapulted the careers of **Carol Channing** and **Angela Lansbury**, respectively. In 1966 composer/lyricist team **John Kander and Fred Ebb**'s *Cabaret* opened on Broadway. Its 1972 film version starred Judy Garland's daughter, Liza Minnelli, who had become a diva figure in her own right.

As musicals became gayer in the 1960s, straight plays made advances in both form and representation of homosexuals. One of the icons of American playwriting, **Tennessee Williams**, had a string of Broadway successes and enjoyed an "openly secret" gay lifestyle not unlike that of Porter and Coward. Williams, too, communicated by code through male characters in his plays—like Tom in *The Glass Menagerie* (1945), the diva Blanche's paramour in *A Streetcar Named Desire* (1947), and Brick in *Cat on a Hot Tin Roof* (1955)—all suffering from an unnamed "secret" or "affliction" that remained a mystery to audience members in denial about homosexuality, but was as clear as day to the gays. Following gay playwright **Edward Albee**'s lead in the hit *Who's Afraid of Virginia Woolf?* (1962), Williams and closeted counterpart **William Inge** began turning to absurdism and a more flamboyant theatrical style, pushing the boundaries of both form and content.

In his continued work in musical theater, which by the 1960s included composing music as well as writing lyrics, Sondheim also experimented with form, often surpassing his book-writer collaborators in sophistication. Work from this period included *A Funny Thing Happened on the Way to the Forum* (1962)—which shocked but successfully intrigued audiences, as it sounded like nothing that had come before—and two more collaborations with book writer Arthur Laurents, the flop *Anyone Can Whistle* (1964) and *Do I Hear a Waltz?* (1965), the latter with music by Richard Rodgers (Hammerstein had died in 1960).

By the late 1960s, fueled by growing political necessity, **Off-Broadway** theater artists started creating honest, realistic depictions of contemporary homosexuals. Among the most important of these works were John Herbert's *Fortune in Men's Eyes*, which had a sizable run at the Actors' Playhouse in Greenwich Village beginning in 1967, and Mart Crowley's 1968 play *The Boys in the Band*, which ran for nearly three years Off-Broadway and was made into a motion picture in 1970. Also in 1968, the free-love rock musical *Hair*, which developed Off-Broadway at **Joseph Papp**'s Public Theater, included the song "Sodomy," which alluded to homosexuality and bisexuality (however vaguely) without stigma. The show ran for 1,750 performances and became the first full representation of rock music and rock culture on Broadway.

Liberation and Representation

Late on Friday night, June 27, 1969, while *Hair* was still playing uptown and *The Boys in the Band* was still running around the corner (coincidentally the same night as icon Judy Garland's funeral), a group of drag queens at the Stonewall Inn, a popular Greenwich Village gathering place, finally resisted what had been protracted police harassment in New York gay establishments and ignited a series of riots that would irrevocably politicize gay culture. One of the immediate effects of the Stonewall riots was a torrent of gays in many walks of life openly declaring their homosexuality. While many gays remained closeted during the remainder of the twentieth century, especially in Hollywood but even on Broadway, regular gay folks "coming out" were welcomed by a very visible, growing, and "proud" community who began to demand representation—politically, socially, and culturally. In the face of considerable opposition, liberation did not happen all at once, but there was no turning back. To the nation's gay community, the battle for equality and acceptance was finally worth fighting on all fronts.

The new sense of political liberation would embolden and expand representation of gay culture in commercial theater, and "out" homosexual characters started to appear on and off Broadway after "Stonewall" (the name by which the riots and the attendant cultural turning point is now known). Coded homosexual "dandy" characters had been found in musicals for decades—including fashion photographer Russell Paxton in *Lady in the Dark* (1941), which launched Danny Kaye to stardom, but openly homosexual characters appearing on Broadway was a post-Stonewall phenomenon. The first such character was the unfortunately despicable Sebastian Baye in *Coco* (1969), played by René Auberjonois (who would go on to perfect the sycophantic dandy ten years later as Clayton Endicott III in the successful television sitcom *Benson*). The next year, Lee Roy Reams played the likeable, openly gay hairdresser Duane in *Applause* (1970), which included a scene in a gay bar. The show ran for two years at the Palace Theatre. **Tommy Tune** won his first Tony Award for portraying a gay choreographer in *Seesaw* (1973).

Not all ensuing portrayals of homosexuality were as positive and openly embraced. After *Seesaw*, director-choreographer–book writer **Michael Bennett** set to work Off-Broadway with a group of dancers on a new musical conceived around the audition process and drawn from the dancers' lives: *A Chorus Line*. The show moved to Broadway in 1975 and became one of the longest-running shows in Broadway history. Paul, a sissy, is the only character in the hit musical about fighters and survivors to elicit pity and condescension. In performance, Paul's speech regularly garnered an ovation from the audience, a patronizing sign of approval. But both Paul and Gregg, the other openly homosexual character, are eliminated from the line in the course of the audition. Audiences were allowed to vicariously experience liberalism without the threat of homosexuals actually sharing in their lives or achieving success. Scholars have postulated that *A Chorus Line*'s depiction of Paul belied the authors' sexuality as an example of gay men keeping themselves and their fellow artists in the closet—acknowledging the existence of homosexuality while denying that there are any homosexuals on the stage.

While depictions of homosexuals in post-Stonewall musicals had peaks and valleys, straight plays on Broadway were boldly tackling the project. Martin Sherman's *Bent* (1979) depicted a heartbreakingly unconsummated homosexual relationship in a Holocaust concentration camp. It ran for seven months and earned a Tony nomination. In 1982, gay impresario John Glines brought **Harvey Fierstein**'s *Torch Song Trilogy* to Broadway, where it was roundly embraced with Tony Awards for Best Play and Best Actor (Fierstein) and a resulting three-year run. Meanwhile, Fierstein collaborated with Jerry Herman and Arthur Laurents on one of the most fabulous and outrageous musicals to date: *La Cage aux Folles* (1983), the story of a gay male couple in show business in St. Tropez, France, who battle the homophobia of their son's future in-laws. The musical won six Tony Awards, including Best Musical, and played at the fabled Palace Theatre. With outrageous dancing girls/boys and a leading gay couple that included one hysterical transvestite, the creators knew that they were exchanging a stronger political message for fantastical broad musical comedy that would mildly challenge but ultimately please middle-class audiences.

The Age of AIDS and the Gay Nineties

Just when representations of homosexuals on Broadway seemed to be making real progress and paving the way for greater acceptance of gays in mainstream American culture, the dynamics changed yet again—this time with dire consequences. In the early 1980s gay men began getting sick and dying in droves, sometimes very quickly. Initially called Gay-Related Immune Deficiency (GRID) and nicknamed "the gay plague," the disease was officially named "Acquired Immune Deficiency Syndrome" (AIDS) in 1982. For gay performers and other artists who had made a home on Broadway, the loss was personally and professionally devastating. Amid a wider America that, from the perspective of the gay community, seemed to refuse to know or care about the crisis, silence was no longer an option. In response to the epidemic and the public response to it, gays in theater began coming out publicly in droves. John Glines risked controversy in thanking his partner during his acceptance speech as producer of *Torch Song Trilogy* at the 1983 Tony Awards, but within a few years such speeches became commonplace.

Gay playwrights quickly began to write about what was happening to their community. Initial efforts appeared Off-Broadway, such as activist Larry Kramer's *The Normal Heart* (1984). Off-Broadway-to-Broadway transfers followed including William Hoffman's *As Is* (1985) and William Finn's musical *Falsettos* (1992). While gay people who had been living through the destruction of AIDS firsthand might have preferred Kramer's Off-Broadway sequel *The Destiny of Me* to Finn's "gay AIDS musical" (however good it was), Finn's *Falsettos* made more of an impact on the predominantly white, straight, middle-class Broadway audience.

The political, the popular, and the important—in both gay and American culture —finally merged on Broadway to much critical fanfare with **Tony Kushner**'s epic play, ***Angels in American: A Gay Fantasia on National Themes*** in 1993. The full play comprises two parts. Part one, *Millennium Approaches*, won the Pulitzer Prize for Drama and four Tony Awards, including Best Play, Best Actor (Stephen Spinella), and Best Director (**George C. Wolfe**). Later in the year part two, *Perestroika*, opened in repertory with the first part and garnered repeat Tony Awards for Kushner and Spinella, who played Prior Walter, a gay man living with AIDS. With new groundbreaking in "legitimate" drama, Kander and Ebb in collaboration with gay playwright **Terrence McNally** created a musical adaptation of Manuel Puig's political novel *Kiss of the Spider Woman* (1993), set in a Latin American prison with a gay protagonist. While it nearly eliminated the politics of the novel, the musical earned rave reviews, six Tony Awards (including Best Musical and Best Actress for diva Chita Rivera), and audiences to keep it running for over two years. The next year, McNally's AIDS play, *Love! Valor! Compassion!*, opened on Broadway and won the Tony for Best Play.

Behind the scenes, the Broadway and gay communities took direct action to help those who were ill. In 1987, Actors' Equity union founded Equity Fights AIDS, followed by the Producers' Group's founding of Broadway Cares. The two organizations merged in 1992 as BC/EFA, the theater community's official response to the AIDS crisis, which has raised over $140 million to help people with AIDS, HIV, or HIV-related illnesses across the country. BC/EFA organizes regular Broadway community fund-raisers, such as the Easter Bonnet competition and the Broadway Bares strip show, as well as semiannual appeals directly to audiences after curtain calls at Broadway and touring shows, ensuring that the AIDS pandemic remains visible until it can be eradicated.

Integration and Post-Gay Broadway

Marking a transitional point in the interrelationship between Broadway and gay culture at the end of the millennium was the musical ***Rent*** (1996), written by straight Jonathan Larson (who died suddenly before the show opened Off-Broadway) and directed by gay Michael Greif. Faulted by some gay critics for its stereotypically safe depictions of homosexuals, the show defiantly won the Pulitzer Prize and five Tony Awards, becoming a pop-culture phenomenon. Set in the

NOTABLE TWENTY-FIRST-CENTURY
GAY THEATRE PROFESSIONALS

The following are openly gay, lesbian, and bisexual ("out") theater professionals with notable Broadway credits since 2000.

Edward Albee: writer, *The Goat, or Who is Sylvia?* (2002), *Who's Afraid of Virginia Woolf?* (2005 revival).

Rob Ashford: choreographer, *Thoroughly Modern Millie* (2002), *The Boys from Syracuse* (2002 revival), *The Wedding Singer* (2006), *Curtains* (2007), *Cry-Baby* (2008).

Christopher Ashley: director, *The Rocky Horror Show* (2000 revival), *All Shook Up* (2005), *Xanadu* (2007); as artistic director of La Jolla Playhouse, producer, *Cry-Baby* (2008).

Gary Beach: performer, *The Producers* (2001), *La Cage aux Folles* (2004), *Les Misérables* (2006 revival).

Douglas Carter Beane: writer, *The Little Dog Laughed* (2006); book writer, *Xanadu* (2007).

Chad Beguelin: writer/lyricist, *The Wedding Singer* (2006).

Michael Berresse: performer, *The Light in the Piazza* (2005), *A Chorus Line* (2006 revival); director/choreographer, *[title of show]* (2008).

André Bishop: as artistic director of Lincoln Center Theater, producer, *Contact* (2000), *The Light in the Piazza* (2005), *The Coast of Utopia* (2006–2007); *South Pacific* (2008).

Walter Bobbie: director, *Sweet Charity* (2005 revival); *Irving Berlin's White Christmas* (2008).

Matthew Bourne: choreographer/co-director, *Mary Poppins* (2006).

Charles Busch: writer, *The Tale of the Allergist's Wife* (2000); book, *Taboo* (2003).

Jeff Calhoun: director/choreographer, *Big River* (2003 revival); director/producer, *Brooklyn* (2004); musical staging, *Grey Gardens* (2006).

Mario Cantone: performer/writer, *An Evening with Mario Cantone* (2002), *Laugh Whore* (2005); performer, *The Violet Hour* (2003), *Assassins* (2004).

Gavin Creel: performer, *Thoroughly Modern Millie* (2002), *La Cage aux Folles* (2004).

Bob Crowley: scenic/costume designer, *Aida* (2000); *The Invention of Love* (2001); *The History Boys* (2006), *Mary Poppins* (2006), *History Boys* (2006); director/designer, *Tarzan* (2006); scenic designer, *The Coast of Utopia* (2006–2007), *A Moon for the Misbegotten* (2007 revival).

Alan Cumming: performer, *The Threepenny Opera* (2006 revival).

Lea DeLaria: performer, *The Rocky Horror Show* (2000 revival).

Rick Elice: book writer, *Jersey Boys* (2005).

Scott Ellis: director, *Twelve Angry Men* (2004 revival), *The Little Dog Laughed* (2006), *Curtains* (2007).

Harvey Fierstein: performer, *Hairspray* (2002), *Fiddler on the Roof* (2004 revival) [replacement]; book writer, *La Cage aux Folles* (2004 revival); book writer/performer, *A Catered Affair* (2008).

William Finn: composer/lyricist, *The 25th Annual Putnam County Spelling Bee* (2005).

Stephen Flaherty: composer/book, *Seussical* (2000); composer, *Chita Rivera: The Dancer's Life* (2005).

Scott Frankel: composer, *Grey Gardens* (2006).

Robyn Goodman: producer, *Metamorphosis* (2002), *Avenue Q* (2003), *Steel Magnolias* (2005), *Barefoot in the Park* (2006 revival), *High Fidelity* (2006), *In the Heights* (2008).

Richard Greenberg: writer, *Take Me Out* (2003), *The Violet Hour* (2003), *Three Days of Rain* (2006); new book writer, *Pal Joey* (2008).

Michael Greif: director, *Never Gonna Dance* (2003), *Grey Gardens* (2006).

Neil Patrick Harris: performer, *Cabaret* (1998 revival) [replacement, 2003], *Proof* (2000) [replacement, 2002], *Assassins* (2004).

Tom Hulce: producer, *Spring Awakening* (2006).

Nicholas Hytner: director, *Sweet Smell of Success* (2002), *The History Boys* (2006).

Cheyenne Jackson: performer, *Aida* (2000) [replacement], *Thoroughly Modern Millie* (2002) [replacement], *All Shook Up* (2005), *Xanadu* (2007).

Elton John: composer, *Aida* (2000), *Lestat* (2006), *Billy Elliot* (2008).

Cherry Jones: performer, *A Moon for the Misbegotten* (2000 revival), *Major Barbara* (2001 revival), *Imaginary Friends* (2002), *Doubt* (2005), *Faith Healer* (2006).

John Kander: composer, *Chita Rivera: The Dancer's Life* (2005), *Curtains* (2007).

Michael Korie: lyricist, *Grey Gardens* (2006).

Lisa Kron: writer/performer, *Well* (2006).

Tony Kushner: book writer/lyricist, *Caroline, or Change* (2004).

Michael John LaChiusa: composer/lyricist/book writer, *The Wild Party* (2000).

Nathan Lane: performer, *The Producers* (2001), *The Frogs* (2004), *The Odd Couple* (2005 revival), *Butley* (2006), *November* (2008).

Arthur Laurents: book writer, *Gypsy* (2003 revival); book writer/director, *Gypsy* (2008 revival).

William Ivey Long: costume designer, *Contact* (2000), *The Music Man* (2000 revival), *Seussical* (2000), *The Producers* (2001), *Hairspray* (2002), *Little Shop of Horrors* (2003), *The Boy from Oz* (2003), *Never Gonna Dance* (2003), *The Frogs* (2004), *La Cage aux Folles* (2004 revival), *A Streetcar Named Desire* (2005 revival), *Sweet Charity* (2005 revival), *Grey Gardens* (2006), *Curtains* (2007), *The Ritz* (2007 revival), *Young Frankenstein* (2007), *Pal Joey* (2008 revival), *9 to 5* (2009).

Anna Louizos: set designer, *Avenue Q* (2003), *Golda's Balcony* (2003), *Steel Magnolias* (2005), *High Fidelity* (2006), *Curtains* (2007), *In the Heights* (2008), *Irving Berlin's White Christmas* (2008).

Craig Lucas: writer, *Reckless* (2004); book writer, *The Light in the Piazza* (2005); writer *Prelude to a Kiss* (2007).

Hal Luftig: producer, *Seussical* (2000), *Thoroughly Modern Millie* (2002), *Movin' Out* (2002), *Whoopi* (2004), *Legally Blonde* (2007).

Cameron Mackintosh: producer, *Oklahoma!* (2002 revival), *Les Misérables* (2006 revival); producer/co-creator, *Mary Poppins* (2006).

Joe Mantello: director, *Design for Living* (2001 revival), *An Evening with Mario Cantone* (2002), *Frankie and Johnny in the Clair de Lune* (2002), *Take Me Out* (2003), *Wicked* (2003), *Assassins* (2004), *Laugh Whore* (2004), *Glengarry Glen Ross* (2005 revival), *The Odd Couple* (2005 revival), *Three Days of Rain* (2006), *The Ritz* (2007 revival), *November* (2008), *Pal Joey* (2008 revival), *9 to 5* (2009).

Jeff Marx: conceiver/composer/lyricist, *Avenue Q* (2003).

Michael Mayer: director, *Uncle Vanya* (2000 revival), *An Almost Holy Picture* (2002), *Thoroughly Modern Millie* (2002), *After the Fall* (2004 revival), *'night Mother* (2004 revival), *Spring Awakening* (2006).

Elizabeth Ireland McCann: producer, *Copenhagen* (2000), *Elaine Stritch At Liberty* (2002), *The Goat, or Who Is Sylvia?* (2002), *Who's Afraid of Virginia Woolf?* (2005 revival), *Well* (2006), *Butley* (2006), *Passing Strange* (2008), *Equus* (2008 revival), *Hair* (2009 revival), *Waiting for Godot* (2009 revival).

Terrence McNally: book writer, *The Full Monty* (2000), *Chita Rivera: The Dancer's Life* (2005); writer, *Frankie and Johnny in the Clair de Lune* (2002), *Deuce* (2007), *The Ritz* (2007 revival).

Jerry Mitchell: choreographer, *The Full Monty* (2000), *The Rocky Horror Show* (2000 revival), *Hairspray* (2002), *Imaginary Friends* (2002), *Never Gonna Dance* (2003), *La Cage aux Folles* (2004 revival), *Dirty Rotten Scoundrels* (2005); director/choreographer, *Legally Blonde* (2007).

Jason Moore: director, *Avenue Q* (2003), *Steel Magnolias* (2005), *Shrek* (2008).

Cynthia Nixon: performer, *The Women* (2001), *Rabbit Hole* (2006).

Jack O'Brien: director, *The Full Monty* (2000), *The Invention of Love* (2001), *Hairspray* (2002), *Imaginary Friends* (2002), *Henry IV* (2003 revival), *Dirty Rotten Scoundrels* (2005), *How the Grinch Stole Christmas!* (2006), *The Coast of Utopia* (2006–2007).

Rosie O'Donnell: performer, *Seussical* (2000) [replacement, 2001], *Fiddler on the Roof* (2004) [replacement, 2005]; producer, *Taboo* (2003).

David Hyde Pierce: performer, *Spamalot* (2005), *Curtains* (2007), *Accent on Youth* (2009).

Jordan Roth: producer, *The Rocky Horror Show* (2000); as vice president of Jujamcyn Theaters, producer, *Curtains* (2007), *Radio Golf* (2007), *A Bronx Tale* (2007), *Gypsy* (2008 revival), *A Catered Affair* (2008), *A Tale of Two Cities* (2008), *The Seagull* (2008 revival).

Scott Rudin: producer, *Copenhagen* (2000), *The Wild Party* (2000), *The Goat, or Who Is Sylvia?* (2002), *Medea* (2002 revival), *Caroline, or Change* (2004), *Who's Afraid of Virginia Woolf?* (2005 revival), *Doubt* (2005), *Well* (2006), *The History Boys* (2006), *Faith Healer* (2006), *The Vertical Hour* (2006), *The Year of Magical Thinking* (2007), *Deuce* (2007), *Gypsy* (2008 revival).

Dick Scanlan: book writer/lyricist, *Thoroughly Modern Millie* (2002).

Thomas Schumacher: as president of Disney Theatrical Productions, producer, *Aida* (2000), *Tarzan* (2006), *Mary Poppins* (2006), *The Little Mermaid* (2008).

Jeffrey Seller: producer, *Private Lives* (2002 revival), *La Bohème* (2002 revival), *Avenue Q* (2003), *High Fidelity* (2006), *In the Heights* (2008), *[title of show]* (2008).

Marc Shaiman: composer/lyricist, *Hairspray* (2002); composer, *The Odd Couple* (2005 revival); composer/lyricist/performer, *Martin Short: Fame Becomes Me* (2006).

Duncan Sheik: composer, *Spring Awakening* (2006).

Martin Sherman: writer, *Rose* (2000); book writer, *The Boy from Oz* (2003).

Christopher Sieber: performer, *Into the Woods* (2002 revival), *Thoroughly Modern Millie* (2002) [replacement, 2003], *Spamalot* (2005), *Shrek* (2008).

Stephen Sondheim: composer/lyricist, *Follies* (2001 revival), *Into the Woods* (2002 revival), *Assassins* (2004), *The Frogs* (2004), *Pacific Overtures* (2004 revival), *Sweeney Todd* (2005 revival), *Company* (2006 revival), *Sunday in the Park with George* (2008 revival); lyricist, *Gypsy* (2003 revival), *Gypsy* (2008 revival).

David Stone: producer, *Man of La Mancha* (2002 revival), *Wicked* (2003), *The 25th Annual Putnam County Spelling Bee* (2005), *Three Days of Rain* (2006), *Next to Normal* (2009).

John Tartaglia: performer, *Avenue Q* (2003), *Beauty and the Beast* (1994) [replacement, 2006], *Shrek* (2008).

Lily Tomlin: performer/producer, *The Search for Signs of Intelligent Life in the Universe* (2000 revival).

Jeff Whitty: book writer, *Avenue Q* (2003).

Scott Wittman: lyricist, *Hairspray* (2002); conceiver/lyricist/director, *Martin Short: Fame Becomes Me* (2006).

George C. Wolfe: director, *The Wild Party* (2000), *Elaine Stritch: At Liberty* (2002), *Topdog/Underdog* (2002), *Take Me Out* (2003), *Caroline, or Change* (2004).

Doug Wright: writer, *I Am My Own Wife* (2003); book writer, *Grey Gardens* (2006), *The Little Mermaid* (2008).

Francesca Zambello: director, *The Little Mermaid* (2008).

—Compiled by Kenneth James Cerniglia

early 1990s but produced at a time when AIDS infection was ceasing to be an automatic death sentence in the United States, *Rent* spoke to a generation of teens who grew up during the height of the AIDS crisis and were ready to find meaning, acceptance, and hope in the future while pretending to be "rebellious" theatergoers.

In the years since *Rent* premiered, Broadway and gay culture have begun to heal from AIDS losses while witnessing the change of a millennium, surviving the shock of 9/11, and continuing the fight for equality. A sign of progress can be found in contemporary Broadway playbills, which are consistently filled with names of out gay writers, directors, and performers (see sidebar "Notable Twenty-First-Century Gay Theatre Professionals"). As Broadway and American popular culture in general have become ostensibly gayer, or at least less overtly hostile to gays and gay life, perhaps the need for a separately identified "gay" culture in discussions of American theater will subside. But even if it does so during this century, twentieth-century Broadway and gay culture were, and in many respects remain, inextricably joined at the hip—as well as joined at the script, the choreography, the score, the libretto, the cast and crew.

Kenneth James Cerniglia

Further Reading

Clum, John M. *Something for the Boys: Musical Theater and Gay Culture*. New York: Palgrave, 2001.

Kendrick, John B. "Our Love Is Here to Stay: Gays and Musicals." Web site: http://www.musicals101.com/ourlove.htm.

Miller, D. A. *Place for Us: [Essay on the Broadway Musical]*. Cambridge, MA: Harvard University Press, 1998.

Wolf, Stacy. *A Problem Like Maria: Gender and Sexuality in the American Musical*. Ann Arbor: University of Michigan Press, 2002.

GERSHWIN, GEORGE (1898–1937), AND GERSHWIN, IRA (1896–1983)
COMPOSER; LYRICIST

Through their innovative, far-reaching, and varied Broadway songs and scores, George and Ira Gershwin introduced to the world new kinds of American songs and new approaches to American music and **musical** theater. Composer George infused his Broadway scores with blues and jazz idioms as well as elements of operatic aria and recitative. Ira, the lyricist, masterfully shaped New York ethnic dialects, colloquialism, and slang into readily singable lyrics and popular hits. In a 15-year collaboration that lasted until George's death at age 38, they wrote

15 musicals together (in addition to those they each wrote separately in collaborations with other people) and dozens of hit songs, including some of the most famous Broadway tunes of the pre–World War II era. In addition, they established the prototype for the durable composer/lyricist team that would define how Broadway musicals would be written and developed in the Golden Age of musicals from the 1940s through the 1960s.

Born two years apart in New York City into a Russian Jewish immigrant family, Ira and George were drawn to their respective callings as lyricist and composer early in life. Intrigued by the humorously complex lyrics of W. S. Gilbert (of **Gilbert and Sullivan**) and the understated wit of British writer P. G. Wodehouse, Ira found great joy in writing limericks and puns using the diversity of urban colloquialisms he heard daily in his Manhattan neighborhood. Younger brother George was a teenaged fan of pub, musical hall, and Tin Pan Alley songs. He also developed an early fascination with ragtime, a new style of music that combined elements of John Philip Sousa's marches with the African-based rhythms emanating from African American neighborhoods and clubs.

As teenagers the Gershwins attended Broadway musicals composed and written by people with whom they would soon compete, collaborate, and become friends, including **Irving Berlin** and **Jerome Kern**. George was captivated by the fledgling musical theater business of the 1910s and longed to be part of it. By age 18 he was picking up occasional jobs as a piano accompanist, using that experience to study the ranges and limits of singers' voices. Meanwhile, Ira was writing witty, sophisticated pieces about the people he observed in the streets of New York, revealing insights into human motivation that would prove useful when he started writing lyrics for his brother's melodies.

Although they are best known as lifelong creative partners, the Gershwins did not actually start writing together until each had experienced some success on Broadway independently of the other. George's first hit composition, "Swanee," was a late addition to Broadway star Al Jolson's revue *Sinbad* (1918). The song, which Gershwin co-wrote with another young New York lyricist/composer, Irving Caesar, was an instant international hit. "Swanee" sold a million sheet music copies and two million records, becoming one of the biggest hits of Jolson's fabled career. The earnings from "Swanee" allowed George, barely 20 years old, to concentrate on more sophisticated works he aspired to compose for Broadway scores and symphonic orchestration.

Prior to working together, George had been more successful than Ira in publishing and popularizing his earliest songs. However, writing under a pseudonym so as not to appear to be exploiting George's success with "Swanee," Ira wrote the lyrics for a moderately successful musical revue, *Two Little Girls in Blue* (1918). Soon thereafter, the brothers' heralded lifelong collaboration began in force. In 1921 the Gershwins wrote their first collaborative musical, *The Dangerous Maid*, which toured but never opened on Broadway. Their first joint Broadway success was their song "I'll Build a Stairway to Paradise," which appeared in *George White's Scandals* revue in 1922.

"I'll Build a Stairway to Paradise" was the hit of the production. In addition, George composed a 20-minute mini-opera, *Blue Monday*, embedded in the middle of the show. *Blue Monday* introduced a Gershwin technique to Broadway—the use of the "blue note" (technically a flatted third or seventh note in a major chord or scale) to signal conflict or disruption. He would later perfect and immortalize this technique in his groundbreaking 1924 jazz concerto *Rhapsody in Blue* and then again in numerous memorable songs, such as "The Man I Love" (with lyrics by Ira).

Rhapsody in Blue, which incorporated blue notes and syncopated jazz rhythms, seemed to function as a musical distillation of all the unsettled sounds of urban, ethnic New York along with the bold confidence of America's new standing as a powerful force in the world. It solidified George Gershwin's role in the new American music scene and, to this day, is considered a small masterpiece of modern musical composition. "The Man I Love," which was originally written for and then withdrawn from the 1924 Fred Astaire musical *Lady, Be Good*, made its impact as a popular single. It is the first of many songs the Gershwins wrote for a character in a particular play or that stands on its own when played anywhere. (It was later introduced in their 1930 satirical Broadway show *Strike Up the Band*.) The song's subtle interplay of words and music, of hope and despair intertwined, provoked a strong response in listeners. Now a standard and one of the most famous torch songs of the twentieth century, it has been recorded by such stars as Ella Fitzgerald, Barbra Streisand, Kate Bush, and even by crooner Tony Bennett (as "The Girl I Love"). Another song from *Lady, Be Good*, "Fascinating Rhythm," cleverly addressed the phenomenon of black-influenced music sweeping the nation, even as the song itself showcased the syncopated swing rhythms and blue notes that white audiences in particular found so fascinating.

Subsequent Gershwin brothers' Broadway shows, *Oh, Kay!* (1926), *Funny Face* (1927), *Girl Crazy* (1929), and *Of Thee I Sing* (1931), provided evidence of their growing sophistication as writers. Ira's witty lyrics used casual language and the slang of the day to set up situations, capturing subtle moods of their shows' characters. George's music showed increasing use of sudden changes to evoke dramatic uncertainty while his bold melodies showed a certain ease and nonchalance. More hits and standards emerged from their growing repertoire. "Someone to Watch Over Me," a wistful ballad written for musical comedy star Gertrude Lawrence to perform in *Oh, Kay!*, became a pop standard, as did " 'S Wonderful" from *Funny Face*. In this song, Ira's now well-known facility with colloquialism dominated the lyric. He slashed off word endings ("pash" for passion, "devosh" for devotion) and slurred words together (" 's wonderful, 's marvelous") to build romantic excitement while humorously undercutting any clichéd sentiment surrounding yet another song about a couple falling in love.

George took some time off from Broadway musicals in 1928 to work on what would become his masterpiece: *An American in Paris*. This full-length orchestral concert work incorporated elements of French classical music and American blues. (This composition, along with other Gershwin tunes chosen by Ira, formed the musical center for the classic **film** *An American in Paris*, which starred Gene Kelly in 1951—14 years after George's death.)

Back on Broadway a year later, the Gershwins found even greater success with *Girl Crazy* (1930), which introduced to Broadway 19-year-old future dance sensation Ginger Rogers and 18-year-old future Broadway diva **Ethel Merman**. Audiences warmed to Rogers's "Embraceable You," but they exploded whenever the school-aged Merman belted out "I Got Rhythm." That song and her shake-the-rafters delivery became her career signatures. Merman was still performing "I Got Rhythm" in concerts when she was in her seventies.

Between 1927 and 1933 the Gershwins worked with **playwright George S. Kaufman** on three politically satirical musicals: *Strike up the Band*, *Of Thee I Sing*, and *Let 'Em Eat Cake* (1933). Unlike Kaufman, who had established himself as a brutally funny social critic, the Gershwins' shows and songs, for all their currency and ingenuity, had been generally void of sharp-edged satire or ridicule. Nevertheless, the combination worked as the Gershwins' witty yet gentle lyrics and warm melodies saved the shows from being unduly harsh. Although *Let 'Em Eat Cake* flopped, the other two fared well. *Of Thee I Sing* even became the first musical to win the Pulitzer Prize for Drama.

In 1933 George worked with DuBose Heyward to adapt his novel *Porgy* into what George called an "American folk opera," using blues and jazz idioms in the score. The story concerns Porgy, a crippled man from the tight-knit African American community of Catfish Row, and his brief love affair with Bess, a complex woman tempted by the violent men from her past. Gershwin hired an all-black cast of classically trained singers to perform the show. The result was a critical success, appealing to both opera and Broadway enthusiasts. The production closed after a disappointing 124 performances. However, the show proved to be popular on tour and in revivals over the next several years (including a decidedly more successful 1942 Broadway production). The show drew some criticism for its rough-edged, even stereotypical portrayal of black life, and even today it is occasionally sited in discussions of racial "authenticity"—the presentation of blacks in works by well-intentioned white artists. However, the show's score—one of the richest troves of hit songs from any American musical—mesmerized audiences all over the country. "Summertime," "A Woman Is a Sometime Thing," "It Ain't Necessarily So," and "I Got Plenty O' Nuthin' " are familiar to millions of people who have never even heard of the show much less seen it.

In 1936 and 1937 the Gershwins took what they thought would be a hiatus from Broadway to work in Hollywood. They wrote songs for the Fred Astaire/Ginger Rogers song-and-dance films *Shall We Dance* and *A Damsel in Distress*, including two of the dance masters' best-known songs: "Let's Call the Whole Thing Off" and "They Can't Take That Away From Me." Shortly thereafter, George began suffering from severe headaches caused by a brain tumor. He died on July 11, 1937, in Beverly Hills, California.

Devastated by the death of his brother, Ira struggled to find composers with whom he could collaborate. His one Broadway success after George's death came in collaboration with Kurt Weill, writing the lyrics for Weill's music in *Lady in the*

Dark (1941). Although the show was a hit and Weill would go on to become one of the more intriguing musical theater composers of the decade, Ira stayed in California and worked on lyrics for film musicals for the remainder of his career. Unlike his brother, Ira lived to see their Broadway shows and songs become cornerstones of American music and theater history.

Ira remained in California until his death in 1983 at age 87.

Sue Ann Brainard

Further Reading

Furia, Philip. *Ira Gershwin: The Art of the Lyricist*. New York: Oxford University Press, 1997.

Pollack, Howard. *George Gershwin: His Life and Work*. Berkeley: University of California Press, 2007.

Rosenberg, Deena. *Fascinating Rhythm: The Collaboration of George and Ira Gershwin*. New York: Dutton, 1991.

GILBERT, W. S. (1836–1911), AND SULLIVAN, SIR ARTHUR (1842–1900)
LIBRETTIST; COMPOSER

In terms of sheer numbers of Broadway productions, nineteenth-century English operetta librettist W. S. Gilbert and composer Sir Arthur Sullivan were twentieth-century America's most prodigious creators of musical theater. Apart from the volume of productions that bear their names (approximately 150 New York revivals of 11 different **operettas** between 1900 and 1980), Gilbert and Sullivan whetted America's appetite for sophisticated, clever musical theater. The characteristic witticisms and satirical elements of a Gilbert and Sullivan show exerted a powerful influence on the direction that the emerging American **musical** would take throughout the century. Since the 1970s, with the advent of the concept musical and the megamusical, commercial interest in their works has waned noticeably. Nevertheless, Gilbert and Sullivan maintain a strong presence in American theater and popular culture to this day.

W. S. Gilbert was born in London on November 18, 1836. A lawyer by training, he began writing short stories, comic rants, and theater reviews while in his thirties to supplement his income. He frequently complemented his written works with original comical illustrations. These illustrated writings were so popular that he published a collection of them (*Bab Ballads*, 1868). The absurd situations presented in his illustrations anticipated some of the distinctive qualities of his later operetta libretti, such as ridiculous plotlines with ridiculous dilemmas and no less ridiculous solutions. Gilbert would eventually turn his interests away from short novelty pieces toward writing plays and libretti.

Arthur Sullivan was born on May 13, 1842, in Lambeth, London. He became interested in music during childhood. As a teenager he attended the Royal Academy of Music on a one-year scholarship, so impressing the faculty that they extended his award to three years. After leaving the Academy in 1861, he began composing suites and incidental music, eventually taking on the more advanced challenges of composing ballets and opera. He composed his first comic opera, *Cox and Box*, with lyricist F. C. Burnand. The work opened in London in 1866. Future collaborator Gilbert, who happened to be reviewing the production in London, observed that Sullivan's score was "in many places, of too high a class for the grotesquely absurd plot to which it is wedded." This very incongruity, of course, would eventually characterize Gilbert and Sullivan's best work.

Gilbert met Sullivan in 1869 through a mutual friend. At that point, each had achieved success in his respective field. Gilbert's cleverly comical poems and plays had made him popular in theatrical circles, and Sullivan's orchestrations had garnered considerable praise from his peers. Their reputations thus inspired producer John Hollingshead to hire them to write lyrics and music, respectively, for *Thespis* (London 1871), a burlesque comic operetta about a theater troop that switches places with the Greek gods. The show was a moderate success in the West End and played for 63 performances. Now largely forgotten, it was never published and has never been produced professionally in New York.

The two collaborated on a few more operettas, notably their first Broadway transfer, *Trial by Jury*, a more streamlined, fast-paced, and witty piece than the broadly farcical *Thespis*. *Trial by Jury* opened at London's Royalty Theatre in March 1875; an American production went up in November at the Eagle Theatre on 33rd Street and played for one week.

H.M.S. Pinafore (London 1878; Broadway 1879) was their first major hit in America. The story of a naval admiral's daughter who falls in love with a lower-class sailor, *Pinafore* satirized the rigidity of Britain's class system as well as its politics and military. It opened to high acclaim in London from **critics** and audiences alike. Demand for American productions was immediate inasmuch as Broadway was long accustomed to welcoming British hits, and word of *Pinafore*'s triumph in London reached America very quickly.

Much of the success of the London *Pinafore* can be attributed to Gilbert's casting and direction of the production. Demanding a more naturalistic approach to acting than was typically associated with operetta, Gilbert integrated sophisticated comedic acting and timing into a genre whose musical elements usually overwhelmed all other considerations. This altogether advanced concept of musical staging exerted an enormous influence on the development of later musical theater in London and America.

The first blush of *Pinafore*'s influence in America proved highly problematic for the show's creators. Taking advantage of lax copyright laws, upwards of 100 American theater companies mounted their own unauthorized versions of *Pinafore* all around the country, making whatever edits or reconstructions of the show they chose. In an effort to head off future thefts of this kind, Gilbert and Sullivan arranged for their next production, *The Pirates of Penzance*, to open in New York (1879) before it opened in London.

By 1881 a London producer, Richard D'Oyly Carte, had built the Savoy Theatre as a showcase for Gilbert and Sullivan, whose works were now the most popular musical theater fare in the West End and on Broadway. The first theater ever to be lit entirely by electricity, the Savoy became the home for all subsequent Gilbert and Sullivan openings. (Eventually, the term "Savoy Operas" became associated with all Gilbert and Sullivan operetta; the phrase is sometimes rather loosely expanded to include works by contemporaries who wrote or composed in the style of Gilbert and Sullivan.) By the 1880s, their popularity and marketability were sufficiently powerful that many subsequent Gilbert and Sullivan hits, such as *The Mikado* (London and New York 1885) or the *Yeomen of the Guard* (London and New York 1888) opened almost simultaneously in New York and London, sometimes within a matter of days of each other.

Gilbert and Sullivan's Broadway audiences seemed particularly taken with the recurring lampooning of British wealth and privilege and made perennial favorites of *Pinafore*, *Pirates*, and *The Mikado*. *Pirates*' bumbling Major General, whose "The Major General's Song" is arguably the most famous in their catalog, is among their most popular foils. Awarded his lofty position by birth and connections, rather than merit, he boasts in song of his knowledge of everything but military matters. *The Mikado*'s setting allowed Gilbert and Sullivan the opportunity to criticize the British allegorically through a story set in mythical Japan. The last shows to follow their trend of satirizing British nobility and aristocracy were *The Yeomen of the Guard* and *The Gondoliers* (1890). The two shows were moderately successful in their own right, though less so than *Pinafore*, *Pirates*, and *The Mikado*.

Over the years, the working relationship between Gilbert and Sullivan became strained despite the continued success of their productions. Sullivan began voicing disapproval of Gilbert's repetitive "topsy-turvy" plots, and Gilbert's famously overbearing personality placed a strain on Sullivan. They ended their partnership after the West End premiere of their last collaboration, *The Grand Duke* (London 1896). Sullivan died four years later. Gilbert published a few unsuccessful plays over the next ten years. He died of a heart attack in 1911.

Gilbert and Sullivan's works were popular on Broadway throughout most of the twentieth century. To date, there have been 32 Broadway revivals of *The Mikado*, 26 of *Pirates*, and 29 of *H.M.S. Pinafore* alone, not to mention countless professional, semiprofessional, and amateur productions. The most recent Broadway success of a Gilbert and Sullivan show was **Joseph Papp**'s pointedly updated 1981 revival of *The Pirates of Penzance*, starring Kevin Kline and pop/rock singer Linda Ronstadt. Contemporary popular instrumentation and arrangements replaced the traditional orchestration, and some purists cringed as synthesizers, electronic keyboards, and pop singers blared out "The Major General's Song," "With Catlike Tread," and the show's other hits. But critics and New York audiences adored the contemporary take on the classic. The show was moved from Central Park's Delacorte Theater to Broadway's Uris Theatre (now the George

Gershwin) to critical praise. The show won three Tonys, including awards for Best Direction of a Musical and Best Reproduction (Play or Musical), and ran for nearly 800 performances.

Commercial musical theater interest in Gilbert and Sullivan began to fade at the end of the twentieth century (although they are very still popular with American light opera companies). Concept musicals like *A Chorus Line* (1975) and *Dancin'* (1978) drew interest away from traditional light opera and, its progeny, the American book musical. Mass appeal megamusicals like *Les Misérables* (1987) and *The Phantom of the Opera* tend to veer away from melodic and verbal subtlety. However, Gilbert and Sullivan's influence upon twentieth-century Broadway was unmistakable. **George Gershwin**, **Oscar Hammerstein II**, **Cole Porter**, and **Lorenz Hart**, all acknowledged Gilbert's wit and cleverness as inspirations for their own musicals (Bargainnier 1989, 125). **Victor Herbert** openly acknowledged the duo's influence and their greatness, and **Stephen Sondheim** tipped his hat to Gilbert and Sullivan in the song "Please Hello!" from *Pacific Overtures* (1976). Their ability to integrate story, lyrics, and song to form a highly integrated whole anticipated groundbreaking American musicals like *Show Boat* (1927) and *Oklahoma!* (1943). Countless updates and reimaginings of their works have been produced in the latter half of the twentieth century, both on film and on stage.

Gilbert and Sullivan also have infiltrated other areas of popular culture. Parodies of their popular songs, notably "The Major General's Song" and "Three Little Maids" from *The Mikado*, often appear in cartoons, sitcoms, and movies. The rock group Pink Floyd sampled the quote "A short, sharp shock" on their famous LP, *Dark Side of the Moon*. The late Supreme Court Justice William Rehnquist, a Gilbert and Sullivan fan, alluded to Gilbert's lyrics in public speeches and statements. A film biography of the two men, *Topsy Turvy* (1999), won two Oscars and numerous other awards.

In the ongoing debate over whether the Broadway musical is a distinctly American art form or a Euro-American hybrid, the legacy of Gilbert and Sullivan presents strong evidence for the persistent influence of the mother country.

Thomas A. Greenfield and Mary Hanrahan

Further Reading

Ainger, Michael. *Gilbert and Sullivan: A Dual Biography*. New York: Oxford University Press, USA, 2009.

Bargainnier, Earl F. "W. S. Gilbert and American Musical Theatre." *American Popular Music: The Nineteenth Century and Tin Pan Alley*, ed. Timothy E. Scheurer. Bowling Green, OH: Bowling Green University Popular Press, 1989.

Bordman, Gerald. *American Operetta: From H.M.S. Pinafore to Sweeney Todd*. New York: Oxford University Press, 1981.

Lamb, Andrew. "From Pinafore to Porter: United States–United Kingdom Interactions in Musical Theater, 1879–1929," in *American Music*, Vol. 4, No. 1 (Spring 1986), British-American Musical Interactions, University of Illinois Press.

GILPIN, CHARLES S. (1878–1929)
ACTOR

Charles S. Gilpin was the first African American actor to achieve fame in Broadway legitimate theater and the first to play a lead dramatic role in a major Broadway play. As Brutus Jones in **Eugene O'Neill**'s *The Emperor Jones* (1920) Gilpin paved the way for **Paul Robeson**, **Rose McClendon**, and other African Americans to secure serious acting roles on Broadway and in legitimate theater throughout the country.

Gilpin was born and raised in Richmond, Virginia, performing in local amateur shows as a child. From his late teens through his twenties, he sang and acted in a number of African American touring choirs and minstrel troops, including the Hamilton, Ontario's Canadian Jubilee Singers, **Bert Williams**'s *Abyssinia* (singing in the chorus when the show appeared on Broadway in 1906), and the Original Smart Set. From 1907 to 1911 he began his career as a stage actor with Robert T. Motts's Pekin Theater in Chicago, the first black-owned professional theater in the country. After four years with the Pekin company, Gilpin returned to touring as a singer for about a year. He finally settled in New York circa 1912 at the dawn of the Harlem Renaissance theater movement.

In 1913 and 1914 Gilpin performed for Alex C. Rogers and Henry S. Creamer (the leading African American musical composers and lyricists of the day) in their revue *Old Man's Boy*, which played at Harlem's Lafayette Theatre. The show toured briefly thereafter. In 1915 he performed with the Anita Bush Players, another major black New York theater company. In 1916 he became a leading actor for the Lafayette Theatre.

Gilpin was among a handful of African Americans who used their prominence in Harlem community theater as an entree to Broadway and other "mainstream" performing opportunities. Gilpin made his Broadway debut as Rev. William Curtis in John Drinkwater's successful *Abraham Lincoln* (1919), which had a successful 193 performance run. Gilpin's performance impressed **playwright** Eugene O'Neill, who cast him as Brutus Jones in *The Emperor Jones* (1920), produced by the **Provincetown Players**. The show became an early major hit for O'Neill and Provincetown and, as such, it propelled Gilpin into realms of fame and professional acclaim that no African American actor had ever achieved. For example, in 1921 he received a citation from the Drama League of New York for outstanding contributions to American theater—the first African American ever so honored. He toured in *The Emperor Jones* in 1921 and 1922, meeting with praise throughout the tour. He also starred in two of the three subsequent Broadway revivals during the 1920s.

By the mid-1920s, however, O'Neill and Gilpin were feuding over the play. O'Neill accused Gilpin of performing the role badly, even drunk, and changing lines arbitrarily. Gilpin, who had come to believe the frequent appearance of the word "nigger" in the play did harm to blacks and the play itself, resented O'Neill's intractability against making any modifications in wording. The dispute led to Paul Robeson being cast in the role for the first Broadway revival in 1925.

Although Gilpin appeared in two later New York revivals of the play (both in 1926), the fallout from the dispute with O'Neill led to the curtailment of Gilpin's career. He formally retired from theater in 1928 and suffered a nervous breakdown shortly thereafter.

Gilpin died in 1929 in Eldridge Park, New Jersey.

Thomas A. Greenfield and Nicole Katz

Further Reading

Krasner, David. *A Beautiful Pageant: African American Theatre, Drama, and Performance in the Harlem Renaissance, 1910–1927.* New York: Palgrave Macmillan, 2002.

Peterson, Bernard L. *A Century of Musicals in Black and White: An Encyclopedia of Musical Stage Works By, About, or Involving African Americans.* Westport, CT: Greenwood Publishing Group, 1993.

GLASPELL, SUSAN (1882c.–1948)
PLAYWRIGHT, ACTIVIST, THEATRICAL PRODUCER, NOVELIST

Susan Glaspell, whose birth year is a matter of dispute among historians, was a prominent **playwright** of the early twentieth-century independent American "Little Theatre Movement" and a co-founder of the **Provincetown Players**. She was among the first American women playwrights to see her plays produced professionally in New York theaters. Her realistic works centered on the lives of women and, thus, paved the way for later American women playwrights and feminist movements within New York theater.

Born in Davenport, Iowa, Glaspell attended Drake University in Des Moines, Iowa, receiving a bachelor's degree in 1899. She went on to do graduate work in English in 1903 at the University of Chicago. After marrying playwright George Cram Cook in 1913, Glaspell moved east, living in Greenwich Village, New York, and Provincetown, Massachusetts. Soon thereafter she began to write plays, both independently and in conjunction with Cook. Her first Broadway play, *Trifles* (1916), which ran in repertory with several other new American plays, is considered to be a canonical text in modern American feminist theater and is still widely produced and studied in universities. Her collaborations with Cook included her longest-running Broadway play, *Suppressed Desires* (1917), which ran for six months.

In 1915, Glaspell and Cook had co-founded the Provincetown Players. Inspired by revolutionary theatrical movements in Europe, Glaspell and Cook established the Provincetown Players to nurture new experimental, intellectual American theater artists and bring their work to the attention of the theatergoing public. In the late 1910s and early 1920s Glaspell and Cook's efforts proved to be highly successful, principally through their discovery and support of the then unknown **Eugene O'Neill**, but also with productions of plays by Edna St. Vincent Millay, Paul Green, and Glaspell herself. In addition to *Trifles* and *Suppressed Desires*, Glaspell enjoyed critical success with *A Woman's Honor* (1918) and *The Verge* (1921).

In 1922 Glaspell and Cook left the Provincetown Players due to what they took to be a loss of the group's original pioneering sense of purpose. They moved to Greece where Glaspell remained until Cook died in 1924. Glaspell returned to the United States and remained active in theater throughout the 1930s. Her play *Alison's House*, based on the life of Emily Dickinson, won the Pulitzer Prize for Drama in 1931. From 1934 to 1935 she was director of the Midwest Play Bureau, an agency of the **Federal Theatre Project**, eventually resigning due to illness. She continued writing novels and articles well into the 1940s.

Glaspell died in Provincetown in 1948 from viral pneumonia. To this day, scholarly and popular interest generate continuous study and admiration for her plays, novels, and advocacy for an intellectual and socially conscious American theater.

Thomas A. Greenfield and Kaitlin Snyder

Further Reading

Carpentier, Martha Celeste. *Susan Glaspell: New Directions in Critical Inquiry.* Newcastle, U.K.: Cambridge Scholars Press, 2006.

Gainor, J. Ellen. *Susan Glaspell in Context: American Theater, Culture, and Politics, 1915–48.* Ann Arbor: University of Michigan Press, 2001.

GREY, JOEL (1932–)
PERFORMER

Although born after the age of **vaudeville**, Joel Grey embodies the spirit and persona of the old-time song and dance headliner more than any other contemporary performer. The son of a dance band leader and a "discovery" of vaudeville great **Eddie Cantor**, Grey's most significant stage roles—particularly that of the Master of Ceremonies in the stage and film versions of *Cabaret*—have placed him squarely in the tradition of music hall history.

Grey was born Joel David Katz on April 11, 1932, in Cleveland, Ohio, to Grace and Mickey Katz. His father's career as a comic musician shaped Grey's childhood. Katz's dance band and *Borscht Capades* show toured for two decades (including a three-month stint in 1951 at Broadway's Royale Theatre, now named the Bernard Jacobs Theatre). Grey's involvement with a local Cleveland juvenile company led to his first role in an adult production at the age of ten. Afterwards,

Joel Grey, in the role of Master of Ceremonies, stands on the piano during the "Money Song" with the ensemble in the original Broadway musical Cabaret *at the Broadhurst Theatre in New York City, 1966. (AP Photo)*

Grey moved with his family to Los Angeles, completed high school there, and at age 16 began appearing in the *Borscht Capades*, often impersonating his father.

After seeing the *Borscht Capades* during its Broadway run, Eddie Cantor booked Grey for his television program. Leveraging the television appearances, Grey was able to get bookings at well-known nightclubs. He formally changed his name from Katz to Grey and set about pursuing a show business career in earnest. True to the traditions of his music hall upbringing and talents, Grey's show included patter, singing, and dancing. Although his shows were generally well reviewed and he secured engagements at famous venues, he seldom got top billing—quite possibly owing to the nostalgic quality of his act.

After a few years, frustrated with touring, the alcohol-fueled ambiance of night-clubs, and the low status of nightclub performers in the theater world, Grey began studying acting at the **Neighborhood Playhouse** in New York City, coached there by **Sanford Meisner** and, later, Wynn Handman. His Broadway debut came in Vernon Duke and Ogden Nash's *The Littlest Revue* (1956), appropriately an updated 1920s style, multi-act song and dance show. The production had garnered a respectable following **Off-Broadway** before moving to **Broadway** for a four-week run.

An appearance in the title role in *Jack and the Beanstalk* for an NBC television special in September 1956 temporarily diverted Grey away from live theater toward **television** and minor **films**. He appeared on more than 50 television shows, including those of Dean Martin and **Ed Sullivan**, and released several musical recordings after playing a rock and roll performer on the television series *December Bride*.

He returned to Broadway in the early 1960s in substitute and understudy roles. In 1961 he replaced Warren Berlinger as Buddy Baker in **Neil Simon**'s first Broadway hit *Come Blow Your Horn*; in 1963 he replaced Anthony Newley as Littlechap in *Stop the World—I Want to Get Off*; and in 1965 he replaced Tommy Steele as Kipps in *Half a Sixpence*.

His 1966 breakthrough role of Master of Ceremonies in **John Kander and Fred Ebb**'s *Cabaret* earned him the Tony Award for Best Supporting Actor in a Musical. Grey's portrayal of the metaphoric, nameless emcee masterfully blended the careless decadence of 1930s European burlesque with the looming menace of the Nazi insurgence. He triumphantly reprised the role in the 1972 film, winning an Oscar for Best Actor in a Supporting Role (thus becoming one of only a handful of performers to win an Oscar and a Tony for the same role).

His second Broadway triumph came in the title role as Broadway song-and-dance icon **George M. Cohan** in the musical *George M.!* Written expressly for him, *George M.!* opened at the Palace Theatre to enthusiastic reviews. The show ran for over a year earning Grey a Tony nomination for Best Actor in a Musical. The show was also broadcast in a television adaptation on the NBC network in September 1970.

In the late 1960s Grey also made several best-selling albums for Columbia Records. He had, of course, been a featured performer on cast albums for *Cabaret* and *George M.!*, but in 1968 he released a hit solo album, *Only the Beginning*. The following year he released his next Columbia album, *Black Sheep Boy* to good reviews and strong sales. After a several year stint on the nightclub circuit that began in 1972, Grey returned again to Broadway in acclaimed roles. He received best actor nominations for *Good Time Charley* in 1975 and *The Grand Tour* in 1979. More recently, he appeared in the 1996 Broadway revival of *Chicago* in the role of Amos Hart and in the 2003 production of *Wicked* as The Wizard of Oz. Although hardly typecast and clearly capable of commanding a variety of roles and challenges, Grey is strongly identified with *Cabaret* and his extraordinary achievement in compellingly bringing old-time music hall song, dance, and bawdy humor to bear on the most serious and somber of subjects.

James A. Kaser

Further Reading

Eichenbaum, Rose. *The Dancer Within: Intimate Conversations with Great Dancers.* Middletown, CT: Wesleyan University Press, 2008.

Katz, Mickey. *Papa, Play for Me; The Autobiography of Mickey Katz.* (Foreword by Joel Grey.) Middletown, CT: Wesleyan University Press, 2002.

GROUP THEATRE
THEATER COMPANY, PRODUCERS

Founded in New York City in 1931, the Group Theatre is best remembered for discovering the successful **playwright Clifford Odets**, training a generation of future stage and film actors in the techniques of Method Acting, and imbuing the New York theater scene with a palpable sense of political commitment and artistic innovation during the Great Depression. The Group Theatre was one of several companies that sprang from the Little Theatre Movement in lower Manhattan during the 1910s and 1920s. It expanded upon the Movement's ideals of securing a place for socially and artistically progressive drama in the world of commercial theater.

Drawing inspiration and some personnel from predecessors such as the **Provincetown Players**, the **Neighborhood Playhouse**, and the **Theatre Guild**, the Group Theatre distinguished itself by its efforts to emulate Russia's Moscow Art Theatre and its principal director Konstantin Stanislavky's theories of Method Acting. In the late nineteenth century Stanislavsky had developed a series of theories and actor-training methods that compelled actors to use their own emotions to create the most psychologically true portrayal of a character as possible. In the summer of 1931 Group Theatre co-founders **Lee Strasberg**, Cheryl Crawford, and **Harold Clurman**—all members of the Theatre Guild—broke off from the Guild to pursue a more experimental, ensemble-oriented approach to theater than the relatively cautious Guild could support. The trio shepherded 28 young like-minded actors to a rustic summer retreat in Brookfield, Connecticut, for weeks of intensive instruction in Stanislavky's acting theories, as overseen and interpreted by Strasberg, and preparation for the Group's first New York production that fall, Paul Green's *The House of Connelly.* This initial production was artistically and critically successful, buoying the ambitions of the young experimenters. However, productions over the next three years yielded mixed results, and Strasberg's intensity as well as his authoritarian regimen grated on some members. These factors in combination with the financial pressures of the Depression led to personal fissures and dissent within the ranks.

In the mid-1930s, the Group recovered their momentum as well as their finances through their unlikely discovery, star playwright Clifford Odets. Odets originally joined the Group Theatre as an actor. Although he was one of the Group's weaker performers, he ultimately flourished in its iconoclastic environment and eventually turned to playwriting. Between 1935 and 1939 the Group Theatre mounted nine original and revival Broadway productions of his plays, including *Awake and Sing*, *Waiting for Lefty*, *Till the Day I Die*, and *Paradise Lost* (all 1935), *Golden Boy* (1937), and *Rocket to the Moon* (1938). Although the Group still produced works by other well-regarded playwrights, including John Howard and William Saroyan, the Odets plays stand as the company's most successful and best-known productions.

Odets's plays would later serve as an inspiration for American social dramatists writing after World War II, including **Arthur Miller**, **Lorraine Hansberry**, and Paddy Chayefsky. The Group Theatre's greatest legacy to American theater, however, was to be found in its contribution to the training of actors. The Group's extraordinary roster of actors, actresses, and directors who worked and or trained with the company and thereafter achieved considerable success in Hollywood and Broadway includes Clurman, **Elia Kazan**, **Lee J. Cobb**, Stella Adler, **Sanford Meisner**, John Garfield, Will Geer, Howard DaSilva, and Franchot Tone. Strasberg left the Group Theatre in the mid-1930s as a result of disputes with other members over the artistic direction for the company. Clurman eventually became the Group's artistic director, a position he held until the official demise of the company in 1941.

The Group Theatre is credited with expanding the knowledge base of American professional theater and infusing the training of American actors and directors with an enlarged sense of intentionality and theoretical analysis. Many contemporary professional acting companies and theater training programs, most notably New York's famous **Actors Studio** and the Neighborhood Playhouse, readily acknowledge the influence of the Group Theatre in their own contemporary practices.

Thomas A. Greenfield

Further Reading

Clurman, Harold. *The Fervent Years: The Story of the Group Theatre and the Thirties.* New York: Harcourt Brace Jovanovich, 1975.

Smith, Wendy. *Real Life Drama: The Group Theatre and America, 1931–1940.* New York: Knopf, 1990.

GYPSY

Broadway Run: Broadway Theatre (May 21, 1959–July 9, 1960); Imperial Theatre (August 15, 1960–March 25, 1961)
Opening: May 21, 1959
Closing: March 25, 1961
Total Performances: 702

Composer: Jule Styne
Lyricist: Stephen Sondheim
Book: Arthur Laurents
Director/Choreographer: Jerome Robbins
Producer: David Merrick and Leland Hayward
Lead Performers: Ethel Merman (Rose), Sandra Church (Louise), and Jack
Klugman (Herbie)

A success from its premiere, the **Arthur Laurents/Jule Styne/Stephen Sondheim musical** *Gypsy: A Musical Fable* represents for many the climactic achievement of the integrated musical in the **Rodgers and Hammerstein** mold. Ostensibly the real-life story of Louise Hovick's transformation from shy young girl into the burlesque star Gypsy Rose Lee, *Gypsy* is really the story of her mother, Rose, a ferocious stage mother determined to make her daughter a star at any cost. Originally played by **Ethel Merman**, Rose is one of the most sought-after roles in all of American musical theater, a magnificent monster who demands the best from any actress who takes her on.

Gypsy originated in Gypsy Rose Lee's 1957 publication of *Gypsy: Memoirs of America's Most Celebrated Stripper*, which was both a critical and a popular success. Seeing the dramatic potential in her already somewhat dramatized stories, a number of **film** and theater **producers** expressed interest in the rights. Surprising many, Lee selected theater producer **David Merrick**'s offer of a stage musical adaptation over the Hollywood producers bidding for the book.

Despite Merrick's faith in the material, the adaptation process was not, at first, a smooth one. Merrick initially contracted composer Jule Styne and lyricists/playwrights **Betty Comden** and **Adolph Green** to generate a libretto. When they found themselves unable to create a compelling adaptation, they dropped out of the project. Merrick's producing partner, Leland Hayward, sought out another writer, Arthur Laurents, to do the book, with Laurents's *West Side Story* (1957) collaborator **Jerome Robbins** as director/choreographer. Laurents came on board not out of interest in Lee, but of her mother, Rose. Originally quite reluctant, he met a woman at a party who announced that Rose had been her first lover, and described her in terms at least as colorful as those in the memoir (where she was a main, and quite eccentric, character). Laurents decided that in Rose, with her relentless drive to turn her children into stars, he had a character worth centering a musical on and agreed to the project under those terms.

With Rose now set as the starring role, a major star was needed to fill it. Laurents approached Ethel Merman, known for her powerful belting voice and stage presence. Merman was eager to take it. Having read the memoir, she saw in Rose a chance to prove herself as a serious actress. With a star like Merman came conditions, however. When Robbins suggested a third member of the *West Side Story* team, Stephen Sondheim, as the composer and lyricist, Merman vetoed the idea. She would accept a young lyricist, but she wanted a tried-and-true Broadway composer, one who knew her voice. Sondheim, eager to compose as well as write lyrics, was reluctant to accept another lyrics-only position as he had for *West Side*

Story. However, he eventually signed on to collaborate on the score with composer Styne.

Sondheim, Laurents, and Styne eventually forged an enormously successful team. The three communicated often and well, with the result that the songs—both music and lyrics—stemmed directly from Laurents's book, seamlessly advancing the stories and characterizations. The collaboration with Robbins, however, was more troublesome. Robbins preferred the kind of creative control he had held on *West Side Story* and was somewhat frustrated to find that it was Laurents's vision, in collaboration with Sondheim and Styne, that fueled the show, not his. Robbins, for example, intended to stage extensive **vaudeville** and burlesque performances. As Laurents developed the book, however, it became apparent that he was writing a much more intimate and family-centered show: a backstage musical, yes, but driven more by Rose's relationships with the other primary characters, and her need for success, than by the razzle-dazzle of their show business world. In the end, Laurents's take on the material triumphed.

Gypsy follows a traditional two-act musical structure. The first act follows Rose's determination to turn her daughter, June, into a vaudeville star. Rose will stop at nothing to achieve her goal—from pawning her father's prized plaque for travel money, to kidnapping boys to appear in the act, to seducing a candy salesman (Herbie, who becomes her love interest) into becoming her manager. Her older daughter Louise, meanwhile, sews costumes, performs as half of a cow her mother dreams into the act, and generally takes a distant second place as the decidedly less talented child. Act one ends with the announcement that June, weary of her show business life and her overbearing mother, has eloped with one of the male performers, destroying the act but only temporarily thwarting Rose's ambitions.

June's departure leads into the showstopping number "Everything's Coming Up Roses." Terrifyingly optimistic, in this song Rose turns her ferocious determination on Louise and swears to make her a star. The second act sees this goal accomplished. After being booked into a burlesque show by mistake, a mortified Louise ends up performing a striptease at her mother's urging. While she succeeds in making her daughter a star, Rose also loses everything: the beleaguered Herbie leaves her, and Louise, who discovers that she actually has a gift for burlesque, finally claims her independence. The show's finale, "Rose's Turn," is a *tour de force* that takes elements from earlier songs and rearranges them into a musical nervous breakdown, as Rose finally recognizes that her dreams were for herself, not for her daughters.

While the bulk of the musical numbers are entirely character-driven, the show also incorporates elements of vaudeville performance via the acts Rose creates for her daughters. Vaudeville also appears as a design element, as placards locate the scenes. There are also two key burlesque numbers: the instructional "You Gotta Get a Gimmick," in which three strippers tell Louise what it takes to succeed in their business, and the crucial sequence where the persona of Gypsy Rose Lee is born and grows into a success. In this extended section, we follow Gypsy from her first, awkward strip through a number of ever more elaborate performances at ever more elite burlesque houses. Her ascendance is performed with no need for expository scenes to interrupt the flow.

In the original Broadway production, *Gypsy* was well received by audiences and **critics** alike. While the show's initial success is impressive, however, *Gypsy* is as notable for how well it has aged as for its original reception. Today it is one of the most admired musicals of its time and type. It continues to be produced regularly, with a remarkable four successful Broadway revivals in less than 50 years. As for the original Momma Rose, it is debatable whether Merman's wish, to be seen as a serious actress through her work in *Gypsy*, came true. Her performance is remembered more for the quality of her singing and the overwhelming energy she brought to the role than for the nuances of her characterization. Still, Rose proved the crowning glory on Merman's already glorious Broadway career, and Merman remains almost synonymous with the role. Later Broadway Roses, **Angela Lansbury**, Tyne Daly, Bernadette Peters, and **Patti LuPone** were all more accomplished stage actresses and put their own stamps on the role. But while Lansbury won the role's first Tony, it is Merman whose ghost continues to haunt the part, and to whom every later Rose is compared.

In the end, *Gypsy* is not a show known for the innovations it brought to the Broadway stage. While *Gypsy* departed from some key tenets of the book musical (not least in rejecting a happy ending for the romantic couple, and making the mother-daughter pair primary instead), in many ways, it is the epitome of the form. Every element in *Gypsy* serves the characters and the story. The book is dramatic and tight, the songs come directly from the needs of the action, and the use of vaudeville and burlesque styles not only entertain but also offer a history of those forms. And the role of Rose remains *the* tour de force for musical theater actresses. Of the five actresses to take Rose to Broadway, all received Tony nominations, and three have won (Daly and LuPone in addition to Lansbury). The mere fact of four revivals—not to mention a film adaptation and a televised production—over the less than 50 years since the show premiered testify to the enduring popularity and resonance of this quintessential backstage musical.

Michelle Dvoskin

Further Reading

Bryer, Jackson R., and Richard Allan Davison. *The Art of the American Musical: Conversations with the Creators.* New Brunswick: Rutgers University Press, 2005.

Garebian, Keith. *The Making of* Gypsy. New York: Mosaic Press, 1998.

HAGEN, UTA (1919–2004)
ACTOR, TEACHER

From the time she performed the role of Ophelia at age 18 in **Eva Le Gallienne**'s production of *Hamlet* until her final stage appearance in Richard Alfieri's *Six Dance Lessons in Six Weeks* in Los Angeles in 2001 at the age of 82, Uta Hagen dazzled audiences with the range, power, and truthfulness of her acting. She is best known for co-starring as Desdemona in the famous "**Paul Robeson**" *Othello* (1943) and originating the role of Martha in **Edward Albee**'s *Who's Afraid of Virginia Woolf?* (1962). In later years she became equally well known as an acting teacher with the HB Studio in New York. In addition, she wrote two highly regarded books on acting, *Respect for Acting* (1973) and *A Challenge for the Actor* (1991), as well as a memoir, *Sources*. She won three Tony Awards, including one for lifetime achievement.

Hagen was born in Göttingen, Germany, the daughter of art historian Oskar Hagen and opera singer Thyra Leisner. After attending her first play with her parents, a production of **George Bernard Shaw**'s *Saint Joan* in Berlin, Hagen knew she wanted to be an actor. The family moved to Madison, Wisconsin, when she was seven. A voracious reader, by the time she was 16 she had read the major plays of **Shakespeare**, Molière, Goethe, Ibsen, Shaw, and all the plays of Chekov. From the outset of her 60-plus year acting career, she worked with some of the legendary figures in American theater, eventually becoming one herself. Immediately following her professional debut with Le Gallienne she debuted on Broadway as Nina in Chekov's *The Seagull* with **Alfred Lunt and Lynn Fontanne** (1938). As Desdemona opposite Paul Robeson in the historic *Othello*, she co-anchored the longest Broadway revival of a Shakespeare play in history. She played Blanche

DuBois to Anthony Quinn's Stanley Kowalski in the national tour of **Tennessee Williams**'s *A Streetcar Named Desire*, eventually replacing Jessica Tandy in the Broadway production opposite **Marlon Brando** (1948). Hagen won her first Tony Award for Best Actress in a Play as Georgie in **Clifford Odets**'s *The Country Girl* (1950)—a performance that revived the playwright's faltering reputation and fortunes. In 1951 she played Saint Joan on Broadway, the role that had inspired her passion for acting.

In the 1950s Hagen's work on the Broadway stage gave way to her involvement as teacher and director for HB Studio, an experimental theater workplace and residency in New York. Founded in 1945 by producer and director Herbert Berghof, HB studio welcomed as students and resident artists Anne Bancroft, Jack Lemmon, **Jason Robards Jr.**, Geraldine Page, Maureen Stapleton, Al Pacino, Whoopie Goldberg, and Matthew Broderick. (Hagen and Berghof were married in 1957.)

Blacklisted in the early 1950s, Hagen had few Broadway appearances from 1955 to 1961 and did limited **film** and **television** work. In 1962, with the effects of the blacklist waning, Hagen returned triumphantly to Broadway as Martha in *Who's Afraid of Virginia Woolf?* She received her second Tony Award for her *tour de force* performance, which helped elevate Albee's stature from that of a promising avant-garde **playwright** to an important voice in American theater. The production is a milestone in American drama since World War II.

Throughout the rest of her life, teaching and acting continued to overlap. Subsequent notable roles reflected her lifelong dedication to modern masterpieces and experimental new works. She starred as Madame Renevskaya on Broadway in *The Cherry Orchard* (1968) and **Off-Broadway** as Mrs. Kitty Warren in Shaw's *Mrs. Warren's Profession* (1985). She also played the title role in Nicholas Wright's *Mrs. Klein* (1995), for which she won an Obie Award.

Hagen died on January 14, 2004, at her home in New York City.

Ellen Herzman

Further Reading

Hagen, Uta. *Sources: A Memoir.* New York: Performing Arts Journals, 1987.

Spector, Susan, and Steven Urkowitz. "Uta Hagen and Eva LeGallienne." *Women In American Theatre*, ed. Helen Krich Chinoy and Linda Walsh Jenkins. New York: Theatre Communications Group, 2006.

HAIR

Broadway Run: Biltmore Theatre
Opening: April 29, 1968
Closing: July 1, 1972
Total Performances: 1,750

Composer: Galt MacDermot
Lyricist: Gerome Ragni
Book: Gerome Ragni
Choreographer: Julie Arenal
Director: Tom O'Horgan
Producer: Michael Butler
Lead Performers: Steve Curry (Woof); Lorrie Davis (Abraham Lincoln, Member of the Tribe); Ronald Dyson (Ron); Sally Eaton (Jeannie, Mother); Lynn Kellogg (Sheila); Melba Moore (Dionne); Shelly Plimpton (Crissy); Diane Keaton (Waitress, Parent, Member of the Tribe); James Rado (Claude); Gerome Ragni (Berger); and Lamont Washington (Hud, Father, Principal).

Hair introduced the Broadway **musical** to rock music, the excesses of 1960s counterculture, the convention-shattering experimentation of 1960s Off- and Off-Off-Broadway, and nudity. Wary at first, Broadway soon marveled at how this unvarnished (for its time) presentation of the heretofore forbidden worlds of rock music and radical youth rebellion not only brought newer, younger audiences to the theater but also charmed the middle-aged crowds it purported to offend. Broadway never looked back. Rock music, political and social commentary, self-conscious theatrical innovation, and sexual adventurousness have since become almost commonplace, if not yet clichéd, features of almost any Broadway season. Thanks to *Hair*, Broadway has maintained a generally sustainable consumer base

The entire cast of the upcoming Broadway production of Hair *poses for photographers during a photo call on the first day of rehearsal at the Union Square Theatre in New York, 2009. (AP Photo/Mary Altaffer)*

among adolescents and young adults ever since, a market that for all intents and purposes hardly even existed in the years between World War II and *Hair*'s opening night. As the first production of **Joseph Papp**'s Off-Broadway Public Theater, *Hair*'s astonishingly successful transfer to Broadway repositioned Papp, **Off-Broadway**, and eventually **regional theaters** outside of New York as major sources for new American-grown Broadway plays and musicals.

Hair was the brainchild of two little-known young New York actors, James Rado and Gerome Ragni, who conceived the show in the hopes of disrupting Broadway's theatrical conservatism in a manner worthy of the counterculture that inspired them. Both actors had worked on Broadway in the 1960s but were drawn to New York's Off-Broadway fringe and street theater movements. Unlike Broadway, Off-Broadway and fringe theater of the late 1960s had no hesitation in taking on the major social issues of the day, including the Vietnam War, racism, sexism, sexuality, and drug use.

Rado and Ragni saw as the key to their book a 1960s sociosexual phenomenon: young adults foregoing couples dating in favor of group-centered romances and liaisons that sustained themselves within the framework of a larger collective of peers. The two writers adapted for *Hair*'s dramatic center the quasi-tribalism they saw in co-ed groups of a dozen or so young adults perpetually hanging out together in college dorms or cramming themselves into three-bedroom urban "communes." The self-proclaimed "tribal" musical would use the sexual and emotional energy of the ensemble to trump Broadway's standard boy-and-girl love story.

In 1966 and 1967 Rado and Ragni shopped an early treatment of the musical unsuccessfully around Broadway. Eventually they attracted the attention of Joseph Papp who, as founder of the New York Shakespeare Festival, was well respected as a producer of Off-Broadway public theater but at the time had no commercial theater record to speak of. The iconoclasm of *Hair* appealed to Papp's artistic sensibilities but it needed a formal score. Ragni and Rado had befriended Galt MacDermot, a veteran jazz composer with little commercial musical theater experience, and had him write the score to the original script and lyrics. Papp booked the more or less finished product for a limited run as the first show of his new Public Theater, whose mission was to complement his **Shakespeare** productions with new works and innovative revivals. *Hair* and Papp's Public Theater opened on October 17, 1967, for a limited run through Thanksgiving. The show drew favorable reviews and terrific word of mouth response, especially in the counterculture neighborhood of Greenwich Village where the Public Theater was located.

The show would likely have folded after its run in the Public Theater but for Michael Butler, a businessman and self-described peace movement activist, who had seen the show at the Public and fell in love with it—to the point of wanting to manage its future. As a stopgap for developing the show for an as yet uncertain Broadway opening, Butler, Papp, Rado, and Ragni arranged to have it run briefly in a midtown disco during the early evenings before the late-night dance crowd came in. In the interim, Papp withdrew from further interest in the project, the writers expanded and refined the score and script, and Tom O'Horgan, a fixture in New York's Off-Off-Broadway scene, was hired to direct the erstwhile bound-for-Broadway version of the show. Butler, O'Horgan, et al. put together a new cast and went into rehearsal for several months. Thanks to Butler's negotiating skills and persistence, Broadway's Biltmore Theatre agreed to stage the show. The new *Hair*, complete with Broadway musical theater's first documented nude scene, opened on April 29, 1968.

More than a hit, *Hair* was a sensation. The 30-song score (almost double the number of a typical musical), produced numerous mainstream commercial hits, including the songs, "Aquarius," "Easy to Be Hard," "Where Do I Go?" and "Good Morning, Starshine," along with counterculture-inspired stunners "Hashish," "Sodomy," "Colored Spade," and "Black Boys/White Boys." O'Horgan's staging included the outlandish physical movements and actor/audience interaction of street theater as well as lighting effects reminiscent of "acid rock" concerts. Teenagers and young adults came to the show in droves, many dressed in the then outrageous couture of the cast. Traditional middle-aged audiences, familiar with the counterculture from the experiences of their children and the political-centered coverage of daily news broadcasts, became fans of the show as well.

No Broadway musical had made more than a modest impact on popular music and **radio** airplay since rock and roll music took over the radio airwaves in the 1950s. Yet for the next two years, cuts from *Hair*'s soundtrack and covers of the show's hits played on radio consistently. Young adults flocked to a Broadway theater in droves for the first time in a generation, creating a whole new youth-oriented postwar market for Broadway theater. Although subsequent Broadway revivals of *Hair* have not been successful, the show has become one of the most successful **touring**, community theater, and school musical franchises in history —notwithstanding having to face some censorship battles and local protests along the way.

Hair's influence on future Broadway shows became apparent almost immediately. The success of *Hair* prepared Broadway audiences for such youth-centered rock-and-roll–based hits as *Jesus Christ Superstar* (1971), *Grease* (1972), and *Godspell* (1976). More recent shows that carry the mark of *Hair* include *The Who's Tommy* (1993), **Rent** (1996), and *Spring Awakening* (2006). *Hair* is also credited with anticipating the 1970s "concept" musical, of which **Stephen Sondheim**'s **Company** (1970) and **Michael Bennett**'s **A Chorus Line** (1975) are among the most notable examples. Although Papp and the Public Theater benefited only marginally from the show's astonishing income, *Hair*'s Off-Broadway rags to Broadway riches production history serves as both an inspiration and a blueprint for **producers** and theater artists aspiring to merge artistic innovation with commercial success. Papp himself went on to oversee other transfers of experimental shows to Broadway success, most notably *A Chorus Line* and ***for colored girls who have considered suicide/when the rainbow is enuf*** (1976). Numerous other Off-Broadway theaters and regional theaters have since followed suit.

Thomas A. Greenfield and Megan Zeh

Further Reading

Horn, Barbara Lee. *The Age of Hair: Evolution and Impact of Broadway's First Rock Musical*. New Haven, CT: Greenwood Press, 1991.

Wollman, Elizabeth Lara. *The Theater Will Rock: A History of the Rock Musical, from Hair to Hedwig*. Ann Arbor: University of Michigan Press, 2006.

HANSBERRY, LORRAINE

See A Raisin in the Sun.

HARRIS, JULIE (1925–)
ACTRESS, AUTHOR

With five Best Actress Tony Awards for plays as diverse as the historical tragedy *The Last of Mrs. Lincoln* (1972), the romantic comedy *Forty Carats* (1968), and the solo performance masterpiece *The Belle of Amherst* (1976), Julie (Julia Ann) Harris is among the two or three most venerated American stage actresses of the twentieth century. Yet, despite an all-but-unmatched theatrical career and dozens of noteworthy **film** and **television** performances, her name and face are only vaguely known to the general public. Nevertheless, among directors, **producers**, and fellow actors, she is revered for her astonishing depth and range, her artistic durability sustained across six decades, and her lifelong disregard for celebrity and self-promotion.

Harris was born in Grosse Point, Michigan. She became stagestruck after performing the lead role in a high school play and committed herself to life as an actress on the strength of that experience. In 1944, she enrolled in Yale University's drama department and shortly thereafter traveled to New York to read for a part in the 1945 production of Curt Goetz's comedy *It's a Gift*. She landed the role and debuted on Broadway in the six-week engagement before returning to Yale to finish the school year. She left Yale the following year to pursue professional acting full time.

During the next five years, Harris played a number of comedic and serious roles on Broadway, working with some of the most influential talents of the time. She appeared in **Elia Kazan**'s *Sundown Beach* (1948), impressing audiences and **critics** alike. The following year she appeared in a **Harold Clurman** production of *The Young and Fair*. In 1950 Clurman directed the 24-year-old Harris in her breakthrough performance as the 12-year-old Frankie Addams in Carson McCullers's *The Member of the Wedding*. The show was a critical and commercial hit, and the role gave Harris immediate fame as well as stature within the Broadway community.

The 1950s and 1960s saw Harris in a dozen different productions encompassing a variety of roles and winning her additional critical acclaim. She won her first Best Actress Tony as the brazen Sally Bowles in the original production of John Van Bruten's *I am a Camera* (1951), which would later serve as a source for the musical *Cabaret* (1966). Harris recreated the role in the 1955 film adaptation of the play. She won her second Best Actress Tony Award as Joan of Ark in **Lillian Hellman**'s adaptation of Jean Anouilh's *The Lark* (1955). Harris's performance became the subject of a cover story in *Time Magazine*—rare national recognition for a Broadway performer—wherein theater grande dames **Helen Hayes** and **Ethel Barrymore** essentially coronated the 29-

Actress Julie Harris, 24 years old at the time, is shown in the role of 12-year-old Frankie Addams in The Member of the Wedding, *in New York City, 1950. (AP Photo)*

year-old as her generation's best actress. She also played the lead female role in the highly successful stage farce *A Shot in the Dark* (1961) and won another Best Actress award as Ann Stanley in the comedy hit *Forty Carats* (1968).

In the 1970s Harris appeared in six different Broadway plays, including two productions in which she gave landmark performances. In her role as Mary Todd Lincoln in *The Last of Mrs. Lincoln* (1972) she set out to redefine and redeem the historical reputation of the much maligned late first lady without sentimentalizing the character or sidestepping historical facts. The effort was a theatrical triumph. As Emily Dickinson and 14 other characters in *The Belle of Amherst* (1976) Harris revitalized the genre of the one-character play and redefined what a single actor could do within its framework. The two productions resulted in her fourth and fifth Tony Awards.

Throughout most of her career Harris also showcased her talent in films and television, somehow avoiding becoming famous on a level commensurate with her abilities and longevity. She performed in some very noteworthy films, including *East of Eden*, *Requiem for a Heavyweight*, *The Bell Jar*, and *Gorillas in the Mist*. She performed on television periodically from the late 1940s through the 1980s, including a six-year stint as Lilimae Clements on the long-running CBS prime-time soap opera *Knots Landing*. She received Emmy Awards for her acting in two *Hallmark Hall of Fame* specials, *Little Moon of Alban* (NBC, 1958) and *Victoria Regina* (NBC, 1961). She earned a third Emmy for her voice-over work in the PBS documentary *Not for Ourselves Alone: The Story of Elizabeth Cady Stanton & Susan B. Anthony* (1999).

Harris remained active in the theater through the late 1990s even after having survived breast cancer, a backstage fall that resulted in cranial surgery, and a stroke. She took on three Broadway productions in the 1990s, including *Lucifer's Child* (1991), another solo play about Danish writer Isak Dinesen. Harris was still playing the 53-year-old Emily Dickinson in *The Belle of Amherst* on the road at age 75. Her last appearance on Broadway was in 1997 in a revival of D. L. Coburn's *The Gin Game*, for which she won a Tony Award nomination for Best Actress.

All but retired from commercial stage acting by the early 2000s, Harris received additional accolades with a Tony Award for Lifetime Achievement (2002) and the Kennedy Center Honors (2005). The highly decorated American stage actress Harris still does occasional voice-over work for television and film and supports a professional theater near her home in Massachusetts.

Helen Isolde

Further Reading

Bryer, Jackson R., and Richard Allan Davison. *The Actor's Art: Conversations with Contemporary American Stage Performers*. New Brunswick, NJ: Rutgers University Press, 2001.

"A Fiery Particle." *Time Magazine* (cover story). Original, November 28, 1955.

Kufrin, Joan. *Uncommon Women: Gwendolyn Brooks, Sarah Caldwell, Julie Harris, Mary McCarthy, Alice Neel, Roberta Peters, Maria Tallchief, Mary Lou Williams, Eugenia Zukerman*. Piscataway, NJ: New Century Publishers, 1981.

HARRISON, REX (1908–1990)
ACTOR

Although he enjoyed a varied, 65-year career in London theater, British films, Hollywood **films**, and Broadway shows, Rex Harrison is best remembered for originating the role of phonetics professor Henry Higgins in **Alan Jay Lerner and Frederick Loewe**'s *My Fair Lady* (1956), one of the truly distinctive roles in the history of Broadway **musicals**. A brilliant veteran stage and screen actor but an absolutely incompetent singer, Harrison deftly talked his way through the intricate pacing and phrasing of Lerner and Loewe's songs. His distinctive "singing" performances, including "The Rain in Spain" and "I've Grown Accustomed to Her Face," are still well-known artifacts of Broadway's Golden Age of musicals even though Harrison barely sang a note in any of them.

Born March 5, 1908, in Lancashire, Reginald Carey Harrison's acting career began in 1924 as a bit player with the Liverpool Repertory Theatre Company. After several years of performing in various English regional and touring theater troupes, Harrison debuted in London's West End in 1931. He spent most of the rest of the decade alternating between London stage productions and countryside touring companies, developing a reputation as a deft practitioner of wit-laced light comedy. In 1936, he took some time away from England to act in his first Broadway play. *Sweet Aloes* was staged by friend and fellow Englishman Tyrone Guthrie, who was trying to carve out a name for himself as a Broadway director. The show closed in a month, and neither Harrison nor Guthrie would work again on Broadway for over a decade. Upon returning to London, Harrison landed a co-starring role in Terence Rattigan's comedy *French Without Tears*, which became a huge hit in the West End and made Harrison a genuine star of London theater.

By the 1940s Harrison began to supplement his theater work with roles in British films, including *Sidewalks of London* (1940), *Night Train* (1940), **George Bernard Shaw**'s *Major Barbara* (1941), and Noël Coward's *Blithe Spirit* (1945). All of these films were distributed in the United States and provided the means by which American audiences were introduced to both Harrison's on-screen roles and off-screen image as the consummate debonair English wit. Buoyed by his success in British films and eager to work in the more dynamic and lucrative Hollywood movie industry, Harrison signed a three-picture deal with 20th Century Fox. *Anna and the King of Siam* (1946), *The Ghost and Mrs. Muir* (1947), and *Foxes of Harrow* (1947) earned Harrison a sizable American following and made him a star on both sides of the Atlantic. For the rest of his career he would work prodigiously in both England and the United States.

In the late 1940s Harrison, now a solid "draw" for American audiences, went back to work on Broadway for the first time since the disappointing venture with Tyrone Guthrie in 1936. His first Broadway role, King Henry in **Maxwell Anderson**'s drama *Anne of the Thousand Days* (1948), earned him the first of his two Best Actor Tony Awards. He worked steadily in Broadway stage comedies for the next five years.

My Fair Lady, Lerner and Loewe's musical adaptation of George Bernard Shaw's 1916 play *Pygmalion*, would elevate Harrison at age 47 from mere stardom to the status of Broadway legend. Notwithstanding the fact that Harrison had never worked in a musical, much less tackled a lead singing role, director Moss Hart counted on Harrison's charm, familiarity with Shavian comedy, and born-for-the-part persona to win over the audience. The serious singing chores would be left to the 22-year-old English actress Julie Andrews as Liza, Higgins's untamable pupil and heart's desire, as well as a supporting cast of British music hall veterans. Harrison dutifully endured weeks of singing lessons throughout rehearsals and tryouts, all to no avail. Making a virtue of necessity, Harrison and Hart gave up on the effort, agreeing to have Harrison more or less talk his way through his numerous singing parts. The result proved to be a critical element in the show's appeal and coherence. Harrison's conversational delivery of his lyrics provided a perfect contrast in song between Higgins's seeming emotional disconnectedness and Liza's soaring romantic reverie ("I Could Have Danced All Night") as well as her tender vulnerability ("Wouldn't It Be Loverly?").

Harrison won the Tony for Best Actor in a Musical for *My Fair Lady* but remained in the part for only 20 months of the show's six and a half year run. However, he is so closely identified with the part that even knowledgeable Broadway followers "remember" him in the role for the entire run of the show. Harrison won the Oscar as Higgins in the 1964 film adaptation of *My Fair Lady*, making him one of only a handful of actors or actresses to win a Tony and an Oscar award playing the same character.

Harrison did very little work on Broadway in the 1960s, but in the 1970s he returned in a string of productions that would carry him, literally, to the very end of his life. His later work showed considerable variety, including an admirable performance in the title role of Pirandello's difficult *Henry IV* (1973), a return to his beloved Shavian comedy in *Heartbreak House* (1983), and a decidedly anticlimactic return, at age 73, as Professor Higgins in a short-lived revival of *My Fair Lady* (1981).

Harrison worked right up to his death of pancreatic cancer on June 2, 1990, in New York City. The previous month, he had been doing eight performances a week on Broadway in Somerset Maugham's *The Circle*.

Thomas A. Greenfield

Further Reading

Harrison, Rex. *A Damned Serious Business*. New York: Bantam Books, 1991.

Walker, Alexander. *Fatal Charm: The Life of Rex Harrison*. New York: St. Martin's Press, 1993.

HART, LORENZ (1895–1943)
LYRICIST

Lorenz Hart brought a fresh new feel to Broadway **musicals** of the 1920s, 1930s, and 1940s, turning out intricately rhymed lyrics to accompany composer partner **Richard Rodgers**'s lilting melodies. Like the **Gershwins**, Rodgers and Hart established an early prototype of the modern era composer/lyricist team that works together over decades and creates a style and identity uniquely its own. Hart's addiction to alcohol eventually robbed him of his ability to work, forcing Rodgers to seek a new lyricist, **Oscar Hammerstein II**. Although Rodgers and Hammerstein's body of work would eclipse that of Rodgers and Hart, Lorenz Hart's prodigious output and signature cleverness helped establish the urbane, witty Broadway musical of the modern era.

Born into a German Jewish family in New York City, Hart learned about theater and music at the upstate New York summer camps he and his brother attended as children. A smart but embarrassingly undersized kid (he barely reached five feet even as an adult), Hart threw himself into writing lyrics for summer camp plays and skits. He would later enter Columbia University only to drop out in 1917 to devote himself to writing. In 1919 he met a brilliant 15-year-old musician, Richard Rodgers, the younger brother of a Columbia schoolmate. Hart, by then a cigar-smoking wild, unruly 23-year-old, saw immense talent in the serious, straight-laced Rodgers. Rodgers, still an adolescent, loved Hart's ebullient spirit, charming wit, and talent for songwriting, but found his new collaborator's late night drinking and carousing troublesome. The pair made concessions to each other's habits and began writing songs that quickly caught the attention of major Broadway figures including producers **Lew Fields** and the **Shubert Brothers**.

Between 1919 and 1926, Rodgers and Hart had several songs interpolated into Broadway shows. The first hit written almost entirely by the duo and generally credited as a "Rodgers and Hart" show was *The Garrick Gaieties of 1926* (1925), which featured the hit song "Manhattan." Within the next two years Rodgers and Hart would establish themselves as the standard bearers for a new, urbane witty Broadway musical with shows like *The Girl Friend* (1926), *Peggy-Ann* (1926), and *A Connecticut Yankee* (1927), each of which ran for over 300 performances. Critics and theatergoers alike particularly loved the lively, witty songs they produced. *A Connecticut Yankee*, based on Mark Twain's tale of love in King Arthur's Camelot, was a particular favorite owing largely to Hart's remarkable ability to combine medieval references and modern slang.

In the early years of the Depression, Rodgers and Hart wrote several minor Broadway hits and some flops. They also wrote some film musicals. (They wrote one of their most memorable songs, "Blue Moon," for the 1934 film *Hollywood Party*.) They hit it big again on Broadway in 1935 with *Jumbo*, which featured the song "Little Girl Blue," and with *On Your Toes* (1936), a frequently revived musical featuring classical dance and the hit song "There's a Small Hotel."

Despite their success, Rodgers and Hart did not enjoy an easy partnership. Rodgers, a disciplined musician, wanted to work 9 to 5 and then go home to his family. Hart regularly partied late into the night. Egged on by a motley crew of disreputable characters, Hart's involvement with the homosexual underground in New York City conflicted with his bubbly if straight-laced business persona. Rodgers also became increasingly dissatisfied with Hart's uncontrollable drinking. Even so, when pressed Hart could redeem himself by writing spectacular lyrics in a very short period of time, as evidenced by the pair's success with *Babes in Arms* (1937), *The Boys from Syracuse* (based on **Shakespeare**'s *Comedy of Errors*, 1938), and *I Married an Angel* (1938), three big hits in short succession. Two songs from *Babes in Arms* have become time-tested American standards and have been recorded hundreds of times. "The Lady Is a Tramp" is a jazz standard that spoofs high society, and "My Funny Valentine" has been recorded by performers as diverse as Frank Sinatra, Barbra Streisand, the Supremes, and Elvis Costello. (In 2009 the song was even a youthful contestant's choice to sing on television's *American Idol*.) After several more minor hit shows, Rodgers and Hart wrote their most famous show, ***Pal Joey*** (1940). In what was then an unprecedented move for a commercial musical, *Pal Joey* focused on the sordid life and loves of an altogether unsavory cad rather than a likeable sympathetic figure. Rodgers and Hart triumphed in creating music and lyrics that brought the listener to some sort of uncomfortable understanding of the play's seedy protagonist. It was a huge hit on Broadway and its most memorable song, "Bewitched, Bothered, and Bewildered," is among the most popular and admired examples of American songwriting in history.

Rodgers and Hart's final Broadway show was the virtually forgotten *By Jupiter* (1942), a critical and financial success. At 427 performances, *By Jupiter* was the longest-running show of the pair's career despite generating no lasting hit songs. After *By Jupiter* Hart's physical and emotional decline drove Rodgers to seek out another lyricist and, with Hart's blessings, Rodgers immediately went to work with Hammerstein.

A dissipated Hart died in New York City at age 48 on November 22, 1943, of complications from pneumonia.

Sue Ann Brainard

Further Reading

Mordden, Ethan. "The Age of Rodgers and Hart." *The Richard Rodgers Reader*, ed. Geoffrey Holden Block. New York: Oxford University Press, 2002.

Nolan, Frederick W. *Lorenz Hart: A Poet on Broadway*. New York: Oxford University Press, 1994.

HAYES, HELEN (1900–1993)
ACTRESS

Known through much of her career as "The First Lady of American Theater," Helen Hayes (Brown) appeared on Broadway in 47 productions spanning a stage career of eight decades. The winner of two Best Actress Tony Awards and numerous other honors, she was one of the few American women born in the twentieth century to achieve international fame primarily through her work as a Broadway actress. Her early success as a child Broadway performer led to a prodigious **film** career that peaked in the 1920s and 1930s. Toward the end of her professional life, she garnered new fame with post–World War II baby boomers through a flurry of commendable if not entirely distinguished **television** roles in network television series, and the occasional prestige television drama. Along the way she became one of only a handful of people to have won at least one Tony, Oscar, Grammy,

Helen Hayes poses with James Stewart at New York's Anta Theatre, 1970, following the opening of Harvey, *a revival of the Pulitzer Prize–winning Mary Chase comedy of 1944. (AP Photo)*

and Emmy award. However, Helen Hayes's legacy stands first and last as a foundation block of Broadway history.

Pushed onto the stage as a child in her native Washington, D.C., by a star-struck mother (although by her own admission Hayes required little pushing), she was discovered at age five in storybook fashion by Broadway comic and **producer Lew Fields**, who just happened to see her in a local hometown performance. Drawn by her talent and stage presence, Fields promised big things to Helen and her mother—and he delivered. In 1909 at age eight Helen Hayes debuted on Broadway in very elite company. *Old Dutch*, with young Hayes, starred Fields along with headline performers John Bunny and Eva Davenport. The show's composer was **Victor Herbert**, whose 1905 *Babes in Toyland* was one of the first major hit American **musicals** of the new century. *Old Dutch*'s musical director was Louis Gottschalk whose previous effort, *The Merry Widow*, had just completed a then staggering 400-plus performance run. Produced by Fields and the **Shubert Brothers**, *Old Dutch* ran for a respectable 88 performances in the popular Herald Square Theatre. Thereafter, Hayes performed continuously throughout her childhood. Through her teens Hayes appeared in eight Broadway productions, touring intermittently (with mother in tow) as a performer in Fields's road companies. By her twenty-first birthday, Hayes had worked with almost every major American theater artist and producer of the day. As a Broadway actress Helen Hayes "had arrived" without ever having been "on her way."

Fate and her considerable talent spared Hayes the common crises of aging child stars. Leading roles in major productions started arriving almost matter-of-factly in her late teens and early twenties as her artistic and career interests evolved from Fields's **vaudeville**-tinged musicals to the sophisticated stage comedies and dramas of producers like Charles Frohman, a co-founder of the **Theatrical Syndicate**. A large role in the original production of James M. Barrie's *Dear Brutus* (1918) brought Hayes her first significant press notices as an engaging, if not flawless, practitioner of wit-laced comedy of manners. Sophisticated stage comedy became her stock-in-trade over the next decade as she built her reputation and resumé on contemporary comedies by such **playwrights** as Booth Tarkington, **George S. Kaufman**, and Barrie as well as revivals by **George Bernard Shaw** and Oliver Goldsmith's Restoration-era classic *She Stoops to Conquer*. During the week she turned 20, Hayes earned her first Broadway above-the-title billing ("Helen Hayes in *Babs*"), the youngest person ever to have had that honor and marketing ploy conferred upon him or her. From that point, Hayes was recognized, if not always lionized, as a Broadway star.

Working continuously and successfully in both theater and film for the next 20 years, Hayes achieved her most important theatrical successes in the title roles of two historical dramas: **Maxwell Anderson**'s *Mary Queen of Scots* (1933) and Laurence Housman's *Victoria Regina* (1935 and revived with Hayes in 1938). Notwithstanding her decades of achievement in comedies and musicals, neither Hayes nor any other actress could have conceivably achieved the status of "First Lady of American Theater" without commanding the stage in at least one dramatic or epic leading role. With these two back-to-back triumphs of high drama, Hayes assumed the regal stature of her characters and vaulted herself into the realm of Broadway greatness. With the end of the run of *Victoria Regina*, Hayes, while not altogether exempt from occasional less-than-flattering notices, was generally spared press excoriation from then on. She had been too successful too often to be subjected to the harshest of critical vitriol. She was widely, and correctly, considered to be one of the reasons why people loved Broadway and came to Broadway shows.

The 1940s and 1950s saw continued success as Hayes aged gracefully into middle-aged damehood—grand or common as the roles demanded. She inaugurated the 1940s with a successful Broadway turn in **Shakespeare**'s *Twelfth Night*. In 1947, she enjoyed one of her strongest performances of the postwar era in Anita Loos's *Happy Birthday*, for which she won the first-ever Tony Award for Best Actress with co-winner Ingrid Bergman. The 1950s saw Hayes make a success of her first performance in a play by the then deceased **Eugene O'Neill** (*A Touch of the Poet*, 1958), who did not particularly like her acting when he first saw her perform in the 1920s. She won her second Best Actress Tony in the English-language adaptation of Jean Anouilh's *Time Remembered* (1958) opposite Richard Burton. Hayes took a five-year hiatus from Broadway appearances from 1959 to

1964, her longest such absence since her 1909 debut, but returned to do some of her most memorable work in the final five seasons of her theatrical career. Her final Broadway performance, the 1970 wistful revival of Mary Chase's *Harvey* (1944) with Jimmy Stewart, holds a special place in the memory of theatergoers who saw the production, notwithstanding its limited run.

For all her awards and honors, Hayes garnered no greater praise than having two Broadway theaters named for her during her lifetime. The Fulton Theater on 46th and Broadway was renamed for her in 1955 and bore her name until it was torn down in 1982, replaced by a portion of the Marriott Hotel complex that now dominates the block. Hayes acted in the first Helen Hayes Theatre in O'Neill's *A Touch of the Poet*. In 1983, Broadway's famed Little Theatre (two blocks from the *old* Helen Hayes Theatre) was renamed for her. To this day, her name still tops the marquee above the title of whatever show is running there in a fitting reminder of when she became Broadway's youngest marquee star in 1920.

Hayes died of natural causes in Nyack, New York, in 1993.

Thomas A. Greenfield

Further Reading

Hayes, Helen, and Katherine Hatch. *My Life in Three Acts*. San Diego: Harcourt Brace Jovanovich, 1990.

Murphy, Donn, and Stephen Moore. *Helen Hayes: A Bio-Bibliography*. Westport, CT: Greenwood Press, 1993.

HELLMAN, LILLIAN (1905–1984)
PLAYWRIGHT

For four decades, Lillian Hellman was a prominent and often controversial figure in American theater. Enjoying some stage successes and weathering some failures, she wrote eight original dramas and four full dramatic adaptations that were produced on Broadway, the most for any solo woman **playwright** after the Depression era. Dismissive of public recognition as a "woman playwright," Hellman dealt with a wide range of serious themes in plays that were often characterized by an ironic view of human nature and a strong moral voice. Her outspoken support of left-wing political positions propelled her beyond Broadway into the national spotlight, particularly as a blacklisted writer who defiantly refused to "name names" when subpoenaed by the House Un-American Activities Committee (HUAC) in 1952. Her controversial writings, a celebrated love affair, her numerous public feuds, and shocking public pronouncements—including unapologetic allegiance to Stalinism in the face of the Russian dictator's mass murders of his own people—embedded her deeply into the history of Broadway, America's literary intelligentsia, and the culture of her time.

Lillian Hellman smiles in this late 1970s photo taken on Martha's Vineyard. (AP Photo/The Estate of Lillian Hellman/HO)

Hellman was born in New Orleans, Louisiana, in 1905. She attended New York University and Columbia University in the early 1920s, but dropped out of college to take a job as a manuscript reader for a New York publishing house. In 1925, she married Arthur Kober, a publicist and minor playwright. The two moved to Hollywood in 1930, where she began publishing stories while working for Metro-Goldwyn-Mayer (MGM) as a script reader. She also met and began a 30-year friendship, professional collaboration, and gossip-generating affair with novelist Dashiell Hammett. Hellman and Kober divorced in 1932 and Hellman returned to New York. At this point Hellman turned most of her professional attention to writing plays for Broadway but over time would become a fixture in both New York and Hollywood literary, left-wing, and celebrity circles.

Hellman's Broadway career began with *The Children's Hour* (1934). The successful play ran until 1936, completing a total of 691 performances. Despite praise from critics, the play created controversy due to a plotline centered on public frenzy over a child's whispered accusation of a lesbian relationship between two teachers. Subsequently, scheduled productions were banned in Boston, London, and Chicago, and the play was spurned for Pulitzer Prize consideration on the basis of its controversial content. Moreover, finding actresses to play the roles of the two teachers, Martha Dobie and Karen Wright, proved difficult.

However, the 1952 Broadway revival of *The Children's Hour* was directed by Hellman herself, following her controversial appearance before HUAC. Hellman clearly wanted the public to draw a connection between the injustices of the HUAC hearings and the public hysteria portrayed in *The Children's Hour*. This time casting was less of a problem. Stage and film star Kim Hunter, herself a blacklist victim, and Patricia Neal, a young but established actress and a friend of Hellman's, played the leading roles. *The Children's Hour* has since become a significant work in the canon of American social drama. It continues to be studied as a searing portrayal of mob mentality, an early representation of homosexuality in mainstream American theater, and an auspicious beginning to one of America's most dynamic and controversial literary careers.

Hellman did not have another Broadway hit for five years after the first run of *The Children's Hour*. *Days to Come* (1936) lasted on Broadway for only one week.

A labor strike drama in the political mold of **Clifford Odets** and other left-wing dramatists of the decade, *Days to Come* lacked the crisp pace and dramatic intensity of an effective social protest play. However, her next work, *The Little Foxes* (1939), was very successful and has gradually achieved the status of a significant work of American dramatic literature. It has had three Broadway revivals since its original production, a major national tour, and a highly regarded film adaptation for which Hellman wrote the screenplay. The play produced Hellman's most famous character, the cunning Regina Hubbard, who inspired a Marc Blitzstein musical *Regina* (1949).

Two political plays followed *The Little Foxes*. *Watch on the Rhine* (1941), an indictment of appeasement with European fascists, and *The Searching Wind* (1944), an exploration of diplomatic stagnancy prior to World War II, both enjoyed respectable 300-plus performance Broadway runs. In 1946 Hellman brought to Broadway as author and director an ultimately unsuccessful prequel to *The Little Foxes* entitled *Another Part of the Forest*. In 1951 her play *The Autumn Garden* offered a departure from her usual, conventional, well-made play structure and plotline. The action of *The Autumn Garden* focuses on multiple character revelations in a manner reminiscent of Chekhov. (An ardent admirer of Chekhov, Hellman published an edition of his letters in 1955.) Dedicated to Dashiell Hammett, *The Autumn Garden* was Hellman's favorite play. Hellman's final original Broadway play, *Toys in the Attic* (1960), is regarded by many critics as Hellman's best work. It, too, invited comparisons with Chekhov and gave Hellman her longest Broadway run after *The Children's Hour*.

In addition to her original plays, Hellman wrote four dramatic adaptations for Broadway. Of these, *The Lark* (1955) enjoyed the most success, running for 221 performances. The others, *Montserrat* (1949), *Candide* (1956), and *My Mother, My Father, and Me* (1963), had disappointingly short stays. She also wrote screenplays for her own plays and three best-selling memoirs: *An Unfinished Woman* (1969), *Pentimento* (1973), and *Scoundrel Time* (1976).

Hellman's life has been the subject of two Broadway plays: *Lillian* (1986), a biographical solo performance based on Hellman's writings starring actress Zoe Caldwell, and *Imaginary Friends* (2002), Nora Ephron's dramatization of Hellman's feud and defamation lawsuit against author Mary McCarthy. (In the 1970s McCarthy famously condemned Hellman's nonfiction writings as fabrication "including the words 'and' and 'the.'")

After a slow physical decline over a period of years, Hellman died of heart failure in Vineyard Haven, Massachusetts, on June 30, 1984.

Thomas A. Greenfield and Christy E. Allen

Further Reading

Horn, Barbara Lee. *Lillian Hellman: A Research and Production Sourcebook*. Westport, CT: Greenwood Press, 1998.

Martinson, Deborah. *Lillian Hellman: A Life with Foxes and Scoundrels.* New York: Counterpoint, 2005.

HERBERT, VICTOR (1859/1860–1924)
COMPOSER, MUSICIAN

An Irish-born cellist and composer of **operetta**, Victor Herbert was Broadway's first major celebrity composer/orchestrator of the twentieth century. Working in Broadway, operetta, Tin Pan Alley, **radio**, **film**, and recorded music he became one of the most prolific composers and songwriters in American history, as well as a pioneer in the development of modern music business practices.

Having achieved early success as a young musician and composer in his native Dublin, Herbert immigrated to New York City at 27. Shortly thereafter he became the lead cellist for the Metropolitan Opera Orchestra. His proximity to New York's burgeoning musical theater industry at the turn of the century aroused his interest in composing for Broadway, which warmly welcomed his facility with romantic, comic, and choral music as well as his astonishing level of productivity. By the end of his American musical theater career, which extended from 1897 until his death in 1924, Herbert had composed music for over 50 Broadway original productions and major adaptations. In addition, Herbert began contributing musical numbers to **Florenz Ziegfeld**'s *Follies* in 1917 and became the *Follies*' principal composer from 1920 until his death in 1924.

For most of his career, Herbert routinely had two or more Broadway productions running each year while simultaneously achieving success away from Broadway as a performing musician, orchestra conductor, and composer and arranger of popular songs, classical pieces, and film music. He wrote the music for some of the twentieth century's first important Broadway **musical** hits, including *Babes in Toyland* (1903), which included the now American classic song "Toyland" and the equally famous instrumental composition "March of the Toys." *Mlle. Modiste* (1905), which featured the songs "The Time, the Place and the Girl" as well as a comic hit "I Want What I Want When I Want it," was another landmark Herbert show as was his most famous musical, *Naughty Marietta* (1910). *Marietta*, one of five Herbert musicals adapted as a Hollywood film, opens with the thundering military chorus song "Tramp, Tramp, Tramp" and closes with the cathartically romantic "Ah, Sweet Mystery of Life," which Nelson Eddy and Jeanette MacDonald immortalized on screen in 1935.

While actively writing and arranging his own productions, Herbert was every bit as energetic as a businessman as he was an artist. In 1908 he testified before Congress in support of strengthening copyright laws for ensuring fair payment of composers' royalties for published and performed works. Six years later he cofounded and directed the American Society of Composers, Authors, and Publishers (ASCAP), which quickly became what it is today—the professional songwriters and composers' primary resource for worldwide collection and enforcement of royalty payments.

Herbert died of natural causes in New York City at 84. He was actively writing well into his 80s and opened a new musical, *The Dream Girl*, in the year he died. Herbert's music has found audiences and exerted its influence ever since. Broadway composers, most notably the inimitable **Richard Rodgers**, have named Herbert as a major influence on their work. In 1980, some of Herbert's songs were adapted for the turn-of-the-century Broadway revue *Tintypes*. In 2002 his song "I'm Falling in Love with Someone" from *Naughty Marietta* was incorporated into the successful Broadway run of *Thoroughly Modern Millie*. Opera and musical theater companies still mount productions of his shows, and his life and work constitute major areas of study in modern American music history.

Thomas A. Greenfield

Further Reading

Gould, Neil. *Victor Herbert: A Theatrical Life*. New York: Fordham University Press, 2008.

Kaye, Joseph. *Victor Herbert. The Biography of America's Greatest Composer of Romantic Music*. Whitefish, MT: Kessinger Publications, 2008. (Original, New York: Crown Publishers, 1931.)

HERMAN, JERRY (1931–)
COMPOSER, LYRICIST, ENTERTAINER

Lyricist and composer Jerry Herman created wildly popular shows and kept Broadway "Golden Era" **musical** traditions alive during the latter half of the twentieth century, just as musical theater formats and audience tastes were starting to change. Herman adhered to singable tunes, approachable lyrics, the use of the reprise, and an unflinchingly upbeat spirit just as many of his contemporaries began experimenting with darker themed, emotionally ambivalent songs and scores.

Writing almost exclusively without a composer or lyricist partner, Herman ranks with the likes of **George M. Cohan**, **Cole Porter**, and **Irving Berlin** as one of Broadway's most important solo musical songwriters. He is certainly the most successful since World War II. In the 1960s Herman had three major hit Broadway shows: *Milk and Honey* (1961), *Hello, Dolly!* (1964), and *Mame* (1966). He had less success in the 1970s when concept musicals and rock musicals rose to prominence. However, the 1980s and 1990s saw renewed enthusiasm for his earlier work, as well as the premier of his groundbreaking musical *La Cage aux Folles* (1983).

He was born Gerald Sheldon Herman (in 1961 he legally changed his name) in Jersey City, New Jersey, to Jewish parents of Russian/Polish ancestry. Herman's father Harry, an athlete who successfully operated a summer camp in New York, engaged in outdoor life with relish. His mother, Ruth (neé Sachs), a talented amateur accordionist and pianist, discouraged Harry from coercing Herman into his mold. From the age of six, Herman played piano by ear and was soon improvising his own tunes and riffs with chords and flourishes. He began composing ballads at 13 and wrote his first show when he was 14. As a teenager he saw **Ethel Merman** starring in *Annie Get Your Gun* on Broadway and decided to devote his life to writing songs, especially for strong female leads. He pursued his interest in college, graduating in 1954 from the theater program at the University of Miami where he wrote music for revues and shows.

Directly after graduation, Herman moved to New York and presented a revue of his songs **Off-Broadway** at the Theatre de Lys (now the Lucille Lortel) in Greenwich Village. The revue earned him positive reviews and scored a 54 performance run, a respectable showing at the time for an Off-Broadway show by an unknown composer/lyricist. Shortly thereafter Herman got a job as intermission pianist for popular 1950s cabaret singer Mabel Mercer while she performed in The Show Place, a fashionable New York night spot. Celebrities coming to hear Mercer began asking Herman to write songs for them. These entreaties led quickly to headline appearances at New York piano clubs, during which time Herman developed his first full show, *Nightcap*. The show was first produced at The Show Place in 1958 and was later remounted Off-Broadway in 1960 at the Player's Theatre as *Parade*.

Herman's first Broadway show, *Milk and Honey*, recounts the experiences of a tourist group of American widows and the romance that one develops with an Israeli man. The production opened successfully at the Martin Beck Theatre in 1961 with Molly Picon, a star of New York Yiddish Theatre during the 1920s and 1930s, in the lead role. The show earned Herman his first Tony Award nomination for Best Musical.

An impressed **David Merrick** chose Herman as composer and lyricist for his musical adaptation of **Thornton Wilder**'s *The Matchmaker*. Orginally entitled *Dolly, A Damned Exasperating Woman*, the show underwent multiple revisions and rewrites in out-of-town trials. A pre-Broadway recording of the show's big production number song, "Hello, Dolly!," by Louis Armstrong was one of many factors that led to the final title change. *Hello, Dolly!* was an immediate smash, winning ten Tony awards—the most of any show in Broadway history until *The Producers* (2001) surpassed it almost 40 years later. Herman won for best score (he would win a Grammy for the score as well). The show catapulted **Carol Channing** to stardom and completely revived Louis Armstrong's career. After its seven-year run, the show briefly held the position as the longest-running musical of all time, but it was surpassed soon after by *Fiddler on the Roof*, which opened the same year and ran slightly longer. However, the song "Hello, Dolly!" is now an American pop standard and is one of the most-frequently performed and recorded **show tunes** of the decade. The 1960s also saw the success of *Mame* based on a novel by Patrick Dennis. The play opened at the Winter Garden Theatre on May 24, 1966,with **Angela Lansbury** in the title role. *Mame* earned a Best Score Tony nomination for Herman and a Best Actress in a Musical win for Lansbury, helping her make the leap from perennial supporting actress to star.

Buoyed by the success of *Mame*, which ran for 1,508 performances over the course of three years, Herman decided to initiate his own project. He chose to adapt as a musical French author Jean Giraudoux's modernist novel *The Madwoman of Chaillot* with Lansbury in the starring role. The show opened on February 6, 1969, under the title *Dear World*. Notwithstanding an unprecedented 59 previews, the show ran for a mere 132 performances—and much of that run was attributed to strong advance sales from audiences eager to see another Herman-Lansbury collaboration. Despite the slow box office, Lansbury earned another Best Actress Tony and Herman's music and lyrics earned favorable notices. With *Dear World*, *Hello, Dolly!*, and *Mame*, Herman ended the 1960s having three original shows running simultaneously on Broadway.

Herman's next project, *Mack and Mabel* (1974) dramatized the lives of silent film stars Mack Sennett and Mabel Normand. Booked into the Majestic Theatre, one of Broadway's largest houses, the show struggled against poor reviews and high overhead costs. Producer David Merrick closed the show after eight weeks. (The show would have a surprisingly successful revival in London 22 years later.)

In the 1970s Herman took hiatus from writing. However, toward the end of the decade he was recruited by author Michael Stewart to write the music and lyrics for *The Grand Tour*, a musical adaptation of a story by contemporary Austro-Hungarian writer Franz Werfel. Despite the star power of **Joel Grey** in the leading role, the show closed after 61 performances.

Herman next wanted to work on a musical version of the French film, *La Cage aux Folles*, but the project was delayed by legal disputes over rights to the property. In the interim Herman developed an all-female retrospective of his songs that mounted at New York's Backstage cabaret in 1981 as *Jerry's Girls*. The show moved to Broadway in 1985 where it ran for two years starring Chita Rivera, Leslie Uggams, and Dorothy Loudon.

Legal matters were settled on *La Cage aux Folles* during the cabaret run of *Jerry's Girls*, and producer Alan Carr finally signed Herman to write the adaptation from a book by **Harvey Fierstein**. The show, which starred Gene Barry and George Hearn, opened at the Palace Theatre in 1983 to rave reviews. Groundbreaking as an open celebration of gay love that "mainstream" Broadway audiences fully accepted, *La Cage* is often cited as making a major contribution to the expanding exploration of gay culture in American theater. Herman, who is openly gay, has expressed particular satisfaction over the fact that his song "I Am What I Am" from *La Cage* has achieved informal cultural status as a gay anthem.

Although he has not written or conceived a new Broadway show in over 25 years, Herman's body of work enjoys a remarkable currency. Even as they perform in other shows and venues, the longevity of Lansbury and Channing's careers stand as a tribute to Herman's enduring influence. *Hello, Dolly!* is still a national and international touring standard, rivaling perhaps only *Gypsy* as the best "diva musical" of the past 50 years. In 2009, the **American Theatre Wing** and the Broadway League presented him with a Tony Award for Lifetime Achievement. His two-minute acceptance speech was inspiring, funny, unpretentious, lyrical, and filled with unrestrained joy and affirmation—like the musicals that had brought him to that moment. It brought down the house, too.

James A. Kaser

Further Reading

Citron, Stephen. *Jerry Herman: Poet of the Show Tune.* New Haven, CT: Yale University Press, 2004.

Herman, Jerry. *Showtune.* New York: Penguin, 1996.

HIGH SCHOOLS, THEATER EDUCATION IN

Theater education in America has experienced a remarkable resurgence in the past 30 years due in large part to a national movement to establish the arts as a core academic subject area in the high school curriculum as opposed to the elective, marginal, or even extracurricular status to which it had been historically relegated. The resulting enhancement in theater education has seen a significant expansion of student exposure to dramatic literature in theater and English classes. Although a few Broadway war-horses, such as **Thornton Wilder**'s *Our Town* (1938) and **Arthur Miller**'s *Death of a Salesman* (1947), have been taught in high school classes for decades, new emphases on and approaches to theater education have expanded the range of plays that have found their way into classrooms as subjects of academic study and not simply "school play" productions. In many instances, these works first came to public notice by way of a **Broadway** or **Off-Broadway** production.

Historical Overview: From *McGuffey's Reader* to the Pulitzer Prize

Notwithstanding the relatively recent advances in theater education, the commercially successful American **playwright** was a relatively late entry into America's circle of venerated "serious writers" and, therefore, a late entry into school reading lists and curricula as well. Moreover, with the exception of the works of **Shakespeare**, drama itself has historically struggled for "face time" in literature textbooks and English courses against the primacy of fiction, poetry, and the essay. The *New England Primer* and the famous *McGuffey's Readers* were nineteenth-century examples of early efforts to bring together great literary works for use in the classroom. Although dominated by works of prose and poetry, McGuffey's 1879 editions of his fifth and sixth *Eclectic Readers* contained passages of dialogue from Shakespeare's *Julius Caesar*, *Hamlet*, and *The Merchant of Venice*.

(Shakespeare has remained, of course, the centerpiece of drama-as-literature instruction in American high schools as it was in the nineteenth century.) But the *McGuffey's Fifth Eclectic Reader* also included excerpts from a relatively modern popular drama: Irish playwright (James) Sheridan Knowles's 1825 biographical drama *William Tell*. Although the play had never been produced commercially in New York, other plays by Knowles—*Virginius* (1820) and *The Hunchback* (1832)—did in fact have commercial runs in New York as well as in London. McGuffey's editor acknowledges the fame of these plays in the introduction to the *William Tell* passage (McGuffey 1879, 207). The Knowles excerpt marks one of the first, if not the first, appearance of a work by a modern popular "Broadway playwright," albeit not an American one, in a major American school reading text.

The first part of the twentieth century saw three critical events forge a close connection between contemporary theater and the school classroom: George Pierce Baker's 47 Workshop on playwriting at Harvard, the founding of the International Thespian Society for high school theater students, and the establishment of the Pulitzer Prize for Drama. Arguably the most important advancement in educational theater of the twentieth century was Baker's 47 Workshop at Harvard University. Professor Baker was the sponsor of the Harvard Dramatic Club when it was founded in 1908, and he began a playwriting workshop shortly after—the first known class on playwriting ever taught in an American school or college. Baker's work at Harvard (and later at Yale) provided a springboard for many important theater writers in America, including **George Abbott**, S. N. Behrman, **Eugene O'Neill**, as well as critic John Mason Brown. More significantly for American education, Baker's workshops consecrated theater as a distinct field of academic inquiry and playwriting as a worthy literary genre for classroom instruction. At about the same time that Baker was conducting his playwriting seminars, the International Thespian Society came into being, filling a growing need for recognizing the excellence of theater students and scholar/teachers at the high school level. The organization grew out of the work of Dr. Earl Blank, a teacher at Natrona County High School in Casper, Wyoming, and Dr. Paul Opp, a professor of theater at Fairmont State College in West Virginia. By 1939 the organization would boast 350 members from affiliated schools across the nation. The third major event occurred in 1917 when Joseph Pulitzer established the annual Pulitzer Prize for Drama to honor the best new Broadway play that "best represent[ed] the educational value and power of the stage in raising the standards of good morals and good manners" (Fischer 1997, 3). Pulitzer's endorsement of the educational potential of the commercial stage has clearly influenced educators and textbook publishers ever since. Plays and authors selected for high school literature instruction are still commonly populated, if not dominated, by Pulitzer honorees.

The 1920s: The Broadway Play as School Book

The years between the World Wars saw enormous growth in American textbook and other forms of book publishing, leading to a sustained expansion of available published materials for schools in many disciplines. Harcourt and Brace was founded in 1919 and eventually became the largest textbook publisher in the country. Norton began book publishing in 1923. From the 1960s to the present, Norton's literature survey anthologies, which gradually began to incorporate modern plays in their expansive collections, became the backbone of literature instruction for colleges and helped set the agenda for reading lists in high schools. Founded in 1925, Random House would publish a number of influential popular play anthologies in the 1940s (see "Bennett Cerf and the Anthologies" discussion below).

The first significant introduction of popular American drama into American high schools came by way of Burns Mantle's annual *Best Plays of* (the Broadway Season) reference book series, which became a popular holding in college and high school libraries shortly after its debut in 1920. Started by and named for the drama critic of the *New York Daily News*, the first volumes of *Burns Mantle*, as it was popularly known (now, more commonly, *The Best Plays Theater Yearbook*), offered nearly complete scripts from ten plays, all selected from works that had been performed in New York commercial theater during the previous season. Significantly, Mantle's focus on Broadway induced students and teachers using his books for class assignments to see American dramatic literature and Broadway as Mantle did, namely as one and the same thing (Mantle characterized Broadway in the introduction to the first volume as "the physical source" of drama in America). Among the selections appearing in the first volume was Eugene O'Neill's *Beyond the Horizon* (1920), whose qualities as serious literature Mantle prophetically extolled in the introduction of the volume. *Beyond the Horizon* later became, and remains, a standard college and high school classroom example of the maturation of American playwriting in the early twentieth century. Today the *Best Plays* are selected from Broadway, Off-Broadway, and Off-Off-Broadway, but professional production (usually in New York) is still the defining eligibility criterion for consideration for inclusion.

The success of Mantle's publication was followed by an expansion of play anthologies for general readership, libraries, and school use. In 1923 Houghton Mifflin published *One-Act Plays* edited by James Plaisted Webber and Hanson Hart Webster, principally for "young people's reading." The selected 18 plays, which included modern and older works, were heavily titled toward European playwrights, including A. A. Milne, Lady Gregory, and Edmond Rostand. However, the volume also included two American plays that had previously been produced on Broadway. (Prior to World War II, New York mainstream commercial theater was more accommodating to evenings of one acts and short plays than it is today, especially in the smaller theaters.) New Yorker Edward Knoblock, by 1923 a successful Broadway playwright (*Tiger! Tiger!* 1918) and a favorite of leading Broadway producer **David Belasco**, had one of his less successful Broadway pieces, *My Lady's Dress* (1914) excerpted in the volume. (The excerpt appears as *My Lady's Lace*.) Another associate of Belasco's, Kentucky-born Stuart Walker, was represented in the volume with his piece for teenagers, *Nevertheless*. Walker, a writer and producer who specialized in mounting evenings of short plays with wholesome religious or moral themes, had presented the play in repertory with several other one acts at New York's famous Princess Theatre in 1916. Although both playwrights are virtually unknown today, this early appearance of American-written Broadway plays in a major reading collection for school-age children constituted a noteworthy step in bringing the American Broadway playwright from the adult and, in the minds of some, unsavory world of commercial theater into the protected environs of the schoolroom. Yet, even with Mantle's groundbreaking publication and other appearances of American plays in book formats, the literary status of the American play remained marginal at best through the 1920s. It is telling that the preface of Macmillan's 1927 hefty classroom reader, *The Book of American Literature*, boasts to teachers and other readers that "the major figures of American literature are here generously represented" although there are no plays reprinted or excerpted (Snyder & Snyder 1927, v).

Bennett Cerf and the Anthologies

In the 1930s the elevation of successful American playwrights such as Eugene O'Neill, Thornton Wilder, **Clifford Odets**, **Lillian Hellman**, **Maxwell Anderson**, and **George S. Kaufman** to the status of major Broadway figures gave rise in the 1940s to a marked increase in the publication of theater-related books and popular play anthologies. The Macmillan Company published *One-Act Plays* by Marie Annette Webb in 1940, a collection promoted for classroom study as well as school production. Webb offered a balanced selection of plays from commercial theater and noncommercial youth drama. Her anthology included American Zona Gale's 1917 Broadway hit *The Neighbors* and Englishman Harold Brighouse's popular *The French Maid* (1918). Webb also included Eugene O'Neill's short play *Where the Cross Is Made* (1928). Although the play had flopped on Broadway and was not well known, O'Neill had already won three Pulitzer Prizes, and by this time his name in a collection represented a ready-made selling point for a drama book. In the same year Harcourt and Brace published a collection of Maxwell Anderson's verse plays, including his essays on poetic drama and complete texts to many of his Broadway successes: *Elizabeth the Queen* (1930), *Mary of Scotland* (1933), *Winterset* (1935), and *High Tor* (1937). Anderson's plays and critical writings on the importance of poetry in contemporary drama combined with his record of Broadway success represented a significant case statement for the literary value of popular drama.

Arguably the biggest single force in establishing the commercial American dramatist as a serious literary artist was Bennett Cerf, founder of Random House publishing. Cerf and Random House specialized in mass market, affordable, literary books, including anthologies on almost any literary genre imaginable: short stories, novelettes, poetry, humorous stories, war tales, among others. A Manhattan-bred theater enthusiast from childhood and personal friend of such Broadway luminaries as **Richard Rodgers**, Eugene O'Neill, Moss Hart, and Irwin Shaw, Cerf began editing and publishing play anthologies in the 1940s. His 1941 collection *Sixteen Famous Plays* saw the first mass market anthologizing of

Wilder's *Our Town* (1938) and Clifford Odets's *Waiting for Lefty* (1935), both of which would become mainstays of high school classroom literary study after World War II. The volume also included George S. Kaufman and Moss Hart's comedy *The Man Who Came to Dinner* (1939), which to this day remains among the most frequently produced **high school plays**. Two years later, Cerf edited *Thirty Famous One-Act Plays* for Doubleday, which brought the work of playwright **Susan Glaspell** to a wide audience. Sharing Mantle's vision that the best modern American dramatic literature was to be found among Broadway's successful productions, Cerf came out with *S.R.O.: The Most Successful Plays of the American Stage* in 1944. This volume sought to correct the error of bygone days when American drama was held in low regard among readers, writers, and teachers of literature. Cerf showcased recent Broadway hits, including Howard Lindsay and Russel Crouse's comedy *Arsenic and Old Lace* (1941, another high school production favorite in the middle to latter half of the twentieth century) and Jack Kirkland's adaptation of Erskine Caldwell's novel *Tobacco Road* (1933). Cerf also called readers' attention to early, overlooked American dramatic literature. Mrs. Henry Wood's melodrama *East Lynne* (1869) and Denman Thompson's *The Old Homestead* (1887) were included as examples of unrecognized but once popular and meritorious nineteenth-century American dramas.

Postwar through the 1980s

By the 1950s Random House, Doubleday, Macmillan, among other publishers had collectively introduced so many editions and anthologies of American plays into their literary trade lines that major American playwrights had finally come to be seen by academics, critics, and the book-reading public as genuine literary artists. In 1958 Prentice Hall published an English literature textbook, the *Dramatic Experience*, which included among its dozen exemplary dramatic masterpieces Sophocles's *Oedipus Rex*, Shakespeare's **Othello**, and recent Broadway hits by American authors: William Saroyan's *The Time of Your Life* (1939) and Arthur Miller's *Death of a Salesman* (1947), both Pulitzer Prize winners and commercial Broadway successes. In 1959, Dell launched its *Famous American Plays* of the decade paperback series, which published volumes of five or six best plays of the 1920s through the 1970s, all having enjoyed noteworthy Broadway or, in a few instances, Off-Broadway productions. Edited with introductions by such theater luminaries as **Group Theatre** founders **Lee Strasberg** and **Harold Clurman** and selling in first printings from 50 to 75 cents (about 10–15 cents per play), the books were common in college American literature classes and also popular with a number of high school teachers who had the freedom and resources to order trade books as texts. By the mid-1960s *Our Town*, fast becoming a common high school reading assignment, was available in at least five different American print editions plus two trade anthologies. In 1964, *Our Town* and O'Neill's *Desire Under the Elms* appeared in a Harper and Row drama instruction text, *Studies in Drama/Form B*, along with works by Shakespeare, Chekhov, Ibsen, and Shaw. Tellingly, by 1963

Cliffs Notes, since 1958 the publisher of the infamously popular student "study guides" for frequently assigned high school literary masterpieces, had added *Death of a Salesman*, *Our Town*, and **Tennessee Williams**'s *A Streetcar Named Desire* (1947) and *The Glass Menagerie* (1945) to its titles along with its mainstay studies of Greek classics, Shakespeare, and lengthy novels. Wilder, Williams, and Miller eventually became the most commonly taught American playwrights in high school. (A 1995 study by the Modern Language Association on the teaching of *Death of a Salesman* posited that, up to that time, it was the most frequently taught modern play in the nation in both colleges and high schools, although many scholars and educators believe it has recently been supplanted by Miller's **The Crucible** [Roudane 1995, vi].)

By the 1960s the best of American Broadway drama was firmly established as literature, and the list of plays and authors appearing in classrooms expanded rapidly. Colleges and some progressive high school drama programs started to teach from the newly emerging canon of the Theater of the Absurd; Anglo Irish writer Samuel Beckett's *Waiting for Godot* (1956) and American **Edward Albee**'s *The Zoo Story* (Off-Broadway, 1960; Broadway, 1968) had found their way into high school classes by 1970 and are now common readings. As high schools and colleges sought to diversify their curricula in the 1970s and 1980s, Lorraine Hansberry's **A Raisin in the Sun** (1959) became a popular selection for classroom study. By the 1980s selections from **Ntozake Shange**'s *for colored girls who have considered suicide/when the rainbow is enuf* (1976) made an impact, particularly in schools with sizable African American populations. The women's movement of the 1960s and 1970s had focused new attention on women writers past and present. Among the beneficiaries of the feminist literary revival was Susan Glaspell, whose frequently anthologized one-act play *Trifles* (1916) has become a popular selection in drama and English classes. Today, as African American dramatist **August Wilson**'s plays steadily gain critical attention and acclaim, he has become an increasingly familiar name on school reading lists.

1980s to the Present: From "Enrichment" to Core Academics, and the New "Broadway Babies"

Up until the 1980s, even though American playwrights had held a secure place in English classes for quite some time, theater and arts education as a whole were generally viewed in high schools as an extracurricular activity and only rarely as a central part of the general curriculum. In many schools driver education had more academic status than theater. The upshot of this marginalization of the discipline was that theater education in American high schools had taken on some of the same social class divisions that had characterized Broadway for years: a pricey luxury predominantly for middle- and upper-class privileged students. However, during the late 1980s a sustained surge of public interest in arts education held out some promise that at least class-stratified attitudes about theater and arts education (if not local school curriculum and funding policies) might change.

The surge of interest in high school theater education in America in the late twentieth century can be attributed largely to the federal government. In 1988 a congressional report on the arts titled *Toward Civilization* found significant deficiencies in American arts education and made specific recommendations for moving the arts toward full curricular "legitimacy" and centrality for the first time. *Toward Civilization* prompted additional advocacy movements for arts education in the early 1990s. Eventually, Congress passed the "Goals 2000: Educate America Act," which President William Clinton signed into law in 1994. Significantly, Goals 2000 identified "the arts" as a discrete core curriculum subject, distinct from and of equal stature with English, geography, economics, and civics. The law also called for teaching and competency assessment in all of these academic subjects for "every school in America."

Even though the law could do nothing to change the legal structures by which local communities and state government exercise control over curriculum and school funding, it succeeded in adding momentum to what was becoming a genuine national movement for arts education. In the same year the Consortium of National Arts Education Associations published "National Standards for Arts Education," which included eight rigorous standards for theater education in grades 9–12, ranging from theatrical production to play analysis to scriptwriting. In 1995 Secretary of Education Richard Riley and National Endowment for the Arts (NEA) Chair Jane Alexander (herself a distinguished Tony Award–winning actress) convened a national panel that produced "Arts and Education: Partners in Achieving Our National Education Goals," which echoed Congress's call for the establishment of arts as a core subject in every school in the nation. The result of this unprecedented support for the inclusion and enhancement of arts curriculum in schools inspired arts educators to improve instructional techniques, leading to a vastly improved climate for the arts in the nation's schools over any time in the history of American education.

For theater education, the improving environment for the arts in the high schools during the closing decades of the twentieth century coincided with an enormous growth in the adolescent and youth markets for Broadway "products." As the decidedly grown-up **Rodgers and Hammerstein** era of Broadway **musicals** drew to a close in the late 1960s, youth culture and rock musicals from *Hair* (1968), to *Grease* (1972), to *Rent* (1996), to *Mamma Mia!* (2001), and youth-entrancing European spectacles such as *Les Misérables* (1987) and *The Phantom of the Opera* (1988) developed nationwide followings among school-age children. National tours of Broadway shows, successful **film** adaptations, hit record sales, and, more recently, audio and video downloads of selections from Broadway shows and reality TV–Broadway cross promotions, have given Broadway a large, devoted, and relatively well-informed youth following all across the country. As the government and educator-led push to enlarge the scope of theater education found its way into America's schools, it was met by an eager, Broadway-savvy generation of students who identified far more closely with professional theater as part of their culture than had their baby boomer parents during their school years.

Even the strong surge of government, educator, and student support of theater education in the past 30 years cannot alter the fact that theater and arts education can be expensive, that economic conditions beginning in 2008 and continuing thereafter led to the removal of some high school theater classes, teachers, and productions; and inequities in education funding remain a critical issue in America's schools. But as a whole, the nation's schoolrooms evolved in the twentieth century from an isolated environment void of any mention of American playwriting to many young people's first and best introduction to American theater—and the playwrights who make it possible and marvelous.

Phillip Moss and Thomas A. Greenfield

Further Reading

Anderson, Maxwell. *Eleven Verse Plays*. New York: Harcourt and Brace, 1940.

"Art Education and Human Development." Getty Center for Arts Education Document(s). Los Angeles, CA: Getty Center for Education in the Arts, 1993.

Cerf, Bennett, ed. *Sixteen Famous American Plays*. New York: Modern Library, 1941.

Cerf, Bennett, and Van Henry Cartmell, eds. *S.R.O. The Most Successful Plays in the History of the American Stage*. New York: Garden City Publishing, 1944.

Fischer, Heinz-Dietrich. *The Pulitzer Prize Archive*. New York: Walter de Gruyter, 1997.

Gardner, Howard. *Frames of Mind*. New York: Basic Books, 1983.

The Imagine Nation. http://www.theimaginenation.net/resources.htm.

McGuffey's Fifth Eclectic Reader. Rev. ed. New York: American Book Company, 1879.

The National Standards for Arts Education. http://artsedge.kennedy-center.org/teach/standards/overview.cfm.

Pink, Daniel H. *A Whole New Mind: Moving from the Information Age to the Conceptual Age*. New York: Riverhead, 2005.

Roudane, Matthew C. *Approaches to Teaching Miller's Death of a Salesman*. New York: Modern Language Association, 1995.

Snyder, Franklyn B., and Edward B. Snyder, eds. *A Book of American Literature*. New York: Macmillan, 1927.

Webber, James Plaisted, and Hanson Hart Webster, eds. *One-Act Plays*. Boston: Houghton Mifflin, 1923.

HIGH SCHOOLS, THEATER PERFORMANCES IN

The most common career course for Broadway performers is to begin learning about theater in a high school somewhere in the United States and ultimately end up working in New York. In a curious retrograde vector of that trajectory, Broadway plays and **musicals** that begin their commercial lives in Times Square eventually live out their dotage on the stages of high schools all over the United States. Just how heavily high school theaters rely on Broadway for their repertoire is evident from the annual production survey of member schools conducted by the Educational Theatre Association since 1938. Nine of the top ten musicals in the 2007 survey have a Broadway provenance (see sidebar "The Most-Produced Musicals and Nonmusical Plays in American High Schools, 2006–2007"). The tenth, the fabulously successful **Disney Theatrical Productions'** marketing exercise *High School Musical*, although never produced on Broadway, is essentially a "Broadway show" made for tweens (10–12-year-olds) and teens. All ten of the most popular nonmusical plays in the 2007 survey passed through Broadway on their way to high school stages. (This includes **Shakespeare**'s *A Midsummer Night's Dream*, which, although its origin predates American commercial theater by a few hundred years, was staged ten times on Broadway in the twentieth century.)

High School on Broadway

Clearly high schools love Broadway, and there is increasing evidence that Broadway is fond of high schools, too. Disney's launch of *High School Musical* as a stage property is just one manifestation of a newfound interest in young people and youth culture, both as paying customers and as subject matter, on the part of commercial theater producers and presenters. Although Troy and Gabriella and Sharpay—the starry-eyed principal characters of *High School Musical*—have never been seen on Broadway, they have been just about everywhere else. Starting as a made-for-cable movie in 2006, *High School Musical* has been a concert tour, a soundtrack album, a television sequel, an ice show, a video game, a best-selling young adult novel, and finally, a stage musical that a national road company began touring in August 2007. Moreover, and needless to say, *High School Musical* has been widely produced by high schools all over the country.

The *Wicked* Market

The theater has always been interested in young people—*Romeo and Juliet* comes to mind—but observers trace the most recent Broadway youth movement to the 2003 opening of *Wicked*. A musical adaptation of a popular novel about the lives of the witches from *The Wizard of Oz*, *Wicked* became a surprise hit by drawing to Broadway very large numbers of teen and tween girls, many of whom painted their faces green (in honor of green-faced lead witch Elphaba) and saw the show multiple times. Long concerned about the graying of their audience, Broadway producers took notice and began thinking in terms of drawing the youthful "*Wicked* market" into Broadway theaters. Not surprisingly, by 2008 there were four musicals running on Broadway that featured teenage characters—*Spring Awakening* (2006), *Grease* (1972; revivals, 1994, 2007), *Hairspray* (2002), and *Cry-Baby* (2008). Of those, *Grease* had been cycling through high school drama programs for decades. *Hairspray*, showcased at the 2008 Thespian Festival (the Educational Theatre Association's annual showcase for high school drama coaches and their star students), saw its first high school productions shortly thereafter. In many respects, it would be hard to think of a musical better suited to young performers than *Spring Awakening*, with its rock score, schoolroom setting, youthful rebellion-against-authority theme, and rite-of-passage story line. However, the show's obscenity-laced youth anthem ("Totally F___d") and the explicit sexual expression required of the young male and female leads will deter all but the most progressive and independent school drama programs from rendering a faithful staging of the hit show once it becomes available for amateur production.

The Repertory

Educational theater's reliance on Broadway is not a new phenomenon, as a glance at the first production survey of American high schools, conducted in 1938 will show (see sidebar "The Most-Produced Titles in American High Schools, 1937–1938"). Only two of the ten most-produced plays—the now-obscure titles *New Fires* and *The Adorable Spendthrift*—had no Broadway production history.

That first production survey is notable for the preponderance of drawing room comedies and the complete absence of musicals. It was not until 1949 that a genuine musical (*Meet Me in St. Louis*) cracked the top 20 of the high school production survey, and schools did not really embrace Broadway musical theater until the early 1960s. **Rodgers and Hammerstein**'s *Oklahoma!* (1947) and *South Pacific* (1949) both made the list in 1961. Between 1961 and 1965, several more hit Broadway musicals joined the top 20 list, including **Irving Berlin**'s *Annie Get Your Gun* (1946), **Lerner and Loewe**'s *Brigadoon* (1947), Strouse and Adams's *Bye Bye Birdie* (1960), Meredith Wilson's *The Music Man* (1957), Lerner and Loewe's *My Fair Lady* (1956), and Rodgers and Hammerstein's *The Sound of Music* (1959). However, straight comedies and dramas maintained their historical preeminence over musicals on high school stages throughout the decade.

The first year a musical was anointed as *the* most popular title on high school stages was 1972. **You're a Good Man, Charlie Brown**, based on Charles M. Schulz's iconic cartoon strip and animated television specials, flopped on Broadway in 1971. But the idea of a show based on characters who, within their own "frame" of reality, were younger than the actors who would portray them proved irresistible to high school drama coaches and student actors. They took *Charlie Brown* to America's high school stages a year after its unlamented departure from Broadway. Although artistically unworthy of comparison to the musicals of Rodgers and Hammerstein or Lerner and Loewe, *You're a Good Man, Charlie Brown* is the *Oklahoma!* of high school theater: a breakthrough show that, arguably more than any other, brought the musical to preeminence on the high school stage. By the late 1970s musicals made up half or more of the top 20 and have dominated straight plays in high school production popularity ever since. (In 2002 the Educational Theatre Association began reporting the top ten musicals and the top ten nonmusical plays in separate lists.)

One of the striking things about the high school production survey is that since the year 2000 there has been a complete absence of any contemporary comedy or drama among the top ten nonmusical titles. Even discarding the two classic plays from the 2007 survey—the 400-year-old *Midsummer Night's Dream* and the nineteenth-century comedy *The Importance of Being Earnest* by Oscar Wilde— the median age of the eight remaining plays in the top ten is over 50—a statistic reflective of the first decade of the 2000s. The most recently written straight play on the 2007 survey was Michael Frayn's *Noises Off* (1983), which, at over 25 years of age, is several years older than any of the actors who perform it on a high school stage.

It is no less remarkable that if the high school production survey had been started one year later in 1939 rather than 1938, **George S. Kaufman** and Moss Hart's *You Can't Take It with You*—which is older than virtually all high school teachers and most parents of high school students much less the students themselves—would have had the unique distinction of being included among the most-produced high school plays every year in the history of the list. The Kaufman and Hart comedy broke into the top 20 in 1939, the year after it ended its Broadway run, and has been there ever since. The runner-up for longevity is **Thornton Wilder**'s *Our Town* (1938), which has made the list continuously for over four decades.

The principal reason that the high school repertory of straight or nonmusical plays is skewed toward older work is that the language and subject matter of most successful Broadway plays written since 1970 are considered by many communities to be too mature or "inappropriate" for performance by 16-year-olds on the stage of the local high school. To a large extent, the boundaries of the high school repertory are defined by school principals and boards of education, sometimes with the support of self-appointed moral watchdogs. This situation can lead to contentious disagreements in schools and communities, such as the widely publicized controversy in 2006 when a high school principal in Fulton, Missouri, canceled a scheduled production of *The Crucible*. A leading school board member announced that he feared that some local religious groups, already alarmed by the school's previous fall musical *Grease*, might be offended by the **Arthur Miller** play. The political dynamics of high school theater also inspire a lot of text editing, with or without the required permission from the author, by theater educators who are hungry to expose their students to a broad range of work than might otherwise be possible, even if the text must be bowdlerized to avoid controversy. About two-thirds of the respondents to a 2007 Educational Theatre Association survey on freedom of expression in school theater reported that they have edited scripts to remove objectionable language, smoking, drinking, substance abuse, weapons used as props, violence, sex, and ethnic slurs.

Controversy seems to be less of a problem with musicals than with straight dramas. There are several relatively recent musical arrivals from Broadway near the top of the 2007 high school production survey, including *Beauty and the Beast* (1994) and *Seussical* (2000). One reason for this is that a new musical is somewhat

THE MOST-PRODUCED MUSICALS AND NONMUSICAL PLAYS IN
AMERICAN HIGH SCHOOLS, 2006–2007

Musicals

1. *Little Shop of Horrors*, by Alan Menken and Howard Ashman (Off-Broadway, 1982; Broadway, 2003–2004)

2. *Seussical: The Musical*, by Stephen Flaherty and Lynn Ahrens (Broadway, 2000–2001)

3. *Thoroughly Modern Millie*, by Richard Morris, Dick Scanlan, and Jeanine Tesori (Broadway, 2002–2004)

4. *Beauty and the Beast*, by Alan Menken, Howard Ashman, Tim Rice, and Linda Woolverton (Broadway, 1994–2007)

5. *High School Musical*, by David Simpatico and others (National tour, 2007)

6. *Grease*, by Jim Jacobs and Warren Casey (Broadway, 1972)

7. *Fiddler on the Roof*, by Joseph Stein, Jerry Bock, and Sheldon Harnick (Broadway, 1964–1972)

8. (tie) *Bye Bye Birdie*, by Michael Stewart, Charles Strouse, and Lee Adams (Broadway, 1960–1961)

8. (tie) *Oklahoma!* by Richard Rodgers and Oscar Hammerstein II (Broadway, 1943–1948)

10. (tie) *Anything Goes*, by Cole Porter, Guy Bolton, P. G. Wodehouse, Howard Lindsay, and Russel Crouse (Broadway, 1934–1935)

10. (tie) *Guys and Dolls*, by Frank Loesser, Jo Swerling, and Abe Burrows (Broadway, 1950–1953)

Full-length Plays

1. (tie) *Arsenic and Old Lace*, by Joseph Kesselring (Broadway, 1941–1944)

1. (tie) *A Midsummer Night's Dream*, by William Shakespeare (First recorded New York production, 1826)

3. (tie) *The Importance of Being Earnest*, by Oscar Wilde (First New York production, 1895)

3. (tie) *The Odd Couple*, by Neil Simon (Broadway, 1965–1967)

5. *You Can't Take It with You*, by George S. Kaufman and Moss Hart (Broadway, 1936–1938)

6. (tie) *The Diary of Anne Frank*, by Frances Goodrich and Albert Hackett (Broadway, 1955–1957)

6. (tie) *Our Town*, by Thornton Wilder (Broadway, 1938)

8. *The Curious Savage*, by John Patrick (Broadway, 1950)

9. *Noises Off*, by Michael Frayn (Broadway, 1983–1985)

10. *Fools*, by Neil Simon (Broadway, 1981)

Source: Educational Theatre Association

THE MOST-PRODUCED TITLES IN AMERICAN
HIGH SCHOOLS, 1937–1938

1. *New Fires*, by Charles Quimby Burdette (Professional production history unknown)
2. *Big Hearted Herbert*, by Sophie Kerr and Anna Steese Richardson (Broadway, 1934)
3. *Growing Pains*, by Aurania Rouverol (Broadway, 1933)
4. *Spring Fever*, by Vincent Lawrence (Broadway, 1925)
5. *Fly Away Home*, by Dorothy Bennett and Irving White (Broadway, 1935)
6. *Little Women*, adapted from the Louisa May Alcott novel by Marian De Forest (Broadway, 1912–1913)
7. *Seventeen*, adapted from the Booth Tarkington stories by Hugh Stanislaus Stange and Stannard Mears (Broadway, 1918)
8. *Spring Dance*, by Philip Barry (Broadway, 1936)
9. *Night of January 16*, by Ayn Rand (Broadway, 1935–1936)
10. *The Adorable Spendthrift*, by Roy Briant (Professional production history unknown)

Source: Educational Theatre Association

A note on the production survey. The survey has been conducted annually among schools affiliated with the Educational Theatre Association's Thespian Society branch every year since 1938. Since the survey does not include non-member schools, it is not comprehensive, but the EdTA is the most reliable source of data on play and show production in U.S. high schools.

more likely than a new straight play to be what publicists call "family friendly." Another is that contemporary musicals are being marketed very vigorously to high schools. Music Theatre International (MTI), a private company that controls amateur licensing for a large catalog of recent show titles, offers "School Edition" versions, with simplified scores and carefully edited books, of many of them. MTI has also recently supported showcase productions of *Ragtime* (1998), *Thoroughly Modern Millie* (2002), and *Hairspray*, cast with students from throughout the United States, at the annual International Thespian Society's festival, an annual festival for high school theater teachers and their best students. The 2008 festival featured, in addition to *Hairspray*, a number of titles that are somewhat more adventurous than the mainstream fare represented by the play surveys, including **Rent** (1996, an MTI School Edition show), Athol Fugard's South African apartheid drama *"Master Harold"... and the Boys* (1982), **Stephen Sondheim**'s bloody *Sweeney Todd* (1979), and David Auburn's intellectual drama *Proof* (2004).

Current Trends

The increasing number of new Broadway musical productions aimed at a youthful market suggests that Broadway will continue to serve as a powerful inspiration for high school theater for the foreseeable future. Not only do Broadway **producers** and theater educators accept this assumption, so does the youth-driven reality **television** industry. In 2007 NBC aired *You're the One That I Want*, a season-long national audition for young unknown performers to land the lead roles of Danny and Sandy in the fall 2007 Broadway revival of *Grease*. The television show was a success, finding a large young television audience (the two eventual winners were both 21), and the new revival of *Grease* has enjoyed a healthy and profitable run. The following year, MTV and the producers of the running Broadway hit *Legally Blonde* (2007) successfully aired a similar audition show to find a replacement for the starring female role of Elle Woods. The classic Rodgers and Hammerstein–era musicals will likely maintain a place in high school drama programs for some time, but they face ever-increasing competition for the hearts and minds of school-age performers against the ever-growing body of newer, teen- and youth-centered shows.

Stage dramas and comedies, with their more adult, occasionally controversial content and usually smaller casts (giving fewer families an opportunity to buy multiple tickets and cheer for the school theater program), will certainly continue to enjoy less visibility than musicals in high school production. However, since the end of World War II, twentieth-century American dramas and some comedies have earned increasing respect in the academic world, and many American **playwrights**, such as Arthur Miller, **Tennesee Williams**, **Lorraine Hansberry**, and **Edward Albee**, have assumed the status of "required reading" in high school English and theater classes. That list has expanded in recent decades to include **Ntozake Shange** and **August Wilson** among others. The presence of first-rate American drama in the high school English curriculum, combined with drama teachers' commitment to the art of literary playwriting ensures that, as long as Broadway continues to support superior dramas, high school theater programs will do so as well.

Donald Corathers

Further Reading

Corathers, Don, and John Marshall. "Under the Chestnuts: What the Annual Play Survey Doesn't Reveal about School Theatre." *Dramatics* 81, no. 2 (September 2009): 22–23.
Miller, Bruce. "Kids Today: A Veteran Teacher Addresses the Problems of Today's Students." *Teaching Theatre* 20, no. 4 (Summer 2009): 21–27.

HWANG, DAVID HENRY (1957–)
PLAYWRIGHT

Playwright David Henry Hwang is America's best-known and most successful **Asian American** playwright. He is the first Asian American to win the Tony

Award for Best Play and the Pulitzer Prize for Drama—both for *M. Butterfly* (1988), his tour de force about gender and race politics. In addition to writing plays, Hwang has also penned libretti for Broadway **musicals**, operas, screenplays, **television** dramas, and essays.

Hwang, the first-generation son of Chinese émigrés, hails from Los Angeles where his earliest exposure to theater was at East West Players. As an undergraduate at Stanford University, he tried his hand at playwriting. His initial effort, *F.O.B.*, written in 1978, examines the shaping of ethnic identity through the eyes of two "ABCs" ("American-Born Chinese") contrasted with the "Fresh Off the Boat" character of the title. Following a year of study (1980–1981) at the Yale School of Drama, Hwang wrote dramas for regional and **Off-Broadway** venues. Eight years would elapse before Broadway took notice of his work.

Tony Award–winning playwright David Henry Hwang is shown at The Public Theater in New York in November 2007. (AP Photo/Jim Cooper)

When it did, *M. Butterfly*'s (1988) overwhelming success catapulted Hwang, then 32, into the public limelight. Drawing upon true events surrounding a 20-year affair between a French diplomat and the Beijing opera star he mistakenly believed to be female, Hwang painstakingly interwove Asian and Western performance traditions to create a compelling drama about how racial and sexual stereotyping shape global and individual perceptions. In 1990 Hwang galvanized Asian American theater artists to protest casting discrimination and the use of "yellowface" makeup. Hwang and his colleagues appealed to Actors' Equity Association (AEA) to prohibit British producer **Cameron Mackintosh** from casting a Caucasian actor, Jonathan Pryce, as the Eurasian "Engineer" in the Broadway-bound musical *Miss Saigon*. Although Hwang's efforts to pressure Mackintosh to replace Pryce were unsuccessful, Mackintosh agreed to eliminate yellowface makeup for the Broadway production and cast Asian American actors as Pryce's replacements.

Hwang has continued writing for Broadway, although he has yet to match *M. Butterfly*'s success. An attempt to revisit issues raised in the *Miss Saigon* casting controversy, *Face Value* (1993), flopped resoundingly, closing before it opened. Critics gave Hwang's domestic memory drama *Golden Child* (1998) a warmer reception, and his colleagues honored the work with a Tony nomination for Best Play. However, audiences did not take to the production and its Broadway life lasted a mere 69 performances. With his reworking of **Rodgers and Hammerstein**'s 1958 *Flower Drum Song* (2002), Hwang became the only dramatist ever granted permission to rewrite a work in Rodgers and Hammerstein's repertoire. Hwang's adaptation eliminated ethnic stereotyping evident in the original text and focused instead on the characters' struggles to define themselves culturally and generationally. The play was nominated for a Tony for Best Book of a Musical but played to mixed reviews and closed after 169 performances. Hwang's libretti for musicals on non-Asian themes, *Aida* (2000) and *Tarzan* (2006)—both written for **Disney Theatrical Productions**—have met with greater box-office success.

Hwang has created a large body of dramatic work that explores issues of race and ethnicity, and gender and sexuality, for regional and Off-Broadway theaters where he has been enormously successful. He has also written lyrics and libretti for contemporary compositions, including Philip Glass's science fiction musical drama *1000 Airplanes on the Roof* (1988), Bright Sheng's fusion opera *The Silver River* (1997), and Howard Shore's opera *The Fly* (2008). In 1991, Los Angeles's East West Players, where Hwang was initially exposed to Asian American theater as a boy, created the David Henry Hwang Playwriting Institute in recognition of Hwang's commitment to mentoring the next generation of Asian American playwrights.

Randy Barbara Kaplan

Further Reading

Liu, Miles Xian. *Asian American Playwrights: A Bio-Bibliographical Critical Sourcebook.* Westport, CT: Greenwood Publishing Group, 2002.

Sponberg, Arvid. *Broadway Talks: What Professionals Think about Commercial Theater in America.* Westport, CT: Greenwood Publishing Group, 1991.

&

IN THE HEIGHTS

Broadway Run: Richard Rodgers Theatre
Opening: March 9, 2008
Closing:
Composer: Lin-Manuel Miranda
Lyricist: Lin-Manuel Miranda
Conceived by Lin-Manuel Miranda
Orchestration: Alex Lacamoire and Bill Sherman
Director: Thomas Kail
Choreographer: Andy Blankenbuehler
Producer: Produced by Kevin McCollum, Jeffrey Seller, Jill Furman, Sander
Jacobs, Robyn Goodman/Walt Grossman, Peter Fine, Sonny Everett, and Mike
Skipper
Lead Performers: Lin-Manuel Miranda (Usnavi), Andréa Burns (Daniela), Janet
Dacal (Carla), Robin de Jesús (Sonny), Carlos Gomez (Kevin), Mandy Gonza-
lez (Nina), Christopher Jackson (Benny), Priscilla Lopez (Camila), Olga Mere-
diz (Abuela Claudia), Lin-Manuel Miranda (Usnavi), Karen Olivo (Vanessa),
and Seth Stewart (Graffiti Pete)

In the Heights, named for the Upper West Side Manhattan neighborhood of Washington Heights, is the first successful **Latino American**–themed mainstream
musical in Broadway history. The author, composer, lyricist, the lead, and most
supporting roles, as well as the actors who performed them, are Latino as are the
setting, major musical and dance influences, and predominant themes of the play
—collectively a first for a major Broadway musical. Written in English, the production immersed itself in Spanish dialogue, idioms, and lyrics, stopping far short

The cast of the Broadway musical In the Heights *performs at the 62nd Annual Tony Awards in New York, June 2008. (AP Photo/Jeff Christensen)*

of creating a genuinely bilingual mainstream musical but taking a noteworthy step in that direction.

Although derivative of countless other Broadway shows—from its New York street set, to a father's misguided disdain for his daughter's suitor, to a plot-cementing neighborhood dance scene at the end of Act I—the show was an instant hit with **critics** and audiences. Lack of originality in the plot and some weaknesses in character development were more than compensated for by a dynamic and eclectic score, a spot-on high-energy chorus/dance ensemble made up almost entirely of Broadway newcomers, and a well-publicized rags-to-riches story of how the show itself came into being. The conspicuous success of the show both raised and partially redressed the question of how mainstream Broadway could have paid so little attention for so long to Latinos—the largest, fastest growing ethnic population in the entire nation, much less New York City.

The show was the brainchild of first-time Broadway composer, lyricist, and male lead performer Lin-Manuel Miranda, himself a product of Manhattan's Upper West Side. Like his show's female lead character, Miranda attended an elite, out-of-state private college (he at Wesleyan in Connecticut, she at Stanford in California). He wrote the first songs for the musical while majoring in theater at Wesleyan, developing his songs around the familiar tension between ethnic neighborhood identity and "American Dream" ambition. After college Miranda moved back to New York City in the early 2000s, where he worked for several years in the high-energy, low-paying worlds of improvisational comedy and hip-hop club performance. During this period he developed what would become the first production version of *In the Heights*. He also befriended many young artists, several of whom he would later recruit as members of the original production company. Quiara Alegria Hudes, an established author and **playwright**, wrote the book, and Miranda eventually secured backing from several **producers**, including two of the original producers of *Rent* (1996). In January 2007, at age 27, Miranda opened a low-budget version of *In the Heights* **Off-Broadway**.

The reception that greeted the Off-Broadway production of *In the Heights* was, in fact, fortuitously reminiscent of that for Jonathan Larson's initial Off-Broadway production of *Rent* 11 years earlier. New York audiences thrilled to it and critics raved. For an Off-Broadway show, *In the Heights* drew a larger than usual number of "mainstream" tourists, many who just happened to hear about the show in casual conversation with friends. It also attracted large Latino audiences—a rarity for both Broadway and Off-Broadway productions. The Off-Broadway success led to sufficient public attention and additional investor interest to warrant a full-scale production on Broadway. *In the Heights* opened at the Richard Rodgers Theatre in March 2008.

The show's Off-Broadway success proved to be a reliable predictor of its Broadway reception. Notwithstanding the fact that the show is filled with achingly familiar Broadway formulas, audiences and critics celebrated the show's infectious score and choreography, its successful translation of Latino urban culture to the Broadway musical form, and the "in with a bang" arrival of a promising new star in Miranda. The Broadway community responded in kind, awarding Miranda and his co-creators the Tony Award for Best Musical, a Tony to Miranda for Best Original Score, plus additional Tony Awards for Choreography and Orchestration.

Miranda's artistic achievement in scoring the show was particularly remarkable. He molded an effective, true-to-the-moment combination of hip-hop, salsa, Latin-pop dance tunes, urban rock radio, and brassy "big score" Broadway arrangements. (The "score" actually begins with the jarring sound of a boom box–carrying graffiti artist impatiently switching channels from one urban musical track to another—a 45-second multicultural kinetic sound barrage that effectively substitutes for a conventional overture.) If not quite the first "hip-hoperetta" star, Miranda deftly used hip-hop lyrics to provide background information, establish character, and effect story line transitions—essentially performing the fundamental groundwork of traditional librettists but using decidedly new tools to do it.

While hardly intended as searing social drama, *In the Heights* more than touches on genuine political issues, noting both unity and some tension within the neighborhood's diverse population. The author also tweaks at neighborhood resistance to grassroots political mobilization with a passing joke about community self-assertion. (During a summertime electricity blackout, a frustrated beauty shop owner turns to her equally frustrated Heights neighbors and shouts, "What are we going to do? Organize or complain?" From the community comes a thunderous collective response: "COMPLAIN!" The line gets a laugh but also makes its point.)

Miranda's use of Spanish dialogue and lyrics was also highly innovative. Broadway songwriters will occasionally introduce into a show a song containing some lyrics in a language other than English. However, the songs themselves generally provide their own English translations, sparing the monolingual theatergoer any confusion over what the lyrics mean. ("Dites-moi" from *South Pacific*, "To Life! [L'chai-im!]" from *Fiddler on the Roof*, and "Wilkommen" from *Cabaret* are examples of self-translating songs.) Miranda, however, plays by new rules. *In the Heights* contains several songs and dramatic interludes wherein Spanish is featured to the point of dominating an occasional dramatic moment or song lyric. At times, if only briefly, non-Spanish speaking audience members do not receive a full literal English translation beyond that which they must infer from context. One of the show's subtle messages to twenty-first-century Broadway seems prophetic: learn Spanish or pay attention—preferably both! The successful opening of *In the Heights* suggests the possibility that Broadway might be ready to hear that message—if only, for now, mostly in English.

Thomas A. Greenfield

Further Reading

Isherwood, Christopher. "The View from Uptown: American Dreaming to a Latin Beat." *New York Times* (online), March 10, 2008. http://theater2.nytimes.com/2008/03/10/theater/reviews/10heig.html?scp=1&sq=%22in%20the%20heights%22&st=cse (accessed March 20, 2009).
Murphy, Tim. "Lin-Manuel Miranda of 'In the Heights' on No Longer Being in the Heights." *New York Magazine* (online), March 7, 2008. http://nymag.com/daily/entertainment/2008/03/linmanuel_miranda_of_in_the_he.html (accessed March 10, 2009).

INGE, WILLIAM (1913–1973)
PLAYWRIGHT, JOURNALIST, SCREENWRITER, NOVELIST

The author of several successful Broadway dramas, William Inge rose to popularity in the 1950s for his vivid, naturalistic portrayals of the American Midwest. In contrast to some of Broadway's cheerful, sentimental depictions of rural America, such as those seen in the musicals ***Oklahoma!*** (1943) and *The Music Man* (1957), Inge's plays explored the psychological isolation of small-town society.

Born and raised in Independence, Kansas, Inge attended the University of Kansas in 1930. After graduating he had hoped to pursue a Broadway acting career but financial pressures prevented him from traveling to New York. Instead, he entered graduate school on a Peabody scholarship for teachers. While a graduate student, Inge suffered periods of severe depression, which would later provide him with source material for his characters and plotlines. After pursuing a series of jobs ranging from radio host, road gang laborer, high school and college teacher, and newspaper editorialist, Inge met **playwright Tennessee Williams** in 1944. Conducting an interview for the *St. Louis Star-Times* on Williams's newest play *The*

Glass Menagerie, Inge became fascinated with playwriting and relinquished his dreams of an acting career.

After seeing *Menagerie* and entering into a brief romantic relationship with Williams, Inge began work on his own dramas. Inge's first Broadway production, *Come Back, Little Sheba* (1950), ran for six months. Despite the impressive run for a dramatic Broadway debut, the production struggled financially, causing the play's director and some cast members to take pay cuts in order for the play to run as long as it did. Set in a fictitious Midwest community, the play's lead characters, Doc and Lola, share an abysmal marriage in which they cannot communicate meaningfully. The play earned for lead actor Sydney Blackmer, a 30-year veteran of Broadway, the only Tony Award nomination or award he ever received and for lead actress Shirley Booth, a 25-year veteran, her first Tony Award for a leading role.

Inge pursued the theme of tension and frustration in Midwest everyday life in his next play *Picnic* (1953), which would win the Pulitzer Prize. The play is notable for Inge's in-depth portrayal of isolated unmarried women of varying ages and social positions. The show provided the Broadway debut and professional breakthrough for the then unknown "bit part" television actor, Paul Newman, who landed his first movie contract shortly after his run in *Picnic*. The play was a critical success as was the highly successful 1956 **film** adaptation. Inge's third Broadway play, *Bus Stop* (1955), was a hit as well. A romantic change of pace for Inge, the play dramatized a five-hour encounter among strangers in a Midwestern diner and became popular for its realistic portrayal of Midwestern dialect and idiom. It, too, was adapted into a successful film in 1956 starring Marilyn Monroe.

After undergoing psychoanalysis in the mid-1950s, Inge explored the oedipal complex in his subsequent dramas. *The Dark at the Top of the Stairs* (1957), directed by **Elia Kazan**, explored the mysterious mother-son relationship and the Freudian concept of internal emotional repression. But Inge was never again able to please Broadway **critics** or audiences. While *Dark* proved successful, 1959's *A Loss of Roses*—involving a complicated love triangle among mother, son, and babysitter—was universally panned. His play *Natural Affection* (1963) disturbed audiences with its onstage portrayal of a young boy fatally stabbing an innocent woman.

After this string of failures on Broadway, Inge turned his attention to Hollywood. He wrote 1963's *Splendor in the Grass*, for which he won an Academy Award for Best Original Screenplay. Despite this success, Inge continued to suffer from deep depression, which was certainly exacerbated by his inability to create Broadway hits beyond his initial triumphs. His last original Broadway play, *Where's Daddy?* (1966) received negative reviews and closed in less than three weeks.

Inge continued to write fiction and short plays. He suffered from depression for the remainder of his life, at times requiring hospitalization. On June 10, 1973, Inge committed suicide by carbon monoxide poisoning in the garage of his Hollywood home.

Thomas A. Greenfield and Robert A. Adamo

Further Reading

Leeson, Richard M. *William Inge: A Research and Production Sourcebook.* Westport, CT: Greenwood Press, 1994.

Shuman, R. Baird. *William Inge.* New York: G. K. Hall & Co., 1999.

INTERNET

See **New Media and Technology**.

Jewish American Musicals

In Monty Python's hit Broadway musical comedy *Spamalot* (2005), a medieval British knight, Sir Robin sings: "You just can't succeed on Broadway if you don't have any Jews." These satirical lyrics jokingly underscore a widely acknowledged strong connection between Broadway and Jewish American culture. Coming to New York City primarily from Germany (in the nineteenth century) and Eastern Europe (at the turn of the twentieth), Jewish immigrants and their descendants were instrumental in shaping Broadway history. Offstage and on, from **producers**, directors, and authors to performers, many key figures from all aspects of the Broadway world have been Jewish. Some of these artists placed high importance on their Jewishness while to others it meant little personally. Some were practicing Jews, while others were not religious. Some addressed Jewish themes or concerns in their work, while others ignored them. Regardless of personal attitudes, Jewish Americans have had a profound effect on the history of Broadway, and, in turn, Broadway has had a significant impact upon how Jewish immigrants and their progeny have assimilated into American society and culture.

Jewish Culture and Theatricality

There are various explanations for the preponderance of artists of Jewish heritage in the theater. Scholars have described Judaism as a "performative" religion, with particular events, such as the Bar Mitzvah (the ceremony marking passage into adulthood), making performance of text and song central to religious ritual. Purim plays (in celebration of the Jewish holiday honoring Queen Ester) also demonstrate the centrality of performance to the Jewish religion. Scholars point to the tradition of a wedding jester, called a *badchen*, as a link between Jewish religious ritual and comic performance. Some also argue that early Jewish leaders and scholars interpreted the Second Commandment, prohibiting the making of graven images, as disapproving of the visual arts, thus privileging writing and performance as artistic outlets for Jews. Additionally, traditional Jewish religious music stresses solo performance by a cantor (who sings Hebrew prayers in temple), whereas Christian tradition places a greater emphasis on choral singing.

As for their involvement in American theater specifically, Jews emigrating to the United States in the early twentieth century faced a considerable amount of prejudice, which limited their opportunities in a number of businesses and professions. However, many in America's established upper and middle classes considered working in the theater to be a lower-class and/or morally suspect activity, allowing Jewish immigrants access to the business and performance aspects of New York's growing theater industry while facing relatively little anti-Semitic resistance. Additionally, the centers of media and art in America have been, since their emergence in the late nineteenth and early twentieth centuries, coastal phenomena: largely in the urban centers of New York and Los Angeles where Jewish populations have historically been proportionately larger than in other areas of the country. Residing in these cities encouraged Jews to take part in the local, urban-based theater and media industries while, correspondingly, the relatively large Jewish populations moving into these cities helped to make them cultural and media centers. Moreover, the same trends that have historically encouraged Jews to become theater professionals apparently have emerged in the evolution of the commercial theater audience. While there are no verifiable statistics regarding the ratio of Jewish to non-Jewish Broadway ticket buyers, it has been widely understood, or at least assumed, for decades by producers, writers, and backers of commercial theater that Jewish people attend Broadway shows at a very high rate, certainly disproportionately to their small numbers nationally—and this persistent assumption has also impacted the character of commercial theater in New York.

Jewish Culture and the Roots of Broadway Theater

The theatrical roots of Broadway theater and particularly of the American **musical** include **operetta**, minstrelsy, and **vaudeville**. Jewish artists played pivotal roles in the development of each of these entertainment forms. European Jews Jacques Offenbach, Emmerich Kalman, Sigmund Romberg, Oscar Straus, and Rudolf Friml became major figures in American operetta in the first two decades of the twentieth century. Jewish performers also took part in the problematic minstrelsy tradition. Most famous among these were **Eddie Cantor**, who performed in blackface during some of his early appearances with the *Ziegfeld Follies*, and Al Jolson, who "blacked up" in many of his stage appearances as well as in the first sound picture, *The Jazz Singer* (1927). Jewish performers such as Jack Benny, **Fanny Brice**, Cantor, the Marx Brothers, Anna Held, Jolson, Molly Picon, and Sophie

Tucker were successful as vaudeville performers and correspondingly as pioneers in the emerging tradition of American comedy. Many of these performers crossed over from variety acts into other entertainment forms. Fanny Brice (born Fanny Borach) was hired out of vaudeville to perform in the *Ziegfeld Follies* on Broadway where she sang songs such as, "Yiddle on Your Fiddle, Play Some Ragtime," by Jewish composer **Irving Berlin**. (Two generations later Brice was immortalized on Broadway in the biographical musical *Funny Girl* [1964], which provided an early star vehicle for another rising Jewish female performer, Barbra Streisand.)

Yiddish Theater

Yiddish theater was also influential in shaping Broadway. Yiddish, a Germanic language written with the Hebrew alphabet, was the primary tongue of immigrant Eastern European Jews and, thus, the primary language of early professional, if decidedly low-budget, community-based theater of New York's Jewish immigrants. Theater produced in the Yiddish language included revues, melodrama, operetta, musical comedy, and naturalist or expressionist drama. Professional Yiddish theater in the United States dates from approximately 1876, and its ultimate epicenter proved to be Second Avenue on New York City's Lower East Side—a downtown neighborhood packed with newly arrived Jewish immigrants. Yiddish theater began to decline in the 1930s as immigrants moved up and out of the Lower East Side. However, as Jewish entertainers who either started out in Yiddish theater or attended Yiddish theater productions in their youth moved into mainstream commercial entertainment, the influence of Yiddish theater persisted throughout the twentieth century in **radio** comedy, early **television**, and certainly Broadway musicals, comedy, and straight drama. A number of Yiddish theater performers even crossed over into successful Broadway performances. Molly Picon, generally acknowledged to be the leading lady of New York's Yiddish theater in the 1920s and early 1930s, later starred in **Jerry Herman**'s musical *Milk and Honey* (1961) and replaced **Helen Hayes** in a 1970 revival of Ben Hecht's *The Front Page*. Another veteran of New York Yiddish theater, Paul Muni, had a distinguished career in both **film** and theater, including a Tony Award for Best Actor in the original production of *Inherit the Wind* (1955).

Important Jewish Figures on Broadway: Producers, Directors, and Choreographers

There have been and remain many men and women of Jewish heritage behind the scenes on Broadway, including a large percentage of Jewish producers and theater owners. Notwithstanding the occasional anti-Semitic Jewish conspiracy myths that appear as "explanations" of this phenomenon, Broadway in the early twentieth century offered to Jewish business people, much as it did to performers, a relatively prejudice-free outlet for investment and entrepreneurship compared to many other businesses or professions.

The early history of Broadway features the rivalry of two production entities or theater owners, the **Theatrical Syndicate** versus the **Shubert Brothers**. The Syndicate, an alliance of theater owners (many Jewish) from across the country led by Abraham Lincoln Erlinger, held a choke hold on much of the theater activity of early Broadway. The Shubert Brothers, Lee, Sam, and JJ (birth names Levi, Shmuel, and Jacob Szemanski) led the opposition to the Syndicate with their own empire, eventually winning the war, decimating the Syndicate, and replacing it as the major theater owners on Broadway and across the nation. Although considerably smaller now than in its 1920s heyday, when it owned or managed hundreds of theaters nationwide, the **Shubert Organization** remains a strong influence on Broadway, along with other Jewish-led family organizations such as the **Nederlanders** and the Minskoffs. Various famous, or infamous, producers through history have also been Jewish, including **David Merrick** (originally named Margulois), "the abominable showman" of the 1970s and 1980s, and **David Belasco**, who either produced, wrote, or directed over 100 Broadway plays between the years 1884 and 1930. **Florenz Ziegfeld**'s aforementioned *Follies* was a Broadway institution for 30 years and transformed the show-girl number from an adult burlesque entertainment to a more or less wholesome staple of mainstream twentieth-century musicals. Ukrainian immigrant Sol Hurok mounted over 70 Broadway productions from the 1920s to the 1970s. Although he produced a number of Shakespearean and other European classic plays as well as original modern pieces, Hurok specialized in short-run (usually between one and three weeks) dance spectaculars featuring stars like Katherine Dunham and Rudolph Nuryev or dazzling globe-trotting touring companies from Spain, France, or Russia. **Joseph Papp** is another Jewish producer/director who changed the face of New York theater although Papp, through his founding of the Public Theater and the New York Shakespeare Festival, often worked just outside the Broadway milieu.

Many major Broadway directors and choreographers both past and present, have been Jewish. Max Reinhardt, the Austrian director and producer who founded the Salzburg Festival, moved to America when the Nazis took over Europe, became an American citizen in 1940, and directed several important Broadway productions. Michael Kidd, born Milton Greenwald on the Lower East Side, choreographed and/or directed musicals such as *Guys and Dolls* (1950) and *The Rothschilds* (1970). **Jerome Robbins** (born Rabinowitz) directed and choreographed such pivotal musicals as ***West Side Story*** (1957), ***Gypsy*** (1959), and *Fiddler on the Roof* (1964). To this last he brought interest in his own Eastern European Jewish heritage and a desire to memorialize the community depicted. **Harold ("Hal") Prince**, the most successful and prolific director/producer of the past four decades, served as producer of *Fiddler* as well as another highly visible Broadway production with Holocaust echoes, *Cabaret* (1966). He also has collaborated with **Steven Sondheim** on many of his famous and genre-changing musicals such as ***Company*** (1970) and with Sir Andrew Lloyd Webber on such major hits as ***The Phantom of the Opera*** (1988), the longest-running show in Broadway history. The first woman to receive a Tony Award for direction of a musical, **Julie Taymor**, is Jewish, and brought her innovative staging techniques to the Disney-produced musical *The Lion King* (1997).

Musical Theater

The mainstream Broadway musical, in its various incarnations from the days of Tin Pan Alley to the present, has been largely created by Jewish composers and songwriters. Jewish composers have written 70 percent of the scores nominated for a Tony Award since the award's inception in 1947. Even a partial list of Jewish musical theater creators accounts for a majority of the most commercially successful and historically significant Broadway musical productions. In the 1920s and 1930s **Jerome Kern**, Irving Berlin, **George and Ira Gershwin**, and **Richard Rodgers** and **Lorenz Hart**—all of Jewish heritage—reigned among the elite of Broadway's musical creators. Of their contemporaries only **Cole Porter** (who was not Jewish) achieved comparable levels of success.

In the 1940s through the mid-1960s, sometimes referred to as Broadway's Golden Age of Musicals or, more pointedly, the **Rodgers and Hammerstein** era, saw a similar domination by Jewish composers and lyricists. Among the leading lights of this period were, of course, Rodgers and Hammerstein themselves (the latter Jewish on his father's side), **Frank Loesser**, **Jerry Herman**, **Leonard Bernstein**, Cy Coleman, the newly emerging Steven Sondheim, and the teams of **Alan J. Lerner and Frederick Loewe**, **Betty Comden and Adolph Green**, and Jerry Bock and Sheldon Harnick. In the years following the mid-1960s, Sondheim, Herman, and Bock and Harnick maintained positions of prominence on Broadway, and the team of **John Kander and Fred Ebb** emerged as writers of sophisticated, sometimes edgy hit musicals such as *Cabaret* (1969), *Chicago* (1975), and *Kiss of the Spider Woman* (1993). In the 1970s and beyond European musical spectaculars made a large impact on the Broadway scene, led by the musical theater's most successful composer of the modern era, Andrew Lloyd Webber (who is not Jewish). Yet Jewish American composers and songwriters, including Stephen Schwartz (*Pippin* 1973), Jonathan Larson (*Rent* 1999), Sondheim, and Kander and Ebb, continue to succeed on Broadway even in the wake of Webber and the "invasion" of the **European megamusical**. The team of Alain Boublil and Claude-Michel Schoenberg, both French Jews, was an integral part of this "British invasion" with their English-produced megahits *Les Misérables* (1987) and *Miss Saigon* (1991).

Jewish Musical Influences and Jewish-Themed Musicals

Cole Porter, one of the major exceptions to the usual ethnic background of major musical theater composers, coming from a Midwestern Protestant family, always held that he wrote "Jewish music." An apocryphal story holds that Porter asked composer George Gershwin how to be successful in musical theater writing. Gershwin's answer, according to the story, was "Write Jewish." In a story with a similar point, Jerome Kern, writing a musical about Marco Polo, was asked what kind of music he would write. He replied, "It'll be good Jewish music." According to these popular stories at least, many Jewish composers were quite conscious of the Jewish influence on Broadway music in general and even their own compositions. Sheldon Harnick, lyricist of *Fiddler on the Roof* (1964), has argued that the cantor tradition conveys emotion well and that is why Jewish composers are suited to theater material. Some Jewish composers came directly from a Jewish musical tradition; Irving Berlin's father was a cantor, and the composer took the liturgical melodies he grew up with and blended them into jazz and ragtime. Scholars have found similarities between George Gershwin's ***Porgy and Bess*** (1935) spiritual "It Takes a Long Pull to Get There" and a Jewish folk song "Havenu Sholem Aleichem." However, all Broadway music composed by Jews, of course, is not restricted to Jewish melodic themes. Instead, Jewish idioms of musical phrasing and chord structure were intertwined with American sounds, such as jazz and ragtime, to form a new music all its own.

Jewish themes sometimes appear in musicals and plays that do not explicitly concern Jewish culture. Between the 1920s and the 1950s, Jewish songwriters and authors, sensitive to the need to appeal to a broad-based audience, tended to avoid direct representation of specifically Jewish themes or characters. The world of early mainstream Broadway operettas, revues, and comedies that Jewish theatrical artists first entered did not lend itself to specific explorations of Jewish ethnicity. Moreover, many Jewish artists wanted wider recognition, larger audiences, and more money than were available in Yiddish or other Jewish-centered theater. Moreover, in the 1940s and early 1950s, fear of provoking anti-Semitism in a period that featured the HUAC blacklists (which affected directly a large number of prominent Jewish authors and artists), McCarthy hearings, and the Rosenberg espionage trials, made explicitly Jewish themes seem too risky for the commercial stage.

As a consequence, Jewish writers of dramas and musicals frequently created characters who were not overtly Jewish but instead, through their outsider status seemed to have implicitly expressed the tenuous security immigrant and first-generation Jewish Americans felt in an often anti-Semitic climate. Jewish authors in this period also could express their heritage through highlighting concerns important to their community. Themes such as assimilation, ethnic and racial harmony, and persevering through obstacles are often argued to be "Jewish" themes in such classic American musicals as ***Show Boat*** (1928), *Porgy and Bess* (1935), *South Pacific* (1949), and *The King and I* (1951), all written by Jews without Jewish characters or explicitly "Jewish content."

However, beginning in the 1960s Jewish producers and creators of Broadway musicals both sensed and created a shift in Broadway audience sensibility, and the decade ushered in musicals with explicit, rather than sublimated or semi-hidden, Jewish material. If, in the Broadway musical's early and Golden Age years, Jews wrote about nuns, frontier folk, and the King of Siam, some Jewish writers of musical theater turned their attention toward subjects closer to their own experience. Broadway soon saw musicals about the new state of Israel (*Milk and Honey*), life in the Eastern European *shtetl* or small Jewish village (*Fiddler on the Roof*), the difficulties of life in anti-Semitic Europe (*Cabaret*), and other challenges of life as a minority in America.

This new willingness on the part of Jewish producers, writers, and composers to present explicitly Jewish themes in musicals coincided with several social and cultural phenomena that reduced long-standing Jewish American anxieties about their place in society. By 1960 a whole generation of American-born children of Jewish immigrants had grown up in America. Most had become well assimilated into American society by being educated in American schools, sharing in the defining national experiences of the Depression and World War II, succeeding in professions and businesses that were generally off limits to their parents, and moving into middle-class urban neighborhoods and burgeoning suburban communities. On the political front, President John F. Kennedy's 1960 election defeat of Vice President Richard Nixon, who first came to prominence as a "Red Scare" congressman in the 1940s, implicitly dated McCarthyism and the Rosenberg trial as vestiges of a past era. Moreover, from the early 1950s until the mid-1960s Presidents Eisenhower, Kennedy, and Johnson unwaveringly touted Israel as a critical American Cold War ally and an oasis of pro-American democracy in an otherwise intractable Middle East region. Correspondingly, as World War II made its way into American history books, a unifying national pride solidified around the country's role in conquering Adolf Hitler and ending the Holocaust—effectively making the rescue of imprisoned Jews a validation of America's oft-touted position as postwar leader of the free world. Significantly, the 1961 televised trial and subsequent execution of Adolph Eichmann, at the time the most notorious of the fugitive Nazi leaders, refocused the world's attention on the horrors of the Holocaust and reinforced America's feelings of pride in its role in ending the Nazis' reign. With the politically ambiguous aftermath of the Middle East oil crisis and related regional conflagrations still years away, the early 1960s represented a high point of Jewish cultural, social, and political acceptance in America.

Yet even in the late 1950s, Jewish creators of musicals were still skittish about staging Jewish themes in the still socially and politically tame genre of musical theater. For example, the original concept for Bernstein and Sondheim's *West Side Story* (1957) involved Jewish versus Italian Catholic gangs. However, the idea was quickly abandoned, and the Jets and Sharks gang rivalry became a conflict between American-born whites and immigrant Puerto Ricans. It was not until 1961 that Broadway saw its first uncompromising portrayal of Jewish life in *Milk and Honey* with music and lyrics by Jerry Herman and book by Don Appell. The show marked the new decade as one that would now directly approach issues of Jewish life and culture on the musical stage. Taking place in Israel, the show celebrates Zionism and American Jewish pride in that state, relatively new when the musical premiered. The show had a healthy 500-plus performance run and launched Jerry Herman's career.

Cabaret (1966) by John Kander and Fred Ebb examines the growing power of Nazis in prewar Germany, including its effect on a Jewish character. *Fiddler on the Roof* (1964), with book by Joseph Stein, music and lyrics by Jerry Bock and Sheldon Harnick, directed and choreographed by Jerome Robbins, told of life in a small Jewish village in Russia, earning the label of the quintessential "Jewish musical." In 1970, Bock and Harnick turned to a new project: *The Rothschilds*, a story of the growth of the famous and wealthy Jewish European banking family, from patriarch Mayer Rothschild's humble beginnings in Frankfurt's Jewish ghetto. Later works, including *Ragtime* (1998), *Parade* (1998), and *Caroline, or Change* (2004), examine Jewish themes, and references to Jewishness abound in other modern musicals, such as *The Last Five Years* (2002), *Dirty Rotten Scoundrels* (2005), and, bringing us back to our starting point, Sir Robin of *Spamalot*'s homage to Broadway and American Jews.

Jessica Hillman

Further Reading

Bial, Henry. *Acting Jewish: Negotiating Ethnicity on the American Stage and Screen.* Ann Arbor: University of Michigan Press, 2005.

Boyarin, Jonathan, and Daniel Boyarin, eds. *Jews and Other Differences: The New Jewish Cultural Studies.* Minneapolis: University of Minnesota Press, 1997.

Buhle, Paul. *From the Lower East Side to Hollywood: Jews in American Popular Culture.* London: Verso, 2004.

Jones, John Bush. *Our Musicals, Ourselves: A Social History of the American Musical Theatre.* Hanover, NH: Brandeis University Press, 2003.

Most, Andrea. *Making Americans: Jews and the Broadway Musical.* Cambridge, MA: Harvard University Press, 2004.

Shapiro, Samantha M. "A Jewish Street Called Broadway." *Hadassah Magazine* 86, no. 2 (October 2004). http://www.hadassah.org/news/content/per_hadassah/archive/2004/04_OCT/art.p.

Whitfield, Stephen J. *In Search of American Jewish Culture.* Hanover, NH: Brandeis University Press, 1999.

www.jinfo.org.

JEWISH AMERICAN PLAYWRIGHTS

Much as the performance aspects of Jewish ritual encouraged many Jewish Americans to become actors, singers, and comedians, the strong emphasis on textual study in Jewish religious upbringing is widely viewed as a key factor in the large number of American Jews (relative to their total population) who have become teachers, editors, publishers, and professional writers—including **playwrights**. Jewish Americans have written approximately one-third of the plays and **musicals** that have won the Pulitzer Prize for Drama. The two most successful comedic playwrights in Broadway history, **George S. Kaufman** and **Neil Simon**, were both Jewish. The overall impact of Jewish American playwrights on Broadway has been lasting and profound.

Dramatists

The first Jewish American dramatist to find success on modern Broadway was Elmer Rice. From the late 1910s into the 1950s Rice saw numerous Broadway productions and revivals of his hard-edged social dramas—serious, sometimes tragic, tales of everyday men and women confronting day-to-day economic and social struggles. Among his more noteworthy productions were the Pulitzer Prize–winning *Street Scene* (1929) and the expressionistic tragicomedy *The Adding Machine* (1923), one of the first American plays to gain widespread admiration and acceptance in European theater circles. Rice's plays anticipated the overriding concern with contemporary social themes that would characterize much of the Jewish American drama that followed. **Clifford Odets**, a member of the **Group Theatre**, became the premiere social dramatist of the 1930s with the radical labor play *Waiting for Lefty* (1935) and the highly influential Depression-era family drama *Awake and Sing* (1935), among other works. The former play includes a scene in which a Jewish doctor confronts anti-Semitism at work, and the latter portrays the daily life of one of the first specifically Jewish families presented in a serious, full-length Broadway drama. **Lillian Hellman** wrote intense dramas on a variety of subjects and themes, including one of Broadway's first considerations of prejudice and homosexuality (*The Children's Hour*, 1934) and the rise of the Nazis in Germany (*Watch on the Rhine*, 1941), as well as the less overtly political *The Little Foxes* (1940). Hellman and other Jewish playwrights' choice to write antifascist plays like *Watch on the Rhine* (plays that addressed Nazism during World War II from a not yet fully informed perspective on the unfolding Holocaust) can certainly be related to their Jewish heritage and attendant concerns over Nazi treatment of the Jews of Europe.

World War II and the postwar period provided fertile ground for all American social dramatists, Jewish and non-Jewish. The war itself, the suburbanization of America's cities, the Cold War, McCarthyism, and the social upheavals of the 1960s kept the attention of authors and audiences focused on current controversial issues.

Crusading social consciousness on the part of Jewish playwrights has often been related to Jewish teachings on community, equality, and justice. The premiere American social dramatist of the late 1940s and 1950s was **Arthur Miller**, a first-generation Jewish American from Brooklyn. In the years immediately following World War II, Miller created a sensation on Broadway with a series of highly successful socially conscious and sometimes controversial dramas. His first Broadway success, *All My Sons* (1947), examined issues of family dynamics and personal morality in the context of war profiteering and business ethics. *Death of a Salesman* (1949) explored the challenges of maintaining a life of honesty and dignity in the pursuit of success. *The Crucible* (1953), Miller's well-researched staging of the seventeenth-century Salem, Massachusetts, witch trials, was a thinly veiled, or really unveiled, indictment of Congress and Senator Joe McCarthy's investigations of alleged communists and "fellow travelers" in government, education, and the entertainment industry. Miller wrote prodigiously until his death

GROUP THEATRE AND METHOD ACTING IN AMERICA

The emergence of many Jewish playwrights in the first half of the twentieth century coincided with Jewish leadership in the development of new approaches to American acting. The most influential force in modernizing training and theory for American actors was the Group Theatre, which flourished in New York during the 1930s. It was a collective of politically and artistically self-conscious actors, writers, and directors who were committed to producing socially meaningful dramas and exploring new approaches in acting and staging. Two of the three founders, **Harold Clurman** and **Lee Strasberg**, were Jewish. Members Jacob Adler, a famous Yiddish theater actor and director, and his children Stella and Luther Adler also helped shape acting techniques in the 1930s and 1940s that influence the theater to this day.

The impact of Strasberg, Clurman, and the Adlers on current American acting styles cannot be underestimated, especially with respect to the introduction of Method Acting (or "the method"). The principles of what Americans came to call Method Acting, in which actors use their own feelings to create a complex psychological and emotional reality for the fictional characters they portray, were developed in Russia at the end of the nineteenth century by Moscow Art Theatre director Konstantin Stanislavsky. Strasberg became America's leading proponent of Stanislavsky's approach and infused its systematic, theoretical teachings into the Group Theatre's productions and organizational culture. Stella Adler, while beginning her career with the Group Theatre, later made a break with their teachings. After working personally with Stanislavsky in Russia, she concluded that Method Acting as taught by Strasberg relied on poor translations of Stanislavsky's work and overemphasized the importance of having actors recalling their own emotions ("emotional recall technique") as the basis of building their characters. She started her own studio in the 1940s and taught her version of Stanislavsky to students such as **Marlon Brando**.

Although Stanislavsky and Strasberg's original teachings have been modified over time, modern-day actors such as Dustin Hoffman, Robert Duvall, and Al Pacino all received training in Method Acting in their careers from teachers or disciples of the Group Theatre approach. Today the **Actors Studio**, New York's premiere advanced training ground for new theater artists, maintains in name and history an explicit allegiance to the traditions of the Group Theatre and its philosophy of theoretical-based training for actors.

in 2005. Although he is best remembered for *Salesman* and *Crucible*, which are among the most influential and best-known American plays ever written, he did explore Jewish themes in two later less well-known plays. *Incident at Vichy* (1964) dramatized Nazi Holocaust practices in the presumably unoccupied, "free" territory of France in the early 1940s. *Broken Glass* (1994) centered on Miller's belief that American Jews were painfully slow in recognizing the significance of Nazi brutalization of German Jews in the 1930s.

Miller's contemporaries during his peak years included other Jewish playwrights who found success with highly regarded, if now less well-known, serious plays. **Arthur Laurents**, best known for his books for the musicals *West Side Story* (1957) and *Gypsy* (1959), wrote *Home of the Brave* (1945) and *The Time of the Cuckoo* (1952). Paddy Chayefsky's *The Tenth Man* (1959) and *Gideon* (1961) enjoyed favorable reviews and moderate commercial success. Toward the end of the twentieth century a new generation of Jewish playwrights made their names on Broadway, including Pulitzer Prize–winning playwrights David Mamet (*Glengarry Glen Ross*, 1984) and **Tony Kushner** (*Angels in America: Millennium Approaches*, 1993). Multiple Tony Award winner **Harvey Fierstein** (*Torch Song Trilogy*, 1983), in addition to writing plays, also writes musicals and acts in and directs Broadway productions. Each of these playwrights has made Jewish characters central to some of his works, Mamet most particularly after he rediscovered his Jewish faith in the middle of his career. While Kushner and Fierstein are not as wedded to the gritty social realistic dramatic tradition as were predecessors Rice, Odets, Hellman, and Miller, their plays follow in the Jewish American dramatic tradition of exploring controversial contemporary social themes, especially with respect to gay/lesbian issues and culture.

The three most prominent British playwrights on the Broadway scene are of Jewish heritage. Although their plays generally open in London first, Tom Stoppard, Harold Pinter, and Peter Shaffer have established very strong followings among Broadway producers, directors, actors, and audiences. Stoppard has won the Tony Award for Best Play for four of his plays: *Rosencrantz and Guildenstern Are Dead* (1967), *Travesties* (1975), *The Real Thing* (1984), and *The Coast of Utopia: Part 1—Voyage* (2006). Harold Pinter, the 2005 winner of the Nobel Prize in Literature, has been writing plays steadily for 40 years but is best known in America for his notable early works. *The Caretaker* (1961) and *The Homecoming* (1967) have each had two revivals since their Broadway premieres. Peter Shaffer is best known for his two Tony Award–winning plays, *Equus* (1974) and *Amadeus* (1980). Stoppard, Pinter, and Shaffer rarely if ever explore Jewish themes directly and, not surprisingly, their plays do not offer realistic portrayals of American society, much less Jewish American culture.

Comedic Playwrights

The success of Jewish American comedy writers and performers—whether on Broadway or in **radio**, **television**, **film**, and night clubs—is one of the most extensively studied and discussed aspects of Jewish American culture. Jewish Americans' highly visible presence in professional comedy, in addition to providing Jewish immigrants and their descendants with important creative outlets and financial opportunities, has been a potent force in dampening anti-Semitic sentiment in America, hastening the assimilation, tolerance, and acceptance of Jewish people in mainstream society.

Many of the first Jewish Broadway stage comedy "writers" were the turn-of-the-century **vaudeville** and sketch comics who generally needed little more than a few minutes of jokes, banter, gags, and small stage gimmicks ("shtick") to last an entire season of Broadway performances and touring. Performers like **Eddie Cantor**, **Fanny Brice**, and Al Jolson, variously wrote, improvised, and swapped material for their early stage shows—although in his later career, particularly in radio, Cantor became a prolific comedy writer as well as a performer. Arguably the most versatile Jewish American figure of the vaudeville era was director/writer/producer/tour manager/performer **Lew Fields** (born Moses Schoenfeld) who, working either on his own or with partner Joseph Weber, participated in the writing of some 50 Broadway shows (mostly revues and burlesques) between 1899 and 1932.

All during the vaudeville era, plays in the mode of British sentimental comedies and "comedy of manners" held a measure of popularity on Broadway, mostly with prosperous middle-class and upper-class audiences. In most cases these plays were, in fact, British imports from the pens of **George Bernard Shaw**, James M. Barrie, or Oscar Wilde, as well as some successful American purveyors of the genre such as Booth Tarkington. However, Jewish stage comics of the time, for the most part, appealed to lower-class audiences and participated minimally in high-style British-type comedy. Vaudeville, burlesque, revue, and musical theater remained the principal genres of the Jewish stage comedy writer/performer until the advent of New York–based network **radio** in the late 1920s.

Radio created a sudden pressing need for full-time professional comedy writing in New York. Vaudeville and burlesque comics seeking to make the lucrative jump from early Broadway to radio discovered, in some cases to their shock, that a year's worth of stage material could be used up in a single weekly broadcast—and time-filling sight gags were of virtually no use at all. In short order, high-quality and high-volume writing became essential to the New York comedy industry. The old vaudeville comedy of one-liners, setups, and punch lines, sight gags, and shtick evolved into extended conversational dialog laced with jokes, comebacks, witty repartee, and increasingly sophisticated observational humor.

The move to wit and word-centered comedy in radio had a corresponding impact in print and on Broadway, and Jewish writers were at the forefront of providing these new, wit-laced American stage comedies. George S. Kaufman, a legendary New York City wit and theater **critic**, became a playwright in the 1930s and dominated Broadway stage comedy for two decades. Eminently quotable ("Satire is what closes on Saturday night"), Kaufman integrated the fast pace of vaudeville punch-line delivery into whole scenes of witty conversational dialog among various comedic characters. A versatile collaborator, Kaufman wrote his most famous plays in partnership with another Jewish writer, Moss Hart. Their most notable works include the Pulitzer Prize–winning *You Can't Take It with You* (1936) and *The Man Who Came to Dinner* (1939). Kaufman had received an earlier Pulitzer Prize for writing the first musical ever to receive the drama prize, the political satire *Of Thee I Sing* (1931).

Other Jewish comedic playwrights were also successful at the time. Sidney Howard, a prolific writer of both comedies and serious drama, won a Pulitzer Prize for his comedy *They Knew What They Wanted* (1924). Edna Ferber, in addition to writing the novel **Show Boat** (1926), which was made into the hit musical of the same name, wrote several comedic hit plays with Kaufman, including *The Royal Family* (1927). Kaufman's contemporary, Ben Hecht, left an impressive legacy of Broadway comedies including the oft-revived *The Front Page* (1928) and *The Twentieth Century* (1932). S. N. Behrman wrote and produced plays from the 1920s through the 1960s but concentrated on writing stage comedies during the 1920s and 1930s. His most successful works of this period include *The Second Man* (1927) and *End of Summer* (1936).

Kaufman's status as America's premiere comic playwright was readily surpassed in the 1960s with the arrival on Broadway of **Neil Simon**, the most successful playwright in American history, comic or dramatic. Growing up in the 1930s in a middle-class Brooklyn Jewish household—a background that would appear repeatedly in his plays—Simon was an avid fan from childhood of radio comedy and worked in television comedy before becoming a Broadway legend. Simon shared Kaufman's gift for witty dialog and the perfectly timed "killer" line, but Simon surpassed Kaufman in his ability to shape his laugh lines to the nuances and vernacular of each character and the textured dynamics of each scene. Simon's major hits—*Come Blow Your Horn* (1961), **Barefoot in the Park** (1963), *The Odd Couple* (1965), *Last of the Red Hot Lovers* (1969), *The Prisoner of Second Avenue* (1971), and *The Sunshine Boys* (1972)—were all made into Hollywood films. These plays are revived continuously in community theaters and schools throughout the country and now collectively set the modern standard for American stage comedy writing.

Simon's influence and style can be seen in the work of other Broadway comedic playwrights working during "the Neil Simon Era," more or less 1961 to 2000. Joseph Stein, best known for writing for musicals, scored a success with a witty backstage comedy *Enter Laughing* (1963). Although not nearly as prolific as Simon, Herb Gardner won many admirers with his slightly edgier humor in such plays as *A Thousand Clowns* (1962) and his Best Play Tony Award–winning *I'm Not Rappaport* (1985). **Wendy Wasserstein**, the most successful American woman playwright since Lillian Hellman, brought sharp wit and irony to her observations about the changing roles of women in *The Heidi Chronicles* (1989), which won the Tony Award for Best Play, and the critically acclaimed *The Sisters Rosensweig* (1993).

Jessica Hillman and Thomas A. Greenfield

Further Reading

Bial, Henry. *Acting Jewish: Negotiating Ethnicity on the American Stage and Screen.* Ann Arbor: University of Michigan Press, 2005.

Boyarin, Jonathan, and Daniel Boyarin, eds. *Jews and Other Differences: The New Jewish Cultural Studies.* Minneapolis: University of Minnesota Press, 1997.

Buhle, Paul. *From the Lower East Side to Hollywood: Jews in American Popular Culture.* London: Verso, 2004.

Epstein, Lawrence. *The Haunted Smile: The Story of Jewish Comedians in America.* New York: Public Affairs, 2002.

Jones, John Bush. *Our Musicals, Ourselves: A Social History of the American Musical Theatre.* Hanover, NH: Brandeis University Press, 2003.

Most, Andrea. *Making Americans: Jews and the Broadway Musical.* Cambridge, MA: Harvard University Press, 2004.

Shapiro, Samantha M. "A Jewish Street Called Broadway." *Hadassah Magazine* 86, no. 2 (October 2004). http://www.hadassah.org/news/content/per_hadassah/archive/2004/04_OCT/art.p

Whitfield, Stephen J. *In Search of American Jewish Culture.* Hanover, NH: Brandeis University Press, 1999.

www.jinfo.org.

JONES, JAMES EARL (1931–)
ACTOR

Although more famous for his 170+ **film** and **television** roles than his stage performances, James Earl Jones is one of Broadway's most venerated dramatic actors and the only African American ever to win two Best Actor Tony Awards. Despite a universally lamented 16-year absence from Broadway (1988–2006), Jones's 15 stage appearances (eight in starring roles) comprise one of contemporary Broadway's most extensive, distinguished, and varied bodies of dramatic work.

Jones was born in Mississippi in 1931 and was raised by his grandparents. Jones overcame a serious childhood stuttering problem before pursuing public speaking and oration in high school and then drama at Michigan State University. After graduation he moved to New York, working when possible in **Off-Broadway** and small theater productions. He made his Broadway debut in a minor role in Dore Schary's hit play about Franklin Delano Roosevelt, *Sunrise at Campobello* (1958). Jones went on to perform in various productions over the next ten years, including a handful of unsuccessful Broadway plays. He also became a familiar figure in New York's African American theater scene, which flourished as part of the Civil Rights and black consciousness movements of the 1960s.

Jones's breakthrough Broadway performance came as Jack Jefferson, the lead role in Howard Sackler's *The Great White Hope* (1968). Jones played a fictionalized representation of heavyweight champion boxer Jack Johnson, whose 1910 victory over the reigning white champion led to increased racial tension in the United States as well as government harassment of the flamboyant new champ. Jones won the first of his two Best Actor Tony awards for *The Great White Hope*

Director Debbie Allen, left, and actor James Earl Jones on stage for the curtain call, opening night for Cat On A Hot Tin Roof *at the Broadhurst Theatre, March 2008, in New York. (AP Photo/Evan Agostini)*

and reprised the role in the 1970 film adaptation of the play. His film performance earned him a Best Actor Oscar nomination—only the second time an African American had ever been nominated for that award.

Jones's successes with *The Great White Hope* enhanced his marketability in Hollywood, and he gradually became a highly visible film and television performer. He used his trademark resonant basso profundo speaking voice to particular advantage as the voice of arch villain Darth Vader in the *Star Wars* films and the voice of lion patriarch Mufasa in Disney's animated hit *The Lion King* (1994). In addition, he also contributed his considerable acting talents to such films as the baseball-themed *Bingo Long Traveling All-Stars & Motor Kings* (1976) and *Field of Dreams* (1989).

Jones continued to work on Broadway after *The Great White Hope*, focusing on a variety of challenging dramatic roles that stretched both his abilities and his reputation as a powerful, versatile lead dramatic actor. He appeared in **Lorraine Hansberry**'s posthumous experimental drama *Les Blancs* (1970). He later triumphed in the daunting role of Hickey in **Eugene O'Neill**'s *The Iceman Cometh* (1973), the first Broadway revival of the play in which the original Hickey, **Jason Robards**, had launched his own career and ignited a national revival of interest in O'Neill. Jones's performance as the disturbed man/child Lenny in a revival of John Steinbeck's *Of Mice and Men* (1974) also met with glowing reviews as did his performance in the star vehicle Philip Hayes Dean's *Paul Robeson* (1978). In the early

1980s Jones helped introduce the work of South African social dramatist Athol Fugard to American audiences, starring in Fugard's *A Lesson from Aloes* (1980) and taking the replacement lead role in the 1982 Broadway production of *MASTER HAROLD . . . and the Boys.* He also starred as Othello opposite Christopher Plumber's Iago in 1982, earning still more plaudits for his well-honed performance.

From the late 1960s through the mid-1980s Jones neither particularly sought nor found the kind of high-profile, commercial stage success he enjoyed with *The Great White Hope.* However, in 1987 he helped secure **August Wilson**'s place as a new major American dramatist. Starring as a former Negro Leagues baseball player, Troy Maxson, in *Fences* (1987)—the second of Wilson's nine plays produced on Broadway—Jones won his second Best Actor Tony. Running 525 performances for 15 months, *Fences* became the longest-running production of Jones's and Wilson's respective Broadway careers.

This latest stage success further enhanced Jones's steadily expanding film and television resumé to the point that Hollywood and other projects would keep him away from Broadway until 2005. During this period Jones became a familiar face and voice on series television in ventures ranging from the sitcom *Frasier*, to the "cop show" *Homicide: Life on the Street*, to the animated juggernaut *The Simpsons*. He won three Emmy awards for his television performances during the 1990s. He also continued working in movies, such as the Eddie Murphy comedy *Coming to America* (1988), the African apartheid drama *Cry the Beloved Country* (1995), and *The Lion King II: Simba's Pride* (1998).

Jones has since returned to Broadway in two revivals. His starring role as the aging former English professor in Ernest Thompson's *On Golden Pond* (2005) was a critical triumph. However, Jones contracted pneumonia during the run, which forced an earlier than anticipated closing of the production.

Jones's recent Broadway appearance as Big Daddy in an all–African American cast revival of **Tennessee Williams**'s *Cat on a Hot Tin Roof* (2008) was a disappointment only in that it fell short of being a major triumph. Reviews were positive but not typical of the raves he had enjoyed routinely after *The Great White Hope.* Audiences thrilled to his bombastic second act entrance and enjoyed his robust performance as the field boy who grew up to be an imposing, power-wielding plantation master. But they did not favor Jones with the kind of "street buzz" that a season-making role invariably generates among Broadway theatergoers. That audiences expected nothing less than greatness—again—from the 75-year-old actor serves as a measure of how much Broadway has come to rely upon Jones to command any production with his riveting sound and splendid fury.

Thomas A. Greenfield and Caitlin Klein

Further Reading

James Earl Jones, Academy of Achievement Biography. Retrieved March 27, 2009, from http://www.achievement.org/autodoc/page/jon2bio-1.

Jones, James Earl, William Niven, and Penelope Niven. *James Earl Jones: Voices and Silences.* New York: Simon & Schuster, 1993.

KANDER, JOHN (1927–), AND EBB, FRED (1933C.–2004)
COMPOSER; LYRICIST, AUTHOR

John Kander and Fred Ebb comprised one of the most influential and enduring composer/lyricist teams of the last half of the twentieth century. They were best known for creatively adventurous hit **musicals**, including *Cabaret* (1967), *Chicago* (1976, current revival 1996), and *Kiss of the Spider Woman* (1993). In January 2009 the revival of *Chicago* surpassed ***Rent*** (1996) to become the seventh longest-running production in Broadway history. It is also Broadway's second all-time longest-running revival, behind the 1976 revival of ***Oh! Calcutta!*** Their numerous career honors include four shared Tony Awards, two shared Emmy Awards (Ebb won a third), and the Kennedy Center Honors.

John Kander was born to a musically inclined middle-class family in Kansas City, Missouri. He began taking piano lessons as a child, trying his hand at song composition while still in grade school. He obtained a B.A. degree at Oberlin in 1951, and completed his M.A. in music composition at Columbia in 1954. Kander began his career as a freelance accompanist in New York. A friendship with fellow pianist Joe Lewis led to his replacing Lewis as pit pianist for the original ***West Side Story*** (1957), entering into the circle of Broadway's creative community at a particularly flush period for musicals. After *West Side Story*, Kander worked as audition pianist for the original ***Gypsy*** (1959), eventually writing dance arrangements for that show and *Irma la Douce* (1960). His first Broadway composing credit came in 1962 for *A Family Affair*. Although unsuccessful, the show marked Kander's first work with director **Hal Prince**, who would figure prominently in Kander and Ebb's career.

Fred Ebb, notoriously circumspect about his birth date, was born in Manhattan to a working-class family. Despite a general lack of family support for his musical interests, Ebb participated in talent shows as a teenager. While attending NYU, he sought out composers for songwriting collaborations. In 1953 he had an early success with the song "Heartbroken," cowritten with Philip Singer ("Santa Baby") and recorded by Judy Garland. Throughout the 1950s Ebb continued to write for music publishers, revues, and club acts.

In the early 1960s, Kander and Ebb were introduced by their music publisher. The two hit it off immediately as friends and musicians. Their first hit as a team was a pop song, "My Coloring Book," which was recorded by several singers, including Barbra Streisand, and earned the new team a Grammy nomination. Their first full musical, *Golden Gate*, was never produced, but they later adapted some songs from that show for later projects, including their next musical, *Flora the Red Menace* (1966). Produced by Prince and directed by **George Abbott**, *Flora* was 19-year-old Liza Minnelli's Broadway debut. The show was not a complete success but Minnelli won the Tony as Best Actress. The duo forged a close relationship with Minnelli that would benefit them all throughout their respective careers.

Kander and Ebb followed *Flora* with their most important show, *Cabaret* (1967), which became one of the defining musicals of the decade. The two primary sources for *Cabaret* were Christopher Isherwood's *Berlin Stories* and the successful play based on the book *I Am a Camera* (1951) by John Van Druten. The production reunited Kander and Ebb with Prince, who commissioned them to write the score notwithstanding the short run of *Flora*. (Prince attributed *Flora's* shortcomings to the book, not the score [Prince 2003, xviii].) *Cabaret* pushed several musical boundaries, including imposing the dark theme of rising Nazism into the normally upbeat and/or sentimental universe of mainstream musical plots. The show's structure—a decadent cabaret variety show interlaced with the ill-fated romance of an English cabaret singer and an American writer—provided a purposefully fragmented story line that anticipated the concept musical of the 1970s and 1980s. **Joel Grey**'s performance as the emcee imbued the show with an eerily effective mix of comedic ribaldry and looming menace.

During previews Prince received protest letters regarding a line in the song "If You Could See Her through My Eyes," in which Grey as emcee sings to his gorilla-costumed dance partner, "if you could see her through my eyes, she wouldn't look Jewish at all." Kander, Ebb, and Prince, all of Jewish descent, intended the line to show how insidiously anti-Semitism can imbed itself in ostensibly casual humor and sentiment. To stave off further protests, they substituted "She isn't a '*meeskite*' "—a Yiddish term for an ugly woman that somewhat blunts the Jewish specificity of the line. The original lyric was restored to the **film** version of *Cabaret* as well as the 1987 and 1998 revivals with no repercussions.

Cabaret ran 1,165 performances over the course of three years, winning eight Tony awards, including Best Musical and Best Composer and Lyricist. Following the triumph of *Cabaret*, Kander and Ebb wrote the music and lyrics for the moderately successful shows *The Happy Time* (1968), which was a triumph for director/

choreographer **Gower Champion** more so than Kandor and Ebb, and *Zorba* (1969), again for director/producer Prince. Their first genuine flop was *70, Girls, 70* (1970), a musical about larcenous septuagenarians that missed its mark and closed after 35 performances.

The 1972 film version of *Cabaret* enriched the legacy of the original Broadway show in ways that few Broadway musical film adaptations do. Jill Haworth had originated the lead role of Sally Bowles on Broadway, but the film role went to Minnelli, who by 1972 was an established **television**, recording, and nightclub star. The film won eight Oscars, including Best Actress for Minnelli and Best Actor in a Supporting Role for Grey. Kander and Ebb were nominated twice in the Best Original Song category for "Mein Herr" and "Money, Money." Anti-Semitism charges surfaced again, this time over the powerful anthem "Tomorrow Belongs to Me," written by Kander and Ebb for the original Broadway score and not, as some assumed, adopted from an actual Nazi propaganda songbook. The film's use of close-up and zoom-out photography on the lead Nazi youth singer allowed the song to morph from an innocent pastoral to a chilling battle cry for world domination. Complaints notwithstanding, the film was a triumph. The musical has since become one of the treasure troves of school, summer stock, and **regional theater** repertoires. "Wilkommen" and the title song "Cabaret" are now pop standards. The American Film Institute named the movie as one of the top 100 films ever made, one of two Broadway musical adaptations (along with *The Sound of Music*) so honored.

Kander and Ebb's association with Minnelli broadened their careers beyond Broadway as Minnelli became a ubiquitous figure on television and in Las Vegas in the 1970s. They wrote for her 1974 television special, *Liza with a Z*, which won Kander one Emmy and Ebb two. In 1974, they wrote for her one-woman show, *Liza*, which ran for 23 performances on Broadway and subsequently provided material for her stage shows and concert tours. They also wrote the score for the Barbra Streisand film *Funny Lady* (1975). The sequel to *Funny Girl* (the saga of **vaudeville** comic and singer **Fanny Brice**), *Funny Lady*'s reviews and box office were generally good, but not spectacular. Kander and Ebb received an Oscar nomination for the song "How Lucky Can You Get?"

Their next musical, *Chicago* (1975), a roaring 1920s style, dance-centered comedy directed and choreographed by **Bob Fosse**, ran for two years and 936 performances. Although reviewed enthusiastically and received well by audiences, it was overshadowed by Broadway phenomenon, *A Chorus Line*. Opening the same year as *Chicago*, *A Chorus Line* swept the Tony Awards and went on to an historic 6,000-plus performance run. The 1996 revival of *Chicago* has met a decidedly better fate. As of June 2009 it had exceeded 5,000 performances with no closing date announced or anticipated. The show has toured with great success throughout North America, and a 1998 London production was hailed as a triumph. The revival's soundtrack album earned Kander and Ebb a Grammy Award. The film version of *Chicago* (2002), currently the highest grossing Broadway musical film of all time, won six Oscars including Best Picture—the first time a musical had won the Best Picture category since *Oliver!* in 1968.

"THE KISS OF THE *NEW YORK TIMES*"

An early version of the *Kiss of the Spider Woman* (sans Rivera) staged at SUNY Purchase, a college campus located some 30 miles outside of New York City, in 1990 generated controversy when *New York Times* drama critic Frank Rich decided to review the Purchase production. Many Broadway producers, not just the backers of *Spider Woman*, protested this decision on the grounds that out-of-town, pre-Broadway runs need to be off limits to reviewers so that shows can be developed properly before the press renders a judgment. *The Times* countered that the *Spider Woman* production was not billed as a workshop (which, by agreement, would not be open to reviewers), the show was using standard professional theater admission prices and practices, and the production involved some of the most newsworthy figures in theater. *The Times* ran the review, which was extremely harsh, to the dismay of Prince, Kander, Ebb, and others. Despite the setback, the creative team proceeded with the musical, eventually bringing a stronger version to Broadway in 1993. Rich reviewed the Broadway show as well, acknowledging that it was much improved over the Purchase version. However, he was still very critical of Kander and Ebb's score.

Their next Broadway projects included a successful star vehicle for Minnelli, *The Act* (1978), and *Woman of the Year* (1979) with Lauren Bacall. *The Rink* (1984), starring both Minnelli and Chita Rivera, was only marginally successful. Along the way Kander and Ebb wrote the song "New York, New York" for Martin Scorsese's film of the same name (1977). Although sung in the film by Minnelli, a cover version by Frank Sinatra became an instant hit, eventually moving City Mayor Ed Koch to declare it New York City's official anthem.

Their next Broadway success was *Kiss of the Spider Woman* (1993) starring Chita Rivera. They teamed again with Prince to take on material whose edginess far exceeded that of *Cabaret*. *Spider Woman* dramatizes the passionate and violent fantasies of one Luis Alberto Molina, a gay window dresser imprisoned in Latin America on a morals charge. His principal fantasy object is the Spider Woman (Rivera) whose kiss is lethal. The fantasy plot is offset against "real life" conflict with a straight cellmate who is a torture victim. Prince, Kander, Ebb, and writer **Terrence McNally** figured correctly that 1990s Broadway audiences, now accustomed to the darker material introduced by the likes of Kander and Ebb and **Stephen Sondheim**, could handle this electrifying, if dark, material if it were presented properly. Nurturing the show through three years of tumultuous development, *Kiss of the Spider Woman* ran for over two years and won seven Tony Awards, including Best Musical for production company Livent and Best Score for Kander and Ebb.

Kander and Ebb had several projects in the works when Ebb died of a heart attack on September 11, 2004. Among the most notable was a backstage mystery musical comedy, *Curtains* (2007), which Kander completed with librettist Rupert Holmes (*The Mystery of Edwin Drood*, 1985). *Curtains* enjoyed modest success, largely through the marquee power of David Hyde Pierce, a veteran actor who had risen to star status in the television series *Frasier* and the original Broadway cast of *Spamalot* (2005). *All About Us*, a Kander and Ebb musical adaptation of **Thornton Wilder**'s *The Skin of Our Teeth*, played in regional theater after Ebb's death but has not yet been staged on Broadway.

John Kander continues to work but may well be permanently known as half of Broadway's most enduring and successfully adventurous composer/lyricist team of the latter half of the twentieth century.

Shannon Kealey

Citations

Prince, Hal. "Introduction." In John Kander and Fred Ebb, *Colored Lights: Forty Years of Word and Music, Show Biz, Collaborations, and All That Jazz.* New York: Faber and Faber, 2003.

"Reviewed over Protest." *New York Times*, June 1, 1990. Retrieved June 22, 2009, from http://www.nytimes.com/1990/06/01/theater/reviewed-overprotest.html?scp=13&sq=%22kiss%20of%20the%22%20review&st=cse.

Further Reading

Kander, John, and Fred Ebb (as told to Greg Lawrence). *Colored Lights: Forty Years of Word and Music, Show Biz, Collaborations, and All That Jazz.* New York: Faber and Faber, 2003.

"Landmark Symposium: *Cabaret.*" *The Dramatists Guild Quarterly* 19, no. 2 (Summer 1982): 13–28.

Leve, James. *Kander and Ebb.* New Haven, CT: Yale University Press, 2009.

Kaufman, George S. (1889–1961)
Playwright, Director

George Simon Kaufman was the most successful writer of Broadway comedy in the first half of the twentieth century and one of the most prolific comedy writers in Broadway history. He wrote more than 40 plays, almost all of them in collaboration with other writers. Complementing the turn-of-the-century London style of Oscar Wilde and **George Bernard Shaw**, Kaufman integrated into his plays highly quotable acerbic witticisms on human behavior and society and, in so doing, helped establish the artfully turned ironic observation and the well-timed wisecrack as staples of American comedic playwriting.

George S. Kaufman, left, and Moss Hart, who together won the 1937 Pulitzer Prize for drama for their work You Can't Take It with You, *collaborate at the typewriter. (AP Photo)*

Born in Pittsburgh, Kaufman attended public schools in Pittsburgh and Paterson, New Jersey. After trying other careers, including time at law school, he began to contribute humorous writings to Franklin P. Adams's column in the *New York Evening Mail*, a popular daily newspaper. Adams recommended him for a position at the *Washington Times* in 1912. Kaufman went on to work at the *New York Evening Mail* and the *New York Tribune* until becoming **critic** and drama-page editor of the *New York Times*, a position that he was to hold from 1917 to 1930. During this time he became a member of the celebrated Algonquin Roundtable, Manhattan's unofficial "Olympic team" of celebrity writers and raconteurs whose daily luncheons at the Algonquin Hotel produced an endless supply of witticisms, cleverly spun gossip, and repartee. The best of these bons mots would be quoted in each other's newspapers to the delight of their large midtown following and even wind up in their plays and novels.

Kaufman began his career as a **playwright** with the flop *Someone in the House* (1918), cowritten with successful stage actor (but decidedly less successful playwright) Walter Percival. Kaufman would not collaborate with Percival again. Kaufman went on to a far more fruitful collaborative relationship with Marc Connelly. Their first comedy, *Dulcy* (1921), was highly successful and launched a series of Kaufman-Connelly hits, including *Merton of the Movies* (1922), the **musical** *Helen of Troy, New York* (1923), and their most successful (and final) collaboration, *Beggar on Horseback* (1924). In the late 1920s and 1930s, Kaufman wrote successfully with a number of collaborators, most notably Morrie Ryskind, Edna Ferber, and Moss Hart. Kaufman and Ryskind wrote two musicals for the Marx Brothers, *Animal Crackers* (1928) and *The Cocoanuts* (1925) as well as the pair's most enduring Broadway achievement, *Of Thee I Sing* (1931). The first musical ever published as a commercial trade book and the first ever to win the Pulitzer Prize, *Of Thee I Sing* was an uninhibited satire, if not outright mockery, of American presidential politics and one of American musical theater's first unadorned forays into wholesale contemporary political criticism. During that same period Kaufman also collaborated with Edna Ferber. A Pulitzer Prize–winning novelist (*So Big*, 1925) and author of the 1926 novel *Show Boat*, which inspired the groundbreaking musical of the same name, Ferber's partnership with Kaufman produced three successful comedies, *The Royal Family* (1927), *Dinner at Eight* (1932), and *Stage Door* (1936).

Notwithstanding his prodigious output of successful plays with partners Ryskind and Ferber, Kaufman began the most famous and successful collaboration of his career in 1930 when he teamed up with a young and generally unknown writer/actor named Moss Hart. Fifteen years Hart's senior, the established veteran Kaufman greatly admired Hart's talent and work ethic, crediting Hart with most of the work on their first hit collaboration *Once in a Lifetime* (1930). Kaufman and Hart's other plays included two plays that are now considered to be classic American stage comedies: *You Can't Take It with You* (1936), which ran for an astonishing 800 performances, and the Pulitzer Prize–winning *The Man Who Came to Dinner* (1939), a comedy about an injured critic. Their other plays, all of which enjoyed commercial and critical success, were *Merrily We Roll Along* (1934), *I'd Rather Be Right* (1937), *The Fabulous Invalid* (1938), *The American Way* (1939), and *George Washington Slept Here* (1940).

A man with a wide variety of talents, unparalleled skills in collaboration, and boundless energy, Kaufman also had a successful career as a director, staging productions on Broadway that included *The Front Page* (1928) and John Steinbeck's *Of Mice and Men* (1937). He won a Tony Award for Best Director for the classic **Frank Loesser** musical *Guys and Dolls* (1950).

Kaufman's legacy to Broadway was the edginess of his wit and comedy, which, while without being mean or malicious, was devoid of sentiment and romanticism. Along with his collaborators, especially Moss Hart, he set new, higher standards for wit, comic timing, and ironic turn of phrase for American stage comedy.

Kaufman died of a heart attack in New York City on June 2, 1961.

Thomas A. Greenfield and Kevin Cunningham

Further Reading

Goldstein, Macolm. *George S. Kaufman: His Life, His Theater.* New York: Oxford University Press, 1979.

Gale Pollack, Rhoda-Gale. *George S. Kaufman.* Boston: Twayne Publishers, 1988.

KAZAN, ELIA (1909–2003)
DIRECTOR, ACTOR, PRODUCER

Elia Kazan (Kazanjoglous) was the single most important figure in the development of serious, high-quality drama on Broadway after World War II and, along with **Eugene O'Neill**, arguably the person most responsible for the fact that artistically ambitious drama even has a presence in American commercial theater at all. The most respected and honored drama and film director of his time, Kazan figured prominently, if sometimes controversially, in most of the milestone events in the development of quality American drama on Broadway from the 1930s to the 1960s. He was centrally involved in the success of the **Group Theatre**; the revolution in psychologically based training for American actors; the launching of the careers of **Arthur Miller**, **Tennessee Williams**, and **Marlon Brando** among other luminaries; the "naming of names" in testimony before the House Un-American Activities Committee (HUAC); and the founding of the **Actors Studio**. Revered for his ability to guide both film and stage actors toward career-making performances, actors who worked with him often identify him as the best American director who ever lived. As of 2008 he was the only person ever to have won two or more Best Director Tony Awards (three) and two or more Best Director Oscars (two).

Of Greek descent, Kazan was born in Constantinople. His family emigrated to New York City when he was a young child. Kazan went to public school in New York and attended Williams College. He claimed to have grown up feeling as if he were an outsider to his peers, and as a young adult committed himself to addressing this early sense of alienation by besting rivals in work and stealing other men's wives and girlfriends. Much of his personal and professional life would reflect the durability of this motivating principle.

Kazan was one of the early members of New York's Group Theatre, joining principally as an actor in 1930 at age 21. Over the next seven years he established himself as a capable member of the troupe, performing in some of the Group's legendary productions including *Men in White* (1933), *Waiting for Lefty* (1935), *Paradise Lost* (1935), and *Golden Boy* (1937). He also did some stage-managing and developed an interest in directing. During this period, he became interested in Marxism. He often socialized with theater people who had varying degrees of interest in Marxist philosophy and/or the American Communist Party. These relationships, some only casual, would play a large role in Kazan's life during and after his HUAC testimony in 1952 (see sidebar "Elia Kazan, Arthur Miller, and HUAC").

Kazan's first directorial efforts for the Group Theatre, including Robert Ardrey's *Casey Jones* (1935) and *Thunder Rock* (1939), earned him a moderate level of peer respect, although both closed in less than a month. His first commercial hit, Hy S. Kraft's comedy *Cafe Crown* (1942), ran a respectable four months on Broadway and established the 32-year-old Kazan as a promising theater director. While *Cafe Crown* was still running, he opened Paul Vincent Carroll's *The Strings, My Lord, are False*, which folded instantly.

Film director Elia Kazan, center, is flanked by playwrights Tennessee Williams, left, and Arthur Miller at Brentano's bookstore in New York City, 1967. (AP Photo/J. J. Lent)

Kazan's third play of 1942, **Thornton Wilder**'s *The Skin of Our Teeth* ushered in Kazan's golden age. *The Skin of Our Teeth* was very successful (359 performances over ten months), earning the Pulitzer Prize for its author and a first professional directing honor for Kazan—a New York Drama Critics' Circle Award. As Kazan's interest in directing grew, so did personal and philosophical conflicts with the Group Theatre's founding principal director, **Lee Strasberg**. Believing more in the director's function to channel an actor's instincts rather than Strasberg's strict Russian-based theoretical probing of an actor's inner emotions, Kazan eventually won converts to his directing style among many New York stage actors.

The end of World War II launched a 17-year period in which major new American plays, **playwrights**, and dramatic actors came to the fore on Broadway as they had at no time before or since. Kazan was at the center of the action. He directed Arthur Miller's second Broadway play and first success *All My Sons* (1947), earning for the two men, respectively, their first Tony Awards for Best Director and for Best Play. The production launched Miller's astonishing 60-year writing career

ELIA KAZAN, ARTHUR MILLER, AND HUAC

The House Committee on Un-American Activities' (HUAC) most famous, or infamous, investigations involved the film, theater, and broadcast industries, conducted on a more or less ongoing basis from 1947 to 1956. These investigations brought celebrity witnesses and sensational press coverage to HUAC's proceedings and generated a series of controversies whose implications stretched beyond the realm of show business and the confines of those few years. Kazan's involvement with HUAC is the best known of the Broadway-related controversies.

During the 1930s Kazan had been a member of the Communist Party in New York. Like many idealists who joined during the Depression, he eventually quit, having grown disgusted with the Party's intolerance of internal dissent and stupefying indifference to Russian dictator Josef Stalin's murderous suppression of his own people. Kazan testified before HUAC twice. In January 1952, he renounced his own past communist affiliation without naming others. However, he was called back to testify in April when he would have to name names or face charges of contempt of Congress and certain loss of his newly flourishing career in Hollywood. He named 13 living and three deceased theater people whose communist activity he recalled from the 1930s.

The significance of Kazan's April testimony had actually originated five years earlier with "the Hollywood Ten." In 1947 nine Hollywood writers and one director, all with alleged previous communist associations, were called to testify before HUAC. All ten refused to testify and were subsequently blacklisted, leaving their careers in ruin.

Six of the Hollywood Ten (John Howard Lawson, Albert Maltz, Alvah Bessie, Herbert Biberman, Ring Lardner Jr., and Lester Cole) had worked on Broadway and still had ties to the New York theater community. Many had hoped that Kazan, by 1952 arguably the most accomplished stage and film director of the day, would defy the committee and expose its recklessness.

and forged a friendship between the two that in and of itself would become part of American cultural history. In the same year Kazan opened Tennessee Williams's *A Streetcar Named Desire*, making stars of young cast members **Marlon Brando**, **Jessica Tandy**, and Kim Hunter, and establishing Williams as a major American playwright. In 1948 he directed a well-received if undistinguished Alan J. Lerner–Kurt Weill musical, *Love Life*. However, he created a sensation on Broadway again in 1949 with Arthur Miller's ***Death of a Salesman***. Choosing to cast as Willy Loman, *Salesman*'s exhausted despairing hero, a broad shouldered, thick-chested actor, **Lee J. Cobb**, rather than a "shrimp" of a man as Miller originally

Kazan cooperated and was reviled by many within the theater, Hollywood, and academic communities for the rest of his life. Kazan's best friend and most important collaborator, Arthur Miller, who would eviscerate HUAC in his play *The Crucible* (1953) and would himself refuse to name names when he was subpoenaed a few years later, cut off their relationship for over ten years; they never entirely reconciled despite working together in 1964 on Miller's *After the Fall.*

The enmity against Kazan never fully subsided. It resurfaced with a vengeance 47 years later when he was awarded a Special Oscar for lifetime achievement at the 1999 Academy Awards' ceremony and broadcast. Pre-broadcast publicity and noticeable protests in the audience (withholding applause or standing with backs turned to the stage) rekindled familiar debates about Kazan's decision to name names.

Kazan's reasons for testifying are somewhat ambiguous, even from his own writings. He believed that the United States had enemies operating in-country and was proud to aid in efforts to identify them. (His classic film *On the Waterfront* [1954] was by his own open admission an in-your-face justification to his critics on the subject.) In the 1930s he had clashed bitterly with communist ideologues in the Group Theatre and the New York Party, whom he felt had humiliated and mistreated him. And he openly acknowledged that lucrative film opportunities were a motivating factor. At the same time, he had acknowledged that HUAC had brought harm to innocent people.

Defenders of Kazan argue he acted out of honest conviction to protect America from sworn enemies. Furthermore, Kazan had been no more cooperative with HUAC than numerous other artists, many of whom faced relatively little recrimination from colleagues and went on to enjoy their fellowship in ways Kazan never would again.

Kazan's testimony and the controversy surrounding it remain a permanent part of his considerable legacy and a lasting symbol for the culture wars of the time.

---

envisioned the character, Kazan brought forth with Cobb one of the defining dramatic performances of the modern Broadway era. *Death of a Salesman* became one of the most widely read, studied, and performed plays ever written by an American playwright.

In 1947, during the most prolific period of his Broadway directing career, Kazan also cofounded the Actors Studio with former Group Theatre members Cheryl Crawford and Robert Lewis. The Actors Studio was to serve as a training institution for actors and other theater artists generally adapting Strasberg-like theoretical approaches to acting and directing but modernizing to stay current with new American theatrical trends and interests. The Actors Studio remains to this day

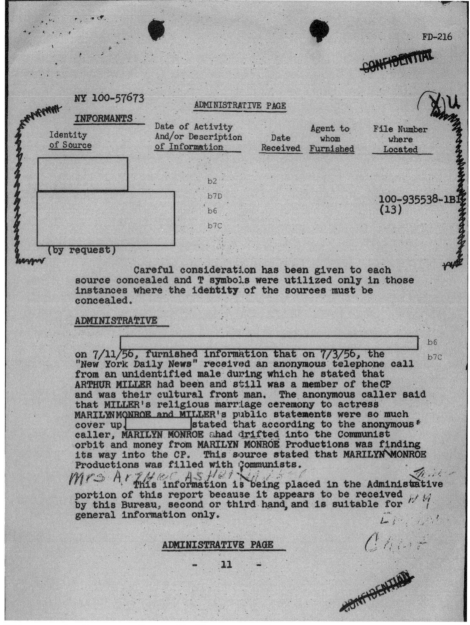

This copy of a document, obtained by The Associated Press through the Freedom of Information Act from playwright Arthur Miller's FBI file, shows an FBI report stating that "the New York Daily News received an anonymous telephone call" on July 3, 1956. The caller, "an unidentified male," stated that "Arthur Miller had been and still was a member of the CP (Communist Party) and was their cultural front man" and that (his wife) "Marilyn Monroe" also "had drifted into the Communist orbit." The file revealed that Miller had been the subject of FBI surveillance for a long time. (AP Photo/FBI)

the most influential training ground for Hollywood and Broadway's leading dramatic actors, boasting Al Pacino, Robert Duvall, Anne Bancroft, Robert DeNiro, and Dustin Hoffman among its alumni.

Kazan worked continuously in both Hollywood and Broadway throughout the 1950s. Not every effort was successful, but he added many major dramatic productions to his already impressive list of credits, including such major plays as Robert Anderson's *Tea and Sympathy* (1953), Williams's *Cat on a Hot Tin Roof* (1955), and *Sweet Bird of Youth* (1959), **William Inge**'s *Dark at the Top of the Stairs* (1957), and Archibald MacLeish's *J.B.* (1959). In the same period of time, he directed in Hollywood several acclaimed films, including *Gentleman's Agreement* (1947), for which he won his first of two Best Director Oscars; the film adaptation of *A Streetcar Named Desire* (1951) and *Viva Zapata* (1952)—both of which starred Marlon Brando and effectively launched his historic film career. He also directed *East of Eden* (1955), which instantly made a cultural icon of young actor James Dean.

Kazan won his second Best Director Oscar for his most controversial film, *On the Waterfront* (1955), which explores not only corruption in the New York City ports but also, pointedly, the courage required to inform authorities on the wrongdoings of one's friends and co-workers. The controversy surrounding *On the Waterfront* was not confined to the film's content. In 1952, Kazan had been called to testify before HUAC named names of former friends and colleagues whom he believed to have been communists—an act that stained Kazan's reputation on Broadway and in Hollywood for the rest of his life. He split with best friend Arthur Miller over the decision—a fissure that would heal, up to a point, more than ten years later when Kazan directed Miller's *After the Fall* (1964).

By the mid-1960s, Kazan had cut back on directing in both film and commercial theater. Broadway production had become increasingly expensive and complicated, and he had achieved everything on Broadway he had ever hoped to accomplish. He became briefly involved in producing for the not-for-profit Repertory Theatre of Lincoln Center. By 1970 he was, largely by choice, essentially an historic figure on Broadway. Later in his life, he wrote novels and a very highly regarded autobiography, *Elia Kazan, A Life* (1988).

In 1999 he was awarded a Special Lifetime Achievement Oscar, an event that rekindled many of the public controversies associated with his HUAC testimony almost half a century earlier (see sidebar "Elia Kazan, Arthur Miller, and HUAC").

Kazan died of natural causes at age 94 on September 23, 2003, at his home in Manhattan.

Thomas A. Greenfield

Further Reading

Kazan, Elia. *Elia Kazan: A Life*. New York: Knopf, 1988.

Schickel, Richard. *Elia Kazan: A Biography*. New York: HarperCollins Publishers, 2005.

Keene, Laura (1826–1873)
Producer, Performer, Director, Manager

One of the most significant women in American theater history, Laura Keene broke important gender barriers in her career as an actress, **producer**, director, and theater manager. Although best known for starring in *Our American Cousin* in Washington, D.C., on the night President Abraham Lincoln was assassinated, Keene's contributions to theater history extend far beyond that fateful performance in Ford's Theatre. Keene led the way for women in Broadway commercial theater management and production, competing successfully in a heretofore all-male field. By mentoring and grooming a female successor to take over her management duties, Keene also laid the foundations for informal and formal networks that would become essential to women's advancement in professional theater during the late nineteenth and twentieth centuries.

Many details of Keene's youth are matters of some dispute or not known. She was born Mary Frances Moss in (or around) 1826 in Winchester, England. The

An illustration of a scene from Laura Keene's Varieties, 1856. *From* Frank Leslie's Illustrated Newspaper, *vol. 1, no. 4 (1856 Jan. 5), p. 52. (Library of Congress, LC-USZ62-79813)*

niece of English actress Elizabeth Yates, she had an early exposure to English theater. While in her teens, she married Henry Wellington Taylor, about whom little is known and less is admired. Taylor would walk out on her some years later, leaving her with their two young daughters. Keene sought refuge and income in theater, obtaining professional instruction and playing roles when she could. Around 1850 she worked for Madame Vestris, a famous actress and theater manager at London's Lyceum Theatre, who took Keene on as an apprentice actress and tutee in theater management. While working with Vestris and developing some measure of audience popularity for her performances, Keene caught the attention of James William Wallack, a London-born actor and producer who had performed frequently in the United States and was eager to manage a theater in New York. He offered to bring Keene to New York as his star actress and she consented, arriving in 1852. Keene performed in New York and toured successfully for Wallack, charming audiences with a demure, delicate, traditionally feminine stage persona that belied her steely determination and ambition.

In 1854 she left Wallack, seizing an opportunity presented by some businessmen to manage a theater in Baltimore. After a brief tenure in Baltimore and sojourns to California and even Australia, Keene returned to New York in 1855, whereupon she leased the Metropolitan Hall theater on Broadway. She immediately appointed herself theater manager, thus becoming the first woman to assume full management and production control of an active Broadway house. She renamed the theater Laura Keene's Variety House and staged both revues and legitimate plays. As director and producer, Keene oversaw every aspect of all her productions, often performing in them when she saw fit. Two years later, she lost the lease but quickly established Laura Keene's Theatre practically next door, inaugurating her new residency with an extravagant production of **Shakespeare**'s *As You Like It*. From 1857 to 1863, Keene mounted some two dozen productions at her theater. She enjoyed some major successes, including the highly popular Broadway premiere of the now infamous *Our American Cousin* (1858) and the daring "leg show" style **musical** *The Seven Sisters* (1860), which ran an astonishing (for its time) 253 productions. She quickly became a formidable competitor for male producers who often frustrated her in their efforts to undermine her. They, in turn, were often frustrated by her resilience, box-office successes, and popularity with the public, to whom she occasionally appealed for sympathy against her ungentlemanly rivals.

Like many other theater managers, Keene struggled financially as the Civil War dragged on, and she eventually tired of the tribulations attendant to management of the theater. She had deliberately set out to teach and anoint a woman to succeed her as manager, having so groomed one of her company's actresses, Mrs. John (Matilda Charlotte Vining) Wood, for precisely that purpose. Upon taking over the theater from Keene in 1863, Mrs. Wood renamed it the Olympic Theatre and began her own highly successful career as a theater manager and producer. In choosing Wood to succeed her, Keene set an important precedent for women hiring other women to assume control of Broadway productions and theater companies. Keene's success, followed by Wood's and subsequently that of other women managers both in and out of New York, led to a greatly improved environment for women to become producers, directors, and managers.

For the remainder of the Civil War, Keene worked primarily as a performing actress away from New York, although she undertook some production and management duties during that time. She was starring in a **touring production** of *Our American Cousin* in Ford's Theatre in Washington, D.C., on the night Lincoln was assassinated. (Legend and some biographical sources hold that she made her way to the president's box and cradled Lincoln's head as he lay dying in her arms.) Her reputation and career suffered somewhat from her association with the assassination. Nevertheless, she continued to tour throughout the decade and spent a year managing a theater in Philadelphia. In 1871 she produced, directed, and starred in *Nobody's Child*, her final Broadway show (and her first since turning over her Broadway theater to Mrs. Wood in 1863).

Keene pioneered an all-important path for women on Broadway. Although not the first woman theater producer in America or even New York, she was the first woman to compete successfully against the leading producers on Broadway and, indeed, the first woman to become one of them.

Laura Keene died at age 47 of tuberculosis in Montclair, New Jersey, on November 4, 1873.

Thomas A. Greenfield and Mary Hanrahan

Further Reading

Cobrin, Pamela. *From Winning the Vote to Directing on Broadway: The Emergence of Women on the New York Stage, 1880–1927*. Newark, DE: University of Delaware Press, 2009.

Curry, Jane Kathleen. *Nineteenth-Century American Women Theatre Managers*. Westport, CT: Greenwood Press, 1994, pp. 93–118ff.

Dudden, Faye E. *Women in the American Theatre: Actresses and Audiences, 1790–1870*. New Haven, CT: Yale University Press, 1997.

Roberts, Vera Mowry. " 'Lady-Managers' in Nineteenth-Century American Theatre." *The American Stage: Social and Economic Issues from the Colonial Period to the Present*. Cambridge, U.K.: Cambridge University Press, 1993, pp. 30–46.

KERN, JEROME (1885–1945)
COMPOSER

Jerome David Kern was one of the most significant figures in the development of American musical theater. Kern's **musicals** were popular on Broadway stages in the early twentieth century and his songs, such as "Can't Help Lovin' Dat Man," "Ol' Man River," "Look for the Silver Lining," "Till the Clouds Roll By," and "The Way You Look Tonight," became enduring classics. His musical theater scores combined a strong lyrical element, rooted in European **operetta** of the late nineteenth century, with a close integration of book (plot and story), lyrics, and music that anticipated what would become the standard for Broadway musicals by the mid-twentieth century. In 1914 he joined with several other major composers as a co-founder of ASCAP (American Society of Composers, Authors [lyricists] and Publishers), which to this day serves as the industry's principal guarantor of songwriters' copyright protection and royalty payments. Later in his career, he turned to composing music for Hollywood musicals, winning two Academy Awards.

Kern was born in New York City where his mother, a pianist herself, began his musical training. In high school, he regularly contributed songs to school musicals and **vaudevilles**. Classmates and teachers hailed him for his prodigious gifts as a pianist and songwriter. Kern dropped out of high school before graduating and enrolled in New York College of Music in 1902 to study piano, composition, and music theory.

During this time his talents as a pianist gained him employment in Manhattan's music publishing houses. In 1903 he went to work for T. B. Harms as a song plugger (a piano player engaged by a publisher to promote new songs to performers and producers). Kern's stint as a plugger put him in contact with most of the major **producers** of Broadway musicals and revues. In addition, as a rehearsal pianist, he was on hand to insert one of his songs or compose one on the spot in the event a new song was needed for a show. By 1912, some 30 Broadway productions contained nearly 100 songs written by Kern.

In the period from 1903 to 1915, Kern traveled several times to London where he absorbed the light operetta style of English musicals and became well-known for songs he wrote for the London stage. The contacts he cultivated while in London included British producer George Grossmith, who introduced London to several of Kern's songs. He also met American producer Charles Frohman, who specialized in mounting popular American adaptations of London musicals. Frohman persuaded Kern to provide songs exclusively for his shows, which further enhanced Kern's reputation on Broadway.

From 1915 to 1918 Kern teamed with lyricists Guy Bolton and P. G. Wodehouse to compose a series of musicals produced at Manhattan's Princess Theatre, a 300-seat house with limited space for orchestra, cast, and sets. These intimate productions, including *Nobody Home* (1915); *Very Good Eddie* (1915); *Oh Boy!* (1917); and *Oh Lady! Lady!* (1918), were very popular with critics and audiences alike. In that these shows (known collectively as "the Princess musicals") presented believable plots and a score that served to further the action on stage, they represented an important departure from typical American musicals, which at the time were generally plot-thin song-and-dance star vehicles with songs collected from various composers.

Between 1918 and 1927 Kern established himself as the most popular and sought after composer on Broadway. In 1918 alone six new productions bore his name. In 1927, together with lyricist **Oscar Hammerstein II**, Kern wrote what was to be his most significant work, ***Show Boat***. Produced by **Florenz ("Flo")**

Ziegfeld, *Show Boat*—based on the novel by Edna Ferber—represented a significant shift in American musical theater. The realistic plot dealt with a troupe of actors plying their trade on a showboat and confronting deep-seated racial and social issues of contemporary American society. Kern's score closely mirrored the characters' dramatic conflicts and gave voice to their emotions. Several songs from the show have become standards in American popular music, including "Ol' Man River," "Can't Help Lovin' Dat Man," "You Are Love," "Why Do I Love You?" and "Bill."

In 1929, like many other songwriters, Kern began composing for the emerging Hollywood musical market. His work in the movies consisted of revivals of his past Broadway musicals, such as *Show Boat, Sally* (1920), and *Sunny* (1925) as well as several original film scores. Productive collaborations ensued, most notably with lyricist Dorothy Fields and the dance team of Fred Astaire and Ginger Rogers. "Smoke Gets in Your Eyes" (1933), "A Fine Romance" (1936), and "The Way You Look Tonight" (1936) were all the product of Kern and Fields and quickly became American popular standards. "The Way You Look Tonight" won for Kern the first of two Academy Awards for Best Song. The second came for "The Last Time I Saw Paris" (1941), which was another collaboration with Oscar Hammerstein II.

Kern returned to New York from Hollywood to work on a revival of *Show Boat* and begin writing a new musical based on the life of Annie Oakley. Prior to beginning work on the Oakley show, he suffered a cerebral hemorrhage while walking in New York City on November 5, 1945, and was famously identified at a hospital emergency room by his ASCAP card. Kern died six days later. (**Irving Berlin** was enlisted to write the new score, which turned out to be the hit *Annie Get Your Gun* [1946].)

Gerard Floriano

Further Reading

Bordman, Gerald Martin. *Jerome Kern: His Life and Music.* New York: Oxford University Press, 1980.

Banfield, Stephen, and Geoffrey Holden Block. *Jerome Kern.* New Haven, CT: Yale University Press, 2006.

KUSHNER, TONY (1956–)
PLAYWRIGHT

Best known as the author of the two-part masterpiece *Angels in America* (1993), Tony Kushner is one of the most influential American **playwrights** alive today. In the venerated tradition of **Clifford Odets** and **Arthur Miller**, his work has revitalized the American theater's commitment to drama that engages and challenges current culture. Yet he is among the boldest experimenters in the dramatic form that America has ever produced and, for the generation of playwrights born after World War II, Kushner has had a profound impact on theater audiences and contemporary playwriting.

Born in 1956 in New York City, Kushner was raised in Louisiana by parents who were both musicians. He earned his B.A. from Columbia University in Medieval Studies then an M.F.A. in Directing from NYU's Tisch School of the Arts. While at NYU he became enamored of the plays and dramatic theories of German iconoclast Bertolt Brecht and turned to playwriting. Kushner's first major play, written while he was at NYU, was *A Bright Room Called Day*. Inspired by Brecht's play *Fear and Misery of the Third Reich*, Kushner set most of the action in Germany in 1932 where a handful of artists and film industry workers

American playwright Tony Kushner, 1993, the year he was awarded the Pulitzer Prize for his play Angels in America. *(AP Photo)*

fails to see the importance of Adolf Hitler's impending grab for power. Their action is crosscut with a contemporary American Jewish woman (Zilla) and a metaphorical figure (Die Alte), who is a precursor to later Kushner characters such as the Angel in *Angels in America.*. Many of his other stylistic hallmarks are also present in this early work, including an unexplained crossing of temporal boundaries, a mix of highly realistic with symbolic characters, witty dialogue, and complicated social and political questions that evade resolution at the final curtain.

Kushner's next full-length play was *Angels in America*, which mushroomed into two complete plays and catapulted him to the top of his field: *Angels in American Part 1: Millennium Approaches* and *Part 2: Perestroika*. *Angels in America: Millennium Approaches* received the Tony Award for Best Play and Pulitzer Prize for Drama in 1993, and *Perestroika* won him another Tony in 1994. *Part 1* was nominated for nine Tony Awards, the most nominations for any play in the history of the Tonys. One of Kushner's goals with *Angels* was to take the issues of gay men in America in the 1980s, and the government's lack of response in the early days of the AIDS crisis, and bring them to a wide audience. Prior to this play, most plays with gay male protagonists were coming-out stories or, more recently, tearjerkers about the AIDS crisis written and produced to appeal to primarily gay audiences. Kushner wanted to make these stories into distinctly American stories. *Angels* mixed fictional characters with real people (McCarthy era attorney Roy Cohn) and some who were unreal, but no less forceful (Mr. Lies, the Angel). He combined acute analysis of contemporary American political thought with intersections of identity involving not just sexual orientation but religion, race, politics, and family. His feeling that America was on the verge of great change is embodied in the figure of the Angel. While *Part 1* paints a bleak picture of the contemporary American political, social, and moral landscape, Act 2, like other Kushner plays, provides essentially a positive outcome for the characters and is full of hope for the future of America.

His next major production, *Homebody/Kabul*, opened **Off-Broadway** at the New York Theater Workshop at the end of 2001. Although it was set in 1998—well before the Twin Towers fell and the United States invaded Afghanistan—the play is remarkably prescient. The character of the Homebody delivers a monologue, comprising the entirety of Act 1, that recounts the war-torn history of Afghanistan through the eyes of this middle-aged Englishwoman who loves the country. We see Afghanistan as a nation on the verge of chaos, and, when the Homebody disappears there after Act 1, her family's search for her provides the main action of Acts 2 and 3. That any American in 1998 would think to write a play about Afghanistan's history and its contemporary relationship to the West further consecrated Kushner's importance as a visionary dramatist.

Caroline, or Change (2004), a musical for which Kushner wrote the book and lyrics, is his most recent Broadway success. The story is Kushner's most autobiographical. It is about his own youth in Louisiana during the Civil Rights Era. Caroline is the maid of a Jewish family in 1963, with the boy Noah representing Kushner. This story brings Kushner back to his Brechtian roots with the inclusion of music that often defies musical theater convention, as when appliances sing or Caroline, the heroine, expresses herself in sad, stoic songs. Like most of his works, *Caroline* is ultimately optimistic about the United States.

Like Arthur Miller, whose early plays he edited for publication in 2006, Kushner has used his fame to become an outspoken voice for several political causes, including gay rights and government funding for the arts. Although much of Kushner's work has appeared Off-Broadway—and will likely continue to do so owing to his political and intellectual bents—his impact on all of contemporary American theater as a writer of bold, inspirational conviction and astonishing imagination is profound.

Melanie N. Blood

Further Reading

Fischer, James. *Understanding Tony Kushner*. Columbia: University of South Carolina Press, 2008.

Geis, Deborah R, ed. *Approaching the Millennium: Essays on Angels in America*. Ann Arbor: University of Michigan Press, 1998.

L

LANE, NATHAN (1956–)
ACTOR

Nathan Lane is widely considered to be the most versatile and bankable Broadway **musical** and comedy Broadway actor of the 1990s and early 2000s. His boisterous emotional performances draw upon a number of stage comedy traditions from **vaudeville**-style physical comedy, to rubber-faced mugging, to knife-sharp delivery of banter and one liners, to deadpan stares and pauses. Although he has played a wide variety of roles in numerous theatrical productions and movies, he is best known for his triumphant Tony Award–winning performance as Max Bialystock in Mel Brooks's ***The Producers*** (2001), which won the largest number of Tonys of any musical in history. Lane also has achieved critical success as an actor in both serious dramas and nonmusical stage comedies. In addition, for most of his career he has been an activist for gay/lesbian rights both inside and beyond the Broadway community.

Lane was born Joseph Lane in Jersey City, New Jersey, in 1956. He attended St. Peter's Preparatory High School where he was elected Best Actor in 1974. After high school, Lane changed his first name to Nathan in honor of the lead character Nathan Detroit from *Guys and Dolls* (1950).

Lane came to New York shortly after high school, electing to forgo college in order to pursue a Broadway musical theater career. His first performance on Broadway was in a revival of the Noël Coward comedy *Present Laughter* (1982). He quickly followed up with hilariously bombastic roles as Prince Fergus in a production of *Merlin* (1983) and as Toad in the short-lived *The Wind in the Willows* (1985). Lane would play Nathan Detroit, his namesake, on Broadway in the 1992 revival of *Guys and Dolls*. The show ran for three years, an exceptionally strong run for a post-1990 revival of a "Golden Era" musical and elevated Lane's status from that of a well-respected musical comedy actor to a Broadway star. Lane went on to play Max Prince, a character modeled after 1950s television comedy star Sid Caesar, in **Neil Simon**'s *Laughter on the 23rd Floor* (1994). He also starred as Prologus in an acclaimed revival of **Stephen Sondheim**'s *A Funny Thing Happened on the Forum* (1996), for which he won a Tony Award for Best Actor in a Musical.

Lane's turn in *The Producers* was noteworthy for a number of reasons over and above the show's record-setting Tony Award wins and exceptional box-office success. (As of 2008 it was the second longest-running show to have opened this century—second only to *Mamma Mia!* [2001].) The show was adapted by Brooks from a 1968 movie of the same title with the role of Bialystock originated by legendary stage and movie actor Zero Mostel. (Lane proved to be a more than worthy heir to Mostel's irresistible outrageousness, adding a made-for-Broadway physicality to Mostel's sad sack screen persona.) The film helped fuel a post-2000 surge of Hollywood/Broadway cross adaptations, further evidenced by films like *Chicago* in 2002, **The Phantom of the Opera** in 2004, and *Dreamgirls* in 2005.

Lane shared critical and audience plaudits for *The Producers* with young screen actor Matthew Broderick as Bialystock's neurotic and reluctant junior partner in crime, Leo Bloom. Recognizing each other's value to the production, Lane and Broderick became close friends. During the run of the show they did little to dampen theatrical and press hype surrounding possible further collaborations between the two. (Many hoped the duo would be to Broadway what Robert Redford and Paul Newman once were to Hollywood: chemistry-infused buddies whose collaboration would translate into box-office success and the stuff of industry legend.) A subsequent Broadway reunion did, in fact, occur, in 2005 when the two revived Neil Simon's two-man 1960s hit and subsequent summer-stock standard, *The Odd Couple*. Perhaps the vehicle was too obvious or the material too dated; both Lane and Broderick's performances were panned by **critics** and the show muddled through a one-season run. In the same year Universal Studios released a Christmas-season movie adaptation of *The Producers* with Lane and Broderick reprising their famed Broadway roles. Surprisingly, the picture died at the box office against competition from *Brokeback Mountain*, *King Kong*, *The Chronicles of Narnia*, and other seasonal releases.

Lane continues his work, both in Hollywood and on Broadway. Most recently, he has starred in two very different Broadway plays that demonstrate the range of his comedic talent. In David Mamet's political satire *November* (2008), he was a satiric, jaded president of the United States, up for reelection and fully aware of his unworthiness. The sure-footed Lane delivered many of the satiric lines at his character's own expense, bringing his considerable gifts for verbal timing and pace to bear on the knowing world of a morally corrupt White House. One year later, as one of Samuel Beckett's clueless desperate souls in a revival of the absurdist masterpiece *Waiting for Godot* (2009), knowing is not the order of the day.

In the poignancy of his verbal and physical clowning, Lane's conveyed movingly the human comedy of trying to impose certainty upon a decidedly uncertain universe.

Thomas A. Greenfield and Sean Roche

Further Reading

Bryer, Jackson R., and Richard Allan Davison. *The Actor's Art: Conversations with Contemporary American Stage Performers.* New Brunswick, NJ: Rutgers University Press, 2001.

Prono, Luca. *Encyclopedia of Gay and Lesbian Popular Culture.* Westport, CT: Greenwood Publishing Group, 2008.

LANSBURY, ANGELA (1925–)
ACTRESS

Broadway and network television's consummate late bloomer, Angela Brigid Lansbury began her New York stage career at the relatively advanced age of 31 to become one of Broadway's most successful and best-known musical comedy actresses. Born in London, Lansbury was encouraged by her mother, Moyna Lansbury, a stage and screen actress, to study acting as part of her formal education. Lansbury moved with her family to the United States in 1940, becoming a working Hollywood film actress while still in her late teens. Under contract to MGM from 1943 until the early 1950s she appeared in such **films** as *The Picture of Dorian Gray* (1945), *The Three Musketeers* (1948), and *Kind Lady* (1951). She was well established as a Hollywood film and **television** actress when she branched out onto Broadway.

Lansbury debuted on Broadway in 1957 as the high-strung Marcelle in *Hotel Paradiso*. She achieved public and critical success with her performance in *A Taste of Honey* (1960), a well-received dramatic piece whose English setting demanded the talents of a predominantly British cast that included herself and English theater stalwarts Joan Plowright and Nigel Davenport. She achieved Broadway star status originating the title role in the **Jerry Herman** hit **musical** *Mame* (1966), a performance that won her the first of her four Tony Awards for Best Actress in a Musical. (In 2009 she won a fifth Tony as Best Featured Actress for *Blithe Spirit*.) In an unusual move for a leading actress at the time, Lansbury toured with *Mame* for a full two years, establishing a national following for her work as a musical comedy star. That reputation was to enlarge itself in various Broadway performances over the ensuing years, most notably in *Dear World* (1969), a highly successful revival of *Gypsy* (1974), and, in what is largely considered to be one of the most impressive musical theater performances of the last 30 years, Mrs. Lovett in **Stephen Sondheim**'s *Sweeney Todd* (1979). She won the Tony Award for Best Actress in a Musical for each of those three shows.

Angela Lansbury as Mrs. Lovett in the original Broadway production of Sweeney Todd, The Demon Barber of Fleet Street *(1979–1980), for which she won a Tony Award for Best Actress in a Musical. (Courtesy of Photofest)*

Following a brief revival of *Mame* in 1983, Lansbury's Broadway career came to a sudden if propitious halt. In one of network television's more improbable success stories Lansbury, at age 58, became a sensation in 1984 as star of the CBS series *Murder, She Wrote.* Series television, then as now infamous for its dearth of roles for older women, launched Lansbury to a whole new level of fame during *Murder*'s 12-year network run and supplemental cable and international airings well into the 2000s.

After a 24-year hiatus Lansbury, who makes her home in Los Angeles and continues to work occasionally in film and television, returned to Broadway opposite Maria Seldes in **Terrence McNally**'s *Deuce.* She played a retired tennis star who reunites with her former professional rival during a personal appearance. Reviews were charitable, but not enthusiastic. However, Broadway audiences, including younger fans who knew her only through *Murder, She Wrote* sat breathlessly during her performances and mobbed her at the stage door after the shows. Perhaps invigorated by that experience, she returned to Broadway two years later as the medium Madame Arcati in a revival of Noël Coward's *Blithe Spirit.* This time **critics** thrilled to her wit, intensity, and, at age 83, her dancing and athleticism. Her record-tying fifth acting award shared next day press headlines with the three teenage boys who collectively won as Best Actor for sharing the title role in *Billy Elliot: The Musical* (2008).

As a Broadway star Ms. Lansbury, having first bloomed late, apparently blooms in perpetuity.

Thomas A. Greenfield and Kevin Cunningham

Further Reading

Bonanno, Margaret Wander. *Angela Lansbury: A Biography.* New York: St. Martin's Press, ©1987.

Gottfried, Martin. *Balancing Act: The Authorized Biography of Angela Lansbury.* Boston: Little, Brown, 1999.

LARSON, JONATHAN

*See **Rent**.*

LATINO AND LATINA AMERICANS

While Latin American culture and drama have grown in visibility and stature within the United States since its early beginnings, their presence, thus far on Broadway, has been minimal. Latin American drama has been showcased more frequently in various festivals and nontheatrical public spaces than on the main stages of Broadway. Even now, the amount of published Latin American drama in the United States hardly reflects the wealth that exists, either in South American nations or in the United States itself. Although a disproportionately small part of the American commercial theater history, Latino culture and drama have a unique presence in Broadway, including some promising breakthroughs and modest surges of activity in recent years.

Early History of Latin American Drama

Part of the reason for the lack of broad access to and distribution of Latin American plays is that most Latin American **playwrights** wrote almost exclusively in Spanish until the 1970s, when there was a decided shift toward English among writers in the United States as immigrants became more assimilated into mainstream American society. Early Latin American theater in the United States was related to politics and patterns of immigration, initially dominated by melodrama and the Spanish *zarzuela* (a style of **musical**), and later on by revues influenced by Mexican *revistas* and Cuban *bufos*, both farcical genres. Little of it was performed in English. Early Latin American theater was "community theater" in the truest sense of the term—community-based theater aimed at a specific immigrant lower-class population rather than a broad, more affluent audience.

Although there have been writers of serious Latin American drama in the United States since the nineteenth century, few managed to hit the critical radar until the 1970s. Spanish presses in New York had been publishing drama, both local and imported, since the 1830s, but there is little evidence of any productions of these plays, and actor Louis Baralt's sporadic performance schedule between 1892 and 1899 of a variety of Spanish melodramas and Cuban plays, such as *De lo Vivo a lo Pintado* by Tomás Mendoza, were only token offerings. Up to that point, Broadway had seemed singularly resistant to Spanish-rooted drama of any sort. Established Spanish playwrights rarely saw their works translated and/or imported to Broadway. Of the few notable exceptions, Gregorio Martinez Sierra had five of his plays produced on Broadway in the 1920s and 1930s. English impresario Harley Granville-Barker had translated a number of Sierra's works for production in England. Sierra's translated plays caught the attention of such influential American theater dynamos as the **Shubert Brothers** and the Barrymores, who facilitated the mounting of Sierra's Broadway productions. In the 1920s and 1930s English translations of several plays by Spanish producer, director, and playwright Jacinto Benavente were staged by some of the more progressive Broadway **producers** of the day, including the **Theater Guild**, The Washington Square Players, and Crosby Gaige. In addition, the La Compania Dramatic Espanola engaged the New Yorker Theater for *Pluma En El Viento* in 1932 and the Spanish Theater Repertory Company mounted seven plays in a month at the end of 1953.

Notwithstanding Broadway's vaunted affection for the works of modern European masters such as Henrik Ibsen, **George Bernard Shaw**, and Anton Chekhov, Spain's most important twentieth century playwright, Federico García Lorca—widely viewed as one of the six or seven greatest European playwrights of the last century—has had a total of only three productions of his plays ever mounted on Broadway (including only one production of his masterpiece *Yerma* [1966]).

Even since the 1970s, few critically acclaimed Latino playwrights have seen their work produced on Broadway, although there is a vibrant Latin American dramatic scene **Off-Broadway**, Off-Off-Broadway, and in a variety of festivals and symposia. Among the most influential of these has been **Joseph Papp**'s Latino Festival, which began in 1984 as the Latino Theater Festival, but has since expanded to include **film** and music, and the TENAZ group (El Teatro Nacional de Aztlán). Founded in 1971 the TENAZ group operates as an umbrella organization for numerous student and community groups. Latino performers have been similarly disregarded by Broadway. Only a handful have maintained a palpable sense of their ethnic identity with respect to their public image and performances without becoming either assimilated or cast in stereotypical roles that hardly reflect the reality of Latin American culture.

The rare creditable presentations of Latin American culture that have reached a Broadway stage either before or after 1970 have generally failed to generate sufficient box-office business to encourage future investment in such productions. Apparently such drama is most appreciated by Latin Americans, who make up only a small percentage of Broadway audiences. Figures collected by the League of American Theaters and Producers for the 2004–2005 season found Latin American attendance at Broadway shows at its highest peak since such data had been collected. That particular season was unusual in that it had two popular Latino-based shows: the revue *Latinologues* and the surprisingly successful revival of the 1990s music and dance hit *Forever Tango*. Nevertheless, even at its statistical peak, the Latin American audience comprised less than 6 percent of the total Broadway audience that season. A hoped for production of a $12 million musical version of *Mambo Kings* in 2005, despite the success of the 1992 movie version, failed to find a place on the Great White Way, and Broadway continues to remain disproportionately non-Hispanic, both on and off stage.

Development of Latin American Drama in the United States

While the roots of Latin American drama reach back into American Indian ritual and European-influenced religious theater, it was a more popular, secular folk play that came to dominate early Latin American theater of the seventeenth and eighteenth centuries. Latin American drama developed in the United States by the middle of the nineteenth century in those areas where Latin Americans initially settled: New York, Florida, and the Southwest, especially California. The plays performed were mostly musical melodramas or comedies in Spanish, produced by a variety of newly formed Latin American acting companies. New York saw these shows mounted in prominent commercial spaces at the turn of the century, such as the Leslie Theater, Amsterdam Opera House, and Carnegie Hall. The Mexican Revolution of 1910 increased the influx of refugees to the United States and saw a resultant growth in theatrical activity. In 1916, the Cuban actor and impresario, Manuel Noriega, performed in a comedy at the Ambassador Theater to packed houses, and soon after founded the Compañía Dramática Española. In 1919, this company became resident for a time at Park Theatre, which Noriega renamed El Teatro Español.

While the predominance of Latin American plays that were produced anywhere in the United States were imported from Europe or Mexico City, the Southwest, in particular, began to encourage local playwrights to write serious dramas about concerns faced by Latin American immigrants. Of these, Adalberto Elías González was the most prolific and, being translated into English, reached a wider audience with plays in the mid-1920s like *The Missionaries*, *The Expatriates*, and *The Assassin with the Hammer, or Tiger Woman*, which was even turned into a movie. His *The Loves of Ramona* (1927), an adaptation of Helen Hunt Jackson's Californian novel, *Ramona: A Story*, broke box-office records in Los Angeles with 15,000 people attending its first eight performances.

But the rise of **vaudeville** leavened the move toward serious drama and heralded an age of revues in the late 1920s, penned by such writers as Guz Aguila. He modeled his writing on the farcical Mexican *revista* that dealt with the life and culture of the working class through music and slapstick comedy. Given the strong presence of Cubans in New York City during the 1920s, Latin American revues in New York were modeled on the *obra bufa cubana*, a kind of Cuban blackface farce that had developed out of Cuban circus routines. Writers Alberto O'Farrill and Juan C. Rivera specialized in developing these kinds of shows.

The 1930s, however, sent much of Latin American theater underground as the Depression hit and movies began their rise. No less significant was the U.S. government's Mexican repatriation policy of the early 1930s, deporting or inducing hundreds of thousands of people of Mexican and Mexican American descent to repatriate to Mexico in what amounted to an effort to free up the American job market for white people. Latino theaters and companies folded in droves. Some companies, such as New York's long-lived El Teatro Hispano survived by producing a series of lowbrow community entertainments for Latin American interest, but there was little serious commercial drama in New York for some years outside of the Spanish language productions of Rolando Barrera's Futurismo group or Edwin Janer's La Farándula Panamericana. During the 1940s, Futurismo staged four productions a year of European works in Spanish translation, and, beginning in 1950, La Farándula Panamericana offered a similar annual output that included contemporary Spanish and Puerto Rican works. The next important event would be produced by Puerto Rican director Roberto Rodriguez.

In 1954 Rodriguez successfully produced the work of his countryman, René Marqués's *The Oxcart*, in a Manhattan church. Its dramatization of the troubles of rural immigrants coming via San Juan to New York City hit a realistic nerve, and its success led Rodriguez and actress Miriam Colón to form El Circulo Dramatico (The Drama Circuit), a Latin American theater group with its own 60-seat theater. This has typified the development of Latino drama in the United States since, predominantly through small theater groups outside the purview of mainstream theater. Luis Valdez's El Teatro Campesino, initially formed in 1965 from local Chicano farm workers, saw its shows produced in Europe and on Broadway. But his success was hardly the norm. Valdez's group did, however, inspire many similar groups to evolve out of their communities.

Recent Latin American Drama and Broadway

By the 1970s a number of Latin American playwrights within the United States, including Luis Valdez, Carlos Morton, Eduardo Machado, Maria Irene Fornés, and Cherríe Moraga, were achieving notice, but mostly in theaters outside of New York. Puerto Rican playwright Miguel Piñero's *Short Eyes* (1974) appeared on Broadway. The play received outstanding critical notices for its riveting, gritty portrayal of prison life. Argentine-born playwright Ariel Dorfman had a single Broadway success, *Death and the Maiden* (1992), which was directed by **Mike Nichols** and starred a powerhouse cast with Glenn Close, Richard Dreyfuss, and Gene Hackman. The harrowing revenge tale of a woman who is raped while she is a political prisoner is possibly set in Chile and confronts issues raised by authoritarian Latin America, but its characters need not be Latin American. Despite the successes of these first Broadway efforts, neither Piñero nor Dorfman has followed up on these Broadway hits.

The work of the renowned Cuban playwright Maria Irene Fornés regularly appears Off-Broadway. Only one of her plays, *The Office* (1966), briefly previewed on Broadway, but never officially opened. Audience and critical responses during previews were disappointing despite the fact that the play was directed by Broadway legend **Jerome Robbins** and produced by movie and theater mogul Joseph E. Levine. Her success with various experimental plays, including *Fefu and Her Friends* (1977), *The Conduct of Life* (1985), *And What of the Night?* (1990), and *Letters from Cuba* (2000), has been outside of Broadway, though nonetheless influential for other Latin American dramatists.

Representation on Broadway: Latino Actors and Directors

Latin American actors and directors have found more success on Broadway than have Latin American playwrights. Panamanian **José Quintero**, in addition to being the most prominent Latino Broadway director in Broadway history, is one of the most important drama directors in the history of American theater. Quintero directed more than two dozen Broadway shows and garnered four Tony Awards for his efforts. Largely associated with the plays of **Eugene O'Neill** and other "mainstream" writers, Quintero never directed a Broadway play with a Latino or Spanish cultural theme.

A number of Latino performers have found some measure of success on Broadway, some as far back as the early part of the twentieth century. Leo Carrillo made a lucrative living playing Latin American stereotypes in a series of Broadway shows in the years following World War I and would go on to do the same in Hollywood. His comic characterization of Tito Lombardi from *Lombardi, Ltd.* (1917) was successful enough to be revived in 1927, but his work would later be criticized as contributing to early stereotyping in film and theater. Carmen Miranda and Desi Arnaz, relatively well-known Latin American performers in the United States, first appeared on Broadway in 1939. Miranda was featured as Carmen in the musical revue *Streets of Paris*, and Arnaz appeared in the musical comedy *Too Many Girls*. The presentations they gave in these initial Broadway roles, along with those they subsequently performed in movies and on **television**, contributed further to the stereotypical characterization of Latin Americans in the United States. Objectified and typecast, Miranda and Arnaz's portrayals presented what would become a durable stereotype of Latin Americans as musically inclined and highly sexualized hotheads. It seemed the only other pre–World War II alternative for Latin American actors who desired commercial success was to obscure their ethnic heritage in presenting themselves to Broadway producers and audiences. It was a "de-ethnicized" and renamed William Gaxton (born Arturo Antonio Gaxiola) who wooed Ethel Merman in *Anything Goes* (1934). Gaxton also performed in a number of other successful Broadway shows in the 1930s.

In the 1970s and 1980s Raul Julia became an internationally known actor of stage and screen before his early death at age 54. But, as with Gaxton, representation of his ethnicity or cultural heritage did not factor into his career advancement as his main successes were in non-Latin roles. When Julia did portray Latino characters on Broadway, his shows met with quick termination. His first Broadway outing, Jack Gelber's *The Cuban Thing* (1968) closed after one performance, and in the 1970s *The Castro Complex* fared little better with just 14 performances. His biggest stage successes were in plays like *Where's Charley* (1975), *The Threepenny Opera* (1976), *Nine* (1982) where he appeared as an Italian, and *Man of La Mancha* (1992) where he appeared as a Frenchman.

Latino Dancing and Music

The post–World War II era saw increased public interest in Latin American music and dance. Domingo Blazes led his Latin American Orchestra through 835 performances of the musical revue *La Plume de Ma Tante* (1958). Broadway producer Sol Hurok, who carved out a niche in the 1950s by bringing ethnic and international dance troupes to Broadway for limited runs and national tours, brought in Ballet Espanol to the Winter Garden Theatre (1959). By this time Latin dancing had become *de rigueur* in many Broadway musicals—a conga in *Wonderful Town* (1953), the cha-cha in *Bells Are Ringing* (1956), a mambo in *Damn Yankees* (1957), but the actual productions portrayed little about the culture behind such music.

Occasionally a Latin American actress might be showcased in a major show, such as Chita Rivera in *Guys and Dolls* (1950) and *Bye Bye Birdie* (1961), or later on, Rita Moreno in *The Ritz* (1975). But by and large, these Latin numbers and roles were created and danced predominantly by white performers, as was the case in one of the few early mainstream representations of Latin Americans on stage: the Puerto Rican gang in **West Side Story** (1957). Rivera played Anita in this landmark production, but few of those involved were authentically Latin. The same would be the case in the equally popular *Kiss of the Spider Woman* (1993) set in a Latin American prison, with few Latin Americans, other than Rivera, in the cast. The Latin American underclass depicted by **Arthur Laurents** and **Stephen Sondheim** in *West Side Story* were at least sympathetic stereotypes. Their presence in America, having escaped the poverty of their homeland in search of a better life, is a familiar Latin American story, but musical explorations of the Latino experience remain cursory at best. The trope of the Latin as dancer remains a dominant image in American culture. Each one of the 6,137 performances of **A Chorus Line** (1975) included the self-effacing character Paul San Marco (an alter-ego of one of the musical's co-writers, Nicholas Dante, whose real name was Conrado Morale). Through this character, Dante depicted his own feelings of marginalization. One unusual Latin American Broadway hit was the dance revue *Forever Tango*, which opened at Walter Kerr Theatre in 1997 for a healthy run of 332 performances. This compilation of Argentinean music and dance caught Broadway by storm and helped pave the way for the future popularity of the dance spectacle *Riverdance* (2000) and its successors. The more recent *Latinologues*, which spent eight years successfully touring the country and finally came to Broadway in 2005, may have eschewed the dance, but its humor was all based upon the usual comic stereotypes. A collection of monologues, written by Rick Najera and directed by Cheech Marin, *Latinologues* advertised itself as the first-ever Broadway play written, directed, and produced by Latinos and starring an all-Latino cast, But it could not even half-fill the Helen Hayes Theatre, the smallest theater on Broadway, for its limited three-month run, and it garnered only mediocre reviews.

Broadway Plays by Latin Americans about Latin Americans

Luis Valdez is the leading light of current Chicano (Mexican American) theater and one of the most influential figures in Latin American drama. His plays deal with material relevant to the Latino world both past and present. He is best known for the documentary play *Zoot Suit* (1979), which was also the first Chicano play to appear on Broadway. *Zoot Suit* places Mexican Americans into an American historical context as U.S. citizens. Valdez's characters are cross-cultural in everything they do and say, from dancing swing and mambo, to speaking a mix of English, Spanish, and "hip." Despite debts to Bertolt Brecht and the Living Newspaper theater of the 1930s, the play incorporates traditional elements of Mexican theater, including aspects of the political *acto*, with its exposure of social ills, the mythic *mito*, with references to Aztec mythology, and the ballad-style *corrido*, with dance and a musical narrative. The play's narrator, El Pachuco, a spiritual alter ego of its central protagonist, Henry Reyna, offers a powerful commentary on the difficulties of being Chicano in a racist American society. Valdez's 1988 revue, *Canciones de mi Padre*, had a brief run at Broadway's Minskoff Theater, but his work has had far greater success on the West Coast. While *Zoot Suit* had played for well over a year after its Los Angeles premier, it closed after 41 performances on Broadway.

Two other Latin American writers have had some success in the Broadway arena: John Leguizamo and Nilo Cruz. Following Off-Broadway successes that exposed Latin American stereotypes with *Mambo Mouth* (1991) and *Spic-O-Rama* (1993), Colombian-born writer/actor Leguizamo has satirized his personal life in a pair of award-winning Broadway **solo shows**, *Freak* (1998) and *Sexaholix* (2001). Both won Tony Awards that gained their author/star greater notice, allowing the latter a revival in 2003. Awards have also given Cuban playwright Cruz better visibility. When his *Anna and the Tropics* (2003) won a Pulitzer Prize, it gave the play sufficient credibility for a Broadway production. It played at the Royale Theater for a respectable 113 performances, with Jimmy Smits in the role of Juan Julian who reads *Anna Karenina* to workers in a Floridian cigar factory and fires their imaginations. *Anna* earned Cruz the Tony Award for Best Play of 2004.

The highly successful ***In the Heights*** (2008), by the same producers who backed the hit musicals ***Rent*** and *Avenue Q*, is a musical set amid the predominantly Latin American population of Washington Heights. Starring and written by a Latino, Lin-Manuel Miranda, the musical's use of hip-hop combined with its salsa rhythms is aimed at a youth audience as much as a Latin American one. The show proved to be the musical hit of the 2007–2008 season, opening to glowing reviews, winning multiple Tony Awards (Best Musical, Best Original Score, Best Choreography, and Best Orchestration), and turning former hip-hop club performer Miranda into a media sensation.

On occasion Latin American drama can be moderately successful on Broadway, and Latin American theater artists do "make it" to the Great White Way—more frequently as actors and dancers than playwrights, producers, or directors. Notwithstanding the recent success of *In the Heights*, the central truth about the history of Latinos, Latin American culture, and Broadway remains fundamentally unchanged even after a century. Generally speaking we must look away from Broadway to find the wealth that Latin American theater offers.

Susan C. W. Abbotson

Further Reading

Boal, Augusto. *Theater of the Oppressed.* New York: Theater Communications Group, 1985.

Kanellos, Nicolás. *Hispanic Literature of the United States.* Westport, CT: Greenwood, 2003.

————. *Mexican American Theater: Legacy and Reality.* Pittsburgh: Latin American Literary Review Press, 1987.

Ramirez, Elizabeth C. *Chicana/Latinas in American Theater.* Bloomington: Indiana University Press, 2000.

Weiss, Judith A., ed. *Latin American Popular Theater.* Albuquerque: University of New Mexico Press, 1993.

LAURENTS, ARTHUR (1918–)
PLAYWRIGHT, LIBRETTIST, DIRECTOR

Heralded for his career longevity and artistic versatility, Arthur Laurents established himself as a successful playwright, librettist, play director, and musical director in a Broadway career that spans seven decades. Best known as the author/librettist for the hit **musicals** *West Side Story* (1957), *Gypsy* (1959), and *Hallelujah Baby* (1967), Laurents was among a core of New York naturalistic **playwrights** who established a foothold for serious social drama on Broadway in the years immediately following World War II. Unlike some of his fellow dramatists, who denigrated what they perceived as the middlebrow tastes of Broadway audiences and **producers**, Laurents evolved from a respected young playwright into a multifaceted commercial theater artist who combined literary sensibilities with an instinct for creating hit shows.

Laurents was born in Brooklyn and spent much of his youth attending Broadway plays and musicals. He earned a B.A. in English from Cornell University in 1937 and returned to New York City to begin his writing career. In the late 1930s several of his **radio** scripts were produced for broadcast on some of the most successful radio drama programs of the time, including *The Thin Man* and *Lux Radio Theatre.* As a soldier during World War II, he was assigned to the New York City area and wrote training films and radio dramas for the army. The army engaged established show business professionals to help create its wartime **films** and radio programs, and the neophyte Laurents worked with many of them, including film director George Cukor (a friend), playwright/musical author Russel Crouse (a nemesis), and numerous professional actors and directors involved with production of his scripts. Some of Laurents's radio scripts for the 1945 army series *Assignment Home*, short plays preparing the nation for the troops' imminent return, were published in highly respected drama anthologies and drew favorable attention in the New York theater community. As the war ended, Laurents had developed a reputation in legitimate theater circles for writing sharp-edged scripts that confronted serious issues such as anti-Semitism and race relations.

Encouragement from show business colleagues and his own ambition soon moved Laurents to write plays for Broadway. *Home of the Brave* (1945), drawn from his observations and experiences while he was in the army, explored a veteran's mental illness arising from war guilt and anti-Semitism. The controversial play earned Laurents critical plaudits for its toughness, as well as a lucrative sale of film rights (although Laurents did not write the screenplay for the 1949 film). His second Broadway play, *The Bird Cage* (1950), a hard-edged urban drama, failed almost immediately. However, his comedy *The Time of the Cuckoo* (1952), directed by the venerable **Harold Clurman**, was a Broadway hit, running 262 performances and earning the praises of **Brooks Atkinson**, the preeminent theater **critic** of the day.

In the years immediately following the war, Laurents also spent some time in Hollywood writing film scripts. The most notable of these early scripts was Alfred Hitchcock's *Rope*. He returned to New York in the late 1940s to live more or less permanently, although he periodically wrote Hollywood screenplays and teleplays throughout his career.

By the early 1950s Laurents, now a respected member of Broadway's community of up-and-coming young talents, had become friends with **Jerome Robbins**, principal conceiver of what would become *West Side Story*, and **Leonard Bernstein**, the show's composer. Robbins and Laurents had both grown up in New York in the 1920s and 1930s, and the two shared a lifelong love of New York theater as well as knowledge of the city's gang rivalries. With New Englander Bernstein, they also shared the ethnic sensibilities of first-generation children of Jewish immigrants, and all three were gay or bisexual. These commonalities not only solidified the creative team (which included the young lyricist **Stephen Sondheim**), but imbued the show with many of its innovative and even controversial qualities.

The show opened on Broadway in 1957 and was a hit from the outset. Laurents was praised for writing gritty, realistic language for a mainstream musical—a vestige of his hard-edged, social dramas from the army and his early years on Broadway. The concept of entertaining Broadway audiences with a full evening of white/Puerto Rican racial tension—a transposition of Laurents and Robbins's childhood encounters with conflicts among New York's ethnic neighborhoods—also represented a new step for Broadway musicals. The show has been revived four times on Broadway, most recently in 2009 when the 90-year-old Laurents directed it himself.

Laurents and Sondheim collaborated almost immediately thereafter on *Gypsy*, which followed *West Side Story* to Broadway only 20 months later. Again, Laurents wrote the book for the show. The hit-filled score by Sondheim and composer **Jule Styne** accounted for much of *Gypsy*'s popularity. However, Laurents's extraordinary characterization of Mama Rose, played with history-making splendor by **Ethel Merman**, established Laurents as a master writer of Broadway librettos. The monstrously narcissistic but achingly vulnerable stage mother Rose stands among the most coveted female roles in Broadway musicals and is widely regarded by many as the best-written mature female character ever written for American musical theater. *Gypsy* was to remain a large part of Laurents's life. Apart from the fame and fortune attendant to the film adaptation, countless professional production tours, and college and amateur stagings of the show, Laurents himself directed three of *Gypsy*'s four Broadway revivals. The most famous among them being the wildly popular 2008 production, which earned Tony Awards for its three principal performers (including **Patti LuPone** as Mama Rose) and a director's nomination for the then 89-year-old Laurents. *Hallelujah Baby* (1967), his last original musical hit, is decidedly less famous than *West Side Story* or *Gypsy*. However, it won the Tony for Best Musical, earning Laurents the only Tony Award recognition he ever received for writing. (He won as best director for the 1983 musical *La Cage aux Folles*.)

Although Laurents wrote for theater and film throughout his life, by the 1960s he had turned much of his attention to directing on Broadway. In addition to *La Cage*, he directed his own moderately successful stage comedy *Anyone Can Whistle* (1960) as well as three revivals of *Gypsy* plus some less-than-successful plays and musicals. He also continued to write socially conscious plays, often produced Off-Broadway due to the weakening commercial viability of serious dramatic work on Broadway after the 1960s. Laurents 1973 play *The Enclave* dealt with his own experiences of confronting hypocrisy with people's attitudes about homosexuality. His 1992 drama, *Jolson Sings Again*, is a complex treatment of 1950s Hollywood blacklisting. (Laurents had been blacklisted and openly excoriated artists who "named names" at the HUAC hearings—including his friend Jerome Robbins.) The play's title alludes sardonically to actor/singer Larry Kert who, in addition to starring in *West Side Story*, was known for performing Al Jolson tributes and was one of the first celebrities to name names ("sing") to HUAC. Working only occasionally in film after 1960, Laurents had two remarkable screenwriting successes in the 1970s. *The Way We Were* (1973) served as a star vehicle for romantic leads Robert Redford and Barbra Streisand, delighting audiences and earning Oscars for the score and the title song. *The Turning Point* (1977), a thoughtful introspective family drama about a ballerina and her aging dancer/mother, received rave reviews and earned Laurents an Oscar nomination for Best Screenplay Written Directly for the Screen.

As a writer, Laurents holds a unique place in the evolution of Broadway after World War II. He was among the cadre of young artistically ambitious dramatists who energized American playwriting and secured a place for serious drama on Broadway after **Eugene O'Neill**, whose active Broadway career was over by the late 1940s. Although not as important a playwright as the likes of **Arthur Miller**, **Tennessee Williams**, or **William Inge**, Laurents also crossed over into musicals— earning a distinctive place in Broadway history for having enriched the repertoire and literary quality of both the American musical and the modern American play.

Thomas A. Greenfield

Further Reading

Laurents, Arthur. *Mainly on Directing: Gypsy, West Side Story, and Other Musicals.* New York: Alfred A. Knopf, 2009.

———. *Original Story By: A Memoir of Broadway and Hollywood.* New York: Knopf, 2000.

LE GALLIENNE, EVA (1899–1991)
ACTRESS, DIRECTOR, PRODUCER, WRITER

A professional actress in London and on Broadway by age 16 and a Tony-nominated Broadway actress at 84, English-born Eva Le Gallienne was a pioneering performer, director, **producer**, theater manager, and iconoclast. She is best remembered as founder and producing director of the Civic Repertory Theatre in New York from 1926 to 1933—to date one of the most successful attempts to establish a European-model national art theater in America. Her life in theater was no less distinguished by the 60-plus years she devoted to producing, directing, and acting in meticulously crafted productions of modern dramatic masterpieces in an impressively successful, if at times wearying, commitment to sustaining quality drama within the milieu of Broadway.

Le Gallienne was born in London to two well-respected journalists. She took an early interest in performing, influenced by her theatergoing parents. After her parents divorced in 1903, Le Gallienne lived with her mother in Paris. In her teens, she saw Sarah Bernhardt, Europe's leading actress, perform several times. From childhood, young Eva made an idol of Bernhardt, who was 55 years her senior. She studied Bernhardt's acting, followed her career in newspapers, and committed herself to theater through Bernhardt's inspiration.

As a teenager Le Gallienne secured small parts in London thanks to family connections. She earned excellent reviews for a scene-stealing role in *The Laughter of Fools* by H. F. Maltby. She and her mother promptly moved to New York, hoping to convert this success into a Broadway career. For the next five years she struggled on Broadway and performed in stock and touring companies. In 1918, she alienated producer Oliver Morosco during rehearsals of a play. He effectively banned her from major roles for about two years.

She then took small parts in more failures than successes but worked with some of Broadway's most influential people, including producers Charles Frohman in *The Off Chance* and *Belinda* (both 1918), and **Florenz Ziegfeld** in a **vaudeville**-style revue, *Elsie Janis and Her Gang* (1919). She also appeared in a long-running hit, the Frohman-produced comedy *The Swan* (1923), with which she successfully toured. By 1925 Le Gallienne had established herself as a quality dramatic actress, if not yet a bankable star.

Le Gallienne had also begun working in New York's Little Theater Movement that, while struggling to maintain a viable presence in commercial theater, was committed to high-quality, serious drama. She received superb reviews in the **Theatre Guild**'s *Liliom* (1921) and starred in the eighteenth-century British comedy *The Rivals* (1923) for the Equity Players, a producing arm of Actors' Equity Association (AEA). In 1925, she performed in Arthur Schnitzler's modern classic, *The Call of Life*, also produced by the Equity Players (now named the Actors Theatre). By midyear 1925, Le Gallienne's commitment to performing serious, quality theater in New York had come to outweigh the commercial-based ambitions of her youth.

Le Gallienne produced and directed her first Broadway play in 1925: Henrik Ibsen's *The Master Builder*, in which she also starred. Originally planned as a low-budget, four-matinee run, it was a remarkable success and Le Gallienne quickly moved the show into evening rotation. **Critics** were effusive in their praise, and Le Gallienne had herself a modest, profitable 76-performance hit. Three months later she produced, directed, and starred in Ibsen's *John Gabriel Borkman* with some of the same actors from *The Master Builder*. Offering discount tickets at selected matinees, she sold out the house. *Borkman* hardened her resolve to establish a permanent repertory theater on Broadway dedicated to innovative stagings of masterworks and selected new plays at discounted ticket prices.

To build a market for the company, in 1926 Le Gallienne toured the East and Midwest with two Ibsen shows, gaining favorable reviews and publicity. She then formalized plans for a permanent company. She brought together an acting and production team that she named the Civic Repertory Theatre. She also secured a venue, the dark 14th Street Theatre that had been a famous vaudeville house. Le Gallienne did not fit the stereotype of a 1920s theatrical producer, but she was an effective fund-raiser, marketer, and advocate for her company's mission.

In October 1926 Le Gallienne premiered the Civic's first season in the new building. Producing in repertory, she incurred some failures but mounted enough successes to ensure a second season. The Anton Chekhov classic, *The Three Sisters* with producer-director Le Gallienne as Masha, received strong reviews and a modern Spanish play, *The Cradle Song* (1927), also directed by Le Gallienne, was a welcome first-season hit. Over the next six years, the Civic mounted a very impressive record of over 30 productions, ranging from Ibsen and Chekhov revivals, to **Susan Glaspell**'s Pulitzer Prize–winning *Alison's House* (1930), to Le Gallienne's own fantasy adaptation of *Alice in Wonderland* (1932). She kept up the Civic, running it and making a name for itself even through the first years of the Depression when many other producers failed. Several notable actors, including Howard Da Silva, John Garfield, Burgess Meredith, and May Sarton, found early career work and/or instruction in the productions and studio sessions Le Gallienne supervised at the Civic. Margo Jones, one of the pioneers of the modern **regional theater** movement, was also a disciple of Le Gallienne.

In the early 1930s the fortunes of the Civic and Le Gallienne herself took turns for the worse. The weakening economy exacted both an economic and psychological toll, and debts mounted. A closeted lesbian since her teens, Le Gallienne was named as a correspondent in a 1930 divorce suit by the husband of one of her lovers, an actress associated with the Civic. Although the scandalous publicity was relatively short-lived, biographers maintain that she never recovered from the trauma of it. Matters worsened when injuries from a 1931 home propane explosion forced her to take a hiatus from theatrical work. The Civic forged on with its leader functioning in a diminished capacity. The Civic's final resident production, however, was a success—a yearlong run of an adaptation of *Alice in Wonderland* (1932), with Le Gallienne returning as writer, producer, director, and featured actress (the White Queen). But it was not enough. The Civic Repertory Theatre was effectively out of business by 1934.

For the next ten years La Gallienne remained active in theater, both on Broadway and on tour, although at a less frenetic pace. However, her dedication to drama classics never faltered. From 1946 to 1948, she established the American Repertory Theatre with stage veterans Cheryl Crawford and Margaret Webster. Although decidedly less successful than the Civic Rep, the American Repertory Theatre allowed Le Gallienne to pursue her now lifelong commitment to the works of Ibsen (three of the company's eight New York productions were Ibsen plays, with Le Gallienne starring in, staging, and even translating for each show).

As Le Gallienne reached her fifties in the 1950s, Broadway had begun its now half-century-long pattern of mounting fewer new productions at increasingly greater cost and financial risk. Although active in regional and touring theater, Le Gallienne's New York appearances waned, as did general interest in staging classic plays on a for-profit basis. She toured in several productions throughout the 1950s and 1960s (most notably in a triumphant performance in the title role of *Mary Stuart* in 1957) and acted in televised drama programs such as CBS's *Playhouse 90* and *Hallmark Hall of Fame*. From 1962 to 1966 she helped establish the National Repertory Theatre (NRT), which toured high-quality productions of classical dramatic works throughout the country. She also directed and performed in NRT productions. In 1964 she was awarded a special Tony Award, honoring her work with NRT and her fiftieth year as a professional actress.

By the 1970s, Le Gallienne was semiretired from theater but performed occasionally. At age 75, she scored one of her longest-running Broadway acting successes, 233 performances, in a revival of **George S. Kaufman** and Edna Ferber's *The Royal Family*. Her final Broadway appearance came in 1982 as director and actress in a revival of her *Alice in Wonderland* adaptation; she still played the White Queen. Celebrating her eighty-fourth birthday during the run, Le Gallienne earned a Tony nomination for the performance.

Le Gallienne died of heart failure in 1991 at her home in Weston, Connecticut.

Thomas A. Greenfield

Further Reading

Schanke, Robert A. *Eva Le Gallienne: A Bio-bibliography*. Westport, CT: Greenwood Press, 1989.

————. *Shattered Applause: The Eva Le Gallienne Story.* New York: Barricade Books, 1992.

Lerner, Alan Jay (1918–1986), and Loewe, Frederick (1901–1988)
Lyricist-Librettists, Composers

Except for the team of **Richard Rodgers** and **Oscar Hammerstein**, lyricist-librettist Alan Jay Lerner and composer Frederick Loewe were the most important writers of **musicals** of their time. Lerner wrote a total of twelve shows, Loewe eight—seven with one another. Like Rodgers and Hammerstein, they wrote "book musicals"—or "integrated musicals"—beginning in the mid-1940s and continuing for two decades. Loewe's cosmopolitan manner conveyed an illusion of effortlessness in his life and work; his most melodious songs often evoked the flavor of Vienna and the **operettas** of Franz Lehar. Lerner was intensely romantic in his temperament and his lyrics, though he was also capable of great bursts of wordplay and wit. Their most important show, ***My Fair Lady*** (1956), is often considered the greatest theater musical from this period and is one of the great works of the American theater.

Lerner was born in New York City on August 31, 1918, to Joseph and Edith Lerner. His father, a wealthy retailer, often took his son to the theater. Lerner

Composer Frederick Loewe, left, and lyricist Alan Jay Lerner shown in 1956 during work on Brigadoon, *the musical about a Scottish village that reawakens once every 100 years. (AP Photo, file)*

attended Harvard University where he contributed songs to the Hasty Pudding Club shows of 1938 and 1939. Loewe was born in Vienna, Austria, on June 10, 1910, the son of Edmond Loewe, a popular star of operetta, and Rosa Loewe. Fritz—Loewe's lifelong nickname—studied piano and began writing his own melodies while still a child. His first song, "Katrina," published when he was 15, sold 2 million copies. He immigrated to the United States when he was 24, spending the next seven years traveling the country and working odd jobs when he needed money. He settled in New York City in 1931 and earned a living by playing piano in pit orchestras for Broadway musicals. He also began to write songs in the early 1930s, a few of which he placed in revues. In 1938, he and lyricist Earle T. Crooker collaborated on two flops, *Salute to Spring* and *Great Lady*. Thereafter, he wrote only with Lerner in a relationship that was close and quarrelsome. The two met in New York in 1942 and began writing together immediately. Their first three collaborations flopped. However, the third one, *The Day Before Spring* (1945), attracted the interest of Louis B. Mayer of Metro-Goldwyn-Mayer. Mayer bought the rights and, in the bargain, gave both men their first financial success in the theater.

Their fourth show together was their first hit, but its opening did not come easily. They performed the score to *Brigadoon* (1947) for 58 different prospective backers before raising enough money to open the show. It received rave reviews and ran for 581 performances. A romantic fantasy set in a town in the Scottish Highlands that awakens only once every hundred years, *Brigadoon* traces the deepening love between Fiona, a village girl, and Tommy, a cynical New Yorker looking for something to believe in. Despite the upbeat manner of such songs as "I'll Go Home with Bonnie Jean" and "My Mother's Wedding Day," the score's major songs were notable for their touching romanticism, including "Come to Me, Bend to Me," "There But for You Go I," and "The Heather on the Hill."

Because their temperaments sometimes clashed, Lerner and Loewe frequently separated but always returned to work together until Loewe retired in 1960, after they completed work on *Camelot*. The pair quarreled and separated after *Brigadoon*, and Lerner next worked with Kurt Weill on *Love Life* (1948), an innovative "**vaudeville**" about the decline of marriage in the United States from colonial times to the present. The couple through whom the story is told never ages but reappears in era after era until the tensions of modern life make it impossible for the marriage to survive. The production, a modest success, had one song that received some play, "Here I'll Stay with You." After *Love Life* closed, Lerner sought a project that would reunite him with Loewe. First, though, he wrote original screenplays for two Hollywood musicals in 1951, *Royal Wedding* with Fred Astaire and *An American in Paris*, starring Gene Kelly and Leslie Caron. He won the Academy Award for Best Screenplay for *An American in Paris*, which featured the songs of **George and Ira Gershwin**.

Lerner and Loewe agreed that their next musical would tell a story set during the California Gold Rush. Just as *Brigadoon* echoed Scottish music and *My Fair Lady* would later suggest the British music hall, so the score to *Paint Your Wagon* (1951) possessed the bluster and vitality of the American West. "They Call the Wind Maria" among other songs in the score sound more like folk songs than songs for a Broadway musical. The show ran for 289 performances. Like all of Lerner's librettos so far, *Paint Your Wagon* was an original story. At this point, though, he came to believe that his shows would have been more successful if their books had been better. He decided that from then on, he would write only adaptations of successful plays and novels. His next libretto showed the wisdom of that decision.

My Fair Lady, Lerner and Loewe's next to last—and most important—complete Broadway score, was an adaptation of **George Bernard Shaw**'s *Pygmalion* (1916). The well-known story derives from a chance encounter between a London flower girl and a gentleman linguist, Professor Higgins, who is telling a friend that one's use of language determines one's place in society. The next day, Eliza arrives on Higgins's doorstep for language lessons so that she can become a lady and work in a fine flower shop. Their relationship and Shaw's ideas about language and class are at the heart of the play, though the musical version transforms those ideas into such witty songs as "Why Can't the English Teach Their Children How to Speak" and "The Rain in Spain."

The chances for a successful adaptation were considered poor because the original play, like much of Shaw, consists largely of witty talk. Lerner eventually solved the problem of the book by retaining large swaths of Shaw's dialogue and adding new musical scenes as needed. With **Rex Harrison** cast as Higgins and the largely unknown **Julie Andrews** as Eliza, Lerner and Loewe knew that they would have to write for a male star who could not sing and a leading lady with a sweet lyric soprano, a much easier task. For Harrison, they added lines they borrowed from Shaw's dialogue, set them to patter tunes, and encouraged Harrison to talk-sing his songs, each of which revealed a different aspect of Higgins's personality. They included his admiring view of men and condescending view of women in "A Hymn to Him" and his insistence on living his own independent and idiosyncratic life in "I'm an Ordinary Man." Writing for Andrews resulted in such songs of character and situation as "Wouldn't It Be Loverly?" "I Could Have Danced All Night," and—in a moment of anger—"Just You Wait." The score also includes "With a Little Bit of Luck" and "Get Me to the Church on Time," reminiscent of the boisterous English music hall, for Eliza's ne'er-do-well father Alfred P. Doolittle, and the score's most popular song, "On the Street Where You Live," for Freddy Eynsford-Hill. *My Fair Lady* won six Tony Awards, including Best Musical. It ran for 2,717 performances, making it the longest-running Broadway musical for nine years, until *Hello, Dolly!* (1964) replaced it.

Before returning to Broadway, Lerner adapted Colette's novella, *Gigi*, into a screenplay, and he and Loewe wrote the score. The 1958 **film**, which starred Leslie Caron, Louis Jourdan, and Maurice Chevalier, won nine Academy Awards, including Best Picture. Its buoyant score includes "Thank Heaven for Little Girls," "I'm Glad I'm Not Young Anymore," "The Night They Invented Champagne," and the title song.

Camelot (1960), Lerner and Loewe's next Broadway show, tried to follow in the same vein as *My Fair Lady*, though its canvas was much larger. Once again, they cast a nonsinging actor, Richard Burton, as their leading man, and Julie Andrews as a much better known leading lady. Once again, they wrote patter songs for Burton and lyrical melodies for Andrews. But instead of a townhouse in London, they set out to put King Arthur's Camelot onstage, complete with the Knights of the Round Table, the love story of Guinevere and Lancelot, and the nefarious plottings of Morgan le Fay. Lerner based his book on T. H. White's retelling of the Arthurian story, *The Once and Future King* (1958). The book was ponderous and the score, while good, could not match what Lerner and Loewe had written for *My Fair Lady*. The show elevated Robert Goulet to stardom for his large-voiced singing of the popular ballad, "If Ever I Would Leave You." Among the other notable songs in the varied score were the comic "What Do the Simple Folk Do?" and "The Lusty Month of May"; the touching soliloquy, "How To Handle a Woman"; and the romantic "I Loved You Once in Silence." *Camelot* opened to mixed reviews but ran for 873 performances, a disappointment only in contrast to *My Fair Lady*.

In 1962, Lerner and Loewe dissolved their partnership, and Lerner moved on to collaborations with several prominent composers. Loewe preferred retirement, although when their movie, *Gigi*, moved to Broadway in 1973, they collaborated on four new songs. It was their last theater work together. Lerner collaborated with Burton Lane on *On a Clear Day You Can See Forever* (1965) and *Carmelina* (1979), André Previn on *Coco* (1969), **Leonard Bernstein** on *1600 Pennsylvania Avenue* (1976), and Charles Strouse on *Dance a Little Closer* (1983). Only *On a Clear Day* had any sort of success and eventually became a motion picture (1970). Loewe came out of retirement a second time in 1974 to collaborate with Lerner on the film score to *The Little Prince*. Lerner also wrote the screenplay.

Lerner and Loewe were inducted into the Songwriter's Hall of Fame in 1971 and were Kennedy Center Honorees in 1986. Alan Jay Lerner died June 14, 1986, in New York City, and Frederick Loewe died on February 14, 1988, in Palm Springs, California.

Michael Lasser

Further Reading

Furia, Phillip, and Michael Lasser. *America's Songs: The Stories Behind the Songs of Broadway, Hollywood, and Tin Pan Alley.* New York: Routledge, 2006.

Lees, Gene. *The Musical Worlds of Lerner and Loewe.* Lincoln: University of Nebraska Press, 2005.

LLOYD WEBBER, ANDREW (1948–)
COMPOSER, PRODUCER

Englishman Andrew Lloyd Webber is the most influential and commercially successful Broadway composer of his generation. He composed the two longest-running shows in Broadway history, **The Phantom of the Opera** (1988–present)

Andrew Lloyd Webber speaks to the audience during the curtain call following performance number 7,486 of The Phantom of the Opera *at the Majestic Theatre in New York on January 9, 2006. With the performance, the musical became the longest-running show in Broadway history. (AP Photo/Tina Fineberg)*

and *Cats* (1982–2000). He is a pioneer of "Rock Opera" **musicals**, which brought rock-influenced scores and songs to Broadway beginning in the early 1970s. Starting out in London theater, Lloyd Webber was at the forefront of the "British Invasion" in the 1970s and 1980s, which introduced America to **European "megamusicals"**—visually overwhelming productions featuring elaborate staging and operatic pageantry. His shows generated several well-known, familiar songs that broke through stiff competition from country music, disco, hip-hop, alternative rock, and music video to become popular hits in the 1970s and 1980s.

Lloyd Webber was born in London in 1948 to a musical family. His father, William Southcombe Lloyd Webber, was the director of the London College of Music. In childhood Lloyd Webber received training in numerous instruments and took to composing almost immediately. At age nine he composed an original suite, which was published in a professional music educator's journal. In 1965, Lloyd Webber began his university studies, first at Oxford and then at London's Royal College of Music. While in London, Lloyd Webber met a young lyricist, Tim Rice, with whom he would have his first major successes. Their initial collaboration, *The Likes of Us*, was completed in 1996 but has never been produced in London's West End or on Broadway. However, 1968's *Joseph and the Amazing Technicolor Dreamcoat* would give the pair their first public recognition in London. Based on the Old Testament story of Joseph, the show's eclectic score combined rock, church music, and calypso, among other genres. The score became a popular holiday concert piece in England as well as the basis of a 1972 British television production, even though a full stage version would not be mounted in London until 1981 or on Broadway until 1982.

Lloyd Webber and Rice would become internationally famous with their next project, *Jesus Christ Superstar* (1971). Originally released as an album in 1970, *Jesus Christ Superstar* sold in excess of 2 million copies in the United States and received regular **radio** air play for a full year before the Broadway production of the musical opened. Promoted as a "Rock Opera" or "Rock Musical" album and marketed to an audience that generally took little interest in musical theater, the heretofore unheard of practice of releasing a show's soundtrack prior to opening the show itself proved to be as successful as it was revolutionary. By age 24 Lloyd Webber was internationally famous. Within two years after the release of the album, *Jesus Christ Superstar* was being simultaneously produced on Broadway and in London's West End as well as being adapted into a commercial film. Critical praise for the originality of the work combined with attacks by religious groups offended by a rock music presentation of the Passion story gave the show and its young creators widespread notoriety within and beyond the world of theater.

Lloyd Webber's next major success would also be his last major collaboration with Rice. *Evita* (1979), a musical based on the travails of the wife of the late Argentinean President Juan Peron, repeated the *Jesus Christ Superstar* formula. The initial release of a soundtrack record was followed by extremely successful stagings in London and on Broadway, followed in turn by a feverish critical response that generated extensive publicity on both continents. **Hal Prince** directed the production, which opened in 1978 in the West End and a year later on Broadway. The Broadway production dominated the Tony Awards for the year, including Best Original Score for the composer. The album for the show also won a Grammy Award, establishing Lloyd Webber as a force within the recording industry as well as commercial theater.

After the long-awaited 1982 staging of *Joseph* in both London and New York, Lloyd Webber effectively ended his collaboration with Rice and worked for the remainder of his career with a number of other lyricists and text sources. Lloyd Webber's next major success was *Cats*, based on a whimsical collection of poems by the late T. S. Eliot. As with his previous shows, *Cats*' music was "let out of the bag" in the United States ahead of its Broadway premiere; two recordings of the show's hit song "Memory" by Barbra Streisand and Judy Collins were already familiar to American audiences before the Broadway opening in 1982. *Cats* premiered at the Winter Garden Theatre to enthusiastic reviews; it would go on to become the longest-running Broadway musical up to that time and, eventually, the second-longest running show behind Lloyd Webber's *The Phantom of the Opera*.

The period between 1982 and 1988 suggested the possibility that a slowing of Lloyd Webber's meteoric rise was in the offing. A rather unadventurous musical, *Song and Dance* (1985), won a Tony Award for lead actress Bernadette Peters but failed to electrify **critics** or audiences; it ran a respectable 14 months. The all-too innovative *Starlight Express* (1987), which looped a skating track around the audience seating area while dazzlingly costumed actors on roller skates played the role of train cars, ran for two years. It delighted children as well as international tourists, who did not need to understand English to enjoy the gaudy spectacle. However, critics panned the music as soulless and the entire production as pointless eye candy.

Lloyd Webber's next production, the reigning Broadway champion *The Phantom of the Opera*, would quell any criticism that Lloyd Webber had lost the ability to attract an audience (although many critics of *Phantom* complained that Lloyd Webber's scores had become as showy and bloated as the elaborate sets and costumes that had become something of a trademark since *Cats*). With Hal Prince directing, *Phantom* made international stars of the heretofore unknown lead performers Michael Crawford and Lloyd Webber's then wife Sarah Brightman. The show won Tonys for Best Musical, Best Actor in a Musical (Crawford), Best Director (Prince), and Best Book (Lloyd Webber among others), although it did not win for best score. Running in Broadway and London for over 20 years (plus a highly regarded ten-year run in Toronto in the 1990s), the show became not just a theatrical mainstay in these cities but also a staple of their respective tourist industries.

The phenomenal success of *Phantom* and *Cats* may have impeded Lloyd Webber from writing comparably triumphant shows in the 1990s and early 2000s, but he continued to be productive with new shows during this period. *Aspects of Love* (1990), although successful in London, ran for only a year on Broadway—an anticlimactic first venture after *Phantom. Sunset Boulevard* (1995), adapted from the 1950 film, turned out to be a successful star vehicle on Broadway for veteran actress Glenn Close, and Lloyd Webber earned some of his most favorable critical notices in 20 years for his score. He also won Tony Awards for Best Original Score and Best Book of a Musical (with lyricist Christopher Hampton). The show was a solid success, running for nearly 1,000 performances over a two and a half year period. A farcical musical *Jeeves* (2001), adapted by Lloyd Webber and British playwright Alan Ayckbourn from P. G. Wodehouse's dryly humorous stories about an English butler, opened in the wake of 9/11 and suffered the same dismal fate as did most new Broadway shows of that season. Lacking any "name" Broadway or Hollywood celebrities *Bombay Dreams* (2004) starred a number of South Asian actors making their Broadway debuts; the show ran for a year with little notice. *The Woman in White* (2005) paired Lloyd Webber with director Trevor Nunn who had staged *Cats* and *Sunset Boulevard*, but turned out to be one of the only genuine flops in Lloyd Webber's career.

A number of Lloyd Webber's musicals have been adapted for film, with varying degrees of success and usually with some active creative involvement from Lloyd Webber. The film adaptations of *Jesus Christ Superstar* (film 1973) and *Evita* (film 1996 starring Madonna in the title role) are widely viewed as superb, smart screen adaptations of musicals. However the much-anticipated 2004 film of *The Phantom of the Opera* was surprisingly disappointing both critically and commercially.

As heralded as have been his collaborations with Tim Rice, Hal Prince, and other theater artists, Lloyd Webber's most important collaborator has been

Cameron Mackintosh, the producer and marketing mastermind for *Cats* and *The Phantom of the Opera*. Between Mackintosh's vision for marketing megamusicals on an international scale and Lloyd Webber's own considerable business acumen (which he channels through his production company, the Really Useful Theatre Company), the two have redefined the shear amount of money an individual producer and composer can make in the notoriously financially pressed theater trade. The British press reports that, at least in U.S. dollars, both men are self-made billionaires.

Even having gone for over 10 years without composing a new hit show and over 20 years without opening an historic one, Lloyd Webber remains one of the most important figures in contemporary theater. Because of Lloyd Webber's influence, Broadway musical production is more receptive to expensive grand spectacle, rock-influenced music, dominating orchestrations, and "easy listening" hit songs than it was prior to his arrival on the scene. Some observers have also noted that, thanks (or no thanks) to Lloyd Webber, musicals are also a lot louder than they used to be. Hit songs from his shows, which include "I Don't Know How to Love Him" (*Jesus Christ Superstar*), "Memory" (*Cats*), "Don't Cry for Me Argentina" (*Evita*), "Music of the Night" (*Phantom*), and "As if We Never Said Good-bye" (*Sunset Boulevard*), are among the best-known and best-written "signature" **show tunes** of the past 50 years. But perhaps most significantly, with the epic runs of *Phantom* and *Cats*, Lloyd Webber appears to have convinced the cultures of two continents that a single musical—and, by extension, the theater itself—can run for all eternity.

Thomas A. Greenfield and Nicholas J. Ponterio

Further Reading

Snelson, John, and Geoffrey Holden Block. *Andrew Lloyd Webber*. New Haven, CT: Yale University Press, 2004.
Walsh, Michael. *Andrew Lloyd Webber: His Life and Works*. New York: Abrams, 1989.

LOESSER, FRANK HENRY (1910–1969)
COMPOSER, LYRICIST

Although he wrote only five Broadway **musicals**, Frank Loesser was a major theater composer and lyricist because of the quality and variety of his three successful shows, and the particularly artful way his lyrics captured the spontaneity and vitality of American speech in the middle of the twentieth century. His shows varied from musical comedy in *Guys and Dolls* (1949), to romantic sentiment in *Most Happy Fella* (1956), to sharp-eyed satire in *How to Succeed in Business Without Really Trying* (1961).

Frank Henry Loesser was born in New York City on June 29,1910, to Henry and Julia Ehrlich Loesser. Although his parents prized high Germanic culture, Loesser fell in love with show business and began to write songs as a teenager. In 1936, after publishing songs with several early collaborators, Loesser moved to Hollywood to write lyrics for motion pictures. In the 1940s he began writing both words and music to songs, including his first such venture, the wartime hit "Praise the Lord and Pass the Ammunition" (1943), and "Spring Will Be a Little Late This Year" (1944). These songs amounted to his pre-Broadway apprenticeship and demonstrated his range as a songwriter.

By 1948, when he left Hollywood for Broadway, Loesser had written lyrics for more than 100 songs for movies and recordings, including such hits as "I Don't Want to Walk without You," "They're Either Too Young or Too Old," and "Slow Boat to China." In that same year he won the Academy Award for best song for "Baby, It's Cold Outside," an amusing seduction contrapuntal duet, characterized by interruptions, repetitions, and seemingly spontaneous changes in direction. It anticipated some of his Broadway compositions, including "Make a Miracle" from *Where's Charley?* (1950), "Sue Me" from *Guys and Dolls*, and "The Sermon" from *Greenwillow* (1960). His ability to write with the particular mix of wit and sentiment that characterized the best lyric writing between the two World Wars would stand him in good stead in the character songs required in the more sophisticated world of theater musicals. (Loesser returned to Broadway one last time in 1952 to write words and music for the fairy tale musical *Hans Christian Andersen*.)

Loesser was hired to write the lyrics for his first Broadway musical, *Where's Charlie?*, an adaptation of Brandon Thomas's nineteenth-century British farce, *Charley's Aunt*. When composer Harold Arlen withdrew, Loesser persuaded the **producers** to let him write the music as well. The reviews were mixed but the show ran for 792 performances in part owing to star Ray Bolger's elevation of a little **vaudeville** ballad "Once in Love with Amy" into a showstopping *tour de force*. Loesser's songs for *Where's Charlie?* lacked the innovation and range of his later work, yet they were charming and surprisingly diverse for a first effort. They include "My Darling, My Darling," a lovely **operetta**-like ballad, and "Make a Miracle," a witty catalogue of new inventions that so captivates the heroine that she fails to hear a proposal of marriage.

Guys and Dolls (1950), appropriately subtitled "A Musical Fable of Broadway," is Loesser's masterpiece and arguably the greatest of all musicals about New York City. Based on short stories by New York newspaperman Damon Runyon, there is no other show like it. Loesser's score combines comedy, skepticism, and romance; it advances plot and creates character. Isabel Bigley as Miss Sarah sang the lively romantic ballad, "If I Were a Bell." In "I'll Know," she and Sky Masterson (Robert Alda) have an argument in song as they fall in love. Paralleling "I'll Know" is the comic argument "Sue Me" between high rolling Nathan Detroit and Miss Adelaide, his long-suffering fiancé. Although the songs vary widely in style and emotional content, they serve the play's needs perfectly. The opening number, "Fugue for Tinhorns," makes affectionate fun of a classical form to introduce the characters and establish their world. In "Adelaide's Lament," Miss Adelaide (Vivian Blaine) tries self-diagnosis to understand why an "unmarried female, just in the legal sense" cannot get over a cold. The rest of the score demonstrates Loesser's impressive range, from the gentle "More I Cannot Wish You," a father's loving wish for his daughter's happiness, to "Sit Down, You're Rocking the Boat," a rousing revival that reforms the sinners at the end of the show. The production ran for 1,201 performances and won the Tony Award for Best Musical.

Loesser based his third musical, *The Most Happy Fella*, on Sidney Howard's 1924 play, *They Knew What They Wanted*. He composed great quantities of music for the show even though he insisted that it was not an opera, but rather an "extended musical . . . with lots of music." To the requisite Broadway pizzazz, Loesser added arias, duets, trios, quartets, choral passages, even recitative. The result was a combination of Broadway musical and grand opera, a rarity akin to the **Gershwins'** *Porgy and Bess* (1935) and **Andrew Lloyd Webber**'s *Evita* (1979). The show's richly varied score included two numbers aimed directly at the popular song charts, "Big D" and "Standing on the Corner," along with one of the Broadway theater's finest charm songs, "Happy to Make Your Acquaintance." But it also included "Rosebella" and "How Beautiful the Days," two aria-like songs originally performed by opera star Robert Weede in his Broadway debut.

With *Greenwillow* (1960), Loesser had his only flop. Based on a short novel by B. J. Chute, it was a whimsical fairy tale about a family that lived in a make-believe village in a faraway time. *Greenwillow* closed after 95 performances. After this unsuccessful attempt at fantasy, Loesser turned to a satirical view of the here and now of American corporate life. In 1952 Shepherd Mead's cynical book *How to Succeed in Business without Really Trying* offered mock advice about rising to the top of a large corporation. Loesser agreed to write the score for a musical adaptation after **Abe Burrows**, the librettist for *Guys and Dolls*, had signed to write the book. *How to Succeed in Business without Really Trying* opened on October 14, 1961, ran for 1,417 performances, and won both the Tony Award for Best Musical and the Pulitzer Prize for Drama (only the fourth time a musical had received the Pulitzer). Every character in the show is unappealing and all the songs are satiric. Yet Loesser wrote with his customary eclecticism and his lyrics demonstrated his keen ear for corporate blather. "A Secretary Is Not a Toy," "The Company Way," and "Coffee Break" lampoon corporate life; the ironic finale, "The Brotherhood of Man," is a parody of a revival hymn. The score's best-known song, "I Believe in You," is an egotistical tribute the hero sings to himself as he looks in the mirror.

Through the 1960s, as the Broadway book musical began a not-so-slow decline, Loesser worked on several projects that failed to materialize. Early in 1969, he was diagnosed with lung cancer and died on July 26 of that year. He was posthumously inducted into the Songwriter's Hall of Fame in 1970.

Michael Lasser

Further Reading

Furia, Phillip, and Michael Lasser. *America's Songs: The Stories Behind the Songs of Broadway, Hollywood, and Tin Pan Alley.* New York: Routledge, 2006.

Loesser, Susan. *A Most Remarkable Fella: Frank Loesser and the Guys and Dolls in His Life: A Portrait by His Daughter.* Milwaukee: Hal Leonard, 2000.

LOGAN, JOSHUA (1908–1988)
DIRECTOR, PRODUCER, AUTHOR, ACTOR

Joshua Logan, who claimed to view all existence in theatrical terms (such as the timing of sunsets and the suspense of weather changes), was one of the most successful and influential figures during the Golden Age of Musicals in the late 1940s and 1950s. He is best known as the driving force behind the hit musical comedies *Annie Get Your Gun* (1946), *South Pacific* (1949), *Wish You Were Here* (1952), and *Fanny* (1954). However, Logan was also one of Broadway's most skillful directors of serious and comedic plays. His shepherding of *Mister Roberts*, *Picnic* (both 1948), and *The World of Suzy Wong* (1958) in combination with his success with **musicals** established him as a central figure during one of Broadway's flushest periods in its history.

Born October 5, 1908, in Texarkana, Texas, Logan was raised in Louisiana by his widowed mother. After attending Culver Military Academy in Indiana, Logan studied at Princeton University from 1927 to 1931. As a student he was a member of a summer-stock acting troupe called the University Players, which included James Stewart and Henry Fonda, and they all became friends. Before graduation, Logan studied on scholarship with Konstantin Stanislavsky at the Moscow Art Theatre. Logan was completely taken with Stanislavsky's direction, especially his ability to apply to theatrical production the psychological and literary power of music, from interludes to full scores. Logan acknowledged Stanislavsky's influence on his own work—especially his musicals—which placed heavy emphasis on story line and coherence of characterization.

Logan made his Broadway debut as an actor in a play, *Carry Nation* (1932). In the next few years he performed in and staged various other plays, leaving briefly to work in Hollywood in 1936. Logan returned to Broadway as director for Paul Osborn's comedy *On Borrowed Time* (1938), which was a modest hit, running ten months and over 300 performances. He also staged his first two Broadway musicals in that same year, the highly successful *I Married an Angel* by **Richard Rodgers** and **Lorenz Hart** and the disappointing *Knickerbocker Holiday* (1938) by Kurt Weill and **Maxwell Anderson**.

Logan served with the United States Army Air Corps during World War II, but returned to Broadway with a flourish after the war. He achieved immediate and meteoric success directing *Annie Get Your Gun*. Few musicals have ever been created with such an esteemed lineup of Broadway talent: **Rodgers and Hammerstein** produced it, **Irving Berlin** wrote the music, Dorothy and Herbert Fields wrote the lyrics, and **Ethel Merman** starred in the title role. The show was the big success it should have been, running for three years. The Western-themed battle-of-the-sexes romance between sharpshooter Annie Oakley and rival–turned business partner–turned husband Frank Butler has been a summer-stock and touring institution for over 60 years.

Logan followed *Annie Get Your Gun* with three strong showings as a director of straight plays. He directed **Helen Hayes** in Anita Loos's comedy *Happy Birthday* (1946) for which Hayes won the first ever Tony for Best Actress (she shared the honor with Ingrid Bergman). In 1947 he reunited with *Annie Get Your Gun* producers Rodgers and Hammerstein to direct a comedy, *John Loves Mary*, which ran for a solid 423 performances. As co-author and director of the war drama *Mr. Roberts* (1948), Logan was the driving force behind one of the most successful plays staged on Broadway since World War II. Running for three years and over 1,100 performances, *Mr. Roberts* won five Tony Awards, of which Logan won or shared three (Best Play, Best Direction, and Author). Despite greater glory that was to follow, Logan wrote that *Mr. Roberts* was the joy of his theatrical life (1976, 264).

Notwithstanding his string of four hit productions in a row, Logan's crowning achievement came next. Logan was an admirer of James Michener's Pulitzer Prize–winning best seller *Tales of the South Pacific* (1946) and, along with producing partner Leland Howard, secured production rights to the book. Independently of Logan, Rodgers and Hammerstein wanted to adapt the book as a musical. The three negotiated control of the material. Logan contracted to direct the show and produce it "in association" with Rodgers and Hammerstein. As the writing progressed, he also became co-author of the libretto with Hammerstein. Reviews were lavish in their praise and audiences thrilled to every aspect of the production. *South Pacific* was the first musical ever to win the Tony's six major awards: Best Musical, Best Original Score, Best Book, Best Actor (Ezio Pinza), Best Actress (**Mary Martin**), and Best Direction. Logan won or shared four of them. He also shared the Pulitzer Prize with Rodgers and Hammerstein. With 1,925 performances, it was the longest-running show of Logan's career.

In the 1950s and 1960s Logan continued to direct and produce musicals, including the successful *Fanny* (1954). His lighthearted, satiric political musical *Mr. President* (1962) would be composer/lyricist Irving Berlin's last original Broadway show. Despite opening during the Cuban Missile Crisis, which brought the United States and Russia to the brink of war, the show ran for eight months. During this same period of time, Logan returned to staging straight plays on Broadway, including *Middle of the Night* (1957), *Tiger Tiger Burning Bright* (1962), and the aforementioned *The World of Suzy Wong*.

By the mid-1950s, Logan had become increasingly involved in **film** work inasmuch as several of his successful Broadway shows had attracted the attention of Hollywood studios. He returned to Hollywood to co-write the screenplay and help direct the film adaptation of *Mr. Roberts* (1955). He also directed the film adaptation of *Picnic* (1955). Logan eventually went on to direct film adaptations of

Broadway shows he had not directed, including **Lerner and Loewe**'s *Camelot* (film 1967) and *Paint Your Wagon* (film 1969).

From the mid-1960s through the remainder of his working life, Logan devoted much more of his attention to Hollywood than to Broadway, owing to the decline of the traditional book musical. From 1965 until 1980, Logan mounted only three short-lived, unsuccessful Broadway shows, but by then—and arguably of his own choosing—he had already become a central figure in Broadway's storied past.

Logan died in New York City on July 12, 1988, of supranuclear palsy.

Monica Moschetta

Further Reading

Logan, Josh. *Josh. My Up and Down, In and Out Life*. New York: Delacorte Press, 1976.

Sarris, Andrew. *The American Cinema: Directors and Directions, 1929–1968* New York: Da Capo Press, 1996.

Long Day's Journey into Night

Broadway Run: Helen Hayes Theatre
Opening: November 7, 1956
Closing: March 29, 1958
Total Performances: 390
Playwright: Eugene O'Neill
Director: José Quintero
Producers: Leigh Connell, Theodore Mann, and José Quintero
Lead Performers: Florence Eldridge (Mary Cavan Tyrone), Fredric March (James Tyrone), Jason Robards Jr. (James Tyrone Jr.), and Bradford Dillman (Edmund Tyrone)

The 1956 production of *Long Day's Journey into Night* is one of the most important Broadway productions of an American play in the twentieth century. In addition to being widely regarded as the greatest production of **Eugene O'Neill**'s greatest play, it cemented the idea that O'Neill is primarily an autobiographical **playwright**, and this has become central to both the study of O'Neill and the performance of his plays. The American premiere also anointed **José Quintero** and **Jason Robards** as O'Neill's foremost interpreters. (Both had established themselves in the landmark **Off-Broadway** staging of *The Iceman Cometh* in the previous season.) Thus the influence of this production is profound in two ways; it irrevocably connected O'Neill's work to his life and limited the production style of his plays to the psychological realism that prevailed in the middle of the twentieth century. This has also affected the way almost all other American plays are studied in English classes and performed on Broadway.

Ever since O'Neill turned his back on Broadway in 1934, there had been rumors that he was working on his greatest play ever. No less a source than magisterial

Long Day's Journey into Night. *Shown from left: Bradford Dillman as Edmund Tyrone, Jason Robards as Jamie Tyrone, Florence Eldridge as Mary Tyrone, and Fredric March as James Tyrone, from the original Broadway production that ran from 1956 to 1958. (Courtesy of Photofest)*

drama **critic** and O'Neill confidant George Jean Nathan intimated that the playwright was holding back a masterpiece from publication and performance because it was dangerously controversial. Nevertheless, the failed first production of *The Iceman Cometh* in 1946 halted Broadway's interest in O'Neill, even as Nathan continued to suggest that O'Neill had written his greatest play, but would never allow it to be sullied by the grubby fingers of Broadway **producers**. Nevertheless, by the time of his death in 1953, O'Neill was almost forgotten. Depending upon one's sympathies, O'Neill's widow was either desperate to revive her husband's reputation or provide for her old age when she decided to assert her authority as literary executrix and offer *Long Day's Journey* to the public. Carlotta Monterey O'Neill countermanded both Saxe Commins, O'Neill's editor and close friend, and O'Neill's publisher, Bennett Cerf, the head of Random House, who both insisted on sticking to their original agreement with O'Neill. This would have held up publication of the play until 1978, and would have forever prohibited any performance.

Mrs. O'Neill had total control over all aspects of her late husband's work so she was able to make all decisions about publication and production. Cerf removed the manuscript from his vault and handed it over. The Broadway failure of *The Iceman*

Cometh still stung, so Mrs. O'Neill decided that the play should first be performed abroad. Noting O'Neill's affinity for August Strindberg and the regard the Swedes had for him, Mrs. O'Neill opted for a Stockholm tryout. The triumphant February 1956 world premiere at the Royal Dramaten sent transatlantic flashes of the play's magnificence. When the play was published by Yale University Press within days of the Stockholm opening, Broadway was doubly overwhelmed with yearning. Relentless speculation about the inevitable Broadway production began.

Fresh from the acclaim of his Off-Broadway revival of *The Iceman Cometh* the previous season, José Quintero was determined to direct *Long Day's Journey*. He began a deft campaign of wooing the widow, abetted by an equally intent Jason Robards, who had starred in that revival. Over numerous cocktails, dinners, and late-night conversations—sometimes with O'Neill's ghost in attendance, according to the enraptured widow—Quintero and Robards successfully courted her.

Doubts about Quintero's relative inexperience were assuaged by the casting of Hollywood star and respected actor Fredric March as James Tyrone and his wife and frequent co-star, Florence Eldridge, as Mary. Each of the performers received superlative reviews. Indeed, the finale provoked one of the most poignant curtain calls in American theater history. Testimony from the actors and first-nighters attests to the silence that descended after the play's final words. Backstage, an eternity went by as the cast waited in heart-stopped silence. Then suddenly, torrentially, applause shook the walls, floor, and ceiling; it seemed to push the curtain open with its force. As the audience gave their overwhelming ovations, many crowded the front of the house trying to touch the actors, because, as Quintero recalled, they would not be parted from the Tyrones.

Thus a legend was born and Eugene O'Neill transfigured. Never again would anyone question his reputation—he is considered by many the colossus of the American theater. Henceforth, O'Neill's late-blooming genius would eclipse all his other work, just as the Tyrones would the O'Neills. Appropriately, since he was playing an actor, March's performance attracted the most description. Most frequently commented on was his choice to give Tyrone a brogue as he slipped into abyssal despair in the later scenes. Less frequently commented on was the costume he wore, which defied O'Neill's stage directions. March wore an ascot quite different from the knotted handkerchief that O'Neill gives Tyrone. March transformed the unassuming gardener in a threadbare suit "who doesn't give a damn how he looks" to a bespoke-kitted-out gentleman of leisure. Theater historians familiar with the diary of the Monte Cristo company actress Elizabeth Robins are aware that Mr. and Mrs. O'Neill were quite different from Mr. and Mrs. Tyrone. What is more, James O'Neill always had defenders among his surviving contemporaries. Old troupers spoke out against *Long Day's Journey* in 1956, but their voices were overwhelmed. The crushing burden of biography has not only limited academic discussion of the play. It has virtually proscribed the play's performance unless its set conforms to the dimensions of a certain parlor in New London, Connecticut (in the original "Monte Cristo Cottage" where the O'Neills summered).

The bellwether for this was critic **Brooks Atkinson** who declared that the play was "as personal and as literal as drama can be." And productions since have been judged according to a bizarre standard of being true to the life of the O'Neills rather than to the Tyrones. Conversely, since the Tyrones of the original Broadway cast were the embodiment of the O'Neills, it was believed best to follow their example.

A central article of faith in audiences' understanding of Eugene O'Neill's mother Ella (Mary Tyrone in the play) probably never existed: the glorious wedding gown provided by a munificent parent. Ella's father did not contribute anything to her wedding; he had died three years earlier. O'Neill could not possibly have known some of the things about his parents that he seems to be revealing in *Long Day's Journey.*

Nonetheless, biographical issues cannot detract from the play's essential greatness. The final scene is arguably the most harrowing in our drama. The conclusion of Walter Kerr's opening night review sums up the place of O'Neill's masterpiece in American drama: "For any one who cares about the American theater, *Long Day's Journey* is, of course, an obligation. But it is more than that. It is a stunning theatrical experience."

Thomas F. Connolly

Further Reading

Alexander, Doris. *Eugene O'Neill's Last Plays: Separating Art from Autobiography.* Athens: University of Georgia Press, 2005.

Murphy, Brenda. *O'Neill: Long Day's Journey into Night.* Cambridge, England: Cambridge University Press, 2001.

Sheaffer, Louis. *O'Neill: Son and Playwright.* St. Paul, MN: Paragon House, 1990.

Lunt, Alfred (1892–1977), and Fontanne, Lynn (1887c.–1983)
Performers, Producers, Directors

Alfred Lunt and Lynn Fontanne were the most important and most influential stage acting couple in modern Broadway history. For over 30 years "The Fabulous Lunts" seemed by outward appearances to embody the glamour and elegance of a sophisticated yet passionate lifetime love affair, which they played out in public through their performances. After marrying in 1922, they performed together as leading man and woman almost exclusively, developing what many historians consider to be incomparable stage chemistry and perfectionists' technical mastery of performing as a couple. In the years between the World Wars, Lunt and Fontanne (alternately "the Lunts") allowed Broadway fans and the theater press to indulge in the kind of romantic idol worship that the film industry so skillfully cultivated through the Hollywood studio system. In recent years, research on the Lunts has

Lynn Fontanne and Alfred Lunt are shown in a scene from Robert E. Sherwood's play Idiot's Delight, *winner of the 1936 Pulitzer Prize in drama, in New York City, 1936. (AP Photo)*

explored their sexuality and unconventional private lives as part of gay/lesbian scholarship on Broadway.

Fontanne, born in England in the late 1880s (her birth year is the subject of some historical debate owing largely to her notorious lack of candor on the subject), completed chores in exchange for acting lessons. She played small parts in London in the early 1900s, becoming a favorite of famed English actress/director Ellen Terry. She was also a protégé of American actress **Laurette Taylor**, who saw her perform during a London visit and persuaded her to come to the United States.

Lunt grew up in Genesee Depot, Wisconsin, near Milwaukee. In school, he showed an interest in acting, but temporarily put his ambitions on hold to provide for his family after both his father and stepfather died. He eventually moved to Boston and then New York to start his acting career. In 1915 and 1916 he served as an apprentice actor in companies run by Margaret Anglin and Lillie Langtry. Both veteran actresses were impressed by Lunt's talent and charm.

The Lunts claim to have met each other in New York in 1919 at opening rehearsals for a romantic comedy (*A Young Man's Fancy*), which was scheduled for a summer opening in Washington, D.C. Each had been cast separately in the lead roles. The two still-unknown actors reportedly fell in love at first sight and gave standout performances when the show opened—inaugurating what would become the legend of their onstage/offstage romance. However, their respective breakthrough Broadway performances came in separate productions. Lunt's first hit was Booth Tarkington's sophisticated comedy *Clarence* (1919), which ran for 300 performances. Fontanne scored a success in **George S. Kaufman** and Marc Connelly's *Dulcy* (1922), the first of Kaufman's astonishing string of hit comedies. Lunt and Fontanne married in 1922 and, thereafter, concentrated primarily on plays that would feature or star them as a romantic couple. Their first hit as husband and wife was in a **Theatre Guild**–produced comedy, *The Guardsman* (1924), which ran for 248 performances and established the pair as a star couple.

The long run of *The Guardsman* allowed Lunt and Fontanne to develop what would become the trademarks of their onstage teamwork, including finishing each other's sentences, intuitively coordinating exchanges of facial expressions and gestures, and improvising lines. More than the sum of its parts, their masterful, layered onstage interplay became a theatrical attraction in and of itself and the focus of much of the critical attention paid to their performances.

Their association with the Theatre Guild proved highly beneficial to all concerned. The pair appreciated the Guild's willingness to support them in a wide variety of challenging, commercially risky roles, and the Guild was more than happy to employ the popular couple as often as it could. Lunt and Fontanne performed exclusively on Broadway for the Guild until 1933. Among their more notable performances during this period were a 180-performance run in **George Bernard Shaw**'s *Arms and the Man* (1925); an adaptation of Fyodor Dostoyevsky's *The Brothers Karamazov* (1927); Shaw's *The Doctor's Dilemma* (1927); **Maxwell Anderson**'s *Elizabeth the Queen* (1930); and Robert Sherwood's *Reunion in Vienna* (1931). They performed in their first non-Guild production when they starred with friend and playwright Noël Coward in his *Design for Living* (1933), which they also coproduced.

Coward's *Design for Living*, a comedy about a love triangle of two male best friends and the wife of one of them, famously invites speculation about an erotic relationship between the two men. The successful Broadway production was neither Coward's nor the Lunts' biggest hit, but it has become a focus in recent studies of Lunt and Fontanne's public image and private life. Current scholarship now deals openly with Lunt and Fontanne's bisexuality and almost certain intimacies with other partners of both sexes—especially since their private lives contrasted so sharply with the public image of marital devotion they created through performing for decades, ostensibly, as themselves.

The Lunts were extremely popular on tour and apparently loved the touring life. The period between 1938 and 1940 was spent largely on tour in the United States with a small company they put together for repertory performances of Jean Giraudoux's *Amphitryon 38*, Anton Chekhov's *The Seagull*, and Sherwood's *Idiot's Delight*. They moved to England in 1943 and stayed until the end of World War II. Upon arrival they staged a production of Sherwood's Pulitzer Prize–winning war play *There Shall Be No Night*, which they had starred in (and Alfred had directed) on Broadway in 1940. They also starred in Terence Rattigan's *Love in Idleness*, which became one of the biggest Broadway hits of their career when they returned to America and staged it as *Oh Mistress Mine* (1946). Eager to welcome the Lunts back home, Broadway audiences kept the show running for 16 months and 482 performances.

Still dashing and appealing well into their fifties and sixties, the Lunts starred in a string of postwar successes: S. N. Behrman's comedy *I Know My Love* (1949); Giraudoux's *Ondine* (1954); Coward's *Quadrille* (1954); Howard Lindsay and Russel Crouse's *The Great Sebastians* (1956); and their final play together, Swedish playwright Friedrich Dürrenmatt's black comedy *The Visit* (1958). *The Visit* was performed in the newly renovated and renamed Lunt-Fontanne Theatre (formerly the Globe Theatre). Fontanne effectively retired from theater after *The Visit*. Lunt, who had intermittently directed and/or produced some of the pair's plays, lamentably made his last Broadway "appearance" as director of a flop, *First Love* (1961).

Owing in part to the secrecy they had maintained so diligently about their private lives, Lunt and Fontanne's fame faded quickly after their retirement from theater. They had done little television or film work and, despite their fondness for touring, generally discouraged biographers and interviewers. They were awarded Special Achievement Tony Awards in 1970. (Lunt had previously won Tony Awards for Best Director of *Ondine* and Best Actor in *Quadrille*. Fontanne had never won for a performance.) But the Tony Awards, instituted in 1947, could not adequately reflect the Lunts' enormous impact on Broadway during their peak years.

Alfred Lunt died in 1977 in Chicago. Fontanne died in 1983 in her husband's hometown of Genesee Depot, Wisconsin.

Thomas A. Greenfield and Nicole Katz

Further Reading

Brown, Jared.*The Fabulous Lunts*. New York: Atheneum, 1986.

Peters, Margot. *Design for Living: Alfred Lunt and Lynne Fontanne*. New York: Knopf, 2003.

Schanke, Robert A., and Kim Marra. *Passing Performances: Queer Readings of Leading Players in American Theater History*. Ann Arbor: University of Michigan Press, 1998.

LuPone, Patti (1949–)
Actress

Notwithstanding an uneven record of hits and disappointments during her 30-plus-year career Patti LuPone is widely regarded—particularly by Broadway traditionalists—as contemporary Broadway's quintessential female musical theater star. She is best known for memorable "diva" performances (*Evita* [1980], *Anything Goes* [1987 revival], **Gypsy** [2008 revival]) that, more than those of any of her contemporaries, recall the grandiose, song-belting star-vehicle style of Broadway's pioneer diva **Ethel Merman**. Yet, LuPone can also effect meticulously controlled understatement (still fully audible, without microphone, in the balcony seats) and intimacy to a house of 1,000—a skill and sensibility honed in decades as a topflight club and concert singer. LuPone's offstage persona is as irrepressible as some of her signature roles. She chastises sleeping or distracted front-row audience members during curtain calls and famously "shut up" the conductor at the televised 2008 Tony Awards when he dutifully cued the exit music during her long Award acceptance speech. More than those of any other Broadway actor or actress of her time, LuPone's theatrical career and legend evolve symbiotically.

Patti LuPone, left, and Laura Benanti perform a number from Gypsy *at the 62nd Annual Tony Awards in New York, 2008. (AP Photo/Jeff Christensen)*

LuPone was born in Northport, Long Island, near New York City and was raised and educated in the New York area. She graduated as a member of the first class of the Drama Division of the Juilliard School and shortly thereafter became a founding member of John Houseman's The Acting Company. LuPone began performing on Broadway in both plays and **musicals** in 1973. She had her first brush with success (and a Best Featured Actress Tony Nomination) as Rosalinda in the short-lived *The Robber Bridegroom* (1975). She worked steadily on Broadway during the next four years, but did not appear in a hit or a distinctive role until **Andrew Lloyd Webber**, who had launched several successful musicals without big-name stars, cast the still relatively unknown LuPone in the title role of *Evita* (1979). The play and the star effectively launched each other. Her Tony Award–winning performance created a sensation, and her showstopping rendition of the anthem "Don't Cry for Me, Argentina" was the word-of-mouth headline of the show.

Evita ran for four years and established LuPone as a major Broadway star. She followed *Evita* with a highly anticipated revival of *Oliver!* (1984), starring as Nancy. However, the show flopped, closing in three weeks. A straight acting role in *The Accidental Death of an Anarchist* (1984) fared little better. She delivered a hit starring performance as Reno Sweeney in a 1987 revival of **Cole Porter**'s *Anything Goes*, acquitting herself commendably in one of Ethel Merman's signature Broadway creations and inviting comparisons with Merman. In 1993, LuPone starred in London in Lloyd Webber's highly anticipated *Sunset Boulevard*, a musical adaptation of the classic 1950 **film** about a demented, reclusive former silent film star living out her final days in delusional reveries of former glory. The show and LuPone received mixed reviews from the London press, although the West End audiences were more forgiving. As part of her agreement with Lloyd Webber, she was to open the show on Broadway the following year. However, the *New York Times* eviscerated her London performance while highly praising actress Glenn Close, who starred in a Los Angeles production of *Sunset Boulevard* that same year. Lloyd Webber offered the role to Close doubtless knowing he would have to settle matters with LuPone. What might have otherwise been a more or less routine contract buyout became a *cause célèbre* among LuPone fans who decried the composer/producer's treatment of the actress. LuPone herself openly expressed bitterness over the rejection, and the New York theater press covered the dispute widely. Notwithstanding a substantial financial settlement LuPone received from Lloyd Webber and a public announcement of a truce, the controversy may well have enhanced her legend among Broadway enthusiasts as much as any role she might have taken at the time.

Apart from a limited engagement concert run in 1995 entitled *Patti LuPone on Broadway*—as if to underscore the impact of the *Sunset Boulevard* episode—LuPone's next appearance marked something of a career rebound. In 1996 she replaced the Tony Award–winning Zoe Caldwell as opera star Maria Callas in **Terrence McNally**'s *Master Class* (1995). Playing an aging Callas instructing young aspirants in song, performance, and life, LuPone drew an uncommon amount of attention for a replacement role—largely because the show marked her post-*Sunset* return to Broadway. She succeeded in the part and erased any residual doubts that her career had peaked. A solid dramatic acting performance in David Mamet's *The Old Neighborhood* followed (1997) as did a successful comic performance in a 2001 revival of the British farce *Noises Off* (1987) and a moderately successful one-year run as Mrs. Lovett in a 2005 revival of **Steven Sondheim**'s *Sweeney Todd* (1979).

LuPone consecrated her status as Broadway's reigning diva in 2008 when at age 58 she stepped into another Merman role: Mama Rose in the fourth Broadway revival of *Gypsy* (1959). Directed by **Arthur Laurents**, the 89-year-old author of the book, the production was especially demanding physically, with the hyperkinetic Rose running, lifting, and even wrestling with boyfriend Herbie. The equally hyperkinetic LuPone captured Rose's dementia and the depths of the character's narcissism while stopping the show no fewer than three times in the second act. LuPone swept the major awards for the season, winning the Tony, Drama Desk, and Outer Critics Circle awards for her performance. For the generation of Broadway performers in the early part of the twenty-first century, LuPone remains

Broadway's closet link and a worthy heiress to Merman and the Broadway diva tradition.

Thomas A. Greenfield

Further Reading

Hadleigh, Boze. *Broadway Babylon: Glamour, Glitz, and Gossip on the Great White Way.* New York: Back Stage Books, 2007.

Tichler, Rosemarie, and Barry Jay Kaplan. *Actors at Work.* New York: Macmillan, 2007.